TILTING AT WINDMILLS™

By Brian Hibbs

Introduction by **Paul Levitz**

IDW Publishing
San Diego

Tilting at Windmills

A Guide Towards Successful and Ethical Comics Retailing

ISBN: 0-9719775-7-7

06 05 04 03   5 4 3 2 1

Published by IDW Publishing
2645 Financial Court, Suite E
San Diego, CA 92117

www.**idw**publishing.com

Book design by Robbie Robbins

Manufactured in Canada

IDW Publishing is:
Ted Adams, Publisher
Jeff Mariotte, Editor-in-Chief
Robbie Robbins, Design Director
Kris Oprisko, Vice President
Alex Garner, Art Director
Cindy Chapman, Designer
Beau Smith, Sales & Marketing
Lorelei Bunjes, Website Coordinator
Brian Berling, Editorial Assistant

Tilting at Windmills: Preface
By Brian Hibbs

Right, so I thought I should step forward here and prepare you a little bit for what you're about to read.

This book is the more than 100 columns I wrote for the first 100 issues of Comics Retailer magazine, a controlled-circulation trade publication for the comic book industry.

This means that, at times, these pieces will seem a little "insider" and that you may not understand exactly who the players are. I apologize for this in advance. Still, in most cases, specific identity isn't as important as the underlying concepts involved, most of which I am confident you can easily grasp.

The nearly decade-long period this book covers was one of the most tumultuous and transformative eras that the "direct sales" comic book market has ever faced. When this tome opens in 1991, comic shops were rich and flush – sales were beginning to approach the highest levels they had since probably World War Two (peaking shortly after "The Death of Superman" in 1993), and the business environment of comics was at its widest and most open. In 1991 estimates suggest there might have been ten thousand or more accounts serviced by the major distributors. There were nearly a dozen "full line" distributors at that point, as well as scores of other, smaller, regional "sub-distributors."

As the 21st century opened we had lost some 2/3 of the comic book stores (conventional wisdom says we're sitting somewhere just north of 3000 accounts), and there is exactly one national full-line distributor (Diamond) and three smaller, regional ones (Cold Cut, FMI, and Last Gasp).

(Parenthetically, I think that good companion reading to this book is Dan Raviv's Comic Wars, which details the "macro" events at Marvel comics during this period – this book shows you some of the real human costs on the micro level.)

One of my hopes is that this book will serve as a good primer of "how to retail comics" – it's not a nuts and bolts, step-by-step analysis of how to negotiate a lease or who to contact or things like that, but more of the Whys.

One impression you might get from reading these pieces is that "things are screwed." And, through lots of the period of time covered in this book, things were indeed that way. Had you asked me in 1997 if opening a comic book shop was a rational thing, I almost certainly would have said "no. " But here, at the beginning of the 21st century, I can say with all assurance that the business of comics is ready again for new entrepreneurs to come in and light things on fire.

Perhaps the lessons of our darkest days will show you the traps to be avoided, the paths not to take.

The future is in front of us again, bright and shining, and if I can inspire even one person reading this book to take the plunge and open an ethical, forward-thinking business, then my decade reporting the darkest days is all worth it.

This book is dedicated to the entire comics industry – to the stores that survived and thrived despite it all, to the publishers who facilitate the dream coming alive, to the distributors who do the absurdly difficult job they do, to all of the creators with their shining dreams that entertain us all.

And especially to the fans, who know that comics are a limitless medium, a truly American art form, whose time in the firmament of pop culture has finally arrived.

Never stop dreaming, never stop striving!

Brian Hibbs
March 24, 2003

introduction by
Paul Levitz

As you will soon see, Brian Hibbs is often ill-informed, ill-advised, occasionally illogical, and always willing to leap to a conclusion of universal truth based on a rather microscopic sample. On the other hand, he is never ill-intended or in search of small answers to small problems, and most of all, never unwilling to engage in dialogue that might lead to his being better informed, advised, more logical, or closer to the truths for which he searches.

I come into this, you see, as one of the dwellers in the windmills. It is the nature of the comics business that the landscape is dotted with a few rather large, occasionally creaky, structures that cast massive shadows across the fields in which many smaller structures toil. From inside, the shadows we cast look fairly benign as the sun and wind move across our blades and we watch the mill grind slowly, creating fodder for all below. But when you stand in the fields for a moment, it only takes a little imagination to see how the shadowy windmill can become Don Quixote's menacing dragon.

More than imagination, it requires courage to charge the shadow from the field when you believe it's a dragon. Whether that courage comes from insanity like the Man of La Mancha's, or immutable optimism like the Man of San Francisco's, there's a certain nobility to the pursuit. And when you're actually willing to talk to the dragon of your nightmares, in order to persuade it back to its rightful role as a benevolent windmill, you've gone right past Don Quixote's score on the courage index.

In a decade or more of discussion, there has been a tremendous amount that Brian and I disagree about. Some of that comes from our different perspectives on comics, our different preferences, and even a few different aspirations for the medium and the industry. Some undoubtedly comes from the different journeys our lives have taken, personally and professionally. But over the years, I've come to value and enjoy what he brings to the discussions, whether one of us has eventually convinced the other (and each of us has done so on different occasions), or time reveals the answer, or the truth of a matter remains lost in the *Rashomon* of different people's view of the same events.

If you are interested in comics and enjoy disputation, or simply want the vicarious thrill of standing in the shadow of dragons and challenging them, you will find some interesting times in these ten years of Brian's columns. And my, in every sense of the old Chinese curse, what interesting times they've been... made just a little bit more so by the man tilting at windmills...

*Paul Levitz is currently President & Publisher of DC Comics,
and has been active in the field as a writer, editor and publisher
for over 30 years, including columns in the early '70s on Comic
Economics that were as naïve as anything Brian's ever written.*

0

This is *Tilting at Windmills #0*. Its first appearance was in the 9/20/91 issue of *Comic Buyer's Guide,* and then was rerun in *Comics Retailer #1*, without the TaW tagline.

Rereading this really makes me feel old. I can see the beginnings of my writing "style" here, but some of my phrasings really make me wince.

It's really funny how much things have changed over the years (I'd nearly forgotten we once used a newsstand distributor as backup, and who has thought of *Comics Values Monthly* lately?), yet in several fundamental ways, things are exactly the same. Comics retailers still chase the quick buck, and magazines like *Wizard* still tout the monetary "value" of comics as at least equal to the entertainment content. We're pretty fucking pathetic, aren't we?

Actually, interesting side-note: I just realized, after all these years, that in the published versions Krause excised all references to *CVM*. Heh.

Oh, and let's look at my prognostication: today on eBay (June 3rd, 2002), I put *"Ghost Rider #15"* into the search box and got six hits back. Only one of them has even one bid...and that's $0.99. McFarlane's *Spider-Man #1* did a little better – not in the quarter boxes like it should be, but sorting through the ten pages of hits that "spider-man 1" gave me, I don't see a copy going for more than $2.25.

After this ran in *CBG,* I received a call out of the blue from Harlan Ellison. Never had spoken to the man before. "Is this Hibbs? Good job, kid." That call, perhaps more than anything else (well, ok, getting a check and having a bully pulpit each month was attractive, too), was what gave me the drive to push Krause to let me do TaW as a monthly.

Not like it was a hard push, really – there weren't all that many people interested in, or capable of, doing business writing on comics...but I might never have thought of it as a regular gig if it wasn't for Harlan's push.

Here's something funny, too (well, I find it funny, at least)...in that same first issue of *Comics Retailer* is a little squib in the "publisher news" section. "Creators form Image Comics". Hmm, I wonder whatever happened to them?

Anyway, the point I wanted to make was this: here we are in the year 2002, and has much really changed from this article written in 1991? Yah, sad ennit?

• • • • •

ETHICS & THE COMICS INDUSTRY

From numerous conversations in the aisles of San Diego, messages on computer networks across the country, and letters and articles in the pages of many of the industry magazine forums, it is obvious to me that both the industry and medium of comics are presently at an ethical crossroads. Most of the concern comes from ethical questions (not necessarily stated) about the nature of comic book speculation and pricing. From my particular vantage as a retailer, I can see several ways that the retail community can take positive steps to expand the consciousness of the medium as a whole.

Let's take a look at speculation with one of the best-selling comics of recent years. *Spider-Man* #1 had a circulation of something like 2.5 million copies. How many people read comics in this country? No one knows for sure, but let's try to make a guess. If we take it that there are 5000 comic shops in this country (these are "official" figures) and that each shop has around 200 regular customers (and by regular, I mean customers who come in at least once a month). The figure of 200 comes from my customer base (by industry statistics, my store is nearly dead-on average on a dollar value point of view, giving me some measure of justification on this point), this gives us one million comics readers. Note that this is a million readers of comics, not of *Spider-Man*. This means that every person who reads comics bought 2.5 copies of this comic on average. If this isn't ludicrous enough, remember that not every person bought even one copy. This probably brings the average purchase to five copies or more.

Seeing that it's obvious that anyone who wants a copy of this comic more than likely has it already, how can it possibly have skyrocketed in price? The answer lies in the twin facts that the people who set the back issue values of comics are the people with the most to gain from higher prices, and that most people do not truly understand the principle of a price guide.

Aren't back issue prices created by supply and demand? Well, in most cases, yes. I don't think that anyone would claim that most Silver and Golden Age prices are inflated, because these comics are actually scarce in high grades. You just don't see too many mint copies of *Fantastic Four #1* lying around. There is a reason for this. During the Golden Age and the beginning of the Silver Age, no one had any clue that comics could be worth anything as a collectible. The copies that do exist in good condition of these comics are primarily in the hands of people who love their collection, and who won't part with their copies unless they must.

After the publication of Overstreet's first price guide, people perceived an implied appreciation in monetary value and started buying multiple copies of comics as an investment. An interesting idea, but to pick the good investment, you must be able to tell what the public is going to want, before they do. And if you can do it, than probably most other people can do it too (more true today than ever before), thereby making your investment worthless.

Once a businessman sees that people are willing to buy multiples of a book, because it is "hot"(i.e. is liable to sell well in the first place), you can bet your life that he is going to do anything he can to convince you that *you* should buy it. It's in his best (short-term) interests to generate that cash. The qualifier there, of "short term," is at the heart of the ethical quandary that we will explore momentarily.

Can anyone reading this name any "hot" comic that retained its value after, oh, let's say five, years? How about *Howard the Duck* #1? Was about $20, now you're lucky if you can get a buck or two for it in any reasonable amount of time. Ditto for *Amazing Spider-Man* #252. Same thing goes for *New Teen Titans* #1, early Giffen *Legion*s, the *Batman*s with "Death in the Family", and every other "hot" book of the past.

Every week these days I get someone coming in with boxes of multiple copies of "hot" early 80s comics to sell, and I won't (and can't) offer them much more than salvage rates. Why? Because I already have multiple copies in the back room gathering dust! Have no doubt, you will be seeing copies of *Spider-Man* #1 in the 25 cent boxes before the turn of the century, when the "investors" end up dumping them on the market.

Have no doubt, either, that many stores have dozens and dozens of copies of *Spider-Man* #1 sitting in their back room right now. Then why, you ask, are they selling them for $5-10 apiece? Obviously, there is no supply and demand conflict. They have more copies than they can sell. But, from a purely business point of view, it makes a limited amount of sense.

You see, most comic shops get their comics at 50% off the cover price. This basically means that after they have sold the first half of the shipment, everything else is profit (and before anyone lectures me on things like holding costs of unsold merchandise or missed cash flow opportunities, no need. I'm merely trying to show how the average retailer thinks), so that even if sales volume drops to 1/10th of the speed that it was, by selling a comic at twice the cover price, you actually appear to be making three times the profit that you would have (although it's actually one third of the profit you would have made had you sold it at cover price).

I even know of a store that charged $3.50 for *Ghost Rider* #15, the day it came out, *to people who had signed up for it weeks in advance*! This guy evidently thought he was making a killing (and he was – short-term! – of a 400% profit), but his customers were pissed, having to pay the price because most other comic shops had sold out, and it was too late to do anything about it.

(Parenthetically, I just spoke of "having" to buy a comic. Of course, no one ever *has* to buy a comic, at least not in the sense of having a gun being put to your head, as the folks at Marvel Comics are always pointing out. But, part of the joy of comics is the sense of community. When everyone [the publisher, the retailer, and the fan press] implies that you are "missing out on the excitement", by not having all of the variant versions of a particular title, and you're young and impressionable, then you're likely to buy everything you are given.)

"But," the Capitalist cries, "we're only giving them the choice of what to buy. If they choose to be foolish and waste their money, that's not our problem." Unfortunately, this is a short-term decision.

It's the ethical difference between short-term and long-term that has created the buying patterns of the comics industry. In short-term thinking, you make as much money as you possibly can off the consumer, by any means, and that's the end of the relationship. But the long-term view recognizes that the consumer is a customer, that they must receive full value for their dollar, and that the relationship is a lasting one with far-reaching possibilities.

Note that I'm not trying to imply that the retailer is the actual cause of this state of the industry. The consumer, as well, is at fault for allowing himself to be led. I put the question to all reading this: What possible reason, besides the pursuit of money, is there to buy more than one copy of a comic? There is no need to read more than one copy, so why get it?

Comics should be a medium of entertainment, not of avarice. When I put *Ghost Rider* #15 on my shelves, I noted its popularity immediately. I limited sales to one copy per person (unless you reserved more before the order deadline), although few of my regulars even wanted more. Consequently, I had copies for sale the next day, unlike most shops in town.

Virtually every person who bought the comic after that had two distinguishing features: one, they were people whom I had never seen in my store before, and two, they tried to buy *every single copy on the stands*.

Imagine that for a moment. After their normal stores sold out (more than likely to two or three people buying huge stacks – maybe even the same people!), they ran around to every store trying to buy every copy they could get their hands on. I had one guy who, after being told that it was one copy per person (not just day), actually hired bums and winos to come in and buy copies for him!

All these people do nothing less than try to drive the price of a book up, so they can make a killing. Of course, the short-term retailer sees this, and pulls remaining copies (or if he manages to get a reorder, the new copies) off the shelves, so he can be the one making a killing.

After I sold out of *Ghost Rider* #15, I called my newsstand distributor, and ordered every spare copy they received. I put them out at cover price (and realize here that from the newsstand, although they are returnable, I only receive 30% off the cover, meaning I'm actually making less profit than the other books on my racks), and had them up until two weeks ago. A long-term retailer realizes that not every one of his customers comes in every week, and makes sure that there are copies available for them when they do arrive.

A long-term retailer realizes that the goodwill you receive, by having a "hot" comic available at cover price for someone, pays off in not only a sale today, but a sale next month, and the month after that, and so on.

Capitalism does not have to be rapacious. I freely admit that I want as much of my customers' money as I possibly can get, but I want to know that they received value in exchange. This is why they continue to give me their business.

As far as price guides go, I think that they may be the single largest problem the industry has. Unfortunately, few people seem to realize that they are (at best) *guides*, not bibles. Part of the problem is that, despite any disclaimers, most people regard printed statements as fact. Most stores in the Bay Area seem to price comics by *Comic Values Monthly*. *CVM* is (in my opinion) an exercise in ludicrousness. Prices escalate there sometimes by 50% a month. But because it is printed, the consumer regards it as fact, and accepts the retailer's use of it. I know of some stores that change their prices monthly, based on *CVM*, regardless of whether the book has sold at the earlier, lower price. Do they actually sell these comics? They must, eventually, or they wouldn't still be in business. But let's look at two examples why it is bad for the industry.

First, do you remember the craze after *Superman* #50 came out? Man, oh man, comics are getting mainstream attention – articles, and TV stories all over the place! But we blew it. 'Cuz when John Q. Non-comics-reader comes looking in the average comics store to find a copy (assuming he isn't repelled by the clutter, dirt, and "ambience"), he sees that it's $10 (Thanx *CVM*!), promptly spins on his heel, and never enters a comic shop again.

Non-collectors (that's almost everybody else in the world) do not understand how a comic that was released last month can possibly be worth more than six times the cover price today. And they'll never give it another chance. Those casual readers now don't have a chance to ever become a fan.

Second, how much do you think that *Ghost Rider* #15 (or *Spider-Man* #1, or *X-Men* #1, or *Legends of the Dark Knight* #1, or *Silver Surfer* #50, or...) will be worth five years from now? My guess for the *Ghost Rider* is $3.00, but let's be charitable and say $4.00. Now hardly any dealer will give you more than 50% in cash (and some will only give 25%). That means that the comic that you paid $1.75 for is worth $2.00 in actual money now. What kind of investment is this?

But you'll find a private collector, you say. Fine, but your time is worth something, isn't it? Even if you only value yourself at minimum wage, if it takes you longer than a half hour to find a buyer, you'll lose money.

So how does someone react who now finds out that their "hot" collection isn't worth what they paid for it? I'll tell you – they quit buying comics altogether. Now sure, from the short-term point of view, it doesn't matter, because there's always a new load of suckers down the bend. But the long-term recognizes that you want the current group of customers, as well as tomorrow's. I actively encourage my customers not to buy doubles, because I know that they will get burned.

Ethical choices must be made on all levels of the industry. We must all continue to encourage and foster the growth of positive, creative values from consumer, to retailer, to publisher, to creator.

One way or another, comics is coming into its own as a big business. Whether we screw everyone else to get our piece of the pie or work harmoniously to create a lasting structure, we must choose, every one of us. It has been said that "there's no room for sentiment in big business." We are perhaps the only big business that was created by fandom, for fandom. As a reader, as a retailer, as a creator, you have tremendous power. Use it ethically, and we will all be the better for it.

And hey! Did you realize that if there are seven million copies of X-Men #1, that's nearly ten for every man, woman, and child living in San Francisco today?

This was my first "real" *TaW* (written expressly to be a regular column), and, looking back at it (ugh, did I ever write that woodenly?), you can see all of the themes that would become my watchword over the next hundred columns: diversification of your key product line, walking away from speculation-driven marketing, encouraging readership over "collecting for its own sake."

I almost certainly didn't hit the "blame it on Overstreet" premise enough – today, that alone would have filled my 2000 words. But fuck off, I was still learning how to write these things.

I also note this column ran in May of 1992. "Within three years, the gravy train will be at an end." In your face.

Now, why the fuck didn't anyone listen?

Tilting at Windmills #1
(Originally ran in Comics Retailer #2)

The proliferation of the back-issue market (hell, even the existence of an organized back-issue market in the first place), the rise of the comics specialty shop, the collector's mentality, and, probably, the ability for alternative publishers to open shop. All this can be pinned on the *Overstreet Price Guide*.

Don't believe me? The first *Overstreet* was published in 1971. The concept that comics can be worth money started filtering around (remember that prior to price guides, comics were usually [and routinely] thrown out, destroyed, or otherwise disposed of. Why keep them? They were just taking up space).

Comic shops started to spring up all over the place (prior to '71 there were only a handful, scattered all over the country), as people saw how easy it was to open a store (all you needed was a big enough collection and a couple thousand dollars), until there were enough stores to support direct distributors. Once we had distributors for just comic shops, alternative publishers started up (as opposed to undergrounds, which, historically, were primarily sold to a "non-traditional" market – headshops and the like). 1977 saw the birth of *Cerebus*, and 1978 gave us *Elfquest*, neither of which could have made it without organized fandom, and the backbone of the comic shops. These two comics, more than any others, spurred multitudes of creators to create and publish their own material, based on their own desires and visions, rather than the dictates of a company. It is this freedom and variety that will be the impetus for any kind of wide-ranging acceptance of the medium.

And it's all *Overstreet*'s fault, however indirectly.

Overstreet did us all a great favor, by creating an implied value of old comic books. But this opportunity for organization and success carried the seed for its own downfall: the collector's mentality.

How are back-issue prices determined? Well, in theory, by supply and demand. Golden and Silver Age comic books command high prices simply because parents threw out or destroyed 90% of the copies. And 90% of the surviving copies were read, over and over again, until the comic was trashed. They weren't stored flat in plastic bags. They were rolled up in back pockets or haphazardly tossed in piles, pages getting bent, torn and yellow. I mean, who'd thought that old *Superman* comics could be worth money? And that's exactly the reason there are only 100 or so copies of *Superman* #1 in any kind of reasonable condition. No one knew!

But, with the advent of price guides and comic book stores, people started to realize that comics *could* be worth money (implied value), and started taking pains to preserve their comics. What this means is that there is no real scarcity of comics from the last 10-15 years (outside of the few "cult" comic books, which the readers would not part with for love or money anyway. Titles like *Cerebus*, *Sandman*, *Taboo*, *Beanworld*, etc. Just try to find copies of the early issues of these comics at any price). There are tens of thousands of copies of *Batman*, *X-Men*, and *Aliens* out there for the asking, all in mint condition, stored in plastic with a board. I go to comics conventions all the time, and every dealer has the same 50 titles, ten deep, at inflated prices. Can't they see there is no scarcity of these comic books? I've heard from too many customers that they've gone to other comics shops, trying to sell collections of *X-Men*, *Alpha Flight*, *New Mutants*, and the like, and having the stores pick out half-a-dozen books out of a 200+ collection. If you're not buying every comic in reasonable condition that comes into your shop, there is an excess of supply, and your selling price is too high, regardless of what any guide says. At this point, I'm throwing *X-Men*, *Alpha Flight*, *New Mutants*, and the like in the quarter boxes, because that is all I ever see. In just a few months, we'll be doing the same with *Spider-Man* #1, then *X-Force* #1, then *X-Men* #1. There are far more copies of these comics than the market can reasonably support, and all it will take is time before they filter back down into the stores, and the speculators realize they're going to take a bath.

To my eyes, most retail organizations are happy to raise prices, and loathe to lower them, despite the dozens of copies they may have in the back.

As the speculator's disenchantment and suspiciousness inevitably occurs, we're going to see a major crash in prices. It is our duty as retailers, for the continued health of the market, to diversify the types of comics we offer, and to suggest that people do not speculate. There is, I believe, still a chance to lessen the effects of the crash. But the steps must be taken *immediately* to disassociate your store with the collector's mentality, and to not depend on any one type or brand of comics.

Encourage your customers to only buy what they *enjoy*, not to "wait until it gets better." Tell them not to buy multiple copies of *X-Men*; rather, to buy several different comics which they can read and feel happy about the money they have spent. You'll probably even be able to get them to increase their monthly expenditures, as they become happier customers.

I don't expect to make many converts here – if your store is 80% Marvel, you probably think I'm full of shit. Your sales are up, and you're selling more comics than ever before. But I guarantee that within three years, the gravy train will be at an end. In the last two weeks, I've bought five collections, and all of them have had multiple copies of *Spider-Man* #1.

The writing is on the wall. I hope you can see it. For all of our sakes.

This is a pretty boring "nuts and bolts" column...one sad thing (or just about right, depending on your POV) is that SF was down to seven comic book shops by 2001. I recently did a tour of all of them, and concluded we don't have any "competition" within the City – unless you count Borders/Virgin/Tower.

Anyway, let me apologize in advance for boring the non-comics retailers in the audience who are reading this (this is one of the few *Tiltings* not reprinted in our in-store magazine, *Onomatopoeia*).

Tilting at Windmills #2
(Originally ran in Comics Retailer #3)

In my last two columns, I discussed taking a long-term view, and discarding the "collectors mentality." Both of these tacks have many benefits, the most important of which is bringing in new customers. Without new customers, while sales can rise, you are feeding off of a stagnant pool of customers. This is a precarious position to be in, as the loss of a few key customers could spiral into dire financial straits.

Diversification, in both product mix and customer base, is the key to a healthy business and industry, and both are directly tied to one another. New lines of merchandise (if promoted correctly) can bring in new customers, while new customers demand a wider range of material.

In San Francisco, where my store is located, there are over 20 comics shops servicing 750,000 people, making competition extremely fierce. But we're posting an annual increase of sales of nearly 50%. The main reason, in my eyes at least, is that we carefully target new customers, and have created a store and variety of material that is reactive to the new customers' needs.

Possibly the most important thing to remember when you are trying to attract "civilians," is that they have no knowledge (even to the point of not realizing comics are still being published) or understanding of the modern comics market, nor are they particularly interested in acquiring such knowledge. If you showed a person off of the street a picture of the X-Men, they would not likely know (or care) who these character are, yet *X-Men* is the benchmark that comics sales are stacked against.

So, when you design your advertising and promotions, it is important to avoid using characters and images that are not immediately known to civilians. Advertising and window displays should revolve around Batman, Superman, Spider-Man, Hulk, Mickey Mouse, Aliens, Calvin & Hobbes, etc., *not* X-Men, Punisher, Wolverine, Lobo, etc. Once you get them in your door, you can expose them to the variety of material available, but it is imperative to get them in the store first.

Besides promoting characters that are cultural icons, it is essential that you have material that appeals to the new reader and will cause them to come back for more. With very few exceptions, this does not include superhero comics. You need to carefully judge your product mix, both quantitatively and qualitatively.

Let's discuss the former first. I want to stress the importance of keeping careful track of the quantities of various titles you carry, not by eye-balling them, but by having hard copy records you can examine. The most common and useful records you can keep are *cycle sheets*. Simply put, you create an individual sheet for each title, with room for 6-12 different issues. You then count the quantities for 4-8 weeks, and sum up your sales and leftovers throughout the cycle period. By having this information at your fingertips, you'll find it much easier to see what comics you order too many of and what you order too few of. You'll probably find that you are under-ordering many independents and over-ordering many majors. If, for example, you sell out of *Love & Rockets* in the first week on sale, and still have 10% of your *Avengers* left after six weeks, you should adjust your *Avengers* order down and *Love & Rockets* up. You'll find that this basic step keeps you more profitable and responsive to your customers' *actual* needs, rather than what you *think* their needs are.

In my experience, non-mainstream material (despite the company it is from), outside of high-visibility licenses (*Aliens, Vampire Lestat*, or Clive Barker material, for example), is what keeps the new customers coming back. While the exact titles will vary from location to location, I personally have had success with titles as varied as *Sandman, Love & Rockets, American Splendor*, and *Dirty Plotte*. While these may not sell the *quantity* of X-Men or Batman, from a *dollar-value* basis, they frequently do as well, if not better. However, you need to actively *build* the clientele of this type of book. Sales will not just spring up, fully-grown.

There are several tactics you can use to safely increase your sales. The method with the least risk is an in-house subscription service. Create a form listing the titles you carry, and allow customers to sign up, in advance, for the titles they want. By summarizing these quantities, you can see which independents you have customers for, and order them confidently with low risk. Make sure, however, that you promote this service to *all* of your customers, because if they are not aware, they won't sign up. Additionally, you must have the perseverance to offer this service for several months, before you see a large response. Personally, I find that offering a token discount is easily justified by the data you receive, enabling you to order a lot closer to your actual sales. You should, however, make that decision based on your volume and needs.

This type of interactive service need not be formal. The important inference here is that you listen to customer requests, and react to them. If you have a customer telling you he wants a particular item, order it for them, even if you feel that this particular title "doesn't sell." Even if you have to get a token down-payment from the customer, it is imperative that you fulfill their needs. If your distributor has minimum orders on the title the customer asks for, call your local warehouse, and explain the situation to them. It is very likely they will make an exception to make the both of you more profitable. A special effort today can spell many sales down the line.

Another way to begin diversifying your material is to give independent publishers a phone call. Frequently, they are happy to make an arrangement to get their material in your store. You will find some willing to arrange a consignment deal, while others have "sampler" packs, for a low net cost.

As the retailer, you have a lot of authority over your customers' habits and purchases. In my store, if I personally like something, I can sell at least 30 copies, because my customers respect my opinions. You will certainly have some number of customers who will trust your opinion and try a book on your say so. This is why it is important to make a qualitative judgment of the comics in your store. It is important for you to read and assess the comics that you carry. If you read and enjoy alternative material, it will be much easier to lead your customers to it. I read every comic that comes into my store, and am, accordingly, able to match the proper material to the proper customer. Furthermore, the more you know your customers' tastes, and the more you match their tastes to the merchandise, the more they'll trust your judgment. The more they respect your opinion, the more sales you'll make.

Finally, I want to emphasize again that expanding your customer base and tastes is a project that takes some time. As with any new promotion technique, you must have the patience to wait for the months it can take for it to succeed. Don't expect immediate results! But, when the results do come, they will be there day after day, month in, month out, making you more diverse, more profitable, and much happier.

a r t i c l e
3

What really really frightens me in looking back at some of these old columns is how I could make a few word substitutions, and I could run it today, and it would still be just as valid and just as fresh.

No one has really learned anything over the last ten years, have they?

Tilting at Windmills #3
(Originally ran in Comics Retailer #4)

The marketplace has changed dramatically in the last ten years. One of the most significant changes is the sheer quantity of publishers and titles to choose from.

With the majority of comic shops having a very limited amount of floor space, it is a very difficult proposition to carry all the material available, let alone the bulk of it.

There was a time when a publisher could simply solicit the books, and expect a reasonable amount of orders to continue publication. This is far from true today. Many wonderful, creative comics are coming out today that get orders of less than 2000 copies on the first issue, and drop far below that on subsequent issues. I believe that comics such as *Cerebus*, *Love & Rockets*, and *Elfquest* would not survive for long, if they were launched today, in today's market. How many of tomorrow's Wendy Pinis or Dave Sims are being discouraged and run out of business by this turn of events? Where will the next group of unique voices come from?

A lot of effort is being put toward (rightfully so) helping retailers get their acts together – cleaning the store, keeping accurate records, being courteous to customers – in short, being responsible business people. It's quite easy to see most of these flaws – just walk into any comics shop, and you'll notice it right off. But these surface problems mask a much more serious flaw: some (hell, most) people just aren't suited to be business people.

And it's not just limited to retailers.

It is my contention that most publishers, and agents thereof, haven't got a clue as to the reality of life in the trenches and are, at best, poor businessmen.

If they were good businessmen, they'd advertise and promote the titles they produce; they'd actively keep in contact with retailers, trying to meet our needs in format, price point, UPC codes, and packaging; and they wouldn't blame their poor performance on other companies' actions.

Too many publishers produce more books than they can maintain. In today's market, without a surefire license or big-name creators, too few publishers advertise or promote their titles on a regular basis. Then they act surprised that their titles do not sell.

There is so much material available on the market that without a well thought-out and focused advertising campaign, both directed at retailers and consumers, no publisher can expect their material to do gangbusters business.

Retailers must order the first few issues of new titles blind. Unless publishers supply us with sufficient information, we're going to be conservative. I feel that when soliciting all new first issues, or significant changes in a books direction, all publishers (from Marvel right down to In-Our-Basement comics) should be sending out full-issue previews (so we are aware of what exactly it is we're buying), promotional posters we can display in our stores, and an outline of the marketing plans for the title. If the publisher cannot provide the retailer (who pays the direct consequences of the publisher's poor business sense) with these items, then they are probably not suited to being publishers.

How many times have we heard publishers grouse about their poor sales, and lay the blame at the marketplace? I try to be one of the most pro-independent retailers, and even I will only order "onesies or twosies" on items that I know nothing of other than a one paragraph description from the distributor's catalog.

I want to stress, as well, that promotion should not end after the first issue. It is imperative that you continue telling the consumer about your material well past the first issue, as word of mouth often moves slowly. Promotion is not a one-time affair – it must be an ongoing concern

Obviously, I don't believe that publishers must bear the burden of promotion alone. However, if they have plans/ideas of how to work with retailers, they must communicate them to us, as well as how we can get in touch with them. I cannot tell you how many times I have had to go out of my way to track down the address and phone number of some publisher, so I could tell them that I wanted to promote their books! Obviously, this is bad business.

Among others things a publisher should bear in mind is the packaging of the comic, so it is salable by us. This is the only point of comic production where I feel marketing needs must overturn artistic desires. As a rule, comics should always have a logo on the cover (Comics without logos are not "distinctive looking" on the rack, they are invisible – often even when someone is specifically searching for it!), and that logo should be understandable from both the left 1/3 (only) of the cover, as well as the top 1/3 (only). Very few stores have the floor space to give full cover display to every title available. In my store, all I have the room to display is the left 1/3, and if the customer can't scan and spot your comic from that much display, it will not sell. Additionally, the price of the comic should be *prominently* visible on the front cover, as this aids in speed of ring-up, and ease of pricing for the after-market.

Publishers that produce (for example) eight titles in a month should not ship all eight titles in one week. This dilutes the effectiveness of any given title's promotion, and often forces the customer into an all-or-nothing situation. Often they will choose nothing.

The timely shipping of material is absolutely essential. Deliver a book when you promise it, or don't promise it in the first place. Never solicit for a title that you don't have completed work for. Nothing will destroy potential customer interest (and stick retailers with unsalable merchandise, and resentment towards a publisher) faster than late shipping material. Unfortunately, many customers labor under the impression that we create the comics in our own living rooms (this goes for Marvels and DCs, as well), so the bad feelings that are generated are directed toward *us*. Timely shipping goes double for limited series. More times than I want to count, I have been successful with the first issue of a limited series, yet get stuck with vast quantities when the subsequent issues are weeks and months off-schedule.

Publishers must also make sure that reorders are conveniently available. More often than not, distributors are lax about reordering material that is not sure-fire. Go direct to the retailer if you have to, but create a plan for ensuring constant availability, and let retailers know how you plan to handle it.

My final suggestion for today is that publishers should take pains to contact a large cross-section of retailers and not depend solely on information from the store down the block from your offices. There are many needs that retailers have, to sell your material, only a few of which I've touched upon here. Most retailers are happy to answer questions, give input, and otherwise aid you in selling your books. If you do not take every chance that you can to sell your material – use every avenue to advertise, promote, and expand your audience – then you don't avail yourself of the diversity of experiences that retailers have. Whether you are in the ivory towers of Marvel & DC, or a fledging publisher, just opening your doors – you are a poor businessperson.

And you've got no one to blame but yourself.

So, I have never really been all that good at meeting my deadlines. Well, no, I meet them, I just usually don't do it until the last possible second. I figured this out fairly early in the game, so I tried to get a jump on things, and write two columns in one month, giving me a "buffer."

And then K.C. Carlson decided to run them both in issue #4. Jesus.

This ran as "Tilting at Windmills PLUS".

Needless to say, I didn't try that again.

Again, this is pretty "nuts and bolts," so don't glaze your eyes over, Charlie.

Tilting at Windmills #3.5
(Originally Ran in Comics Retailer #4)

As this is an opinion column, I usually have the freedom to write about anything I damn well please. However, this month, K.C. has asked me to write a column about in-store promotion. Well, he certainly couldn't have asked for a harder column, because I have a little secret to share with you: promotion (for me at least) is about 75% inspiration, and 25% perspiration.

Well, I certainly can't teach inspiration to you, it's either there or it isn't. But I can point you towards some of the ways to focus your perspiration.

My single greatest resource for promotions is creator signings, and the best way to entice creators to appear in your store is to speak to them in person. Most of the contacts I make with pros are at comic conventions. I never set up shop at these events, preferring to use my time making connections. Generally, I only attend the larger cons (like WonderCon in Oakland, or the San Diego ComicCon), as the smaller cons usually have a handful of guests, most of whom will attend the larger shows.

(I need to make a digression here. It is important to state from the onset that my store is located in a large cultural mecca, San Francisco, and that my very location provides numerous advantages to facilitating events. Most people *want* to come to the Bay Area, so it is far easier to set up signings here than it would be in, say, Des Moines. Moreover, the Bay Area is filled with local creators, so traveling expenses are negligible. So, some of *my* tactics may prove useless to you, but hopefully you'll be able to extrapolate some underlying attitudes.)

I cannot overstate the value of going to as many major cons as you can afford. The contacts that you can make, if you're prepared to work a little bit, will prove invaluable to you. You will probably find that creators, themselves, are generally prepared to go that extra mile to promote their work directly in your store, whether it be from a personal appearance, to assisting you in getting promotion materials (creating an original piece of artwork or design for your flyers, or making additional phone calls to get promotional material directly to you). Additionally, it is beneficial to create as many relationships as you can with the marketing people from the various publishers. You never know when someone could do you a favor that can create a promotional bonanza.

Of course, I'm discussing here the art of the *schmooze* – another concept difficult to discuss empirically. Let it suffice that if you feel an *itch* to talk to people, to create and broaden your working relationships, then you have the *schmooze*. If you feel none of these symptoms, well, you probably shouldn't even be bothering to read this magazine (or at least this article...).

Anyway, as you make more contacts, more will be available to you. And then more still, and so on.

There are two major expenses involved in creator appearances: Travel/lodging/expenses for the pro, and advertising. In the Bay Area, this is a $500+ commitment (and 80% of that is the advertisement). It is very important to remember that you won't make your money back on the day of the event (normally, at least). Personal appearances will create sales in the long run, not the short run.

You want to make sure that you have at least one month to promote personal appearances. This is the minimum amount of time you'll need to create window displays, send out press releases, create and run flyers and display advertising, etc. While I've always found it a necessity to advertise in local "hip" media, the most effective advertisement is (assuming you have a sufficient lead time) is flyers, displays, signage, and word of mouth. Media advertising merely serves to reinforce your message. Don't forget to send press releases to both your local papers (especially independents) and the *Comic Buyer's Guide*!

It is essential that you treat the pro well. Put them up in a nice place, find out if they have any special desires, provide refreshments for them during the event, and take them out to dinner afterwards, picking their brains for ways you can better promote their material, or if they have suggestions on how to better display their work. While many of their suggestions may prove unusable, I have gotten wonderful suggestions from pros that have helped me sell far more copies of their work.

After the signing, if you had a notable success, or anything out of the usual happened, write a news report and send it to the local media and to the *CBG*. You might as well get your promotion to do double duty for you!

There are pros and cons in working with publishers (as opposed to dealing with the creator directly) – especially with Marvel and DC – on setting up creator appearances. The big pro argument is that if you work with them, many of your expenses for the appearance are eligible for co-op reimbursement. A major con in working with the Big Two is that they are hesitant to schedule too many appearances with their "big gun" talent – especially if they are deadline offenders. The bottom line – most creators are not under exclusive contract to their publishers and will ultimately do what *they* want to do. You may be able to snag them on your own, but you may have to forgo the co-op option if the publisher is not happy about them going on the road.

However, you can save money by doing your own legwork, and still get some co-op support. You know your area better than the folks in New York (or whatever) and can find affordable, but nice, hotels that will save everybody money. And watch for "package tours" forming. Hypothetically, chances are slim that DC will spring to fly Neil Gaiman into South Dakota for a one-day signing, but they may be open to a plan that will take him to several area shops for a short number of days to promote a special project. In fact, such "tours" may be company-sponsored and a phone call may be all you need to get you signed up for a slot.

As I said, creator appearances are my most frequent promotion, but I can suggest a few other ways you can draw attention to your store.

Try to form alliances with purveyors of other media in your area. Talk to bookstores, record stores, video stores, theaters, etc. Look for ways to generate traffic between your store and theirs. For example, theaters (and their publicity departments) are often happy to get you movie posters, pins, and other paraphernalia, if you give it away in your store and help promote the film. They get the additional (and effectively free) potential consumers you appeal to, and you get a good reputation from your customers. When a genre related film runs, you can donate related comics material, to give away, or raffle, at the premiere. You could set up a display in the lobby, or leave flyers. Either way you do it, it's important to not wait until the genre film opens – most theaters will want to see some other participation (on films that really need help) before they'll throw you the bone of a big movie.

Another example of positive use of non-comics connections: When *Alpha Flight* #106 came out, we held a panel at a local gay bookstore, debating the portrayal of homosexuals in comics. We made a couple phone calls to artists and activists, ran off some flyers, and bingo, we had an event. Rather than trying to sell a crummy superhero comic for five times cover price, we pointed out the diversity of material available, in genre and not. For a small investment (less than $30 – and that includes my time), we potentially showed 100 new customers what comics were. (It is important to not let your personal interests limit you to what opportunities you explore. I myself am not gay, nor do I have any interest in gay subculture, but I saw a clear opportunity to introduce a new group of people to comics.)

The final promotional tool you must use is usually the most neglected one: In-store signage and displays. The way your store looks and "feels" is as important as any event or advertising. If you have new faces coming into your store, you must work to keep them there. The front of your store should be clean and neat (not covered in generic superhero posters) and clearly marking your store name. If at all possible, you should try to have some sort of cool display in your front windows. I'm lucky enough to have two deep bays, one of which we use exclusively for "artistic" displays, hyping a specific event or appearance. Your store should be well organized, with signs and placards directing people to specific areas, and bringing their attention to whatever special sales or features of your store. Always try to look at your store as an outsider – someone who has no idea whatsoever as to what comics are, or that they even exist. You'll probably find numerous ways to make your store more palatable to the non-comics person. Listen to your customers! They'll often point out things that you've become blind to.

In summary, keep an open mind and a flexible attitude. Look at the world around you and explore your opportunities. Always remember that most promotions won't show immediate results. You have to have a fair amount of patience. But, eventually you'll see a steady and inexorable growth in sales. Let me close with one recommendation: seek out a copy of Jay Conrad Levinson's *Guerrilla Marketing*. My copy is at the store, as I type this, so I can't give you publisher info, and whatnot, but a few years ago, Marvel was carrying this book. Maybe they can be persuaded to do so again.

Heh. Arguing with other columns I haven't the right to reprint!
You can figure it out, though.

Tilting at Windmills #4
(Originally ran in Comics Retailer #5)

One of the nice things about writing an opinion column is that I can write about anything that I damn well please. If I want to talk about religion or politics, I can (as long as I can at least peripherally tie it in to comics retailing). The soapbox is mine. This being so, I'm going to continue a debate that began in *Comics Retailer* #1, in Pat O'Neill's article, "Stop 'Preaching to the Choir'," and was continued into *Dialog* in *CR* #3, via Lou Bank's letter. Well, I'm bringing it into my column, 'cuz I think Lou is wrong, wrong, wrong.

First off, a couple of disclaimers. *Numero uno*, is that this column is entirely my opinion, and certainly doesn't reflect any views that *CR*, K.C., or Krause might hold. I say this because I figure the last thing this fledgling magazine needs is Marvel honked off at them. Direct your ire straight at me, if you please. Second, Pat certainly doesn't need me acting as apologist for him. Hell, Pat and I disagree on many, many things, but he's on the right track with this one.

Anyway, I'm very surprised that Lou even wrote a letter, seeing that he is not doing much more than parroting what he's said before. It is obvious that his main contentions come from someone who does not work in a store on a day-to-day basis, and, as such, are completely indefensible.

His first contention, repeated in both pieces, is that, "No one's going to walk into a comics shop for a horror comic if they aren't already familiar with the comic format. If they're a big horror reader, I don't think they'll buy a horror comic, unless they're already somewhat familiar with comics."

Well, Lou, I say thee nay! In my store, Clive Barker comics, Anne Rice titles, licensed SF/horror titles (*Twilight Zone*, and the like), and similar comics go in the window. Invariably, we get several people a day wandering in, proclaiming that they didn't even know that comics were still printed, let alone telling stories of characters and stories they are already familiar with. Compare this to when we put a superhero comic in the window. The requests usually border on nonexistent – exceptions being media tie-ins like *Batman vs. Predator.*

Now, I will accept that mass media stories (like Northstar announcing he was gay, Superman's engagement, or Spidey's 30th anniversary) *do* pump the sales way up, but these sales are very problematic. The first problem is that the sales usually go back down to pre-event numbers within 4 months. Yes, we got dozens of civilians walking in looking for *Superman* #50, but exceedingly few of them came back next month for #51. The second problem is that the vast bulk of these additional sales are generated not by civilians, but by speculators, smelling a buck at the expense of the ignorant. *Every* time one of these media-generated hits come out, we have at least two or three unknown (and greedy-looking) people trying to buy out our entire stock. Every time! The end result is that these books become hot within a span of a day, and the civilian perceives comics as a rip-off, because they won't pay $5 for a comic that came out yesterday. My most immediate example is *Spectacular Spider-Man* #189 – the 30th Anniversary issue. The comic shipped on Friday, and by Saturday, most stores were charging $7 for it!

Lou points to the success of the *Batman* movie as proof of his theory. *Batman* was a huge success, and since all those hundreds of thousands of theater-goers got into the idea that a man could dress like a rodent and punch out a clown, they immediately have an innate enjoyment of a totally foreign medium. How the one leads directly to another, I simply cannot fathom. I think it is evident that – while *Batman* sales reached remarkable peaks throughout that summer – by the time winter came, sell-through was at a fraction of what it had been. Even now that the sequel is coming, I see almost no signs of the fad we had last time. In San Francisco, at least, *Batman* sales are equal to or lower than they were this time last year. The same is true of most retailers I speak with in different parts of the country.

So, if you want to talk about follow-through sales, I think it is dead wrong to suggest that anything more than a minuscule fraction is generated by people reading in *USA Today* that Spider-Man is getting married. It is my direct experience that this is not the case. More readers (but perhaps not numerical sales) are grown by intelligent comics and media tie-ins than by super-hero one-hit wonders.

It is important to distinguish between readers and numerical sales. I believe that the number of actual comic readers is stagnant at best, and perhaps even diminishing. Most other retailers inform me that multiple copy sales are beginning to become the norm, rather than the exception. I know of one store where, by the owner's admission, 40% of the stores sales were multiple copies! And this doesn't begin to figure in the copies that are held back for the back issues. I am firmly of the opinion that most mainstream comics have, at best, a readership of half their circulation. The other side of this are so-called "fringe books" like *Sandman*, *Love & Rockets*, or *Hate*, where, while they have smaller print-runs, virtually 100% of those copies are reaching actual readers.

In my experience of dealing with the bureaucracy of the largest comics companies (though not the individuals themselves) the overriding concern is for sales, not readers. It doesn't matter if 90% of the 8-million-plus copies of *X-Men* #1 are ever going to be read by anyone, the only important thing is that it sold more than eight million. I submit that this type of attitude is severely detrimental to the industry itself. What happens when the people finally wake up, and realize that all the cases of *X-Men*, *Robin II*, and *X-Force* they have aren't actually worth a damn thing? They'll stop buying the next "big" thing. And the retailers will be the ones left holding the bag – not the publishers, who just print the books and reap the rewards. It's an easy ride, and I more than understand the underlying reasons that a corporation (and a publicly traded one at that) chooses this path: it is profitable. But I think at the end of the day, it ultimately hurts the marketplace itself – damaging the company in the long run.

So, if the comics-reading public really is stagnant, it is apparent, to me at least, that steps must be taken to create a new readership, and that the key to this is *advertising*. I know that full-page monthly ads in *Rolling Stone* are definitely out, but what about regional editions, local alternative papers, independent radio or TV? There are *dozens* of potential test-markets out here for us to learn how, exactly, to sell comics to civilians. One thing I know is that it won't ultimately be with spandex punch-outs. I'd be happy to advertise and experiment with increasing the sales of, say, *Hellraiser*. More people know who Clive Barker is than who know comics are still published, let alone sold in specialty stores. Sadly, the only ads Marvel sees fit to produce for co-op are garish and project a feel of "Hoo, hoo, bloodcurdling horror, kiddies." I certainly can't see them attracting new readers.

Unfortunately, the great unwashed hasn't a great affinity for the concept of illustrated fiction. And super-heroes aren't going to attract them in droves. I can see no tangible evidence that the current genre as it stands holds anything for the average person. Expanding the genres, advertising options for them, and general accessibility for the truly new reader are the only things that will grow our market.

There are retailers out here who want desperately to expand our audience, who are not content in simple lying back and selling 25 copies of "Hot" book #1 to a decreasing number of customers. There is not one comic book company which is giving their full support to the market. Oh, sure, if I call up, I can probably get someone to work with me, but there are non-existent levels of direct retailer support as a policy. Fuck, *you* should be calling *me*, and the dozens just like me, who are fighting to give our medium the future it deserves, and who desperately show our desire to work with you in that betterment.

But, damn it, we can't do it alone.

So, rather than mouthing vague platitudes to the shrine of the super-hero media stories, why don't we all do some active work in our communities? Spend more than a week working at a comic shop, and it's painfully obvious that we have to work a helluva lot harder to turn our stagnant pool of speculators and fanboys into a swiftly expanding market of a diverse and eclectic group of readers. Our time would be better used by attempting to find new markets, rather than defending the status quo.

Let's all get on the stick, okay?

a   r   t   i   c   l   e

5

I'm not that happy with some of these early columns – I didn't quite have my voice or hit the "right" points in a lot of cases. This one, in particular, I think is shit. It was done at editorial request: "Write something about holiday promotions."

This was the last time (or close to it) that I ever **took** editorial suggestions!

If you're not a comic book retailer, go read another column. Hell, even if you are, go read another one. This is only here for completeness' sake!

Two side notes: this was the month *Comics Retailer* started printing my name as "Brain Hibbs;" and this was quite possibly the most edited column I've ever written. When I compare my original text to what ran in CR...well, then-editor Don Butler...um, **added** about 10% to my word count. Weird.

TILTING AT WINDMILLS #5
(Originally ran in Comics Retailer #6)

Holidays are potentially great sources for sales. The key to realizing the possibilities is, as always, creativity. Anyone can create simple promotions that will bring in immediate sales, but creative solutions can create long-term customers.

One of the simplest promotions is the sale price. Large chains like Macy's have Mother's and Father's day sales every year, where selected merchandise is discounted. It is simple to recreate this type of event in your store, but by putting a spin on it, you can make a routine sale something special.

For example, you could give a discount to anyone bringing their mother or father in, or to anyone with pictures of their children. By using "audience participation", you create a dynamic image in customers' minds. Maybe you could have a contest for the parent and child who look the most alike, with the winning pair given a $50 shopping spree in your store. Remember: when you do a contest or any unusual promotion, take pictures and send a press release to your local media.

More complex promotions could revolve around other holidays. For example, for Easter, you could make up egg-shaped gift certificates, and disperse them randomly in your back issues boxes. During your "Easter Egg Hunt," customers have to look through your stock, hopefully finding something they'd like to buy. April Fool's Day could bring a Wheel of Fortune your customers could spin, bringing them either a random discount, a free gift, or a squirt with a water gun! Perhaps President's Day could spawn a raffle you can enter if you pay with One or Five-dollar bills (pictures of Washington and Lincoln, don't you know). Of course, check with your local and state laws to make sure they do not forbid raffles...

Reward your customers for shopping with you! Giving out $1 gift certificates to your regular customers on Christmas shows them that you care, or perhaps you could set up a birthday club. On Halloween, give out your overstocked comics, instead of candy, to trick-or-treaters.

Get involved in your community. Perhaps on Arbor Day you could sponsor a tree-planting campaign. You can help register people to vote, or give a discount to all voting customers on Election Day.

Remember, the more involved people are in your promotion, the more likely the memory will stick with them. Halloween costume contests, New Year's Eve parties, or "how I spent my summer vacation" cartoon contests with schools on Back to School day are all likely ideas.

The only limit to this type of promotion is your own creativity. One thing that is often helpful is to take out a calendar at the beginning of the year, and find at least one event a month that you could center an event around. Look for themes in the holiday of which you can take advantage. Valentine's Day, for example, is hearts, love, red, and romance. Among the many things you could do is provide a Valentine's Day card free with purchase; 20% off all romance comics; a poll of the greatest comic book romances (Clark & Lois, Peter & Mary Jane, etc.) with a prize given to a random entry; a discount for anyone wearing red; or heart-shaped gift certificates hidden like the Easter Egg hunt. There are dozens (if not hundreds) of other ways you can use the holiday theme to your advantage. The trick is to be creative, and always try something new. You can learn as much (if not more!) from your failures as you can from your successes.

You need not always give a discount or a gift to take advantage of a holiday. For example, a couple of Thanksgivings ago we did a window display of the Doom Patrol fighting a plucked and headless giant turkey – we created a thematic display, that got people talking (and laughing), and coming into the store to find out what it was all about. We sold a greater than normal number of copies of *Doom Patrol* that and subsequent months, just because we saw an opportunity.

What does *Doom Patrol* have to do with Thanksgiving? Nothing at all, but that didn't stop us from finding a creative way to tie the two together.

This is not to say that you always need to stretch credibility, or do a window display, to create a mood in your store. Even simple decorations or music can achieve that end. Christmas might bring a Christmas tree, boughs of holly, or even a little mistletoe, in the store itself. Halloween lends itself to spider webs, a skeleton, and creepy music. Valentine's Day might be hearts and lace. The sky is the limit.

Some of these suggestions might sound corny to you, or inappropriate to your store. I'm not suggesting that you follow these to the letter, or even that you use them at all. Actually, I've not tried many of them, myself. The point is that you look carefully at your options and find the ones that work for you and, more importantly, for your customers, no matter what your inclinations are.

I've used the word "creative" many times in this and other articles. The secret to creating sales is being creative, whether you are creating a holiday promotion, arranging an in-store appearance, or designing an advertisement. Don't stop at your first concept. Work, and think creatively. I cannot overemphasize the importance of "skull time" in running your business. The more you consider, plan, and organize, the less energy you'll waste in implementation.

Our industry is still in its infancy (relatively). The more creative you are, the more you push the envelope, the better we'll all be for the future.

And there's so much future in front of us.

Not much commentary on this column, really. It pretty much speaks for itself.

Pictures from this event (and some of the other signings I've discussed) are on the Comix Experience website – www.comixexperience.com.

Actually, here is one note: we used to do a lot of signings. A **lot** of them. But, then, because we did **so** many...people stopped caring about them **at all.** You **can** overdo a good thing.

Tilting at Windmills #6
(Originally ran in Comics Retailer #7)

I'm writing this on August 3rd. It's one helluva month (past and coming up), so this column will be much shorter (and less controversial) than usual.

On July 24th, we were lucky enough to be able to host the *Sandman: Seasons of Mists* Hardcover tour. We had Neil Gaiman, Kelley Jones, Matt Wagner, Mike Dringenberg, and Steve Oliff all in the store at once. This tour (sponsored and organized by DC comics) was an unqualified success – we had several hundred people waiting more than two hours each to speak with these creators, and spend an average of $40 a person. We had our best day ever ($6316), and all we had to do (practically) was open our doors.

In August, we have signings with Garth Ennis (*Hellblazer*), Jill Thompson (*Sandman*), Lewis Shiner (*Hacker Files*), Dave McKean (*Cages*), and Alan Grant & Norm Breyfogle (*Shadow of the Bat*, and for Grant alone, *The Demon*). In

November, we'll host the *Love & Rockets* 10th anniversary tour, and I'm working on arranging Francis Ford Coppola for *Dracula* (crossing my fingers), and Clive Barker. While I don't expect any of these to do anywhere nearly as well as the *SoM* tour, I am confident that they will all create greater than usual business.

I noted that July 24th was our best day ever — our second best day ever was also a signing (Dave Sim). In fact, seven of our ten best days have been creator appearances.

Pay particular attention to the line-ups we've been having. With the sole exception of the Grant/Breyfogle, not one of them is in support of mainstream projects. Moreover, when we do mainstream signings, they are generally less attended than their "alternative" counterparts. Why? I suspect it is because alternative projects create customer bases that are supremely interested in the people behind the work. When we had Javier Saltares in for *Ghost Rider* (at the time it was just about the "hottest" book around), only four people showed up. At least 100 times that showed up for Dave Sim, and in most stores *Cerebus* is a poor-selling title. It becomes apparent to me, at least, that with mainstream titles, the character is, indeed, more important than the creator. No one cares who draws *Ghost Rider* (as long as he is good), but everyone wants to know about the guy who writes *Cerebus*.

Generally, signings attract an older clientele, who invariably will buy whatever special items you may have. For the Gaiman *et al* signing, we had 20 copies of *Signal to Noise* imported from England. Those 20 copies didn't last an hour (and that's at $40 a copy!) I could've sold three times that, easily. We sold more than 30 copies of *Taboo* #5 (with the Sweeny Todd Penny Dreadful) at $14.95 a book, and nearly 50 copies of the Endless poster. I could go on and on about the extra stuff we sold (on top of the 150 copies of the *SoM* HC, at $30 each), but the point is, that by going the extra mile to make sure we were adequately stocked on "fringe" materials by the creators, we garnered many extra sales. What makes our figure even more unbelievable ($6316) is that it was comprised almost entirely of single copy sales, and there was no gimmick involved. We didn't especially "hard-sell" anyone, nor did we give any special deals to customers. How many of you out there can claim a more than $6000 day without multiple copies, "gimmick" comics, or special incentives? Promotion clearly works.

As I said, we had quite a long line, and to make it pleasant for the customers, we bought everyone in line a Coke (just as, for Dave Sim, we gave out copies of *Cerebus* for them to read in line). If you go that extra mile for your customers, they'll respond! Moreover, when your staff goes above and beyond the call (like mine certainly did), make sure they know that their efforts matter. I kicked them in for 1% profit sharing. At the least, take them to dinner, afterward!

The final point to the *SoM* tour is that at least 40% of the people we saw had never been in the store before. By throwing a professional event, where everyone was happy, I am confident that more than half of those will come in to the store again. The success doesn't stop when the event does!

It is possible to make money (oodles of it) without towing the mainstream line. I prove it, day in and day out. The only thing that matters is that you believe in what you're doing. If you do that, it's hard to fail. A love for comics, the medium, the industry is infectious.

I'll talk to you in a month, with the post-San Diego Comic Con report.

a r t i c l e

7

And finally we get to a column that I actually think is pretty good and well-focused. Took me long enough, eh?

I mean, sure, I'm fucking full of myself.

But I was right.

Heh. Mr. T. Bet you forgot that one, eh?

Tilting at Windmills #7
(Originally ran in Comics Retailer #8)

I was going to write one of those cutesy travel-diaries for my trip to the San Diego Comic Con and Expo. You know:

9 am: Arrived in San Diego

9:15: Arrived at Convention Center

9:20: Went to breakfast meeting

Etc.

Well, that fell through real fast. Within a half hour of reaching the con, I became so overwhelmed with people to meet and greet that any pretense of keeping notes on exactly who and when was thrown right out the window.

So, rather than discuss specifics, I'm going to give some general impressions, feelings, and abstracts on how (among other things) our industry has changed in the last eleven months (the con was in July, not August, last time), how the con has changed with it, and how we, as a retail community, can influence it to change even more for the future. I'm apt to be a little long-winded and philosophical on this one (heck, I might even stray from the point entirely, but free-form has always been my strength – especially when I've only had one day off in the last 22), so please bear with me. I think it'll be worth it.

First things first. I went to this show a little too little. Since we're still effectively a three-person operation, and since I wanted Aldyth, my promotions person, to go down as well, I only went to one of the two days of the trade show, flew back to San Francisco to work the store, then flew back down to San Diego for an evening, a morning, and a full day. That sounds like two days, but, no, it really didn't work out that way in practice.

The show has grown this year. The expo looked 25% better to me, while the con itself was at least 50% larger, if not far more. Absolutely overwhelming. I allotted my time for the smaller space it had last year, and was completely unprepared for this year's demands.

The growth of the con is both a blessing and a curse. Let's take the expo for a moment.

First of all, for those of you who have never attended one of these, what happens is that the various publishers and manufacturers set up booths where they display their upcoming wares. You have a chance to talk face to face with the publishers about what does or does not work in your store, how they can help you better sell their books, and you can view material that is up-coming, to better gauge your orders.

The extra space that the expo had this year means more diversity of publishers and suppliers, both in number and fields, exposing a wider diversity of material that we can carry and become informed about. The downside is that, if you're conducting tangible business (rather than merely running from table to table doing the meet and greet), it becomes nearly impossible to spend much quality time with every exhibitor there. I spent eight hours at the trade show, and I didn't get to visit with nearly a quarter of the exhibitors. I realize that it may not be feasible, but given the escalating number of exhibitors, it would be nice to see at least one more day of the trade show proper. To a certain extent, I think it is unfortunate that the smallest of the publishers are jammed into the back corners, while DC and Malibu are right by the front doors. I'll admit I know absolutely nothing about convention organization, but it seems to me that it would be better if the "big attractions" were further back in the hall – the same way milk is the furthest back item in a supermarket, and the new comics rack is usually the most distant rack in a comics store. You want to have the thing that people want the most farthest in the rear, so people have to walk past all the "B ticket" attractions to get to it, hopefully spending more money, as they go along.

Other than the "not-enough-time" syndrome (which it looks like many people faced), I had a very enjoyable time at the expo. I reacquainted myself with many an old face and friend, while making many new friendships for the future. I fought with some people, shook the hands of others, and generally made my usual impact (no jokes now...).

One of the biggest surprises to me from the whole convention was my newly-found pseudo-celebrity. I had dozens of retailers, publishers, fans, and creators coming up to me (not the other way around) saying that they had been looking for me, and could-I-please-have-a-moment-of-your-time? I gave out advice, I fomented revolution, and shook my head in wonder at the whole thing. Now, I realize that I'm one of the few retailers who is standing up in public, desperately trying to change the status quo, but I labor in solitude 51 weeks of the year, I run my store, mind my own business, and don't hear a peep from anyone else in the industry (that's why the column is titled *Tilting at Windmills*). Sometimes I feel I'm fighting an impossible fight, all by my little old self. So all you people coming to me ("I love your column!"), I wanna thank you for your kind words, but you should get out and write yourselves! If you agree with me or (most especially) if you don't, pick up that keyboard and type a missive – we need all the communication we can get!

This is really what I walked away from San Diego with: an overwhelming certitude that we (as a whole industry) don't communicate enough. If there's a message here today, that's it. And I mean every level, both internally, and externally.

Can I get real here for a moment? Good. We're fucking ourselves up by contracting rather than expanding our lines of communication as our business rapidly grows itself.

The publishers sure as fuck don't know what they're doing. They promote in the wrong way (to a stagnant base rather than reaching out for new ones), choose the dumbest books, with weak creative teams to produce them (I won't insult anyone in particular by naming names, but there was sure a sea of crap floating around this year), and in general seem oblivious to the concept of nurturing a market. They'd far rather flood the market with garbage in a desperate attempt to retain market share (all 40-some odd annuals from Marvel & DC next year introduce new characters? Please tell me where are we going to get the customers to purchase all this merchandise? Anyone?).

The distributors have gotten so big that they are virtually unable to support anything that isn't "hot." Reorders? Hah! What a joke! Nothing personal to the lads and ladies at Diamond & Capital (some of whom I like an enormous deal), but service is at an all time low. Sure, they've both got fancy computer set-ups that (in theory) make reordering easier, but the situation is just as bad, if not worse for anything but the 10% of "strong sellers."

I hear so many of you complaining to me about your similar problems, but how many of you take the time to complain to the companies themselves? One of the most productive meetings I attended was a breakfast with Marvel, billed essentially as a bitch session. Tell us what you think we're doing wrong, and we'll work to change it (telling us what we're doing right is O.K., too!) I got my time to make a couple of points, and while I'm well aware nothing is going to change overnight, at least I think I planted some seeds.

Besides retailers not being willing to articulate their needs and desires, we're still a generally unprofessional bunch. More people were lined up to have their pictures taken with Mr. T than went to the Kitchen Sink booth, for example. Even retailers are as simple and easily directed as our customers.

What can I say? I think we have the power to change the world (or at least the industry) in the smallest of our fingers, if we so desire. This industry is a tiny, aborning thing, and all it takes is a little elbow grease and a loud mouth to make an impact. I've never been one to fool myself. My one little store in San Francisco represents probably less than 1/10th of 1% of any given publishers market. But I know that with a little bit of assistance, a smoothing of the obstacles retailers have to climb, and a dint of hard work, I can become worth far more than that to most of them.

Do you have a problem? Reorder processing too erratic? Price points too high? Worried about speculation and its long term impact on the market? Stand up and say it. Say it loud, and say it clear. Announce your declaration of independence from the tyranny of business-as-usual. 5000 comic shops, people. That's all (and some people say far less). 50 retailers all crowing about the same problem, all suggesting ways to combat it, all working towards a unified goal of the best retail marketplace in the world – that's 10% of their business. And they'll take you seriously.

I worked a five-figure promotion deal with Marvel to try and reach a new market here in the Bay Area. It sure as shit didn't come spontaneously. ("Boy, let's help out that Hibbs guy, he's got such luscious blue eyes...") It happened because I was willing to stand up and criticize, publicly, some of their promotional practices. And, assuming that this works as well as I know it will, I'll be praising their balls to take a chance on a punk like me (that's not to say I'm going to stop criticizing them, mind you — they've got p-l-e-n-t-y of problems that should be addressed. Just like every other publisher). Virtually every week I get some publisher calling me up saying, "I'm working on such-and-such, d'you want to be part of it? Do you have any suggestions?" Not because I'm any big authority, but because I'm willing to address the concerns of the enlightened retailer. (I only get listened to 25% of the time, after all.)

So why don't you do it? No time? Bullshit! I work 80+ hours a week, and I still find time to stir up new shit. No interest? Well, then you're probably not reading these words at all, but it's your future, man! No understanding? Then educate yourself. If you work as hard as you possibly can, trying to make your store the best that there is (something for everyone, fair prices, appealing to a wide demographic base) then it will happen. Communicate your mind, clearly and loudly, and they'll eventually pay attention.

So how does this all tie in to the con? Well, like I said, it was bigger this year than ever before, reflecting the expansion of the industry itself. But, I have noticed that the bigger the con gets, the more fragmented it gets. There was a perhaps higher level of clique-ishness than ever before. But, it's still small enough that we stand a reasonable chance to break down the barriers. But we have to foment change – "A little madness, now and then, is relished by the wisest men." (My obligatory *Willie Wonka and the Chocolate Factory* quote) Speak out, express yourself, and never settle for the status quo. We can make a difference. Go to events like the San Diego con, and speak to as many people as will listen. It's all of our futures.

I can't do it alone.

Neither can you.

And if it's not now, then when?

a r t i c l e

8

Nothing really exciting to say here (so don't be surprised if these introductions kinda become sporadic after this point) other than that the kinds of semantic games we play over arbitrary labels in the comics industry really miss the point. I'm guilty a lot, in the writing of this column, of mistaking the Semantic for the Point. Don't be like me!

Tilting at Windmills #8

Steve Gerber was right.

Several months ago, Steve asked me to write a piece for the freelancers' magazine, *Words and Pictures* (*WAP!*), and we got to talking about the mechanics of writing. Steve said, "You should always take notes, you never know when an idea is going to hit you, and you don't want to forget a great topic."

There's another side to that, as well: you might forget that you haven't talked about a specific topic.

I'm sitting here, thinking what to talk about (and it's got to be something that I burn about, y'know, otherwise it falls flat), and I totally forgot that I hadn't yet talked about how (and why) to sell alternative comics. This may be because it's one of the most frequent questions I answer on the phones and computer bulletin boards, and so I assumed I had already covered it in depth. I touched upon the topic on my piece on diversification, but there are a couple more things to say.

One of things I hear frequently from other retailers is, "I can't sell alternatives, they don't sell, I have no customers for them, and last time I tried to sell them, I almost lost my shirt." All I can say to these people is that they're just not doing it right.

One important thing to bear in mind is that alternatives are not like mainstream comics. Wait, lemme backtrack a touch here and stress that "alternative" and "mainstream" have absolutely nothing to do with what company is publishing them. Marvel and DC publish some alternative comics, and Dark Horse and Eclipse (for example) publish some mainstream material. *Aliens* is a mainstream title, *Sandman* is an alternative. You with me so far?

Overall, the clearest difference between the two is a matter of scale. A mainstream comic is one that appeals (immediately) to a large number of your "typical" comic shop customers, while an alternative has a smaller, more select clientele (but one that's just as passionate – if not far more). Independents can be either mainstream or alternative, as can the Majors.

Since mainstream comics have a more obvious clientele, the tendency is to order high on the assumption that if you don't sell it right away, it'll move as a back issue, somewhere down the line, probably at a higher price. There's not a great deal of (obvious) risk (though this is perhaps a much more insidious trap – but more on that later), so you order with confidence.

Alternatives, on the other hand, having a far more select audience, tend to be ordered down because while you might sell half of your total sales (or more) of a mainstream title in the first week (because of your regular, weekly customers), the alternative customer tends to not be that weekly grazer, so you may only sell 10-20% of your total (that is, potential) sales that first week. The alternative customer may only come in once a month (or even less), making it much harder to readily identify them in your day-to-day sales, especially if you're not using cycle sheets. Often, working in the store daily can blind you to the bigger picture.

The trick to ordering alternatives is not to think of them as mainstream comics – that is, that they'll (effectively) sell themselves, that most of them will sell in the first week (or month even), or that you should expect any significant portion of your customers to buy them (at least initially).

Nor will every alternative sell in your store – even in my "pro-alternative" store, there are many items in which there is nil (or next to it) interest. You must know your customers and their tastes, and you must strive to educate yourself about the material itself (this is work, after all).

Here's a simple way to do it: purchase one copy of a dozen titles you've never carried before (start with titles that have a track record, and/or by creators that have won or been nominated for industry awards), and take them home and read them – chances are, if you enjoy it, you have customers that will as well. Either way, you should be able to write off this expense as research from your taxes. If you find a title that you enjoy, contact the publisher about getting a conservative number of copies on consignment, or with return privileges – make sure you present it to them as trying to expand your product mix! If the particular publisher is unwilling or able to help, go to the distributor. I have found helpful people at both Diamond and Capital.

An important consideration in your initial tests is being conservative. Many a retailer has almost lost his or her shirt by going hog-wild on alternatives after one or two minor successes. If developed carefully, alternative comics can develop into a healthy profit center for your store, but, quite often, while there is a market for some independent sales in every store, it almost always has to be nurtured. On the other hand, many a retailer has almost lost his or her shirt (or is in the process of losing it) by over-ordering – even by as little as one percent – on mainstream material as well.

One major difference is that of frequency, as well. Let's walk through an example using the idea above, using, say, *Hate* as an example. Let's say that you buy one copy of #7 in January for experimentation (It's made it past #3, so it's got some legs, and Peter Bagge has been nominated for several industry awards). You also get the solicitation for #8, which ships in April (*Hate* is quarterly). Since you liked #7, you order, say, five copies of #8. (The exact number will depend on your store, and knowledge of your customers – it could be three, it could be ten, etc.) Even if the solicitation for #9 happens before you get #8, you'll still have your sales figures from #8 before you order #10. Your risk is really minimal, because you're only ordering one (or at most two) issues "blind". Compare this to a new monthly release from Marvel or DC (where you're virtually obligated to carry it), where you're ordering three or more issues blind.

Anyway, if you only sell three of the copies, you'll know to take your order down a bit; while if you sell out, it's easy to build up an increase for the next issue.

I would strongly recommend that you set aside a small amount each month for "experimentation" – say $20, or so. That's only $240 a year, and you should be able to write that off as research. That $20 will get you around six new titles to try out and see.

One last quick bit on selling alternatives: an important thing to consider is how you rack your titles – you can't expect something to sell if you don't rack it properly. Alternatives will not sell if you put them all the way at the back of the small dusty rack in the back of your store. You must give them adequate coverage in a prominent place. In the case of items that you particularly like, you should have them at or near the counter to facilitate your pushing them.

If you make a minor, honest, conservative effort to know your product and customers, you should be able to slowly build alternatives into a nice profit center in your store. How nice is entirely up to you, and how much effort you're willing to put into it. 'Course, if you don't want the money, I'm sure another store would be more than willing....

Don't say I didn't warn ya.

a r t i c l e

9

Speaks for itself, this one does

Tilting at Windmills #9
(Originally ran in Comics Retailer #10)

One of the best perks of owning a comic book shop is the ability to read through your stock at whim – checking through old musty back issues to see what cool stuff you might find. During one of my last whimsical journeys, I stumbled through a back issue of *Eerie*. Issue 81, to be exact (bitchin' cover turn on King Kong, with Fay Wray in the ape's position, and Kong in the girl's). While my general memories of this mag are, shall we say lukewarm, at best (a lot of these stories seemingly existed to show as many scantily clad women as possible, regardless of plot needs), I figured, "What the hey, I've got 10 minutes to waste." The first story basically confirmed my worst suspicions, and a quick flip through the rest clinched it.

But then I hit a column, simply titled, "The Comic Books," by a fellow named Joe Brancatelli. Now what (I suppose to be) a regular column on comic books in general is doing in a black & white "Tits 'n' Screams" magazine, I'll never know, but this column really surprised the hell out of me. It was critical, it was insightful, and, well, it was still relevant to today's market. Anyway, instead of describing it to you, I'm just gonna reprint it, verbatim (to which I owe Meloney Crawford Chadwick of Harris Comics a passel full of thanks – not only was she smack in the middle of launching a new line of comics in today's hostile market, but she found the time to track down obscuro rights to a defunct column for your humble writer. A standing "o" for Meloney, 'kay?)

Before I start the reprint, let me observe something: this column is from 1976. That's a while ago (by comics industry standards, that is), and a powerful lot of changes have elapsed in the industry since then. The most important of which is, of course, the formation (and ascension) of the direct market. No one in 1976 could have predicted how much the industry's health could revolve around the direct sale market. I mean, 16 years ago, Diamond distributors didn't even exist (as such), and a substantial proportion of the Image guys were in elementary school! Anyway, enough with the observations, let's get to the meat, and I'll see you at the end.

•   •   •   •   •

Less is more
By Joe Brancatelli

Enigmatic California governor Jerry Brown gathered reams of publicity from the less-is-more stance he adopted during his quixotic campaign for the Democratic presidential nomination. But both the hype and the substance of the less-is-more doctrine quietly went the way of most campaign rhetoric as soon as Jimmy Carter and Gerald Ford geared up their publicity machines for the quadrennial "Promise More Services and Lower Taxes No Matter What" derby otherwise known as the presidential elections.

Now I'm certainly not going to muse about the politics of America here – all you Americans can jump into the Pacific Ocean for all we New Yorkers care about you anymore – but I am quite willing and even eager to consider less is more as a short-term panacea for what ails the comic book industry. Me, I believe nothing will save mass-market comics as we now know them, but application of less is more might stave off imminent doom for a couple of years.

As opposed to the bedrock American belief that more of anything is peremp-torily better than less of anything, less is more recognizes the equally bedrock notion of a point of diminishing return. While much of the American economy is based on the notion that big volume is its own reward, less is more says it is oftentimes desirous to do less, to produce less, to sell less, because – in the long run – your return will be greater than had you done more, produced more, sold more.

Being as totally steeped in traditional American values as they are, comic book producers have naturally followed the more-for-more's-sake theory blindly in total disregard for what is actually happening in their marketplace. Blithely tripping down the more-is-always-better road, comic-book companies always managed to produce new titles at every turn – even though doing so depressed the margin and profits of the new titles and reduced the sales and profits of the existing ones. Like so many other Americans, comic book moguls have constantly been blinded by the sheer dint of volume to the detriment of the bottom line.

For example, Marvel published only one comic book starring Spider-Man several years ago. It sold, let us say, X number of copies and made Y profits for a cost of Z dollars. By adding a second title starring Spider-Man, Marvel thought it could sell X+X copies and make Y+Y profits for a cost of Z+Z. What happened, however, was that the two Spider-Man titles sold only 3/4X+1/2X and made a profit of only 3/4Y-1/2Y. The cost was the full Z + Z, though.

That's what we call diminishing return, folksies. Rather than get a full X worth of sales and Y worth of profits from the new investment of Z dollars, Marvel got a diminished return on its second investment and a reduced return on its original investment. Similarly, when Marvel then added a third Spider-Man book it was paying Z+Z+Z dollars to do so, but only getting something like 5/8X+3/8X+1/4X sales and only 5/8Y+3/8Y+1/4Y profits.

I chose Marvel for that little demonstration not because it is the only comic book company ignorant of diminishing return – God knows, it is not – but because it consistently manages to be the most oafish in its flouting of it. Marvel actually has three Spidey titles now when you count *Marvel Team-Up* – which always features the Web-Spinner – and each individually sells fewer copies per issue than what the original *Amazing Spider-Man* title sold in a one-book market. Granted, the combined total sales of the three books are higher than the one book's sales ever were, but the three books aggregately return less profit now than the one Spidey book did during its heyday in the late 1960s.

All of which brings us to less is more and its eminent desirability for comic books. What has happened to Marvel's three Spider-Man titles happens in a larger sense to the comic-book macrocosm; all titles compete against each other and take readers and profit away from each other. Moreover, because of the vagaries of the magazine market we discussed in previous columns, there is only a limited amount of space available on retail display racks – distributors estimate there is room for only about four of every 10 comics published today.

So the question, then, is why produce all those additional comics in the first place, comics that will never sell because they will never be seen? The old argument that you have to overproduce to sell notwithstanding, there is no reason to be glutting the market. Distributors say they can only distribute four of every 10, so why give them 10? Give them four because that's how many you know they can distribute.

What I'm proposing is not a reduction in the print run of comic book titles. That would result in only a marginal saving, since the big cost today, despite rising newsprint prices, remains "start-up" dollars needed to produce even one copy of any title.

What I suggest is that the companies cut the number of titles they produce down to the bone, down to the tried-and-true best sellers. If a company publishes 60 titles now, let it cut back to the 15 or 20 most successful ones. With the additional 45 titles out of the way, not only will you be saving the costs of producing those comics, you'll be giving your best sellers a chance to improve their sales performance, too.

For example, if a distributor is committed to giving a retailer only 240 comic books per delivery, he'll probably give him four copies each of those 60 titles. If, however, a company only prints 15 titles, chances are the distributor will give perhaps 15 of each instead. And since the titles around are best sellers, those extra 11 copies will probably sell better than the copies of the fringe titles that once cluttered the stands.

What I'm saying, in a nutshell, is this: I'd be willing to wager that if Marvel and National each cut their number of titles by 50 or more percent, their profits would not only increase as percentage of sales, but also in terms of actual dollars, Sales of the remaining titles might improve from 40 percent to maybe 60 or 70 percent of the press run without adding a dime to the cost.

I'm sure that the total number of all comics sold won't decrease, either. Given the better display, the total sales of those 15 or so best sellers should easily match the total sales of 60 titles which were never displayed properly.

And for National and Marvel, both fighting and losing battles with their bottom lines, a 50 percent or more cutback in titles and costs with no loss of total sales would be very helpful.

So take heed out there, Jerry Brown was right. Less is more – at least for comics.

One caveat, though. Knowing the turkeys in the comic book business, the minute they cut back titles and see sales and profit increases in the remaining books, they'll wrongly interpret it as a new comic book boom and reinstate the old titles.

That'll put us right back where we started.

Again.

(Reprinted from Eerie #81 with permission, © Harris Publications.)

• • • • •

See? Still reasonably relevant, eh? While Brancatelli's proportions may be a bit off, by today's numbers, the premise still holds. These days, there are four monthly Spider-Man books (well, five if you wanna count *Marvel Tales*, or six if you throw *Spider-Man 2099* in the mix, but I personally won't count *2099*, because it's far too new to be able to judge it's long-term impact), and the numbers look like this: *Amazing Spider-Man* sells somewhere between .9 to .75Y (Y being *ASM*'s circulation before the multiple Spidey titles): that is somewhere between 300-330,000 copies, compared to around 370,000 copies in the late 1960's. The best I could find for current circulation was numbers for 1990, but Todd McFarlane was drawing the book then. This is the Spidey's 30th anniversary, so they're probably doing nearly as well, but I'm going to project, based on my store (where *ASM* sales are significantly lower since Todd left), and go with the 300,000 figure. *Spider-Man* (the title created for Todd) currently has sales figures of about .85Y, *Web* is at .7Y, and *Spectacular* hovers at .45Y (these are approximations based on Diamond's sales charts for November, just so's ya know).

So we come to sales of .75Y + .85Y + .7Y + .45Y. Or 2.75Y sales (and profits) for a full cost of 4Z (and maybe higher, since I'll assume that Marvel's paying more, proportionally, today than they did in the 1960's.)

Now, this only covers distributor sales. What actual sell-through may be a whole 'nother matter (I'm thoroughly convinced that actual sell-through is probably less than 75%, nationwide – what store do you know that doesn't have a huge backstock of unsold material?).

Lemme change gears, and use a specific example (from my store) of sell-through. Before they started the second *Ghost Rider* title, *GR* sold (actual sales, not orders) about 57 copies a month. Now that there are two titles (and we're past the initial launch-hoopla), *GR* sells 38 copies a month, while *GR: SoV* sells a piddling 23. We're up a measly four copies (not even 10%!) between two titles, and now it takes twice as much rack space.

That's really where Brancatelli didn't go far enough – rack space. Despite the fact that the distribution network then is absolutely unlike today's in nearly every way (stores now get to actually order material themselves, based on their predictions of what will sell, rather than a distributor's whim and fancy), there is still not anywhere near enough rack space in most stores for the volume of material that is on the market. Brancatelli suggested there was room for only four out of ten titles on the market then, I'd be surprised if it was *two* in ten these days! Perhaps in the more idealistic 70's (hah!), when Marvel was a very different beast, he didn't conceive of this, but today I think it's clear that the majors pump out as much material as they can to crowd other publishers off the rack. If you, as the retailer are taking 200% of your rack space to sell 10% more books, if they sell two *Ghost Rider* titles, then that's one less book that has room to compete with a Marvel.

The thing that *really* wigs me about Brancatelli's piece is that for the longest time, I've thought I was a "lone voice crying out in the wilderness" (or at least the only one who was getting column inches!), but here we've got a guy, 16 years ago, saying basically the same things I am today. During both periods, our industry was at a crossroads of what we would be, of how we would conduct ourselves, and whether it was "something for everyone", or "mostly for us." Brancatelli believed in 1976 that mass market comics as we knew them would disappear within years. And, if it wasn't for the direct market, and the changes (and sophistication!) that it brought, I've little doubt that he would've been right. Sometimes you do get second chances. But, I'll observe, that most of those second chances were for the publishers and the fans only. Very few of the same retail locations are selling comics today as were in 1976! The retail market continues to sell comics because of a paradigm shift in distribution methods. If we do get a third chance that's not generated from within our industry, odds are it'll be a shift away from the comic shops, and towards mass-market locations. You and me are going to have a hard time fighting against the resources of, say, a Blockbuster chain of comics.

Less is more, for our futures – 'cuz those who ignore history....

...and Superman #75 sells for how much now, Martha?

Tilting at Windmills #10
(Originally ran in Comics Retailer #11)

On *Superman* #75: Oy.

No, really, what more can I say?

Although a lot of people have made a bunch of money on this, and everyone's pleased as punch at the success of it, I question whether it will *really* do any good, long-term.

If you're at all like me, you ordered somewhere in the vicinity of 1000+% of "normal" *Superman* numbers. And you *still* sold out the first day.

This has been followed by weeks of "civilians" calling every 3.2 seconds, in one of the largest feeding-frenzies this industry has ever seen.

As I write this, the paperback of the entire series is due out in a couple of hours, and a week from now, we'll see the fourth (!) printing of #75.

I would guess that the total print run for all these printings will end up being near four million copies (if not far more). The initial printings alone hit nearly two million copies.

So there are several points here:

1. In my store, at least, because we ran out so early, we had several forced confrontations with people who believed that they (but no one else) should be privileged to buy as many copies as they liked, despite the need to be fair to all; and since the phone was almost ringing faster than the call-waiting could handle, we were unable to a) deal with our normal needs of business, or b) accomplish almost anything at all. When I look at the extra time that has had to been put in to deal with the madness, weighed against the amount of money that we made, it appears that we actually made *less* of a profit than we would've from a "normal" issue of Supes. (of course, this is compounded by the fact that Diamond was unable to completely fill our orders on the second printing, and seemingly lost *all* orders [throughout their entire chain!] for the third – things *may* slide back in the profitability section, depending on what happens with the TPB).

2. This is a little more insidious: the immediate skyrocketing price (I've heard as high as *$90* less than three weeks after the book shipped!). A lot of this is due to *genuine* "civilian" interest, but everybody is *real* clear on the fact that there is no way in *hell* that this book will keep *any* of this value, right?

Look at the numbers: something nearing 1.6 million copies of the "collector's" edition on the market (and don't forget that DC's original solicitation held forth that we should order more copies of the newsstand version than the bagged, because that's what the civilians would want. It was wrong then, and it was far more wrong on Doomsday, itself). Now, a *substantial* number of these copies actually made it into the hands of real civilians, maybe as high as 50%, but that still leaves *800,000* copies firmly in the market (that's an average of 133 a store!). It may not seem like it, but 800,000 is a tremendously high number. There are not significantly more than that number of people who read comics at all, let alone care about Superman! Within six months after Supes' *inevitable* resurrection, this book is gonna be deader then the big red S, hisself.

Look at history, people! The Death of Robin, the Engagement of Superman, the Wedding of Spider-Man – who cares now?

By *scalping* Superman #75 now at $90 per, *knowing* that it is *not* going to be able to sustain that value, you are an unethical fuckwad (and I really, really, *really* hope that daunting Don Butler, editor-at-large, doesn't edit that last word out. While I may be a filth-mouth in real life, I try to be somewhat gentile in these pages. The swearing is to show my *utter* disdain and offense toward the parasitic scum who take advantage of another's curiosity. Besides, we're all adults in this joint. What kid could bear to read *my* rantings? *[2003 note: Don, of course, did edit it out!]*) You are *clearly* ripping people off, for the sake of a bit more profit, which is a sleazy and slimy stunt. In fact, this is *exactly* the type of crap that's holding our industry back, for if a civilian were to pay that price, then see it dwindle six months later, they'd surely swear off comics for life, spreading the word to all their acquaintances.

Go back and read my article on Ethics back in issue one, for a refresher course.

3. And, of course, this was a pretty bad comic book.

No, really, this was!

Try reading it with the eyes of a non-comics reader.

Every stereotype about how insipid and juvenile comic books are is contained between these covers. It is an *absolutely* mindless slugfest, told in pin-ups with freakishly sappy writing. The conclusion, with Supes and Doomsday killing each other *simultaneously* by *punching each other* is the worst type of cliche. This will *only* confirm: "See, Henry, I told you comic books were for children and morons."

While certainly *some* civilians may get the "bug" from this, it is not *anywhere* near as many as it could have been, had this been a well-told, poignant story. Moreover, I hold that this will do more harm than good in the eyes of John Q. Public.

Maybe I'm an old fart (but I'm only *25*!), but I simply cannot fathom the direction that DC is taking. Between high concept trash like this, the cancellation of a good read like JSA (before the first issue even *ships*), the death of !mpact, the commercial failure of Piranha (but *I* really like [and can *sell*] most of their output), the clumsy handling of the Vertigo launch (hawking an intelligent line for mature readers at collectible nuts is hardly wise marketing), and the soon-to-be failure of the Milestone line (not one of these books have the smell of success, in my oh so humble opinion), it seems to me that DC is stuck down a well, but they keep digging deeper hoping to find a vein of gold. Then maybe they'll be able to buy their way out.

But all they're striking is pyrite.

And the damn shame of it all is that I *like* the majority of their output (and they sell well in my store, at least).

We still drink Anchor Steam on anniversaries!!

Tilting at Windmills #11
(Originally ran in Comics Retailer #12, duh)

<<<<<Hmmmmmmmmmm>>>>>

Happy Birthday to us, Happy Birthday to us, Happy Birthday, dear *Comics Retailer* and *Tilting at Windmills*, Happy Birthday to us.

Welcome back, my friends, to the show that never ends. The party has been going on a while, but there are still a bunch of people hanging around, and I think the keg ain't been dusted yet...hold on, I'll check for you...

Sure enough! Here's a glass of Anchor Steam, and I think we can scratch up some soda or mineral water, if you'd prefer...

You're O.K.?

Cool.

Well, can you possibly believe it's been a whole year? It astonishes me sometimes, too. And look at all that's come and gone in that time: We're on our (technically) 3rd editor now (K.C. is at DC, Maggie is back home at the *CBG*, while good ol' Don is still playing shepherd to this unruly herd), we've had four covers that've had absolutely nothing to do with the insides, we're up to seven regular monthly columns from the five we started with, and I've written twelve opinionated diatribes. Isn't life wonderful!?

I've spoken about Ethics, the Problems of Price Guides, Diversification, Publishers' Responsibilities to the Market (and has anyone listened? Noooooo!), Promotion, Arguing with Lou Bank, Holidays (actually, I hate that one...), Signings, San Diego, and The State Of the Industry, Alternative Titles, Oversaturation, and Ethics Mark II. That's a pretty full plate. The only hard part is coming up with something new!

This last year has been a helluva ride (but haven't you read this a million times before now? Ah, the perils of a two-month lead time!), but I'm gonna ditch on the traditional year-end wrap up, and concentrate instead on what the future holds. And what *you* can do to help.

In 1993, I think we've got one major battle facing us: that of identity. Now, although I've written around this one many a time, and that I've held this opinion for a while, I've finally found the right terms for this argument. Now, I'll freely admit that I've stolen these exact words from Dave Olbrich (publisher of Malibu comics – Hi Dave!), but it crystallized what I've been feeling for a while. The number one problem facing our industry is *what* are we: an *entertainment* industry, or a *collectibles* industry? As Dave has observed, the goals of these two markets are *diametrically opposed*! That which appeals to a market full of readers is not in any way, shape, or form what will appeal to a market of collectors (note that I'm using "collectors" in the speculative sense, *not* as readers who keep their comics after they are done. Technically, we *all* collect comics, in some shape or form, but I'm speaking of those who buy (even one copy) for the express purpose of accumulating value). Now, ignoring, for the moment, that buying "hot" comics in hopes of making a fortune is a sucker's bet, the nuts and bolts mechanisms of selling to these markets have distinct differences (I don't really have to list them, do I?).

The biggest problem facing all the pre-consumer levels of the business is that it's a helluva lot easier to market to the collector than it is to the reader. The collector is looking for something that is "obviously" a good investment: "hot" creators, "special" covers, "word on the street," etc. Manufacturing collectibles is easy: look at how often Marvel does it. On January's order form, I count at least ten "gimmick" issues (and two relists of previous ones), while December had six, as had November. These are the same titles that, naturally, the distributors fall in lock-step behind, and the fan-press hype, and we retailers order in big numbers. So far, this strategy has seemingly paid off: most of us have had a bigger bottom line in '92 than in '93. But, I question whether or not we've a) become more *profitable* because of it (that is, whether our percentage of expenses has stayed consistent with our grosses), and b) whether or not we're actually gaining new *readers* by these events.

I've noticed a sharp drop-off on "midline" Marvel titles, in direct proportion to the number of "hot" books coming out. Lemme digress a moment and mention that after a book has had roughly ten weeks on our racks (two on the "new comics" racks, and two months on the general A-Z), we pull our "par" (What we feel we can sell, without street-purchases, for about a year, depending on the title) for the back issue boxes, then throw the overflow into the quarter boxes. Yep, that's right, we trash them! Inventory that hasn't turned within the time-period gets remaindered: We haven't sold it, and it ain't gonna sell, so why should we be holding on to it? It just absorbed space and cash-flow! Now, given this, what sometimes surprises me is that a disproportionate amount of this "quarterized" merchandise is mid-line Marvel books. Marvel actually only accounts for about 25% of my orders (unlike the industry averages of 45-50 % – so I'll admit I skew a bit differently from most of you), but some 75-90% of the quarterized comics are Marvel "mid-line" books.

O.K., this isn't all that hard to explain: there's only a finite amount of money in the market, especially among Marvel's target audience (boys with fixed allowances), but what I find the most interesting/disturbing is that while the "gimmick" books are great for the collector crowd, they are *discouraging* the readers. A little historical perspective is, perhaps, required. It used to be that if an "anniversary" issue, or a special storyline (like, say, an "Operation: Galactic Storm") was done, the numbers would spike for an issue, then slowly drop back down, as people who saw something they liked stayed on for a few issues to keep giving it a chance. Oh, sure, eventually, due to attrition, the numbers would creep back to where they were before the event, but it would take six months, or more. These days, conversely, I'm often seeing a drop in readership *immediately* after the event, as the core readers of the book are put off by the luring of the collectors, and say, "well, it wasn't that great anyway - besides, I don't want to have to buy six other comics to understand the one I was reading and/or I don't want to pay extra for a gimmick cover." My most recent example? The "X-cutioners Song" in the X-books. Sales were up 20-50% from "normal" X numbers, while they were polybagged, but the first post-crossover issues are *down* from normal numbers as much as 30%! That's a butt-load of unsold copies! The worst part of this is that our numbers are locked in for the next three months, so there can be no national perception of this trend (unless, of course, my store is so abnormal, that I'm the absolutely only person facing this trend, but, based on casual conversation this ain't the case). Now, normally, as soon as I could, I'd drop the numbers to reflect reality, but (of course!) the first post-crossover sell-through issue is *Uncanny* #300, with a foil cover. Obviously, that ish will do better than any around it, perhaps by a factor of two, so the national view of sales are skewed dramatically, since they won't reflect the "fallow" period. Which will only feed into the perception that gimmicky, collector oriented sales are the way to go.

(Another digression, this one parenthetical. One major argument retailers have had is that of returnability. No one wants especially to mess with the status quo of returns, but I think one possible solution would be to allow order *decreases* up to four weeks before the title actually ships. Just as you can place higher advance orders (and if you do it a month or so before, stand a fairly good chance of actually receiving it...), you should be able to cut orders, to reflect your most recent intelligence. I don't think it would cause *too* much extra work on the higher levels (I'd only need it on, say, 5-10% of the titles I order), and it would increase profitability and total dollars available to the market to the point I'd think it would offset it's expenses. Of course, it'd need to be fairly tight, say a maximum of 25%

of your initial, perhaps a per-month limit, like up to 25 titles a month, but I think it would easily prove cost-effective...)

Now, material aimed at *readers* (that is, focusing on the *entertainment* aspect), on the other hand, tends to see a slower, but steady upwards trend in sales, and is not, in fact, affected by one whit when a mega-hyped "collector's item" is released. I've gone from five copies of *Hate*, when the first issue was released, to 100! I didn't even "cram" this one down my customer's throats, like I do with *Sandman* or *Cerebus*. No hologram covers or poly-bagged trading cards, but this title has become one of the most profitable that I've ever carried.

I *want* us to be an entertainment medium, not a collector's market. And I hope that the arguments I've made in the last year, on diversification, oversaturation, ethics, responsibility, the State of the Industry, and how to promote the "oddball" stuff has at least swayed you in that direction as well. But what can you do? I want you all to make the following resolutions in '93 (even if you make them in February, it'll still help), and say them *loud*:

• I resolve to make a modest and sincere effort to carry and *promote* titles that will expand my customer's tastes and my customer base.

• I resolve to become an entertainment store, rather than one appealing *solely* to collectors.

• I resolve to value art over commerce, while staying profitable.

• I resolve to find my *own* Windmills to Tilt at, and never remain silent about the injustices I see.

If everyone in my audience (including those of you outside of the direct retail market) agreed to resolve to at least *one* of these resolutions, this time next year we'd face a much saner and healthy market.

And I, for one, think we can do it.

•   •   •   •   •

I don't usually do this kind of thing, but Scott McCloud was good enough to send me a galley of his new book, *Understanding Comics*. I don't know exactly when this is going to be solicited, but I'd assume it will be sometime around when you're reading this.

Now, I'm not a reviewer by trade, so this won't be all flowery in it's praise, but this is one great book. It's filled with historical perspective, artistic philosophy, scholarly analysis of form and function, plus it's a fun book to read. *And* it's in comics form!

Order one for yourself, and half a dozen for your customers. They'll thank you (and Scott probably will, as well), since this is the best book I'm ever read on the field.

Four stars. *TaW* sez check it out.

There's another column about Challenge #1 coming up, but I'll "spoil" it a bit by noting that Lou Bank (Marvel Comics) was the only publisher's rep to ever take the offer up. I still try from time-to-time these days to get people to do it.

Challenge #2 worked for something like a year before I realized I was doing all of the work, and was really only sending out my own ideas. Since that was utterly not the point, I killed the whole thing.

This column, of course, was from the "pre-internet" days – today organizing such a group would be a snap because of the power of the net. In fact, comic retailers now use Robert Scott's Comic Book Industry Alliance in a manner very close to what I proposed. Access can be gained by going to www.thecbia.com.

Tilting at Windmills #12
(Originally ran in Comics Retailer #13)

This is the first column of 1993 (for me – you're probably reading this in March or so), and this is a serious column. As an industry this new year is bringing us new challenges. I'm here to put my money where my mouth is with two of my own challenges to the industry, each of which is going to involve a shitload of work for me, in addition to running my store, and will, no doubt, win me very little affection.

Both of these involve my contentions that we need to be more responsible to our marketplace (retail and non-retail), and that we need to encourage efficient communication between all levels (consumer, retailer, distributor, publisher, and creator). Sure, some of us are talking back and forth, within our groups, but we need to create industry-wide lines of communication that will benefit us all.

Enough preamble. Read the challenges, and I'll wrap up at the bottom.

•**TaW challenge #1: Publishers going to "retailer school"**

I think it's fairly clear that nearly every publisher, in one way or another, is out of touch with how, and why, retailers work the way we do (sadly, the same can be said of many of us retailers, as well...). The information that the publisher receives only shows them a) raw numbers, based on nationwide orders by retailers, that does not necessarily relate in any realistic way to what the end-consumers may be actually buying, b) direct communication with a small numbers of retailers, many of whom are either telling them what they want to hear, or working their own agendas, or c) contact with consumers at conventions and the like, which is, of course, a skewed picture of what happens in the stores, or the market as a whole. Now there's got to be a way to help fill out the larger picture, for publishers to get their fingers on the "pulse" of the market, filtering out both the retailers sensibilities, and their own pre-conceived notions. This will, I believe, help the publishers focus promotional efforts to programs that are actually useful and directed, and help them see what the consumers are actually buying, not what they think (based on national orders) they're buying. So here's the '93 *TaW* Publisher challenge:

Work in a retail store for a week.

Yeah, I know it's a bizarre idea. But, I think that the information you'll absorb from working the nuts and bolts end of the business will prove invaluable. Most of the Publisher's marketing efforts, and title decisions are made without the input of anyone besides those pre-disposed to contact you (the old saw that positive mail always outnumbers negative mail. Someone with a negative opinion is far less likely to say anything, and just leave, rather than bothering to register their opinions). I'm constantly surprised by the new information that *I* learn every day by directly speaking to the customers. Think how much more you can pick up, by being two steps closer.

Why do I think this is important? Primarily because I see so many programs and items purported to be aimed at the retailers, that when observed from my eyes accomplish nothing or less. We have an unhealthy market right now, where due to the sloth or foolishness of retailers, what is being sold-in is not necessarily being sold-through; where people aren't viewed as customers, but as *consumers* – and I think we can still stem the tide of greed, if we want to. What do you have to gain from it? I mean, a week is a lot of time! You have knowledge to gain, information that can't be seen by looking at a national graph. The forest may be beautiful from miles away, but you have to ensure that the individual trees are healthy, if there's to *be* a forest in the future.

An important note: this is NOT designed to be a direct promotional tool (like, Valiant's Trading Places contest). There's certainly nothing wrong with running promotional events, but any information gained from there is going to be skewed by the knowledge that is what it is.

So, *any* real publisher (let's define this as having published at least a dozen different titles since you've been in business) is hereby invited to contact me, and set up a time for themselves, or one of their trusted minions, to come and work in my store for a week. I'll walk you through cycle sheeting, order forms, racking and promotion (on a practical level), actually selling directly to the consumer, and the dozens of other "behind the scenes" things that make a retail store work. Harbor no illusions: this will be work! You'll be a grunt, a simple counter-person, and no one's gonna know you're a publisher's representative. The only thing I ask is that you come with an open mind, ready to try to fathom *why* we do thing the way we do. I also think this can be a two-way street. *Every* store in the world can benefit from having a fresh pair of eyes viewing it from the inside-out. I'm sure that for everything you learn, I'll learn two more things.

I suppose the question then becomes: why *my* store? After all, my store skews differently from most (though I'd only hope that it is the type of target audience that we'd all like to see, in the long-run), and I'm an opinionated S.O.B.. But getting past all that, I'm not trying to curry any favors, and I've got no ulterior motives. Hell, I'll probably make far more enemies than allies from this (but, hey! I *like* living on the edge!). My store will be open to you, my books will be open to you, and my customers will be open. I don't *want* an ear higher-up, I don't want special treatment from anyone, and I'm not going to color the picture that *your* company is the best thing since sliced bread. My customers will not know who you are, so you won't be answering a bunch of questions about your publishing plans, or asked to look at portfolios. You'll be no more (or no less) than another member of the staff, trying to balance both of our pre-conceived notions of what the market is, or can be, with cold reality.

Frankly, I'd rather that this was opened to the rest of the industry, but at this moment, right now, I'm the only one making the offer. Those retailers that are reading this, and want to make the same offer, I beseech you to do so. The more shades and depths of opinion we can get, the better educated we all can be. I think that this could be a pilot program for the entire industry, with many different strata of retail operations and publishers learning and sharing their information, unfiltered through bureaucracy. As I said, this is a two-way street. I want you to challenge my assumptions as much as I challenge yours. There is no doubt that none of us have *all* the information and knowledge that we need to stay healthy, and to help grow our market for the future. I want to forge a tool to help us build our industry.

As of this writing, I've found a volunteer from Marvel to start this program with me. Yep! Big, bad Marvel, with whom I've had many a flame war, and confrontation with in the past (and *no* doubt the future as well), sees the value in open communication, whether or not I am their audience. Hopefully my plea won't fall on deaf ears, for what this industry needs is more knowledge and more communication. What's a week of your time balanced against the future of our industry?

Can *either* of us, retailer or publisher, afford to *not* take that time to build our tomorrow?

•TaW Challenge #2: The Alliance

Over the course of the last year or so I've become aware that there are a *lot* of articulate, informed retailers out there fighting grass-roots battles to change and transform our industry. We're each cultivating our own gardens, trying to nurture what we find good, and weed out the elements that (to really stretch the metaphor) soak up all the sunlight. The problem is that we're mostly doing it alone. Sure, we meet, in twos and threes, more often by happenstance than by plan. A lot of us are small stores, struggling in a vacuum of self-imposed solitude, not knowing who, or even *how*, to talk to others; a lot of us are managers of locations owned by others, striving to turn around the inertia of standing store policies (that *did* make sense when they were instigated half a decade ago) holding back its full potential, fighting the two-front battle of customers and owners; and some of us *want* to change things, but haven't the tools or the resources to pull it off themselves (lord knows I fall into that category a lot, meself) – they need to work with others, co-operatively, to hit their stride.

Here's what I'm proposing:

The creation of a list of retailers willing to participate in promotional efforts, both between themselves and with others. If I decide it would be really great to have Dave McKean in for a signing, but am unable to scrape up the funds for a transcontinental flight, I can turn to a list of 50, or 100, or 1000 retailers who I know are predisposed to working together. Will *each* of them want to work with me, on *every* project? Probably not. But, at least I have a working knowledge of who to try. Let's say an artist decides that he wants to go to the San Diego Comic Con (he lives on the East Coast), and can't afford it. Boom! He's got an index of dedicated stores to arrange his travel expenses through, in exchange for a signing. I created a cool display or promotion that I want to share? Sure I could send it here to *Comics Retailer*, but if it's time sensitive, it may not work out. Here's a resource list, targeting people who are more likely than not to use it. You're a publisher who wants to send out promotional items, but you haven't the funds to try to scattershot 6,000+ stores? You've got a direct line to the stores that are, more likely than not, going to *use* the things. The uses of this are limitless, controlled only by our efforts (previews of upcoming work: control your orders better, and build advance support; an open network for distribution of ashcans; clearer channels of communication for information that affects *all* of us; etc.).

That's about it. A network, an alliance, a list of people willing to work for *all* our benefits.

This type of structure is inclusive, rather than exclusive. That's the charm of it. Any retailer is welcome, because what you'll get out is what you put in. If you don't make the effort, others won't work with you. The opportunities are what you make of them.

I contend we need an alliance of these stores, a confederation of interests, if you like, for we're not adequately represented by the extant organizations: CBRI (personally, I don't find anything particularly useful in hawking bad mainstream comics to twelve-year-olds on top 40 stations, or getting some actors to dress up as Ren & Stimpy. 'T'ain't nothing *wrong* with this, but it ain't my cuppa tea) or the DLG (which isn't generally open to membership, anyway).

In fact, exactly what we *don't* need is another *organization*. I envision this like, well, the Defenders. A Non-Team. A pool of talent, as it were, working together for the common good. Bring your ideas, but leave your agendas at home. Work in big groups, little groups, whatever you like; it acts as a central mailing list, an *information* list, a resource for us all to affect our environment.

I think we need this non-group because we need to create clear lines of communication between both ourselves and with the creative community. One the most exciting ideas for me, is to clearly link this organization into the creators, most of whom are anxious to promote their work, but are stymied by the barriers put up by publishers and distributors. Realistically, *we* are the creator's true customers. We make the decisions that make their books available, or not; we determine whether they succeed or fail, or whether they can continue to afford to create the merchandise we depend on. And they need to be able to access us, to get our input on what *we* need to make their work sell better, to arrange local and regional publicity, and to be *able* to view us as an ally, not an enemy.

So, I'm asking for a call to arms. I want to create a coalition of retailers who *care*, who want to make the *difference*, and the names and facts I gather will be available to *all*, on any level of the industry. I'll work as the central mailer for the first year, then pass the baton to someone else. We'll attempt to have *some* form of meeting (however informal) at the San Diego con this year. And we want you to join!

Is this for you? Here are my loose criteria:

• Are you open to new promotional ideas?

• Are you willing to experiment, and possibly lose money in the short-term, on projects you believe in?

• Are you willing to expend effort to work directly with creators (and *not* to be a fanboy!) to promote their work specifically?

• Do you value Art over Commerce (though, of course, the goal is that the Art *provides* the Commerce)?

• Are you willing to fight whatever injustices you may find in our industry whenever possible?

• Are you, ultimately, in the business for Love of, and Passion for the Form? Or is it just a Money thing?

If this describes your attitudes to your store, then send me a note with your name, address, Phone and Fax number, and any details you might want to provide about the types of promotions you've done, or want to do in the future. If you've got photos, that'd be cool too. I want to send out a big package as the first mailing, and I'll photo-copy as much stuff as you'd like. Send flyers that you think are cool, or whatever. The more info we have about what one another does, the better we can plan. But even if you've never really done anything before, and you just want to try something new, here's a place to start. No fees to join, and really, nothing to do, if you don't want to. You'll be solicited to work on projects, by creators, publishers, or other retailers (Creator Tours seems like the most obvious idea, a network for ashcans might be another) but you need not accept any particular task (sorta like *Mission: Impossible*). More importantly, if you know someone that would *also* want to be a part of this, pass the information along to them! Sad but true, there's still a bunch of people who aren't plugged into *Comics Retailer*, or any of my other avenues of dissemination. This is about *building* bridges, and the more people involved, the better! We need to transcend the "business as usual" attitude that pervades our business, where even "competitors" need to work together.

This is not about getting things for free, or even at better prices, necessarily, it's a network, not for trading, but for *retailing*, and creative, guerilla retailing, at that. *We* have the power to transform the industry, and the more we work *together*, the more we'll be able to accomplish. Please join me.

It's *our* (inclusive) industry, after all.

I haven't thought of Sandy McMurray in a long time. He used to work for The Silver Snail up in Canada. He wrote a regular review column on CompuServe called "Tidbits." I hope he's still doing well, wherever he is!

Tilting at Windmills #13
(Originally ran in Comics Retailer #14)

This is a special "Tidbits" installment of *Tilting at Windmills* (with a very special Tip of the *TaW* hat to Sandy McMurray for that one) with a bunch of brief bits relating to no particular subject or theme.

• As you read this, I've made a whole bunch of progress on the two challenges in last month's *TaW*.

A) The Publisher Challenge: two weeks ago, Marvel's Director of Sales/Direct Market, Lou Bank, became the first publisher to spend a week working at my store. I'm not going to go into gobs of detail because, hopefully, it will be the focus of next month's column. With any luck, I'll be able to turn a fair chunk of the column over to Lou himself. The only reason I bring it up now is that (I think) it went real well: Lou and I each learned bunches from each other, and I think we both walked away with a much clearer picture as to *why* each one does what they do. By the time you read this, that column will have been out for months. With any luck (and with the success from Lou's run), I'll have three or four more people signed up. To those of you who've told me you want to volunteer *your* store for this type of project I say "do it!" We can do nothing but learn and educate.

B) The Retailer's Non-Organization: Again, as I write this, the column hasn't even seen print. *But* I've already got *134* names to start with! I'm flabbergasted! I can be a tad pessimistic, so I didn't expect to have that many by the end of the summer. I guess I have to upgrade my goal to 250 by the time of the San Diego con...

• On that same note, Don asked me to explain the term "ashcan", which I used a couple of times in last month's column. I'm no expert on historical ashcans (which I believe were pre-publication "dummy" copies to secure copyright), but I can explain the way we use the term today. Basically, it's a set of photocopied 8-1/2 by 11" sheets folded in half and stapled to make a little black & white comic book (though it's not a small as your traditional "mini-comic" which is often a sheet folded in quarters). These are usually pre-publication comics, and often signed and numbered by the artist. They function as at least 3 things: 1) as a cool "collectible" (though I loathe that term...), 2) as promotion for an upcoming title (and, in some ways, as a barometer of how to order a comic), and 3) as a way of financing the production of a comic book. As you should know, the creator hands his work in to the publisher about a month before it ships, so they can get it to the printer. Meanwhile, the publisher doesn't see any money for the book until 30-90 days after it's shipped, so a creator may have a three to six month wait from creation to payment. Now, most publishers do pay out some form of advance on royalties, but when you're self- (or collectively-) publishing, this is not always an option. It's fairly hard to create when you don't have food on your table, or a roof over your head. So, ashcans, sold directly from creator to retailer, create a way to "subsidize" that fallow period without payment.

• Just last week DC's Retailer Participation Program had its annual meeting in Burbank. The one thing that I want to touch upon here is that it *seems* that DC is making a very strong effort to work with retailers this year. DC's theme this year was "The Year of Change," and while I'm not going to try and quantify how much change, and is it enough (in my humble opinion), there are certainly some heartening signs. Besides announcing that they would do no more distributor-coordinated tours (thank God!), they announced that they would be making a much stronger push on retailer driven promotions (such as P.O.P. and co-op). This is good news. Let's hope it works out.

• Coming from that same meeting, I was astonished by how many retailers who have never met me expected me to be some sort of anti-Marvel ogre. No, we don't hunt the Marvel Zombies down, skin 'em, then hang their pelts in the back room as a trophy (and Lou Bank can attest to that...). I don't particularly like *most* mainstream comics (not just Marvel), but that hardly means they're banned from the store, or hidden behind other comics. I carry them, I just don't push them.

I'm going to turn the back half of my column here to my Promotions Director, Aldyth Beltane, since I think she has something valuable to say to retailers at-large. I'm going to sneak out the back door (I've heard the run-through in Dress Rehearsal a whole bunch of times now), but I'll see you in 30...

• • • • •

Women customers and how to keep them
By Aldyth Beltane, Promotions Director, Comix Experience

Once again, the topic of Women in Comic Book Stores, (or Why there are So Few) is the subject of discussion. As a woman who has been on both sides of the counter over the years, I've developed a number of insights and opinions on the matter.

In the more than twenty years that I've been involved with comics, there have been a number of changes in the industry. I've seen the birth of the direct market, and the growth of independent publishing companies, two developments within themselves that help to make comics more attractive for women. I'll explain that presently. In the ten years in which I've been involved with comics professionally, there have been other changes that have helped to introduce women to the comics world, but the changes have been slow, inadequate, and the most effective ones were not even designed with the idea of bringing more women into comics.

One given that I'll use in this column is that we would all like to have more women reading and buying comics. I assume all the retailers reading this are intelligent grown-ups who would not discount a possible income that could be gained from customers based on gender. Not knowing how to encourage a woman as a customer is an entirely different thing from actively discouraging, and at least in theory we've all moved beyond that.

Having said that, there are still two basic "problems" to address. The first is how to bring women into the store, the second is how to bring them back as repeat customers. As a comic reader, I was an easy customer. I learned to read from comics, and progressed swiftly from *Archie* to *Superboy and the LSH*, to whatever comics I could get my hands on every week at the local newsstand. Now those were places to make a young girl uncomfortable – comics and the smell of cigar smoke were linked completely through my early years. But the comics made me so happy that those things didn't matter. One of the best changes of recent years is the development of pride and concern for store appearance and atmosphere. We hear so much more about stores that are clean and well organized, with staffs that are intelligent and articulate. The dark, dusty comic store is swiftly becoming a cliché of the past, which makes the whole idea of comics more appealing to everyone, regardless of gender.

So you have a reputable store, one that you'd be proud to have even Hillary Clinton walk into. How do you get her there? Well, there are comics that women will be inclined to read, and surprisingly enough, different women are drawn to different types of comics, just like guys! Comix Experience has a comparatively large percentage of women as customers, and the only book close to a universal is *Sandman*! Other books that are popular with women are the other Vertigo titles, *Hate*, *Love and Rockets*, *Eightball*, Marvel Mutant titles, *Ironwood*, Ann Rice adaptations, and many others. As one can tell, a varied list indeed. The only thing all these books have in common is that overall, they are story/character driven books. So get these titles into your store! Put them in the window! Take out an ad that features Death, or a Barker book, or *L&R*! On the mainstream books you can get great co-op rates, and as for the independents, refer back to Brian Hibbs' articles on promoting them, lest I reiterate. We just ran an ad in a local paper for *Death: the High Cost of Living*, and among the response we got, were calls from a number of people who had never read comics, but just thought the concept interesting enough to call and ask about it!

So these women see *Vampire Lestat* or whatever in your window or ad, come in to buy it, then what? As with any customer, a smart retailer is interactive. You see (or ask) what a customer is interested in, and build from that base. In general, its the nature of comics to want to read more, once someone enjoys reading comics at all. If she buys *Sandman*, show her *Hellblazer*, *Shade*, *Death*. If a girl's a *Love and Rockets* fan, show her *Madman*, or maybe *Palookaville*. *Hate* and *Eightball* seem a matched set. If a woman comes in with a male friend and seems bored or uncomfortable, show her a *Sandman*. I've had wonderful success selling *Sandman* to "girlfriends" of guys who come into the store.

One important thing – when a woman comes into your store, be as nice and polite as would to any customer, but don't treat her like a girl. Most of your male customers aren't stupid and wouldn't shop with you if you treated them as if they were. Your female customers are the same way.

Now to refer back to what I mentioned earlier, in regards to changes in the comics industry. The changes that have brought more women into the comics industry are not the ones specifically designed to do so! This is something extremely important to realize. Titles designed for specific "female appeal" have, to a one, been insulting and poorly executed. To clarify, I am referring to women here, not kids. The comics that have brought more women into the industry are the ones geared to intelligent people, the ones that have brought more readers into comics. More women involved in the creative process of comics publishing is a subtle but important factor here as well. Yes, women have been cartooning for a century (see Trina Robbins' soon-to-be-published book for more on that subject) but now even more women are taking strong roles in writing and editing. In addition to other things, this eliminates a large amount of the off-hand sexism that often inadvertently slips into comics. I know for many women this makes for a far more enjoyable read. But at the same time, this type of psychological growth should be a reflection of the growth of society itself, so I'm not certain if it's directly related to comics.

Last, don't be afraid to hire a woman to work in your store. But don't hire a token, someone with no knowledge of or interest in comics. That's worse, because it fosters the notion too long held that women don't read comics, by a very public example. I shudder every time someone asks me if I "read comics." There would be literally no reason for me to work in a comics store if I didn't, regardless of my gender.

At a time when the industry is at a crossroads between the innovative and the retread, women and other former non-comics readers are important and necessary to allow for that tilt to the side of growth.

Lou went to work for Dark Horse shortly after this, and I haven't got the foggiest notion what he's doing these days. Don't you think Bill Jemas' be well served to come work at Comix Experience for a week? Or Paul Levitz.

Tilting at Windmills #14
(Originally ran in Comics Retailer #15)

As you (no doubt) remember reading two months ago, I made a challenge to publishers to come and work retail for a week, to get a sense of "how the other half lives." After all, it's damn hard to sell comics if you don't know your customer's needs (and *we*, the retailers, are your *true* customers).

So far, we've had Marvel's Director of Sales Lou Bank come and go, and bites from at least one other publisher (it's Milestone).

I thought that it was important to not only have my impressions, but those of the visitor, as well, so this month, we have a special *TaW Point/Counterpoint* installment.

Without further ado, I'll hand you over to Lou Bank, in his own words...

Lou Bank: Sitting in our high tower on Park Avenue, we tend to expound on the problems and lost opportunities of comics retailing about as frequently as – well, as frequently as retailers expound on the problems and lost opportunities of comics publishing. It's very easy for me to tell retailers to cycle sheet, to cross-promote with other retail venues, to publicize in-store events and to make sales suggestions to customers. Having to do it myself is entirely another story, and that story is the week I spent working for Brian Hibbs at Comix Experience.

Don't take this to mean that I'm lazy; the point I'm making is that the demands of the individual tasks are great and added together are incredible. As well, the abilities that are necessary to complete the various tasks that both maintain a store and create store growth are so varied that no one person could possibly be adept at all of these aspects. The more employees a store has the greater the likelihood that it will be able to grow the store, not just through sheer volume of hands but because individuals are able to specialize at certain tasks and improve their ability to perform those tasks.

Making these tasks even more difficult, you have to expect customers and phone calls to set you off track. I've found that most jobs have a rhythm that builds and allows you to work more quickly once you've found that rhythm. Like a train derailed, once you've lost the rhythm you have to work to get it back again. Obviously you should be appreciative of customers; they're the reason you're able to remain in business. You won't remain in business long if you don't complete the tasks necessary to maintaining a store. It's the worst kind of Catch 22.

Besides the sheer volume of work I discovered a number of other things about comics retailing that week. The first item of note that struck me was the importance of putting bar codes on the comics. When I was faced with having to restock the trade section of the store, I felt like I was working ass-backwards. Listing what you have and searching distributor stock for what you don't have is time-consuming and inefficient, not to mention frustrating.

Having to do the cycle sheets the following day only reinforced this belief. The importance of accuracy in cycle sheeting is the defining purpose of the task; without codes you can neither guarantee accuracy nor efficiently complete the task in a timely manner. To say that I am absolutely astounded that retailers didn't physically assault comics publishers to convince them to institute the direct market bar code system years ago is a dramatic understatement.

A related realization was the danger and complexity of poor sell-through. If a comic suffers from reader drop-off, because of the ordering system and the time it takes to note a real trend in cycle sheeting it can take anywhere from six to 12 months to correct an ordering problem, and in that six to twelve months you can lose an awful lot of money. The result, I would guess, is that the retailer cuts deeper than is probably necessary as soon as he can react in order to ensure that the problem doesn't continue to snowball. The likelihood that the retailer will reorder the title if it sells out is almost non-existent. In order to avoid this problem we really have to take greater measures to produce greater sell-through.

On a different note, I was struck by the enormous range of ages that came through the store. It really increased my belief that comics stores should be organized by genre and interest rather than alphabetically. Racking to appeal to a generic comics fan cannot possibly produce better long-term financial results than racking to market to individual tastes and ages.

I also noticed that most customers complained about the cost of buying everything they wanted. I'm uncertain if the complaint was that they had to pay a lot of money, or if the complaint was that they did not have any more money, but the end result was that they were putting back a lot of comics that they obviously wanted. This in and of itself is not a problem, but the fact that consumers are working off of a budget, self-imposed or otherwise, and retailers (as evidenced by April order numbers) are by and large not budgeting their purchases as title counts increase leads me to believe that there are an awful lot of unsold comics sitting out there, and a lot more on the way.

The other side to that problem is that adequate racking space is rare in today's comics shop. Retailers have to make decisions about the display of new comics. There is no longer space to display two month's worth of comics effectively, and there is no logic in allocating the same amount of space to each title, I suggest that stores analyze sales of new product against two month old issues still displayed on the new comics rack. I suspect we'll find that 90 percent of the copies that are going to sell at all sell in the first four weeks. This being the case, that month old issue is taking up space that could be allotted to better displaying the new titles and perhaps increasing the sales on the new titles. Further, a title like *Spider-Man*, which sells nearly four times as many copies as *Avengers*, should be given better racking. If it sells better already, then the likelihood is that the title has a broader appeal than *Avengers*. By granting it more display space the chance that a new customer will pick it up is increased. When making this type of decision the retailer should always gamble on his best selling titles, whatever they may be. The analysis needed to prove this is obviously great, but once the bar codes are in place and stores are running electronic cycling, this data will be readily available.

At Marvel, we tend to believe that any title selling 35,000 copies has no market appeal. Obviously, that title has an appeal for 35,000 people. It's our job to figure out what it is about that comic that appeals to those 35,000 customers, and flaunt it; find out who the customers currently are, and find more people like them. Similarly, store owners need to not give up on a title. If you're only selling a handful of copies of some comics, find out why those customers are still buying that title. If it's out of force of habit, you're out of luck; if, however, they can explain why they like it, then find other titles that have a similar appeal and self-suggest the lower selling title. You build your customer base from scratch, and even if you influence your customers to a great degree in their reading choices, there is still an enormous range of personalities and tastes. While I hear a lot of complaints that there are too many titles being solicited, I feel that all this means is that retailers are fully armed with as diverse a selection as they could want. Certainly the bulk of the titles fall under similar categories, but there are comics available for every taste conceivable. Order what you know you can sell and build on that business – with all of your free time.

•   •   •   •   •

Lou, you ignorant slut...oh, that's right, this isn't a comedy bit! (sorry, I couldn't resist)

In all seriousness, you can see that Lou walked out of the week with a couple of astute observations.

I ran Lou through (virtually) every aspect of running a store – doing the cycles, taking calls, ringing up customers, pulling the new orders, etc. Just about the only thing we didn't get to was having him do an order form (and it's not my fault – Diamond shipped the catalog a week late, which, might I add, is an extremely screwed thing to do, considering that they didn't extend the deadline to turn it in a single iota...).

Lou seems to think that the panacea for a lot of the time-consuming processes will be bar-coding. While I don't doubt for a moment that it will make life marginally easier, there still a bunch of *different* problems that come from computerized systems. In any event, you *still* need to physically count the stock on a regular basis, and, in fact, I might say that you need to count it *more* frequently (having seen several programs in operation), because if you're not always completely on top of the inventory processes, you can just as easily be screwed, blued, and tattooed. My best example is Last Gasp, the underground distributor in San Francisco. They've got a pretty high powered system that seems incredibly efficient, but I cannot count the number of time the computer has insisted that an item is out of stock (and, hence, they can't sell it to me), and I'll find a six-inch stack sitting on a shelf, somewhere in the warehouse. Another good example is Diamond and Capital's computer systems, which are both, in theory, supposed to automatically shift product from location to location, and place reorders. In practice, of course, these systems barely work.

I'm not trying to cap on bar-coding systems here, but they certainly aren't going to solve problems overnight. Particularly when you factor in the fact that very few of the 6000 stores in this country can actually afford the computer system in the first place, and that smaller publishers show no signs of moving to the bar-coding. Personally, at this very moment, I see it as exchanging one set of problems for another.

I'm very pleased that Lou saw the twin problems of sell-through and lack of customers' funds. Obviously, these two are linked together, at least tangentially. As more and more product (at increasingly higher and higher price-points) comes out, the customer is forced to make immediate decisions on what to buy. The problem comes from the fact that as retailers, we're forced to make wild guesses as to what's gonna ship when, and how our customers will react when it does. More often than not, these guesses are shots in the dark. Even the best retailer doesn't have a crystal ball to arrival dates, and one week can make all the difference between feast or famine.

I notice on a daily basis that after a book has a gimmick (or, if you'd like, you can call them enhancements...), there is a disturbing trend for the title to sell-through at a *lower* amount than it did before the gimmick. Lou saw this as well, looking at the cycle sheets. I think the answer is two-fold: 1) Since gimmick books DO increase sales (on a one-time basis), publishers should *never* raise the cost of that comic book to the consumer. The consumer is sick and tired of paying 1.5-3x as much for some flashy cover, or bagged something. It's a lot easier for them to walk away from the title completely, even though *we* are the ones holding the bag. Lou said to me a week after being in the store that he was going to suggest this to his bosses. Hopefully, they'll listen, because, once again, it's making a short-term buck at the expense of a long-term customer. 2) We should be allowed to make order decreases, up until the print run is finally set for the title, just as we're allowed to place advance reorders. If *Spud-boy* #49 sells 20 copies, #50 (with a gimmick cover) sells 40, then #51 sells only 15, we should be able to drop our orders on #52 & 53, without having to wait until #54 shows up on the order form (and, of course, in a lot of cases, we're ordering #55-60 "blind" as well). I, personally, would call that customer service: a quality that most every distributor is *sorely* lacking. (In fact, to digress a bit, I was mildly amused to note that Lou, who is used to coming in the front door of the warehouse, with the suit and all, getting the "official" view of life at a distributor, was fairly distraught by the utter lack of help the people at the loading dock provide. "They didn't offer any help at all!" said Lou. And that's what it's like in the [not to be pejorative] real world).

Lou goes on to talk about rack space (or the lack thereof), and I agree with him that it's no longer practical to give maximum exposure to every title. I will, however, *mildly* disagree that the best sellers should always get the best exposure. This is, of course, a self-fulfilling prophecy. "Little" books *become* "big" books by promoting them. *Avengers needs* more help and more space than *Amazing Spider-Man because* it doesn't sell as well. It's always bugged me that the comics that get the covers of the distributor catalogs and the ads in the fanzines are always the titles that are sure-fire hits. *Spider-Man* #1 would have sold (in my humble opinion, though, of course, there's no way to *prove* this contention is true) just as many copies, had it not been the focus of that intense ad campaign. And even if it did drop a little, I believe that the profits would have been *more* than made up by the sales of other books that could've used the push. Rather than taking an attitude of "O.K., here's a good comic, let's see what we can do to make it sell better," this industry (as a *whole*) has always fostered the path of "Here's something that's selling *really* well already. Let's remind everyone of that fact." There are far too many unsold comics on the market as it is. Let's help the stuff that needs it.

In any event, the idea of keeping a sharp eye on stock, and racking accordingly, is a damn fine one. Every store should heed this advice, while adapting the *way* you do it to your owns needs, and clientele.

As a final direct note about Lou's piece, I can't help but note that "At Marvel we tend to believe that any title selling 35,000 copies has no market appeal." I suspect that there are several titles that Marvel (and every other company!) produces that have that number of readers, or lower. Based on my (admittedly biased) empirical observations on sell-through, multiple copy purchases, distributor stock, retailer back-issue stock planning, and "I'm-just-buying-it-to-keep-my-collection-current" (to just touch the tip of the iceberg of unsold copies), I suspect that the actual number of *readers* on your average superhero comic book is between 1/2 to 1/3 of the circulation. On some titles, that ratio may be as low as 1:10! There *are* a lot of unsold (and unread!) copies floating around the market, and there *are* going to be a lot more. You're reading this in June, so you'll know by now what some of the effects of the "Summer of Glut" are going to be, but I have a feeling that this time next year, we're going to be facing an entirely different market, with an entirely different set of problems and challenges.

Lou Bank came out and took *my* challenge, and I think he did really well, because he came to it with his eyes and ears open. He came to learn, and learn he did. I honestly don't think that half of what Lou really learned made it into his piece above – there are so many things (that *we* all know) that just can't be articulated. And more than learn, he taught me a few things too, in the way that a new set of eyes on an old problem always will. I believe that this was an invaluable experience for the both of us, and although there are still a dozen things I dislike about Marvel (and I'm sure there are a dozen things Lou didn't like about how I run my store), we both came away with a clearer understanding as to how to try and make it better. I wouldn't trade that time for almost anything, and I hope you can find the time to do something similar. There are hundreds of publishers out there, with thousands of people who need the education that we can help provide. I threw down the *TaW* gauntlet (which, might I add, is still down, with dozens of quarters unheard from), why don't you throw down one of your own?

'Cuz we *all* can use more knowledge.

Heh. This might have been more effective with a less mundane example. I read it most-of-a-decade later and say "jeez, whiner!"

Today, distributors (well, heehee, Diamond) uses centralized ordering for all things. And, yes, it's much more efficient.

Tilting at Windmills #15
(Originally ran in Comics Retailer #16)

Let's talk about distributors. (You had to see that one coming, right?)

Lemme preface these comments with a few disclaimers:

1) *All* opinions included herein are *mine*. *Nothing* I ever say should be interpreted as reflect any views held by Krause, or any of it's employees. I'm a freelancer – I'm allowed to have an attitude.

2) I've also worked at a distributor (for about a year) – I realize the problems of that system, and the constraints they're working under. Most distributors *are* fairly efficient at getting books from A to B, at least of any titles that the preponderance of retailers order in quantity.

3) Although I only use one primary distributor for a majority of the mainstream periodicals we sell, I'm in enough contact with other retailers who use virtually every other distributor, to be able to make some blanket statements, based on common experiences.

I've got two major areas of contention with the distributors: restocking policies, and customer service.

Restocking problems we're *all* acquainted with. I don't know of a single retailer that doesn't have some sort of horror story about foul-ups in orders. The thing *I* resent the most is when I know for a *fact* that the publisher has stock available in their warehouse (in quantity!), I've met both the publisher's and distributor's minimum order, and the items will *never, ever* show up! I mean, what the hell kind of system is it when you have a customer waving around money around on one side (that's us), and a warehouse full of comics (that's the publishers) on the other, and you don't see a transaction? I guarantee you that if any of us ran our stores like that (where the guy behind the counter wouldn't take the customers money), we'd be out of business post-haste.

There are one or two fairly good programs in place that make some headway. For example, Diamond's Star System is a good model. Automatic confirmation of availability, an *extremely* high fill rate, and free freight over certain (modest) ordering levels. The only problem we have here is the very limited breadth of backlist items listed (it's really only stuff that sells well in the first place and, accordingly, probably the type of stuff they were getting high reorders on in the first place, making this just a more efficient system to do what they were before), and the complete lack of any periodicals. We are, like it or not, a periodical driven business, and the lack of a national system, with *every* item that the distributors carry, is holding the market back from achieving it's potential. And, in fact, until we see this, "distributors" are hardly even that – they're mere freight forwarders!

I'm lucky in that the volume of my orders makes it practical for me to restock direct from many publishers. I know that for a lot of stores this is entirely impractical. Let's take a book that I think can easily be built into a strong seller with a little work, but is virtually ignored by the distributors: *Hate*. Let's say that you took my advice from previous *Tilting*'s and ordered a handful of copies, to give it a try. You liked it, it sold through, so you place a reorder. In most circumstances, the distributors aren't going to be able to fill a reorder for one or two copies, so you're SOL if you want to keep giving this book a chance. I think that it's criminal that the system is currently structured to effectively only support the stuff that is going to sell gangbusters in the first place. Sure, I can walk over to Last Gasp (a local "alternative/underground" distributor – a good resource for any store that wants to diversify their stock), or call up the publisher, but that's not an option for everyone.

I tend to suspect that the distributors, as currently structured, are only as good as the local warehouse manager. That is: just like our customers are only able to buy materials that we like and have faith in (past the first few onsale weeks), we're only able to have strong restock on the local manager's likes and faiths. If the local manager thinks *Hate* is a good book, then he'll make sure that there are copies available. And if not, then "oh, well" to that title. The problem stems from the fact that most of the warehouse managers seem to be happy to fall in with "company lines" – they stock in depth what they're told to by "conventional wisdom." That is: the same items that are pushed on the covers (and ads) of the catalogs, or to put it another way, the items that they're paid the most for by the publishers.

Let's, as retailers, face up to a hard truth: the distributors are getting rich off us. They have a guaranteed sale from every item they solicit, while we're completely guessing (even though it's educated, we're still guessing. I was flabbergasted at Steve Geppi's claim that *Adventures of Superman* #500 was a complete sell out! Oh, sure neither DC nor Diamond have any copies leftover, but I sure can see a *lot* of retailers swimming in copies); and they make buckets of money from their catalogs. I've seen some of the checks from publishers for catalog ads, and they are insane! I'm no expert on publishing costs, but my rough calculations show that the distributors are making a fortune from listings of guaranteed sales for them! It makes me pretty ill to think about.

Anyway, let's talk about the second area: customer service. It's hard to discuss in concrete terms, because it's an almost intangible thing. You know when you're not getting it, but defining it is difficult. And it's what separates a good business from a poor one. I think it boils down to the golden rule: do unto others as you'd have them do unto you. Be excellent to one another.

I run my store with that in mind. You go out of your way to do good for a customer, because you're not making just the sale today, you're making a sale for the rest of your life. Yet I hardly see that from the distributors.

I am regularly given misinformation ('course, I know enough people to be able to find out the truth eventually); I have shipments dicked (gee don't you love it when, as a random example, an item like *2000ad*, the British weekly, shows up once every two months? And then it's eight at once, with one of the issues missing?); and to get *anything* out of the norm done, I have to jump through hoops.

Here's an example: we order a case of current comic bags *each* and *every* week. We bag our customers purchases. One week the bags don't show, so I called my distributor, and asked what up?

"Oh, we have no order on record."

But the order *was* placed, by the member of my staff who is the most entirely conscientious guy in the whole wide world, just like he does *every* week, and I have a witness that he placed the order, not that it should be a big deal, mind you, so could you please go slap a UPS tag on a case of bags and get it out right now? And if it's a big deal, screw it, I'll even pay for the shipping.

"Well, we have no record, so we'll have to treat it as a reorder, and we won't get to it until Monday."

Look, we order a case *every* week, and I'm *not* going to sell them – it's *not* a reorder, it's my original order, that you screwed. It's not like I'm ordering 100 *Turok* #1s – it's bags fer-christ's-sake – I need to bag my customers purchases!

"Sorry"

So, I gotta call the main HQ, and bitch to *them*, then have *them* call the local warehouse to do it.

It's bullshit!

And this is the *least* of my tales...

What happened to customer service?

If I can provide it, why can't they?

I'm deadly, powerfully tired of this, and my only possible response is to take my business from them, direct to the publishers. I don't *want* to do this. It's a headache for me, and a lot of damn hard work. But what other choice do I have?

I try damn hard to run the best business I can, but the distributors don't do the same for me.

And it *must* change.

Tilting at Windmills #16
(Originally ran in Comics Retailer #17)

I've been having, in the last few weeks, what might be termed a crisis in confidence.

I've watched this industry spin out of control, every revolution cranking the speed up a notch, threatening to throw the whole show of its axis.

Some symptoms?

• The observation that virtually *every* dealer at the recent WonderCon in Oakland (one of the biggest cons in the nation) had *identical* stock! Every one of them top-heavy with recent "hot" comics, in deep quantities, at exorbitant prices. Here's a great example: on almost every dealers wall sat a "gold" *WildC.A.T.S.* #1, for $100 or more! And they were there on the opening day of the Con, and for the most part, were still there on closing day. If 90% of the however-many-hundred retailers there have the same comics, *none* of those comics could possibly considered "hot!" It's blatantly obvious!

• While channel-surfing the other night, I happened past QVC's comic book segment.

A more nasty & evil thing I can not imagine.

Let's look at some of the prices they were hawking items at:

- $145 for a signed set of *Adventures of Superman* #500, and the four "return" issues. $15.75 retail for $145. $29 an issue. And this is less than a month after the book was on sale.

- $45 for "Ten first issues, including *WILDC.A.T.S.* #1 and *Spawn* #1" (of course they don't mention that five of these first issues are lame garbage like *Armageddon: Alien Agenda* #1. In fact, several of them were cancelled titles. Not much investment potential there).

- $25 for a *Nomad* #1 (regular series) signed by the artists. If your store is anything like mine, you're only selling three or four copies of *Nomad* a month (and considering it's sitting at #179 on Diamond's June sales chart, I don't think I'm far off...), and the demand for a *Nomad* #1 is nil or next to it. With a $2 cover, let's be generous and say it's "worth" $3, so it's $22 for the signatures, or $11 per! For two effectively unknown artists.

- $29 for a *Moon Knight* #1 (first series) signed by Jim Shooter (!). Here's a character who has been cancelled twice (and soon to be thrice, if placing #203 in the charts, and dropping, is any indication), who almost nobody cares about, and a book that I *regularly* put in my quarter boxes! It's not even signed by any member of the creative team, but merely by the Editor-In-Chief! Hey, I know! *I'll* go sign old copies of *Marvel Two-in-one*, and price them at $50 each!

Pshaw.

Not only are these bastards taking advantage of an ignorant buying public (who know *nothing* besides the newspaper reports that "the comics your mom threw away are now worth BIG BUCKS!"), they are, in the long run, screwing *us*. Because, sooner or later, the people who buy into this ridiculous hype are gonna come to us to turn in their "valuable collectible," and they're going to walk away feeling like idiots, when we won't *ever* give them more than half of what they paid (if that).

But, are they going to blame QVC?

Nope. They'll blame *us*.

And then they'll go off and tell all of their friends and acquaintances what a rip-off comic books are.

Everyone these days is trying to tap into the "suckers" market, by hawking "signed collectibles" for exorbitant prices, or by only carrying "hot" books, or by starting up a new superhero universe in the wake of Valiant and Image, everybody is trying to cut their little slice of the money pie, but almost no one is trying to build and protect the market.

It's so easy, and very tempting, to give up the morals for the money. I could quadruple the amount of money I take in if I decided to play the game like everyone else.

But then I couldn't sleep at night.

I couldn't stand valuing commerce over creation, avarice over art, or losing the feeling of a home, or a family, that both myself and many of my customers hold close to our hearts.

So I hold on to my values, for another day, for another week, and I run the kind of store where price is based on value rather than hype, and where value is always stressed.

Y'know why?

Because of the comics, themselves.

Comic books taught me that "With Great Power Comes Great Responsibility," that the value of living is in doing the right thing, of making it better, in the end, for everyone. That being a hero, doing right, was the greatest thing you could ever aspire to.

Today's market is very much like today's comics: KILL! KILL! KILL!!! And whatever is left standing at the end is right. Even if it doesn't have a foundation of substance left to stand on.

Every day, I see another potential hero become an anti-hero, and it makes me want to cry. We need more people willing to fight, willing to kick and scream, willing to drag this industry back from the precipice it's brought itself to.

We need more heroes.

The time has passed for waffling: are you going to wear a black hat, or a white one? And today, right now, gray may as well be black.

Be a hero. Decide that you want to grow the market rather than fragment it. Don't price books by the flavor-of-the-week – use the supply and demand of your *own* store; reduce your dependence on multiple copy sales; encourage your customers to read rather than invest; promote the titles *you* are the most excited about, *not* the "sure-fire investments" (if they're so "surefire," howcum people need to be *told* about them?); concentrate on the *fun* of comics, the *joy* of reading, and all the excitement that caused *you* to fall in love with them in the first place. Make your store a real comics store, not a commodity market.

It's the least anyone can do.

One of the most "important" columns I have ever written.
I quote from it a lot to other retailers.
If **your** store offers a discount, take a close look at that math and tell me if it **really** makes sense.

Tilting at Windmills #17
(Originally ran in Comics Retailer #18)

Deep discounting never made any sense to me.

When I was recently in Kansas City visiting a relative, I went into a local store to buy my cousin a copy of the latest *Sandman*. I was given a 10% discount. I asked why, and the store replied that *every* customer gets a 10% discount, and that regulars do even better. Evidently this is a citywide phenomenon.

I understand in Detroit, discounting *starts* at 20%.

I just don't get it.

Why would anyone give away money, just because a customer happens to walk in your store *once*? I can understand giving a discount for someone who *earns* it, but to any Tom, Dick or Harry? No way, Jose!

At Comix Experience, we give a straight 10% discount to any member of our subscription service. Unlike most stores' pull-and-hold services, we put out a new form monthly, so we're able to get (nearly) instant information about our customers likes and dislikes. So it's worth giving away that discount in the face of the information I take in.

But I'll talk about pull-and-hold systems another day – today the topic is discounting.

Are you aware just how much discounting can cost you? I've prepared the charts below to illuminate my point. First find the chart that corresponds to your discount level (though even stores that get 55% off still have some titles they only make 40% on). I've made four charts, for 55%, 50%, 45%, and 40% discount levels. If you're one of the rarer "odd discount" retailers, I apologize, but hopefully you'll be able to create an appropriate chart with the info I've given here.

Each chart compares six different customer discount levels (none, 10%, 15%, 20%, 25%, and 30%). First you'll see the retail amount a $1.25 comic book sells for at that discount, then the *profit* from that sale. When you give discounts, your *costs* remain the same! Then the chart show how many copies you'd need to sell to make $20 profit. Finally the chart shows how many *more* comics you need to sell to make the same amount of profit. (*All* numbers are rounded to the next whole number.)

Look at the charts, and then we'll talk some more.

Chart #1: $1.25 comic at 55% off • Cost is $.56

Discount Given	None	10%	15%	20%	25%	30%
Retail	$1.25	$1.13	$1.06	$1.00	$.94	$.88
Profit	$.69	$.56	$.50	$.44	$.38	$.31
Number of copies sold to make $20 profit:	29	36	40	46	53	64
% difference from NO discount:	n/a	22%	38%	57%	83%	120%

Chart #2: $1.25 comic at 50% off • Cost is $.63

Discount Given	None	10%	15%	20%	25%	30%
Retail	$1.25	$1.13	$1.06	$1.00	$.94	$.88
Profit	$.63	$.50	$.44	$.38	$.31	$.25
Number of copies sold to make $20 profit:	32	40	46	53	64	80
% difference from NO discount:	n/a	25%	43%	67%	100%	150%

Chart #3: $1.25 comic at 45% off • Cost is $.69

Discount Given	None	10%	15%	20%	25%	30%
Retail	$1.25	$1.13	$1.06	$1.00	$.94	$.88
Profit	$.56	$.44	$.38	$.31	$.25	$.19
Number of copies sold to make $20 profit:	36	46	53	64	80	107
% difference from NO discount:	n/a	29%	50%	80%	125%	200%

Chart #4: $1.25 comic at 40% off • Cost is $.75

Discount Given	None	10%	15%	20%	25%	30%
Retail	$1.25	$1.13	$1.06	$1.00	$.94	$.88
Profit	$.50	$.38	$.31	$.25	$.19	$.13
Number of copies sold to make $20 profit:	40	53	64	80	107	160
% difference from NO discount:	n/a	33%	60%	100%	167%	300%

As you can see, discounting eats into your bottom line dramatically! Let's take a couple of for examples.

Example #1: You're a 50% discount store that gives a uniform 20% discount to *all* customers (a typical Detroit scenario) – you've got to sell 67% *more* comics to make the exact same amount of money if you didn't discount. To put it another way, if you immediately cut the discount, and lost about 40% of your customers, your profit would remain the same! You currently have to sell 53 comics at 20% off to equal the same profit you'd see from selling 32 comics at full retail.

Example #2: you're a small store that gets a 40% discount. You give your customers 10% off. You've got to sell 13 more comics to make the same amount if you gave no discount – that's a third! You could lose 25% of your customers, eliminate the discount, and still make the same amount of profit!

Example #3: You're Bob's Mega-comics, and you get 55% off. You give a 30% discount. You've got to sell *more than* twice as many comics to make the same profit as you would with no discount. You could lose more than half your customers, and still be just as profitable.

Of course, losing volume could affect your discount from your distributor, so it's not like I'm saying to automatically dump the discount. And, of course, all numbers assume that you've got 100% sell-through (an unlikely event across the board) – the poorer your sell-through, the more you've got to sell to make up for it.

I believe that discounting has its place. When someone performs a service for you (like the collection of information from my customers; or the courtesy discount I give to professionals – who supply the material I sell in my shop; or even to other merchants who give you discounts on services for the store), it makes sense to "reward" him or her with a discount. But I think it's inane to "give away the store" to any Joe off the street that hasn't even provided customer loyalty to you.

Use the charts to see what you're *losing*. Then make the appropriate decision, based on your store and clientele. But without the basic information, how will you ever know?

Tilting at Windmills #18
(Originally ran in Comics Retailer #19)

Some days I hate technology.

I spent a solid week on this month's column, with tight arguments weaving in a coherent narrative. It was a thing of beauty.

So then I go to send it off to *Comics Retailer*, and what do I find? It's *gone*. Into the electronic ether. Like it never existed. It's not on my hard drive, it's not on any disk in my possession. It's just *gone*.

>Sigh<

So with my back against the deadline wall, I get to start from scratch. I hope it doesn't lose too much in the rush.

How many titles can the market maintain? How many publishers? How many universes?

I'm rapidly coming to the opinion that our customers have *too many* choices. Obviously we're in the middle of product glut, but the people most affected are us, the retailers.

In Marvel's October 1993 *Sales to Astonish* catalog, it is claimed that Direct Market retailers have a 90-92% sell-through. I find this a little hard to believe, unless it includes sales on the discount racks.

I look at my sales patterns, and the only thing I can safely predict is that I can't predict anything. Books sell without rhyme or reason, with *no* kind of pattern I can discern. As an example, I sell somewhere between one and four copies of *Silver Sable* each month. As far as I can tell, there is no difference in content or packaging as to whether I sell one or four copies. It's not the creative team. It's not guest stars. It's not crossovers or specific chapters in an arc or even the color of the cover. It appears to be complete and absolute whim.

Silver Sable may seem like an extreme example, but the truth is, on one scale or another, almost every comic we carry has a similar situation. *X-Men*, for example, currently sells somewhere between 60 and 85 copies (It used to sell well in the 200 range!). If I order 85, and only sell 60, that's only a 71% sell through! Now, *X-Men* has back-issue potential, so it's not *all* that bad, but the sad truth is that the *vast* majority of titles on the racks have a one-week shelf-life. If it doesn't sell in the first week, it ain't never gonna sell!

The solution to fluctuating sales is to be conservative, of course. But the problem with conservatism is that it doesn't leave much room for increasing sales over time. My observation is that as more and more and more and more product comes out, sales growth only comes from one of two places: 1) quality of the material, and 2) perceived "heat" as an investment item. #2 is *always* short-term, unless #1 *also* exists. But #1, in and of itself, is no longer enough, in the face of ordering conservatism.

I remember, not so long ago, when it was possible to overbuy by a copy or two on most every book. Back in the days where 50 titles was considered a *huge* week (nowadays, that's *tiny*). When you're selling 30 or 40 copies, dependably, an extra few copies still kept you comfortably within an 85% or better sell-through. Sure, every once in awhile you'd choke, but that was the exception. Conversely, these days, as once-dependable titles steadily lose ground (*Captain America* used to sell a steady 25 copies: now it's whittled down to a measly five...), you simply can't afford to stock any extras. Where do the next generation of a title's readers come from, then? If for the last six months I've sold a steady four copies of *Darkhold*, without exception, you can bet the house that unless something truly and awe-inspiring amazing happens, I'm only going to order four copies. Yet another *Ghost Rider* crossover doesn't count as exciting (quite the opposite – it's far more likely today, right now, to drop those sales from four to three). But if I'm only ordering four copies, then it's nearly impossible that the number will *ever* increase. Should I order five copies then? Of course not – if I still only sell four (that's what the cycle sheets say we *will*) then 20% (!) of my orders go unsold. And if they don't sell in the first week, it'll *never* sell.

It takes at *least* six months to accurately determine the real sales of a title (sometimes as much as a year!). That can be a lot of books to eat, if you guess high. And it can be a *lot* of potential sales (long-term) lost if you guess low. Both of these are untenable positions for all strata of the industry – creator, reader, retailer, publisher, we *all* lose when we play conservative. But to do otherwise is the road to financial ruin. So what's the solution?

The only thing I can see is twin programs of focused overshipping and limited returnability.

Focused overshipping is the province of a publisher. They need to assess when retailer advance orders don't show as much confidence in the material as the publisher has. For example, Malibu purportedly spent a million dollars to promote the *Ultraverse* line. While I understand that orders on the first issues were healthy, advances on the second issues dropped as much as 50%. Given that almost all stores reported selling out of the first issues, and that, even after spending a significant amount of money, you've still got a limited window of opportunity, before the consumer forgets the advertising message, I think that some form of overshipping would have been appropriate. These extra books would be shipped fully returnable, on the assumption that very few would be returned in the end.

Limited returnability is a little trickier. What I would suggest is an option between a fixed percentage and a number of copies. For example, 20% or three copies, whichever is higher. In other words, if you order less than 15 copies of a title, you could return up to three copies, while at over 15, you could return 20%, rounded up. If I ordered 20 copies of *Namor*, I could return up to four copies.

The real trick is to discourage retailer "padding" – that is, if I'm selling a steady four copies of *Darkhold*, I shouldn't then jump my order up to seven, simply because I can. I should raise it to five, though, to attempt and find a new consumer, and another long-term sale for the title. I think the best way to discourage "padding" would be to make the returns credit not take effect until six weeks after the on-sale date. To the best of my knowledge, no store has better than 30 day terms, that two week after-the-fact window would make it unlikely that all but the best-capitalized stores could afford to "float" large over-buying. And the well-capitalized stores are that way because they're too smart to play that kind of game.

While it makes the publisher's position a little riskier, in the long run it will prove better for them – they'll get information that much more closely approximates real-world sell-through. Here's an example: Last year, the DC Annuals crossover sold ever so slightly better than the "parent" book each annual was from. The advance orders for this year's crossover seem to support that this was the same for many of you (either that, or we have short memories). This year, however, my experience is that almost all of the annuals did significantly worse than the "parent" (though my orders were slightly higher – that's a lot of books to eat). My understanding is that DC is currently planning next year's "big event" – with the "instant" sell-through feedback of limited returns, maybe they'll re-think the viability.

I know that retailers would think this a good idea, and I suspect that most publishers would ultimately support the principle (there *are* ways to move returned books, especially to expand the audience ultimately – "3-paks" in airports and the like would be but one), but the hard ones to convince are the distributors. They're happy with the status quo, and have no reason to change it. If you think this is a worthy idea, I implore you to write your distributor, as well as many publishers as you can, asking for limited returns to become a reality. This is the type of thing that *must* begin as a grass-roots effort for it to have any effect. As always, it's up to you.

Again, except for the bit about weekly comics, I could just change a few words and rerun this today.

We're caught in an endless cycle!!!

Tilting at Windmills #19
(Originally ran in Comics Retailer #20)

This month's *TaW* is being written post-San Diego Con. That means that I'm far too overworked (and underpaid) to write a long one (even though I spent the week before the con trying to get ahead...). So, instead of my normal scathing indictment of What Is and What Should Never Be (gratuitous Rock reference alert!), we're going to try and keep this one relatively simple.

As you can see from the title at the top of the page, this month I'd like to talk specifically to the publishers out there reading this. There are a number of things you're doing wrong that are (seem?) easy enough to fix that are costing me on my bottom line.

First off, and this one is easy, *spread out your shipping schedules*. Let's take a couple of specific examples so you can see where I'm coming from: Jademan comics (who did the Chinese martial arts comics – are they still in business?) used to publish about six titles. They invariably shipped in the same week. Most small independents seem to follow this pattern. Now if you're a company with no "name" value, you're constantly fighting an uphill battle for the consumer to even *look* at your work. When you dump your entire output on to the market in one week, you've just made that hill a little steeper.

Let's take a moment here to underline a point that is at the center of retailing today: the majority of regular comic readers (not counting speculation) have a *finite* amount of money that they can spend. This is far truer today than it ever has been in the history of the direct market. Prices have escalated rapidly, as has the amount and variety of product that is available on the racks. Customers have more choices than they ever had (too many, in my humble opinion – see last month's column), and the ultimate effect of more choice, without a larger budget, is that the consumer becomes more selective. You have to make it *easy* for them to buy your material.

When you dump all your product on the market in one week, the only thing you've made easy is the opportunity to *ignore* your material. I can remember several months when Valiant, at that point publishing nine or ten titles, would put six of them out in one week. This *always* slowed the sales down in my store, often to never recover, because, that's asking for $12-15 that week! And that's pretty darn near my average customer's *entire* budget for the week! At that point, you're practically forcing the customer to drop one or more of the titles they were "on the edge" with: "I can't afford to get all of these Valiants this week, on top of my other books...well, I haven't been enjoying *Rai* as much as the rest of these, so I'll just stop buying it."

Bearing your customer profile in mind is imperative when you set schedules, as is looking at what else you may be shipping in a given week. As my third "for example" on this bit, I point to Vertigo. *Sandman* and *Hellblazer* are Vertigo's two best-selling books, although *Hellblazer* still only sells a fraction of *Sandman*. The reason why they're the best-selling titles? Because they're the best books in the line (one of the few publishers where this is actually the case). But, let me point out that the average Vertigo customer is typically one with *very* limited funds – usually students, or "disaffected youth" are the top two categories. My experience shows that often the *Sandman* buyer only has enough money at hand to buy *Sandman*: they simply *can't* afford another book that week. I'm positive that if *Hellblazer* came out in a different week than *Sandman*, it would sell better. To make matters worse, the latest catalog lists *Children's Crusade* #1 (the first Vertigo Crossover) as shipping at the same time as *Sandman* and *Hellblazer*. It's written by Neil Gaiman, and illustrated by Chris Bachalo, and it's going to end up competing with *Sandman* (the *reason* why these creators will sell comics) for the customer's money.

The second thing all publishers should do is *only make schedules you can keep!* Yes, I know you've heard this litany many times before, but it's even more important in these times of conservative ordering than ever before. The first thing we need to get rid of is this ridiculous "only late after 90 days" rule. That was just fine five years ago, but today it is absolutely ludicrous. You're late if you don't show up in the month solicited for. Period. I have no slack to cut for publishers who can't deliver on time. Don't waste my time, money, and energy if you can't keep your promises. I have exceedingly little faith in, say, Harris, who were soliciting for #11 of the "monthly" *Vampirella* at the same time they delivered #3; or in Eclipse who've resolicited some issues of *Miracleman* four and five times; or in Continuity, who've had the single most laughable shipping record in recorded history, and then took out all kinds of ads promising the moon and the sun, and after one month went back to their same deplorable patterns. And I'm not even going to mention Image.

This also holds if the market mechanisms can't deliver the product. Sun comics is producing "weekly" manga and *Ripley's Believe It or Not* reprints, and for all I know, they actually do print them and ship them weekly. But I can tell you without a shadow of a doubt that they don't work through the chain like that. We get them monthly at best, and so they sit on the rack, collecting dust.

And let's talk about reprints, shall we? I can understand a *certain* amount of flexibility in the schedules of original material. Creators aren't robots, after all. But reprints? If they're even a *day* late it's because of someone's incompetence. It frightens me when I look at Dark Horse, who've been doing *advance* solicitations of reprint material (like scheduled for August if all the other solicitations are for July), and can't get the book out on time. Yes, reprints have a far longer shelf life than the majority of my store's stock, but given the state of availability of reorders, I'm ordering what I think I can sell in the first 30 days. This is invariably higher than what sells outside of that window, on a month-to-month basis. Why? Because you promote the book, and I promote the book, and the customers are actively looking for it. But if you don't produce it on time the advertising wears off.

Every time a publisher stiffs me on sales because of *their* lateness, I'm less inclined to strongly support their material in the future.

Listen, I don't care what the excuse is. It doesn't matter to me if your production department is overworked (hire more people), or if the editor set an unrealistic schedule (slap some sense into them, or penalize them), or if the talent cannot produce the work on time (get different talent), or whatever your excuse may be. The only thing I know is that there is *no* excuse for not keeping a promise. Shipping schedules represent a promise to the retailer and consumer that the books will arrive at a certain point. If they do not arrive at that point they usually become unsalable. And you've just made it that much harder to sell the next project.

Oh, and if you *do* blow your schedule, #1) tell people about it, so we're not left hanging on your whim, and #2) *never* try and make up for lost time squeezing out issues in a shorter time frame. DC recently had an issue of *JLA* that was a month late. The week after they shipped the late one, they shipped the next issue. Sales on that one were half of what they should've been, leaving me eating comic books. Bad call. When *Next Men* had some shipping problems, Dark Horse started banging out issues bi-weekly. That was when I started experiencing serious dips in sales, which have never caught back up. Don't compound your late shipping problems by "jury-rigging" the schedule – you made the problem, it is *your* responsibility to accept the penalty (taking returns) until the next solicitation where you can fix the problem. If this means you're taking returns on three or four issues, so be it. There is *no* valid reason to stick retailers with *your* mistakes.

I know that a lot of publishers hold many retailers in contempt. I'm also aware that some of these perceptions are perfectly valid, given the mechanisms of the industry, and many retailer practices, but you've got to be aware that respect and faith are two-way streets. Retailers will never support you as long as you engage in practices that cost us money, time, and energy. We're rapidly moving past the idea that all storeowners must be wide-eyed fan boys who'll succumb to any line of hype we're handed. As more and more retailers become professional in their business practices, the more we're going to expect out of you. Ours is a symbiotic relationship, and it's never a good idea to harm your host.

2 0

This is the first attempt at "straight reportage" I've ever made.
Also the last.
It reads fine...but it's not really much of a *TaW*.

Tilting at Windmills #20
(Originally ran in Comics Retailer #21)

A look at the Eisner Nominees

This August, at the San Diego Comic Convention, the Will Eisner Spirit of
Comics Retailing Award was handed out. Fifteen retailers from all over the
country "competed" for the top honor – sort of a retailer "Hall of Fame".

I'm of the opinion that, given that this award isn't a "who's better" or popularity
contest, but rather a one-time "respect of your peers" honor, that the nominees in this
case are equally as important as the actual winners. (And, no, I'm not just saying this
because I didn't win – former editor Don Butler can confirm that I suggested this
the day the nominees were announced!) Since this issue of the *Retailer* should have
a feature on the three winners, I took it upon myself to interview the other twelve
nominees, and to try and show what makes these stores superlative.

I did brief phone interviews with each of the nominees, asking them two
questions: "What are the standout elements of your store that allowed you to be

nominated for this award?" and "What piece of advice do you have for other retailers to help them get nominated next year?" I'll move directly to the responses after one caveat: because of the time difference, and my deadline on this column, I was unsuccessful in getting in contact with anyone representing Forbidden Planet in London. I apologize for this in advance, and want to offer the opportunity for FP to write me at the address at the bottom of the page – I'll run whatever comments you might want to add...

"Why were you nominated?"

Mike Pandalfo of Dr. Comics & Mr. Games in Oakland, California thinks that a comfortable environment is the key. Mike says, "We try to be more of a successful retail store than a hard-core comic book store. Because you say 'comics store' and that turns people off, but you say 'retail store' and then they're much more apt to come and check you out, and then they'll happen to see you have comics."

Central City Comics' (based in Columbus, Ohio) Steve Synder agrees: "We take a little bit different approach in retailing comics. My wife came up with a design, with a designer, six years ago. We put a lot of thought into our design: it's laid out like a Blockbuster. You feel comfortable in any of our shops that you went into, and know where the same things are. We have things laid out by comics genre, which makes it real easy for people to find books within the shop. And we work with our people – most of them love comics as a medium, and it comes across, but we work with them on how to engage customers. Not to make a hard sell, but how to make the customer feel at ease. Like your place of business is a friends house that they stop off at."

Store design is not simply throwing up some racks and calling it done. Thought and care needs to be put to what your store will be. Lyn Pederson of Page after Page in Las Vegas had this to say, "I've always approached retail with a commercial art slant. A lot of people in the business call me about doing those kinds of things. A lot of things we've been doing for years, like standees, are becoming a lot more commonplace for comic companies to do, once they get the budget for it. We've been going outside of the market for a long time: doing presentations at fairs, and home shows – anyplace where they wouldn't expect comics, to try and alert people to the fact that comics are changing, and it's not what they expected."

Echoing the need to create an identity, and expand your individual market is Joe Field from Flying Colors in Concord, California. Joe says, "I think one of the things we've done in the five years we've been open is that we've been able to establish our identity within the industry where publishers, distributors, and creators know that this is a store that is very reader-friendly; it's one that is very forward looking; it's one that is doesn't owe anything at all to speculators; and it's one that would rather sell one copy to 100 people than 100 copies to one person."

As I interviewed the retailers for this piece, certain ideas came up over and over. Speculation, and its effects are among our largest concerns. Most agree that the solution to this is diversification of product in your store, and the love of what you're doing. Says Mike Moynihan of Words & Pictures in Calgary of why he was nominated, "I think it's just a sincere honest appreciation for the medium. I love comics, and I feel that comes across in our store, with displays of particular works, and I think it comes across to our customers, that comics are not an investment thing, like bonds or stocks. We try to teach them that the comics are intrinsically worthwhile."

Three more votes for diversification are cast by Wayne Winsett of Time Warp in Boulder, Bob Gordon of Acme Books & Comics in Peoria, and Joesph Miller of The Comic Store in Lancaster, Pennsylvania. Wayne says, "I think our strongest point is that we carry a complete line of comics, not just the regular Marvel-DC-Image-Valiant type of stuff. We carry...well, not everything, but we have the largest stock of independent titles in the state." Bob Gordon concurs: "I try to work harder with doing small-press publications. I promote a lot of small-press stuff and carry other items outside of comics — a lot of college-oriented stuff. My employees aren't totally immersed in superhero stuff – they read other things too." Joesph Miller adds, "I think people like seeing that kind of support. Even if we're handing one or two copies of real independent stuff, at least it's around, you can see it. Let me add too, that you've got to have a knowledgeable staff. We have a very small turnover. People come in, get their questions answered, get taken care of by people who they know will know what will fit their needs."

Bill Liebowitz of Golden Apple in Los Angeles gives these reasons for his nomination: "We fit all the criteria, and we're a very visible store. We've spent a lot of time, money and effort to promote ourselves, within the comic community, and outside, to attract new people in. We have a 4000-foot store that's stocked with all the breadth of product that's available from the regular distribution channels, plus a lot of extra stuff. We have a very pleasing environment, and we've done an awful lot of things in order to promote comics outside of the community, and to bring people in. We're probably the most visible store in the country." Very true – I've lost count of the number of TV shows that Bill has plugged comics on. Golden Apple is, in many ways, the "point-man" for our industry.

Deep in the heart of Killeen, Texas, Paper Heroes and John Christian don't have very many opportunities to appear on Entertainment Tonight. But he does give us the final "why were you nominated?" quote, and the one that reflects my personal feelings the most, "We were nominated by one of our customers, which is the thing I'm most proud of. He nominated us because of our Standard Operating Procedures: like fairness to our customers, not hiking up prices on `hot' books, our general business ethics that we try to work by, and the way we treat our customers." Hear, hear, John! Our customers are our blood.

The Advice

I'll let these comments stand on their own. See you at the bottom of the page.

Bill Liebowitz: "The first thing is definition. Find out what kind of a store you want to be, and who your audience is, and what kind of services you want to provide for that audience. You've got to understand what it is that you want to do. There's all sorts of a range of different kinds of stores that are available now, and you can pick and choose what your store's personality is going to be, and what your objectives are. Once you do that, it should just be a natural process to accomplish those objectives. I think that a lot of people just go into business and don't take a lot of time, own their own, to think what their objectives are, and who their customers are."

Lyn Pederson: "One thing I've really learned recently: advertise. The industry is talking about doing a national advertising campaign – talking about spending millions on this thing, and I think that's a good idea. But that's probably some years down the road. I would tell everybody out there to get an advertising budget of his or her own, and to use it. We don't need to go out there and spend a million dollars.

We need to spend a hundred dollars, regularly. Also, don't necessarily use publisher co-op ads. I've seen the print ads, and the television ads, and they don't advertise my store. It's very nice of them to try to help us, but I would prefer the ads to be more store, with a sprinkling of their product. You don't get any personality of your store out there."

John Christian: "Put the customer first. Always remember what it's like to be on the other side of the counter. Think of the long-term, and treat your customers right, for the long-term growth of your business, not just trying to make the quick buck."

Mike Pandalfo: "Look at things from more of a retail standpoint, than a comic book store standpoint, if that makes any sense?"

Steve Snyder: "Go into business. It's important that you have a passion for what you're dealing in, that's what separates the men from the boys right now. But, treat things as a business, and do things to promote comics as a medium. Do a lot of community work – we're a flavor of entertainment that a lot of people don't know about, and the more people we can get to know about it, the more sales we're going to have. We just started a library program with 65 different libraries in our area, where we're giving them 5 comic books, four they get to choose, and one we choose for them. We're spending five dollars each on 65 new places to get comics exposed. Through this I've gotten six speaking engagements between now and January. I did one presentation with a Boy Scout troop, and word spread like wildfire — these people are looking for people to come in and put on quality presentations!"

Joe Field: "Try to see forest for the trees – what is good for your store is what is good for the future of the comics industry, and I say that on a commercial level, as well as an artistic level. You should have a wider view when you take a look at what to do with your store. It is very difficult for stores that are undercapitalized, and probably 75-90% are stores in this business are under-capitalized. It's very difficult for these stores to weigh factors from every segment of the business when you're having a difficult time paying your distributor bills. What you have to realize is that if you want to be able to pay your distributor bill, you really need to pay attention to all the creative forces at work in the comics business."

Bob Gordon: "Try and expand your market, and don't do it just by carrying role-playing games and trading cards. To the general public, that stills ties into a general comics store. I carry Escher prints, Pez candy, Einstein Posters, Three Stooges items, monster magazines, other stuff that ties into the nostalgia and collectible thing. I use Diamond, and they do a great job for me, but I use them just as my comics source – there's a million other channels to get posters, and T-shirts, and merchandise from, less expensive, and more timely – and you can always get reorders on it."

Joesph Miller: "Get to know your area, and your clientele – that's what you're got to go for. But at the same time, you need to expand it by sharing other things, turning people on to something rather than the latest issue of *Spider-Man*."

Mike Moynihan: "Promote things that you're genuinely interested in, and take the time to read a new comic. If you like it, let your customers know."

Wayne Winsett: "Go out of your way to find out what the people want. I can carry what I like in the store, but I'm not necessarily an expert on what everybody else is going to like. You have to give them options, and let them see what they can get. You have to definitely keep up on everything that's in print right now, and educate yourself."

When taken together, here's the sense I made of this: Define your store, present yourself as something special. Carry a wide range of material, appealing to a diverse of an audience as you are able. Advertise yourself. Make sure that you and your staff are educated about the breadth of material available. Make sure you have ethical business practices. Be a part of your community.

All sound advice, from many of the "leaders" of the field. Take it to heart, and maybe next year, *you* will be an Eisner Nominee!

Tilting at Windmills #21

(Originally ran in Comics Retailer #22)

No big topic this month, just a few quick hits:

• Remember me telling a year or two back how Marvel was going to give me $10,000 to spend at my discretion to promote Clive Barker comics in the Bay Area, centered around an appearance by Clive? Well, forget about it.

Lou Bank had initiated this program and passed it on to Mike Martin, my local Marvel Field Rep, who was supposed to facilitate the final arrangements. Mike and I had many a meeting trying to get things pinned down, but were ultimately never able to arrange the appearance, all the while stalling the rest of the plans, since they *hinged* on Clive's participation. Now a lesser man might suggest that Mike deliberately scuttled the plans so that he could do his *own* event – the Marvel Mega-Tour (a notion borne out by the fact that Clive was available to make a Bay Area stop on the MMT, but not available for our previously organized event), but I would never say such a thing. Mike and I came up together: we both worked for a Bay Area retailer who caused us to re-evaluate our own roles – I opened my own store, and Mike went to Marvel. I encouraged Mike to take this position, and gave a good word for him to anyone that would listen. I'm just disheartened that we've lost such a good chance to promote intelligent, adult material to its proper audience. Still, Lou's over at Marvel U.K. these days, and the Clive Barker line has been supplanted by generic super-heroes, so I guess it's not such a loss anymore...

• Of course the problem on every retailer's lips these days is that of unsold merchandise – there's too many books coming through the channels, and no matter how tightly we order, we're still leaking product everywhere. There are several things we need to do that'll help solve our problems, and I discussed one of them in detail a few months ago (limited returnability). Let's turn to two other aspects that will, when paired with limited returnability, will get this market back on track: distributor and publisher accountability.

Distributor accountability mostly hinges on the ability to lower our orders before a book ships – just as we have guaranteed advance reorders, so should we have "advance returns." In short, we need the power to adjust our orders *downward* as well as upward. Our market is extremely volatile, and what looked like a sure bet three months ago looks like a turkey today. Simply put, I think it is our *right* to be able to adjust our orders in any way we need to, before the order ships. And in fact, to the best of my knowledge, this is a guarantee in Marvel & DC's trade terms! You should vocally *demand* it of your distributor!

Now contrary to the beliefs of many other people whom I respect, I do *not* think that advance returns, in and of themselves, are going to be a panacea that will heal this industry's woes. For one, advance returns inherently favors the bigger stores, with the manpower available to examine orders on 2400 items three times before they ship. I'm considered by some to be a "large" store, but it's just me and two part-time employees. It's difficult enough to adequately examine each and every item, the demand for it, and its relationship to every other item on the order form, each and every month. It's an incredible strain on my time and resources, and to have to do it more than once fills me with a sense of dread. But there are other problems as well: are advances limited the same way as reorders (that is, you can change the order up to two weeks before it is *scheduled* to ship)? That doesn't solve the problem of late books. And it doesn't seem fair to the smallest publishers: what happens when we have another "Return of Superman"-size week, and retailers everywhere "red-line" their orders to completely eliminate the "marginal" books?

Still, I think it is an avenue that we need to examine closely, because we need as much ordering flexibility as possible.

Publisher accountability holds the publishers to the promises they keep. Currently, the industry determines a company's "on-time" performance by the *month* they solicit. Nonsense!! Our market *has* shifted to a weekly status – *most* books have a real shelf-life of *one* weekend: if it doesn't sell then, it ain't never gonna! The glut of titles on our racks plays havoc with making accurate orders, because sell-through is not only dependent on the merits of the individual title, but of the other items available that week. We've all seen it: one late book or mis-shipped title can play havoc with the spending money of our consumers. *No one* can get it *all* any more, and so hard choices are made that come out of *our* pocketbooks in the form of unsold merchandise.

I think that *all* publishers should *immediately* institute weekly schedules (not merely, "it ships in November," but, "It ships on 11/14") – this will give retailers the kind of information we need to intelligently place orders. If you blow that schedule by more than *three* weeks, the book is 100% returnable. And if you're doing a crossover or a weekly continuity, then that is reduced to *any* late shipping!

Draconian, you say? Maybe so, but I, for one, am tired of getting the short end of the stick because a publisher can't stick to their established schedule! When a late shipping (often even by as little as *one week*!) title doesn't have it's proper sell-through, I'm directly out money. The publisher isn't. That's not right, and if the platitude-spouting "retailer-friendly" publishers really *were*, then they'd take the blame for their own errors, and they'd be responsible to the marketplace.

• In a similar vein never ever forget that we are the publishers' and distributors' *true* customers. Being nice and kissy-face to their faces, while they contribute to the demise of your business, will do nothing more than Maintain the Status Quo. Publishers and distributors don't have to *like* you – they're here to *service* you. Don't let your fears of some nebulous "retaliation" dissuade you from confronting them on the issues regarding your business. Don't worry about "falling out of favor" – the health of our industry *demands* that we all fight for our rights! But having rights means we must live up to our responsibilities. While I may feel that most distributors are money grubbing bandits who *really* know as much about the comics industry as the dead tree stump in my back yard, that doesn't abrogate our responsibility to pay our bills on time, and turn in our order forms before the deadline, or to bring a matter to their attention before "taking it public," in the hopes that they fix the problem on their own. On the other hand, when there is injustice, we *must* fight it by any method at our disposal.

Just don't cow-tow to their whims like meek little sheep – they exist to service *us*, not the other way around.

• Last Item: the *TaW* mailbag. I received the following fax from Joan Gross of Mint Condition in Port Washington, NY: "Great article in Nov. 1993 *Comic Retailer*. As I sit and read *C.R.* [my favorite sections are] your article, Dialog, and Small Store Strategy .

"What can we do as retailers to change the industry? Have you ever heard of the Uniform Commercial Code?

"We could write all the articles and never get an answer. What can we do?? *HELP*"

The biggest problem that we as retailers face is the lack of any kind of coherent consensus as to what to do. We have enormous power, but it is useless, because we don't wield it with any force. We need to "unionize" – dialog on the issues that are facing us and come to conclusions and solutions.

Get in contact with other retailers and industry professionals – communicate to them your dissatisfaction for certain events and propose solutions. Find out how they feel and take these results public. Write to the *CBG*, the *Journal, Comics Retailer*, the distributors, and the publishers with your findings. Push hard, and keep pushing until you find a sizable enough bloc to herd the changes through.

Go to trade shows and collect cards, start your own mailing list of other retailers you can caucus with. The sad-but-true state of affairs today, right this minute, is that we control our own destinies, *but not until we decide to*!!

I'm a loudmouth. I push and I push and I push, and I can see the snowballs I create. I've heard from many of you who took a piece of advice that I've given and used it to great advantage. I've heard from retailers who thought they were alone in perceiving the shortcomings of this business, and now know they aren't. I say to everyone: only *you* can empower yourself. The revolution is ours, and *you* are the leader. And, trite as though it may be, if you're not part of the solution, you're just another part of the problem, so go the hell away and let those of us who want to do the job get it done with faster.

And that's what *I* think. How about you?

See ya'll in 30.

#22

As a historical note, this column was the first that John Jackson Miller was on as editor. He's now about 4 months from his 100th issue, and we finally stopped playing editor-go-round.

Tilting at Windmills #22
(Originally ran in Comics Retailer #23)

There are times that I get *so* sick of the nonsense in this industry; of the lies that are spoon-fed to us, like formula to a baby; of the half-truths and hype that we have to wade through to get even the barest semblance of the accurate information we *need* to do our jobs.

And I say "shame on you" to the purveyors of these lies, to the hucksters of these half-truths – because they do it not because they necessarily believe their own fictions, but because it covers their asses as the ax starts to fall.

I was incredulous (like I hope you also were) at the glowing reviews that Capital and Diamond both gave Marvel's 1994 publishing plan. "Back to basics," they exclaim. "1994 looks Marvel-ous," they cry.

Bullshit, I say.

Let's get real here for a minute: the concept that stories are back in vogue at the "House of Ideas" assumes that there are people there that can recognize them. Seeing how Marvel has not announced any massive changes in the editorial structure recently, one can only assume that the same editors and creators who have been dumping sub-par, barely literate hack-work on the market throughout 1993 are going to be the same people trying to provide "story-driven" material in 1994, no? Without getting too specific and insulting anyone in particular, why should we believe that the editor on, say, the "Midnight Sons" group (which has been particularly filled with moronic cotton-candy in 1993 – to the point of lowering sales in my store to, in some cases, 10% of what they were selling last January) is suddenly going to be able to pull tired and cliché-ridden tripe out of its current tail-spin? If the editor is capable of doing this, then why are they waiting until now? What were they doing in 1993? Twiddling their thumbs? As a retailer and a consumer, I expect *everyone* in this business to be giving it their 100% (or more!) – I do, after all. And why should I expect anything less out of one of my suppliers? If they *haven't* been giving 100%, then you should fire their fool asses, and if they *have* been, then clearly this "back to basic" stuff is rhetoric.

Empty. Hollow. Meaningless. Rhetoric. Full of sound and fury, signifying fucking *nothing*.

You'll note that this is very similar to Peter David's "problem" with Image over the "holding back" statement: If you *have* been "holding back", then you've been cheating us, and why should I trust a cheat? And if you *haven't*, then you're lying, and there's no reason to trust a liar, either.

Speaking of Image, I simply cannot believe the things that *still* come out of their mouths. Specifically Todd McFarlane. In the "E.G.O." column in *Wizard* #28, Todd insinuates that retailers greedily over-ordered *Spawn* #10 because of the Rob Liefeld poster. Since Todd is against greed, he won't accept returns when the book arrives sans poster. That's right: you have leftover returns, not because it was mis-solicited, but because you were greedy! The problem with this is that the only person *demonstrably* displaying greed is Todd. After all, there *are* retailers who have too many copies *because* the poster wasn't there (I know, I've talked to them!), as they expected to be able to sell it to their Liefeld customers who *don't* buy *Spawn* regularly. And if these people are stuck with unsalable merchandise *because* of Todd's inability to get that poster in on time, then who is being greedy? Certainly not the retailers who ordered based on what sales-patterns in their stores show. No, it's Todd, who mis-solicited a product and is refusing to make good on his mistake.

At least Todd is only ignorant (quote [From the interview in 11/92's *Comics Retailer*]: "I'm selling 200 Copies of *Spawn* to a retailer and they're selling five copies of *Wonder Woman*, and I get the same rack space. And I'm going, 'I put in 45 times more money into your pocket, and I get the same rack space as *Wonder Woman*?' It doesn't make any sense to me." Well, a-duh! I could put *Spawn* in a rusted barrel, glowing with green pus, with a ten-foot sign saying "DANGER! RADIATION HAZARD!" blinking in neon lights, and *Spawn* would still sell [O.K., that's an exaggeration, but you know what I mean]. *Wonder Woman*, on the other hand, needs a great deal of help and push for it to perform well. In fact, I would argue that *Wonder Woman requires* more rack space than *Spawn* in order to help it perform), and not willfully idiotic, like, say DC.

DC has fallen into the trap that started crippling Marvel half a decade ago: "If they like it once, they'll *love* it a dozen more times!" You like Superman? Well, here's two more monthly books (*Steel* and *Superboy*)! You like Batman? Here's another couple of books *(Robin* and *Catwoman*, plus the seemingly endless "specials" or mini-series of the month)! You enjoy crossovers? Here's a twenty-eight (!) part one, each one with *another* new character (each of whom will be spinning off in one fashion, or another!). You enjoyed us killing Superman? Cool, we'll maim Batman and make Green Lantern go insane! Yeah, that'll draw in a big crowd. I know I'm sick of it, and look! There go the titles off my customers' subscription forms. Scratch, scratch, and scratch!

And as near as I can tell, these decisions were made by looking purely at the *sell-in* figures. Of course, *sell-through* would've told another story (*Bloodlines* was a dog; Multiple Bat-titles are killing the franchise; and *Knightquest* is the most meager shadow of the Superman success story. How much less *GL*?).

<sigh>

Then there's the "look how 'retailer-friendly' we are" ploy. Take Valiant, for example. They're crowing that they've got an in-house 30-days-late-it's-returnable policy. Whoop-de-fuckin'-do. Never mind the fact that Capital has *already* closed the window to 30 days, and that Diamond long ago announced plans to do the same. Sheesh! What do they take us for? If they're *so* damn concerned with late-shipping books, then why isn't *Deathmate* returnable? I don't *care* that it was the "Image half" that was late...it was a Valiant/Image co-project. And when you partner with someone, *you* are responsible for their mistakes if they won't make restitution. But, no. I see no "friendship" there.

Don't stand for it. Whether it's lies, ignorance, or idiocy, don't put up with it. Raise your voice, make a stink! Because by silence you make it easier for them to lie to us in the future.

#23

This one is odd...it didn't actually run as a *TaW*.

Because I used a letter from Neal Adams as the starting point of this column, J.J. decided that he should run this piece in the letter column of *CR*, rather than as a *Tilting*.

Foo!

Still, in *my* records, this is #23.

Anyway, Neal Adams did a whole-fucking-lot for the comics industry. He was also one of the loudest and most vocal proponents of creators' rights at a time where it was virtually guaranteed you'd get blacklisted for taking that stance.

But he was the *worst* fucking comics publisher you can even *begin* to imagine.

Continuity stopped publishing comic books shortly thereafter.

Tilting at Windmills #23
(Originally ran in Comics Retailer #24's letter column)

Sometimes it's a real struggle to write a monthly column (I don't see how people like Peter David manage to do it on a *weekly* basis): I can struggle for weeks on end to find just the *right* topic at times. Not so this month.

This month I'm a full two weeks ahead of deadline.

Why, you ask? Simple: *Comic Retailer*'s letter column.

This afternoon I received a copy of January's *CR*, and found innumerable grist for my mill. Let's start simple: Neal Adams.

O.K., everyone go to your pile of back issues and dig out January's issue. Flip to page 16, and read the letter from Neal Adams. I'll wait till you're finished...

...all done? Good. Let's begin.

This letter is *so* filled with nonsense, distortions, and just plain ignorance of the way the market functions, that's it's nearly impossible to know where to begin. I'll be linear, start at the top, and move down.

To begin with, the cynic in me inherently distrusts any letter that begins with, in effect, "look how swell we are" – usually this is a clear sign of smoke screens to mask an inferior message. But, since "quality" is an issue that Adams is predominately concerned with (at least insofar of *his* perception of it goes), let's address this head on:

Continuity's books fucking suck.

I'm willing to defend this assertion: Continuity's comics feature wooden writing with inanely simplistic or wholly nonexistent plots. The artwork is bad swiping of Adams' own style. This is not to say that I don't like Adams' art – I quite do. But I (and the majority of my customers) find the slavish aping utterly unappealing. And the editing is atrocious, rife with misspelled words and ungrammatical sentence structure. My opinion is clearly backed up by my customers' buying habits: we now are completely unable to sell *any* Continuity comics at all (customer dissatisfaction is equally clear by looking at the sales charts: Continuity's best-selling title, *Armor*, took a 56% drop from issue #1 to #9 on Diamond's charts, and an astounding 78% drop from #1 to #8 on Capital's charts!).

But let's put that aside for the moment and talk about shipping schedules. Yes, it has been S.O.P. at Capital and Diamond, at least, to require resolicitation or full returnability if an item ships later than 90 days after it was scheduled (though, as we all should know, Capital has closed this to 30 days while Diamond is in the process of instituting 60 days). *However*, the mere *ability* to deliver material late does not imply it is a *right* to do so. Continuity has *long* had the absolute worst performance records in its decade or so (or has it been nearly two? Either way, a *long* time) in the business. "With *Deathwatch 2000* we rededicated our company to a monthly schedule," Neal says, recognizing, one presumes, that it was systematic late shipping that has made Continuity such a joke over the years. And yet Continuity *seems* to think that "April shipping" means "July".

Let me put it this way: most buildings have emergency exits, right? When you want to leave a building in a normal course of affairs, what do you do? Go for the front door? Or make for the emergency exit? Late shipping policies are like emergency exits. If you *have* to, you can use it, but normally it should be avoided, and kept clear for, well, emergencies.

Unfortunately, Continuity (which, let me reiterate, has had a *history* of flagrantly violating the most basic of vendor/merchant contracts: delivering a book when scheduled) once again opted to unfailingly use the emergency exit *right out of the (second) gate*! Want proof? Here's a chart.

Title	Month Solicited to ship	Date Delivered	
Armor #1 (DW 1)	April 1993	5/5/93	(1)
Hybrids #1 (DW 2)	"	5/5/93	(1)
Megalith #1 (DW 3)	"	5/5/93	(1)
Ms. Mystic #1 (DW 4)	"	5/19/93	(3)
Earth 4 #1 (DW 5)	"	6/2/93	(5)
Cyberrad #1 (DW 6)	"	5/19/93	(3)
Armor #2 (DW 7)	May 1993	8/11/93	(11)
Hybrids #2 (DW 8)	"	9/8/93	(15)
Megalith #2 (DW 9)	"	8/4/93	(10)
Ms. Mystic #2 (DW 10)	"	8/11/93	(11)
Earth 4 #2 (DW 11)	"	9/8/93	(15)
Cyberrad #2 (DW 12)	"	9/8/93	(15)
Valeria #1 (incentive)	"	9/1/93	(14)
Armor #3 (DW 15)	June 1993	9/22/93	(12)
Megalith #3 (DW 16)	"	9/22/93	(12)
Ms. Mystic #3 (DW 17)	"	9/22/93	(12)
Hybrids #3 (DW 18)	"	10/5/93	(14)
Earth 4 #3 (DW 19)	"	10/5/93	(14)
Cyberrad #3 (DW 20)	"	—	(24+)
Valeria #2 (incentive)	"	—	(24+)
Armor #4	July 1993	10/13/93	(11)
Hybrids v. 2 #1	"	—	(20+)
Hybrids: The origin #2 (a)	"	12/14/93	(20)
Megalith #4	"	12/1/93	(18)
Earth 4 v.3 #1	"	12/14/93	(20)
Ms. Mystic v. 3 #1	"	9/29/93	(9)
Cyberrad v.2 #2 (b)	"	12/14/93	(20)
Valeria #3	"	—	(20+)
Bucky O'Hare #1 (c)	"	—	(20+)
Crazyman #1	"	8/25/93	(4)
Samuree #1	"	9/1/93	(5)
Armor #5	August 1993	12/1/93	(14)
Hybrids v. 2 #2	"	—	(16+)
Hybrids: The origin #3	"	—	(16+)
Megalith #5	"	12/1/93	(14)
Earth 4 v.3 #2	"	—	(16+)
Ms. Mystic v. 3 #2	"	12/1/93	(14)
Cyberrad v.2 #3 (c)	"	—	(16+)
Valeria #4	"	—	(16+)
Bucky O'Hare #2 (d)	"	—	(16+)
Crazyman #2	"	—	(16+)
Samuree #2	"	10/13/93	(7)
Armor #6	September 1993	12/8/93	(10)
Hybrids v. 2 #3	"	—	(11+)
Hybrids: The origin #3	"	—	(11+)
Megalith #6	"	—	(11+)
Earth 4 v.3 #3	"	—	(11+)
Ms. Mystic v. 3 #3	"	—	(11+)
Cyberrad v.2 #4	"	—	(11+)
Valeria #5	"	12/8/93	(10)
Bucky O'Hare #3	"	—	(11+)
Crazyman #3	"	—	(11+)
Samuree #3	"	—	(11+)

NOTES: There are also 33 titles solicited for October, November, and December that I haven't bothered listing because *none* of them have come in yet!

The numbers in parentheses after the date arrived is the **minimum** amount of weeks the book is late – counting an "April" book as due on the last week of April. Obviously if you hold a more stringent definition, these numbers greatly worsen...

(DW #...) = The chapter number of the
Deathwatch 3000 crossover
a) = resolicited from a **previous** 3/92 due date
b) = resolicited from a **previous** 12/91 due date
c) = resolicited from a **previous** 4/92 due date
d) = resolicited from a **previous** 7/92 due date

Obviously this chart makes it clear that Continuity hasn't *ever* shipped *one single* book during the month it was solicited. Even Image can't make this claim. Not only that, but they can't even put out a crossover in correct order, nor even *complete* it! They shipped *Megalith* #4 & 5 simultaneously; and they completely skipped *Valeria* #'s 2 to 4 (also, *Hybrids: the Origin* is described as a three-issue series, when they later solicited for #4 to 6). I could go on and on.

What a sad and sorry record.

Oh, but Neal Adams and Continuity are nice guys, yes they are! After all, they gave us "premium" comics ("that guarded against any difficulties that might show up"...which is exactly the *opposite* of the *point* of incentive comics: they're not there to "appease" us after we've been screwed, they're to *reward* us for supporting your line!) – Neal even provides a chart of his own to show *how* nice he is...except he forgets to remind us that we needed to invest $12.50 retail for the *Megalith/Hybrids* #0s and $75 retail to receive each *Valeria* premium, and that not all of them made it to retailers: I assume a *Valeria Fur* is supposed to be *Valeria* #2, based on the description of that item, and I've never even *heard* of a *Hybrids #0 Red* (nor is it mentioned in any of Diamond's catalogs in the last 9 months), so instead of $40 low/$105 high it suddenly becomes $20 low/$50 high. A vast difference when you're talking about an average of a $43.75 investment to see that "return."

Of course, the ironic part here is that the "value" of the "premiums" is *due to* speculators, which Adams spends many a paragraph decrying. Stores that sold these books ("guarding" us, I suppose) are selling to speculators, *not* readers. Those of us that gave them away (the *only* right thing to do – we have them *because* the customers wanted the comics) did *not* a priori "assure a solid readership" – the quality of these books were so low that none of *my* customers wanted any more. After the first wave of books, I got cancellation notice after cancellation notice from my subscriber customers for the entire line.

But, before the books actually arrived, there *was* interest. In fact, there was a lot of *speculator* interest: I know of *many* stores that were requiring purchase of all 6 April books to get the premiums. Many (though, admittedly not all) of the purchasers of these sets were looking to make some money of the "value" of the "premiums" *even in "reader-driven" stores.*

O.K., Neal, *let's* talk comics:

1) There are *far* more than 300,000 comic-book readers who shop in U.S. comic shops. There are well over 6000 retail locations in the US. Simple division would mean that the "average" comic shop has a customer base of a measly 50 people! 50 people? It would be nearly impossible to sustain a store on that small of a base

(not that *some* stores aren't that small, but they're the exception rather than the rule) – figure there are *at least* one million people buying comics regularly from the direct market. To suggest less would be absolutely insane!

2 and 3) Market size has *nothing* to do with the basic responsibilities to the market. These include such things as on-schedule shipping, shipping in proper order, accurate solicitations, and not deceiving your customers.

You have the audacity to suggest that retailers who are being hurt by *Continuity's* incompetence are instead for some reason "shifting the blame" to *other* companies? Man, are you way off base! Look at your shipping record, look at your plummeting sales – a lot of retailers got *hurt* by your inability to do your job properly. Yes, we *also* got hurt by other companies, but the issue before us, right here, right now is *your* culpability and flagrant irresponsibility toward the market.

Of course retailers' problems are with Continuity, 2% market share, or smaller. *Any* company that spits on retailers and our customer base needs to be exposed. A defense that "we're smaller than Image or Marvel – go pick on them" just doesn't wash. If you're not with us, you're against us. Are you so wildly out of touch with the way that retailers do business to not understand that by not delivering an April book in April you do *irreparable* harm to the retailer's budget? Many of us have to budget as closely as possible : the decision to carry a Continuity title often means that we'd have to *not* carry something else that would potentially make us money. When that book is not delivered in time it a) *costs* us money (in Loss of Opportunity, among other things), and b) kills the sell-through as the customers (who have budgets too, y'know) spend their money on other things.

You're right, sir, this industry's problems *have* caused a glut and killed many retailers. And you are clearly and without argument guilty of perpetuating these problems: both on the front end of tying up our cash flow, but on the back end as well – by *actively* seeking to attract the speculator dollar: seven out of ten 1993 solicitations feature "incentive" comics, and *all* ten feature "enhanced" covers on the majority of the line!!

You ask if all retailers have become speculators. Beyond the fact that the very nature of ordering in the direct market is a *form* of speculation, *if* retailers turn towards speculation, it's *because* companies like Continuity foster a climate for it to thrive in. Especially when you can't even count on publishers to actually deliver the comics when they *promise.*

No one wants to make you a "scapegoat" (no matter how much rhetoric you try to heap on) – simply to live up to your *responsibility* to the marketplace and to retailers. Believe me, if you were the paradigm of virtue you seem to believe you are, then no one would be making noises. We retailers may be pretty screwed up in a lot of ways, but we don't bitch when we don't need to – none of us have the time to waste.

Finally, you may want to think that the retailer's voice is raised in "animosity and anger", but nothing could be further from the truth. This is merely business. You can't screw the retailer any more, without screwing the *whole* industry even harder. This isn't the comics market of 1985 any more. Hell, this isn't even the market of 1990 any more! Things have changed, and you can't afford to screw up any more. All publishers. Every one of them. You say "cooperation counts". Fair enough. Shape up, live up to *your* side of the agreement and maybe you'll get some good will.

Lord knows you aren't going to get it by screwing the marketplace, then trying to cover it up with empty and hollow rhetoric. I say to publishers large and small, tiny or tall: either shape up or get out. We don't need any more bad publishers who undermine the retailer's ability to survive.

Anyway, enough of that.

I have two more letter column comments yet to go (but I promise I'll make these shorter...really)

To Jerome Piroue: you'll note that in the January issue it went back to "Brain," even though Don & Maggie fixed it in December. <sigh> If it says Brain this month, I'll scream! Anyway, the problem that I see with lower, tighter ordering, with higher publisher overprints is that the reorder mechanism just doesn't work (I placed 18 reorders last week...all on mainstream stuff, too, and had a 0% fill-rate), and that publishers often *can't* get space at the printers in a week. It'll take three or four days to figure out that a book is gone, nationwide, so you figure it'll be at least two weeks before a book can be in our hands (and that's only if we're talking about Marvel or DC, who're buying such massive run-time, they can shuffle things around better. Three to four weeks is far more likely, and, by that point, most material (barring your occasional Death of Superman) is very difficult to sell.

I'll tell you why I want small returns: while I do choke hard occasionally on any given title, I'm generally more affected by the "nickel and dimes" – the three copies of *Captain America* left after cycles, the copy of *Silver sable*. It's deadwood at that point, and any individual book isn't much, but together it's dragging us down. Also, one would think that reorders would be that much more available under a system of returns – what didn't sell for you might be just what you need.

To Craig Stormon: No doubt you could find things I'm doing wrong. I can positively identify at least a dozen of them or so, myself.

I never claimed I was perfect. These are just my observations about the industry. But (permit me to be immodest) I *was* kinda figuring that being nominated for an Eisner, winning "best comic shop in San Francisco" in one of the most crowded markets in the US, and being allowed to write this very column would give me a certain cachet.

Well, perhaps not. Heh.

I'm very sorry for you that your artist left. But it's not the *retailer's* problem.

I'll tell you, what irritates me is publishers' knee-jerk reaction that retailers lobbying for returns are people looking to shift the blame to. It was bullshit when McFarlane said it in *Wizard*, it was bullshit when Neal Adams said it two letters up from you, and it's still bullshit now.

Retailers are asking for returns because the *mechanism* of the direct market doesn't work anymore: cycle sheets are meaningless these days, everything is a shot in the dark. I've been in retailing for nearly ten years in some form or another, and I'm telling you the market has *changed*. Every day I hear a new horror story about stores, *good* stores, mind you, not fly-by-night cardvestites, on the verge of going under. We're not over-ordering *intentionally*, we're doing it because *most* of the numbers are purely *guesses*. Did you know that some 40% of the top 200 comics are at an issue number lower than #6? Given that it takes *at least* six months to find a books true level of sales, that's a *tremendous* amount to guess right!

Every retailer is feeling the pinch right now – this isn't scam artists trying to get over. This industry is going to need a fundamental change in the way we do business, or we're going to lose a lot of good, smart retailers. My opinion is that partial returns, with appropriate charges to offset damage to publisher and distributor is the best of our several options.

But, really, it's not shifting blame, and if you can't see or understand the current state of the market, then why are you in publishing?

Goodnight, my darlings, I'll see you in 30.

...and THIS is what actually ran as Tilting #23.

Previews (the distributor catalog) still sucks, by the way!

Tilting at Windmills #23.5
(Originally Ran in Comics Retailer #24)

This one is going to be much shorter than usual. I'm writing this post-Christmas, and we managed to turn what was going to be our worst December into our best by clearing our dead backstock at up to 90% off. The way I see it, it's far better to make a couple of cents on a book (or even take a small loss), than to have the money tied up in unsalable merchandise and to have to store and pay tax on that sludge.

I've been utterly swamped, and having to rewrite my column didn't help much – the first draft was about Continuity, but, of course, that actually ended up in the letters column, rather than in this space. I don't care much, but it means double work for me the one month I had half the time. But at least the Comic Book Legal Defense Fund will get a double payment this month, right?

I'd like to open *this* month's bitch-fest with some comments about distributor catalogs. I don't know about you, but I'm getting *damn* tired of how many pages in each month's catalog *don't* contain a solicitation. Card inserts, "exclusive" comics, price guide features, etc. These things all have some value in the consumer edition of the catalog, but in the retailer's version they do nothing except make my job that much more difficult and time-consuming.

I'll let you in on a little trick, if you'd like. You would? Oh good. The first thing I do each month when I receive the catalog is to start tearing out pages. Off comes the cover, and the first two dozen pages of "editorial" material; out go the inserts, and the comics, and the price guides; the back cover also goes bye-bye, along with the seemingly endless pages of Marvel hype that are repeated within the body of the solicitations (and their *own* solicitation magazine), right at the back; finally, I remove any page that has an ad on both sides of the page, and the sections of the catalog for which I have no use (like the sports card solicitations). This reduces the bulk of the catalog by at *least* half (this month I was left with 176 pages from 350+), and makes it *far* easier to look up individual title descriptions, and to fill in the order form.

What I'd like to see is two distinctly different versions of the catalog produced: the consumer version, with all the inserts and editorial features intact; and a retailer version with *nothing* except solicitations. If a retailer *wants* all the supplementary material, they can purchase the consumer version, and if not, then they're not subjected to it.

This goes just as strongly for advertisements: I simply don't need to see the vast bulk of them. I'm not a fool. One issue of, say, *Brigade*, is virtually indistinguishable from another. When I place my order for that issue of *Brigade* the full-color ad doesn't sway me one tiny inch on what to order: I go purely by my cycle sheets and the caption in the solicitation. When you're an established company offering a regular book, a distributor-catalog ad is a waste of your time and resources, just as it's a waste of mine. Now I well understand that they're there primarily for the benefit of the consumer, but they get in the damn way when I'm racing to fill out my order form. When I get to that 16-page full-color Image section, I yank it right out, without even looking. There's nothing there that's going to help me order the book correctly that isn't just as well told in an inch of text.

Of course, if you're truly new, or you've got a retailer-based promotion that you want to explain graphically, or you're doing something important to the status quo of your title, advertising may be important; otherwise, *we* know our jobs, and, in my oh so humble opinion, you're wasting your money by simply telling us the same thing month after month. That's what the solicitation information is for.

We've gotten "used to" flashy catalogs, but all the flash does is distract our attention from what *really* matters: the solicitations.

It already takes far too long to do an order form as it is: even a paltry 15 seconds each on the 2000+ items available to us each month means we're spending over eight hours on *one* full pass through! We need that information undiluted by hype and ads. Just the facts, ma'am, to get the closest to the number we're actually going to sell. And the closer we get to that, the better this whole industry will be.

That's it for this month – I'll be back in 30 with a full-sized column. Take it slow.

Tilting at Windmills #24
(Originally ran in Comics Retailer #25)

One of the things that frustrates me the most about this industry is seemingly how little the publishers understand their audience, and how seldom they put themselves in the consumer's position.

Let's take a couple of examples: As we all know, Malibu comics debuted the Ultraverse (as you read this) eleven months ago – in this span of time they've solicited for 122 comics with a total cover price of $239.50. Also, ten of these have come bagged, 27 involved a coupon promotion, 14 have cross-title crossovers, and 25 have had content geared to a line-wide promotion. Eliminating issues that appear on both lists, we're only left with a massive 58 comics solicited solely on the individual contents – that's barely 48% of their output!

Now, on one hand, you have to hand it to Malibu for going full-tilt, with strong promotions and heavy advertising – even outreach to the "civilian" market via advertising on cable. These are valid strategies, and mark Malibu as a "professional" publisher: strong unified strategies working towards a single goal. This should be lauded.

But has it worked? Some stores have reported major successes with the Ultraverse, but other stores, like mine, are watching it stall or drop. I feel that any title that's selling less than 5 copies is a dog. Why? Because of the amount of money that each foot of floorspace costs us, and the amount that processing time (cycle sheets, ordering-in, unpacking, racking, and handling, etc.) costs. Taking my costs into account, I *break even* on floor-space at roughly $12 per rack space per month. Figuring that the "average" comic costs well over $2, that gives me a thumbnail (but, of course, it's not necessarily that of any individual book) of five copies. Six of the 13 regular monthly UV books sell less than five copies each for me.

Now, I'll freely admit, that I'm hardly "gung-ho" about yet another super-hero "universe," and I've never "pushed" the Ultraverse in general (though I have for the individual books that I think are exemplary), but I have given them good display, and when asked for a mainstream action recommendation, have steered customers toward them. But, even given my "passive" involvement, one would think (one would hope!) that the heavy promotion would be bringing people in.

So, I think the problem lies not in how much (or the quality of) the promotion, but rather the *quantity* of material. I have many customers who are super-hero fans. They basically like cross-line continuity and interaction, but few can *afford* 13 monthly titles. I have many customers who *adore* Barry Windsor-Smith. But few of them were willing to shell out $27.50 for the 33 pages of serial that launches his monthly title. The feeling I get from watching my customers in action is that they might be interested in some of the individual titles, but they're *afraid* they're going to get sucked in to the rest of the universe, and they can't afford that, so it's easier for them to skip it all than to try one or two books.

Is that crazy behavior? Well, yeah, possibly, but I know most of my customers, and the majority of them are having a hard enough time paying the bills, and they can't afford to buy into another universe.

And that's what Malibu has been selling: the universe. All of the ads, all of the promo has been selling the Ultraverse, not the individual titles. What the consumer *feels* he's being asked to buy into, right or wrong, is the line-identity, not the individual components. And in the comics market of three years ago, that would've worked just fine – but in this glut, with consumer confidence at an all time low, it's counter-productive.

One more quick Malibu example before I move on would be the Bravura "Are you Fan Enough?" promotion. It should be called "Are you Confused Enough?" – a promotion that can't be explained in two sentences isn't any good. It's another example of throwing more at the consumer than either a) they want to handle and/or b) they are capable of handling.

Moving down the list I look at Marvel's *Spider-Man* Animation Promotion in the April Books. So, great, Spider-Man is a big property for Marvel, and a new cartoon is going to start, and it's a wonderful cross-promotional opportunity to create new consumers, etc. So what does Marvel do? They double the price on the entire line (including the reprint books!) for a month to include a 16-page advertisement and a cel. Now this is all well and fine – a reasonable promotion that might even be cool, if the cels are done right. But it's more likely to alienate core-readers than it is to bring in new readers who'll stay for life.

Look at the scheduled shipping for the first week of April: You have an *Amazing Spider-Man* "ashcan" (advertisement) for 75 cents; two editions of *Spider-Man* #46 for $2.95 & $1.95; two editions of *Spider-Man Classics* #15 for $2.95 & $1.25; 2 editions of *Web of Spider-Man* #113 for $2.95 and $1.50; the *Web of Spider-Man annual* #10 for $2.95; and *Spider-Man 2099* #20 for $1.50. One of each would cost $18.75. Without the variants it's still $14.05 (and before I get a hew and cry from those of you checking my math, I'm using the "enhanced" version as the "keeper" because by looking at the charts, the majority of retailers either don't offer the "unenhanced" version, or carry such an incredibly small number of them that most consumers *have* to choose the higher-priced version). Now maybe it's just me, but I think that's far too much money to ask for from a consumer. Let's face it, *most* people who buy Spider-Man are "Spider-Man Zombies" – they buy *everything* Spider-Man related that they can. But they're not zombies because they *only* like Spider-Man; oh no, it's because they can no longer afford to keep up on Spider-Man *and* the X-Men *and* the Avengers, etc. And many of these people are buying from *nostalgia*: Spider-Man (or whatever) is their last mainstream *habit*...otherwise they only buy the books they enjoy *consistently*. Junkies are a large part of all entertainment industries – people who need their *fix* of product X. But the trick is to balance the needs of the stockholders against the *ability* of the junkie (and I'm sure there are those of you who're going to *cringe* at the metaphor, but, damnit! we're selling *habitual* entertainment...) to sustain that need. The last thing you want to do is give them a reason to question their purchases – *that* is the point where they start to go from junkie to "clean & sober".

Once you start asking them to give you $14 in *one* week you're opening a can of worms. That's the point where it's easier to quit than continue.

In a different way, DC is giving their junkies an "out." Of course we're all aware that Batman has performed less consistently than they have since Bruce Wayne no longer wears the mantle, but I'll focus on *Green Lantern* for today. Unlike the other "big shake-ups" that DC has brought, the change in *Green Lantern* has not grown naturally out of the character, but was clearly imposed from above. The end result has been to horribly alienate many long-term Green Lantern fans. Now, maybe these were a small number, and DC judged it a reasonable risk to court a larger audience with drastic changes, but I believe it is always a dangerous tack to blow off your base in search of an audience that isn't *necessarily* there. The end result is to create *open* animosity from the long-time reader, and not just towards *Green Lantern*, but also to *all* DC universe books. One of my best customers (spending well over $80 a week) informed me that he would no longer automatically buy every DC comic any more...he was going to be a lot more selective because of the events in *Green Lantern*. When you lose the hardest of the hard-core there's something terrible wrong.

In all three of these cases we can see publishers misunderstanding the consumers' interest in or *ability* to follow an expansion or radical change. Now, of course, the publishers will point to sell-in figures and go, "Look, the numbers are up (or at least not down as far as the free-fall of today's market), so we must be doing the right thing," but I say again, sell-in is *meaningless* – all it reflects is *hope and conjecture* on the part of the retailers. And while that stands for *something*, it's hardly the proper benchmark on which to base a line-expansion.

Understand your market. Understand your customers. Understand how retailer orders skew the bigger, long-term picture.

Before it's too late.

• • • • •

I have one last order of business to cover before I lay this to rest this month, and it's a topic that by now you're probably thoroughly sick of hearing about: distributors' penalty fees to publishers.

As you all know, Capital City Distributors announced that, effective immediately, publishers who cancel titles will have to pay $500, or $750 if they have to resolicit. Now, you tell me: is this *right*?

Of course it's not!

Wiser and more eloquent mouths than mine have gone into detail about how this system is inherently unfair to small publishers because their costs and margins are substantially worse than those of a large publisher (the old "economy of scale"). I agree wholeheartedly with these positions.

But (you knew that was coming, right?) I also don't disagree with the *idea* behind this policy. Let's call a spade a spade: there are *far* too many marginal companies producing drek in a market that can't afford it. Further, there are *far* too many creators who are not *yet* of *professional* quality to go the self-publisher route.

It was not very long ago when I felt constrained to carry at least one copy of every comic solicited. I figured it was the least that I could do to support the future of the marketplace, but giving support to anyone who even *tried*.

Well, those days are over. There's far too much product on the market, and there's far too much consumer confusion to play the "support the amateur" game.

Quite frankly, it's *way* too easy to publish your own comic book. $5000 (or less) and you're a publisher. It cost me 4 times that to open my store five years ago (and today, I *know* I couldn't've done it for at least 50% more...)! $5000 is not an insignificant amount of money, but it is still a paltry amount to get national distribution with! So while I *do* actively encourage new and young creators to attack the industry with all the vigor they can muster, and while I *do* **wholeheartedly** embrace the idea that creators should have full control of their creation, I still think it's *far* too easy for any hack with a pen, an idea (it doesn't have to be a *good* one!), and an indulgent parent to put out a comic.

On the other hand, we certainly don't want a system that would destroy a full-blown creative vision like *Bone*, or cripple a soon-to-be vision like *Cerebus* was when it started.

Of course it *does* cost money to process and handle orders on a book that doesn't ship (or ships late). On cycling, ordering, and handling subscriptions for my Saver customers it costs me roughly a minimum of 50 cents to simply carry a book. When that book doesn't ship or has to handled again (resolicited), my costs, of course, jump. Naturally, that 50 cents base is scaled to the volume I'm handling, so that your average issue of *X-Men* costs more for me to process than an issue of *Obscure Comics* #1. And I imagine it's the same for the distributors.

So while I think it *is* fair for a publisher to pay a fee for screwing with the market and the retailers, I hardly think a flat fee is equitable.

What *would* be fair is a per-book fee. Say, five cents a book. What that would mean is that the little guy who is trying to make a serious go of it and only musters orders for 500 copies is only dunned for $25, while the big guy who constantly abuses the system, and gets orders for 750,000 copies is liable for $37,500. "Let the punishment fit the crime."

And to add one last thing: if it *does* indeed cost Capital a minimum of $500 to handle *orders* for a book, then I want to close my shop, and handle order processing for them – I could be making $50k+ a year for doing grunt work ($500 per item with 1200 items a month, assuming 50 employees doing *nothing* but order processing for 22 warehouses gives you $72,000 a year!)!

I urge everyone reading this column to make your dissatisfaction with Capital's policy known.

•   •   •   •   •

One final thing before I go: I just heard that Jack Kirby died. At the point you read this the news is old. I have no doubt that you've read many passionate and eloquent eulogies for one of the few men about whom *every* cliché is true (he *was* an inspiration for thousands, he *was* one of the most prolific & influential artists of all time, etc.) – and I can't add to that. What I can do is ask you all to bow your heads right now in a moment of silence for a man we all owe our livelihoods to. I truly believe if it wasn't for the passion and the life that The King brought to comics there would never have been a need for comic book shops.

A moment of silence, please...

Thank you.

Tilting at Windmills #25
(Originally ran in Comics Retailer #26)

Labeling: censorship? Or providing adequate information? Now there's a fat can of worms.

I was looking through the 1994 *Comics Retailer*'s "list of themes" for each issue this year (yup, it's planned out that far in advance), thinking to myself, "Self, you're just not a team-player." I mean, this space is for Brian's Rant-of-the-Month-Club, what the hell could I say about "store fixtures" or "holiday buying," right? I'd rather expose whatever issue is stuck in my craw this month, figuring if we're all going to get screwed anyway, at least we may as well *know* we're getting screwed. Sometimes this is hard, but mostly it's handed to me on a silver platter by a publisher, distributor, or creator. Anyway, I basically figured I'd never need the "official topics" list – it's just not my bag.

Well, color me surprised when I realized that I wanted to wade in on labeling comics, the same month as this was to be the "official" topic. So, while you shouldn't expect to see me playing in the same sandbox as everyone else again, I'm here now.

Now, I'm in San Francisco, arguably one of the most liberal cities in our country. Further, Comix Experience is located in one of the most "alternative" of neighborhoods in The City: the Haight-Ashbury (you remember the 60s, right?). We've never had problem one with "community reaction" to what we sell, or even the slightest *hint* of a problem. Hell, most of our customers are adults – less than 5% are under 18; and those that are either are regular customers (so I know how far their parents will let them go) or are accompanied by their parents during their visit. So it's pretty much a non-issue for us, right?

Additionally, I make a massive effort to read *every* comic that comes into the store, so it's unlikely in the extreme that I'll ever have someone come back to me in the future claiming I sold them something *I* was unaware of.

However, it is clear to me that few other retailers are in such a liberal geographical location; blessed with an older, more sophisticated customer base like us; or are taking the time and effort to read their wares at all (to say nothing of carefully). While the last could be argued to be the retailer's responsibility (though that ignores the practicality - the *reason* I'm able to stay so on top of it is because *I don't have a life*), the first two are so far out of the retailer's control, that it's clear that there must be some measure of responsibility from the publishers.

By the same token, I subscribe to the notion that the *creator must have absolute control of their own work*, up to, and including, the manner in which it is marketed. If a creator decides that they do not want to label themselves, then we have to abide by that desire. Frank Miller said, in the letters column of *Sin City: A Dame to Kill For #4*,

"I oppose cover advisories because I don't want us to declare ourselves accountable to parents groups or censors. It's a slippery slope. Once the use of labels became widespread enough, there would be calls for a rating system, like Hollywood's MPAA, that would be a nightmare, and would only hurt the quality of comics.

"It would also set a disastrous precedent for us to abide by rules set up for the electronic media. We're in the publishing industry, which has been much more courageous in defending itself against censors.

"Besides, I have received *not one complaint* about *Sin City* falling into the wrong hands. Cover design that accurately represents the contents is much more effective than a little apology in the corner."

I'm behind this sentiment 100%. You don't walk into WaldenBooks and see "Suggested for Mature Readers" plastered all over the cover of the latest Stephen King novel. But by the same token, it is generally understood that if you buy a *Hardy Boys* book, you're not going to be reading about a disembowelment, described in every exquisite detail. The projected audience for the work determines the suitability of violent and sexual situations. This is, of course, eminently sensible.

However, hand-in-hand with creator freedom comes creator *responsibility*. You can *not* have freedom, without assuming the responsibility that goes along with it: responsibility to your marketplace, to the concerns of parents, to your fellow creators. Not holding to your end of the bargain is a craven and selfish thing. Frank is right: *Sin City* is clearly not for kids. You can see that from format, from content, from price point. Given this, I think it's wholly appropriate for *Sin City* to not be cover-tagged. You will note, though, that the book is *solicited* as for "Mature Readers". This is *very* important. The retailer is given the appropriate information as how to handle this title, *before* it arrives in the store.

On the other hand, you have the situation with Image's *Bloodstrike* (which has gotten plenty of press, so I won't say much more) or with Defiant's *War Dancer*

#1. Have you seen this one? The last few pages of this comic book feature a small boy and his dog exploding in extremely graphic detail. This in a title that is described in the solicitation materials as laying "the foundation for the Defiant Universe," a line of comic books clearly aimed at the pre-teen superhero fan. No mention was made in the solicitation materials of exploding children, but we get a lot of frothy hype about *War Dancer* being "Defiant's centerpiece title, meaning that it will serve as the linchpin for their first mega-crossover (Schism) scheduled for July/August 1994! Consider yourself warned!" Sure. Just not about the *right* things.

The worst part about these kinds of abuses of the system is that the publisher will never be held accountable. If Mrs. I.M. Acensor gets upset about her little Johnny buying a copy of *Bloodstrike* or *War Dancer*, who d'you think she's gonna sic the cops on? Rob Liefeld? Jim Shooter?

Or *You*?

So, what do I think should be done? Thanks for asking. If a publisher missolicits a book based on violent or sexual content, they should pay for any and all expenses involved in legal actions against retailers. And, right now, this second, they should donate 100% of the gross amount collected from these comics to the Comic Book Legal Defense Fund. Anything less would be greedy and cowardly.

Other than that, publishers should make sure the content of a specific work is *explicitly* solicited. We don't *need* cover advisories, but we *must* have the proper information to make the choice in the first place. Anything less would be cowardly and does an incredible disservice to we who put our very livelihoods on the line.

'nuff said?

•　　•　　•　　•　　•

On a completely different note, I just want to state for the record how much I *HATE* that Marvel has pulled out of the distributors' catalogs.

It already takes far too long to place my monthly orders. I vehemently oppose any decision to make that job harder or more time consuming.

My records are, and always have been, in alphabetical order by shipping group. Not only is this the most sensible and easiest way to organize the *vast* amount of data that we're forced to collect, it's also the industry standard for all other publishers, and allows us to quickly calculate *weekly* cash-flow (which is all-important to retailers in today's market).

However, Marvel's new system is listed in the rather bizarre alphabetical by "family" group. Not only have I never seen a store that racks books in *anything* like this manner (I know I'd hate to shop in a store like that – talk about confusing), but it adds substantially to the time in filling out an order – first you've got to figure out *where* something is listed before you can access the solicitation.

For my part, I plan on ordering Marvel comics by cycle sheet numbers *only*. I simply don't have the additional hours in the ordering process to mess around with their new system. I've no doubt that this will uniformly lead to lower orders on Marvel comics from me.

2 6

Hahahahaha! "Rumor has it that Marvel is contemplating allowing no reorders." God damn, if that's not a plus-perfect example of "Same Shit, Different Day," I have no idea WHAT is! Why do I have to keep repeating myself, is the question?

Tilting at Windmills #26
(Originally ran in Comics Retailer #27)

Although they're no longer the titans they once were, we still like to think of publishers in terms of the "Big Two": Marvel and DC. Put them together and they represent more than half of the Direct Market, and they're the focus of this month's column.

Marvel has been getting enormous criticism in the last few months, much of it valid, because of the perception that they're abandoning the Direct Market. This is going to sound weird coming from me, but, from Marvel's point of view, it makes a certain amount of sense. After all, we are a fickle and unpredictable market. Orders can fluctuate wildly based on factors outside of their control, and, as a publicly held company, they have an *obligation* to squeeze as much profit as they are able. Marvel, by necessity, must continue to primarily focus on the short term, because the second they "let up", the stockholders are going to take it in the shorts.

Looking at our market from the outside, it's a wonder we can function at all. Information and product is caught in the bottleneck of the distributors, and most retailers haven't anything even slightly resembling healthy business practices (a slight digression: Capital City has just added new features to their Top Comics charts – a percent of total and a cumulative percentage. These two numbers really show how skewed the marketplace is, and how much of our survival is tied to a handful of comics. In the April charts, the top ten comics account for 13.49% of all orders for the month! The top 25 is 26.94%; the top 50 is 42.2%, and the top 100 a whopping 62.14% of *all* orders for the month. This suggests to me that too few stores are carrying *anywhere near* a full line of comics or product of any kind of diversity). If I were head of Marvel Comics I know I would be looking closely at virtually anyway to get away from this sick and self-limiting system. After all, you can hardly sell *anything but* superhero comics in it. Sure, you get retailers like me, and Carol Denbow, and Matt Lehman, and the DLG, and etc., etc., ad nauseam, who are always looking for a new way to expand our marketplace with material geared at a wide variety of consumers, but how often do publishers actually *sell* more than a handful of copies? Not too damn often. The direct market has become a catch 22: non-genre material "won't/doesn't sell" because we're selling to the same, finite group of customers, but we'll never expand that finite group without non-genre material. Marvel has the potential clout to bring in thousands and thousands of new readers, but do they really want them to see the typical, messy, hole-in-the-wall, fanboy comic shop?

Even an outsider like me can make the quick calculations that Marvel could be saving thousands of dollars by eliminating the distributors (we've all heard the rumors that Marvel is trying to buy Capital City, right? Whether true or not [I'd suspect not - seems to me there's some dangerous legal questions there], it's interesting to speculate), and by bypassing the comic shop, they can provide the face that *they* want the consumer to see, rather than the ones *we* want to show them. Do I feel betrayed? Hell, no! It's good business sense on Marvel's part, *but* I do think they should get on one side of the road or another.

The press releases cry, "Hey! We're on your side! We want to be your friend! The Direct Market is our partner, and we're not going anywhere!" yet the *deeds* speak otherwise: Announcing the planning of Marvel stores, the sneak attack of the Marvel Mart, the rumors of No Reorders, (wait! Another digression, if you please: rumor has it that Marvel is contemplating allowing no reorders. The story goes that it's a big strain and hassle when retailers are very conservative on a product (say, the $5.95 *Marvels*), then reorder up the wazoo once it hits the stores. The concept is that by limiting retailers to initial orders only, we'll *have* to show greater faith, or else we might "miss out." And, I betcha most retailers'll play right along. "Don't want to miss the Next *Moon Knight*!" you'll cry [well, maybe not *you*], so you'll up your orders and have an even worse sell-through and cash-flow. Again, as of this writing, it's still only a rumor, so don't panic yet!), all of these actions seem to belie the "commitment" Marvel says it has. It's either one or the other, kids. Don't insult our intelligence by sneaking around behind our backs, please. If you want to hit the road, that's cool, and if you want to stay likewise, but please don't say you're going to stay, then disappear for weeks at a time – in much the same way we wouldn't want you to say you're going, then have you hang around all the time, mooching out of the fridge. Relationships are two-way streets – pick a direction, please.

On the other hand, there's DC. While DC has certainly made their share of bonehead moves (we talked about the *Green Lantern* fiasco within the last few months, as one example; another would be the renumbering the *entire* line to #0 for *Zero Hour* – in a glutted market it hardly makes sense to me to do a one-month event on a line of 40 some-odd superhero books, that *forces* us to throw our cycle sheets straight out the window; one final example would be the revelation that I recently received that neither Mike Carlin nor Paul Levitz reads every book that DC produces. Hell, if *I* can find the time to do so [as well as reading every other comic that comes through my door!], then I am wholly dumbfounded that the Executive Editor and the Publisher can't manage to do the same!), they've never wavered in their support for the Direct Market. DC has historically put more money back into the market then they "should" have (based on things like market share), and has systemically taken such actions as instantly reprinting material (often in a less expensive format) that has sold through faster than we imagined it could (*Death of Superman* being a recent example).

DC also has what appears to be the largest commitment of *any* publisher in stocking trade paperbacks and other backlist material. We all get Coming Comics, right? Look at the backlist pages! There are at least 120 different items listed there. Assuming even a moderate level of stock-depth, they've got to be carrying over a million dollars at full-retail there. What does Marvel have? Eleven books that are listed as permanent stock items, right? I can't speak for anyone else, but in my store it's the new comics that provide the bread and butter for keeping the doors open, but it's the trades and the backlist that makes me profitable and allow me to expand my business beyond the tiny fanboy ghetto that we, as an industry, have become.

The last thing we can laud DC for is their commitment to non-genre material, in a *serious way*. Vertigo has been strongly supported by the company, and one can only hope that the new Paradox line will get the same support. Hardly anything from these lines has/is going to set the Direct Market on fire with their sales, which makes the support DC gives even that much more amazing, but *without* that support, such lines invariably fizzle (can anyone say "Epic?" I thought you could...). And DC consistently gives new launches from the imprints the *same* level of support that it gives to any of the super-hero line.

Again, I've had more than my share of problems with DC in the past (Right, Bob? Right, Bruce?), and I have less than no doubt that I'll take them to task over hundreds of issues in the future (that's why I have a column, after all); and, when given the choice, I will *always* opt for creator-driven business rather than corporate-driven (any given corporation might be our best hope today, but, in the end, their only allegiance is to furthering themselves - it's the individual people who make a corporation good or bad, and the "good" ones could be gone tomorrow, leaving you nothing but ashes – the day Dave Sim leaves *Cerebus*, or Peter Bagge leaves *Hate*...well, that's the day those books go away forever), but when forced to choose between the "Big Two." I don't think there is any question where our support must go.

I'll be back next month with more pissed-off ramblings.

While I still believe in the ultimate message of individuals over companies, thank you very much, my examples at the middle-end make this an amusing column to read years later. James Owen of Starchild **did**, in fact, ultimately screw-up and go away. Still, reading this all these years later I think, "God, did I really believe all my own hype back then?" Now that I'm older, and maybe even a smidge wiser, I kinda cringe at the raw arrogance my early self displayed in the first few paragraphs here...

Tilting at Windmills #27
(Originally ran in Comics Retailer #28)

In the May issue of *Comics Retailer*, we have a Small Store Strategy by Preston Sweet, entitled "A Modest Proposal" where he talks about a (mythical?) organization called CRAPO (Comic Retailers Are Pissed Off). While his simile may not by directed *squarely* at your humble columnist, there are certain elements that I figure are intended as a slight barb to my own self (before we go any further, let me observe that, while Preston and I may bicker on any number of issues that face retailer-dom, I like the man personally, and I can state with some degree of certainty that he has fought for more than one program [the Small Press Sampler leaps immediately to mind, as does the "40% direct from publisher to retailer, they pay shipping" {it needs a catchphrase} plan] that will benefit each and every one of us). However, I come today, not to praise Caesar, but to argue with him.

I've made it clear, more than once in this column (and elsewhere), that I have no great love for companies. My argument runs as follows: no company, at any time in the history of civilization, cares one iota for *you*. Oh sure, *individuals* within those companies may be on "your side," but the company itself *never* is. I can state this with a great deal of certainty having, over the years, watched one company after another dick around with the individuals within – individuals who gave all of their lives and passion to that company. No matter how noble the intentions (look at Tundra), no matter how long the association (how about Chris Claremont and the X-Men?), no matter the length or breadth of the promises (look at, say, Marvel Mart...), inevitably they'll stick it to you.

In my mind a company says to you: "Look, you won't mind if we put a finger up your ass, do you? It's just our policy, and besides, it won't hurt you *too* much. Nothing personal, you know." So you say, "Well *nngggh* O.K. As long *nngggh* it's just *nngggh* this once *nngggh*." So, you accept it, and you walk around with a thumb in your ass for awhile. Now, at the point where you've basically gotten used to the pressure, someone from the company will come to you and say, "Look, I know we said it would just be a finger, but, well, some things have changed, so now we've got to use this broom handle. It shouldn't bug you *too* much, after all, you've already got a finger up your butt." "Well, O.K., *nngggh* that's certainly *nngggh* inescapable *nngggh* logic *nngggh*. Go ahead *nngggh*." Months pass (years even, maybe), and your sphincter adjusts, then they come back holding a baseball bat: "Look, we're sorry about this, but it's a new policy. Everyone else has a baseball bat, so we're going to have to insist you get one, too. We can't cut a special deal just for you – that wouldn't be fair, and, besides, there's already a broom-handle sticking out of your asshole." And if you accept that, then next time it's a sapling, then a small car, and so on, until they manage to cram the Statue of Liberty in your nether-regions. They keep going, until you're more a hole than a human, at which point they say, "Thanks for playing, but we've got a new contestant."

Let's face it, there's really only two kinds of people who decide to go into comics retailing: those who can't hack it in the "real" world, holding down "straight" jobs; and those who think they're going to make *a lot of money* (hah! – show me a *rich* comics retailer, and I'll buy that premise). We "misfits" don't want to be beholden to anyone but ourselves, yet by and large, we end up getting in bed with the large publishers, with the cry "but that's what our customers *want*." Well, I can't speak for anyone else, but I'm not especially fond of anal intrusion, so that's why I decided quite some time ago not to play *that* game.

I was at the Capital City trade show the beginning of May, and I had a *lot* of you come up to me complimenting me on this column (hey, thanks!), yet entirely oblivious to it's contents ("What do you mean, cycle sheets?" <sigh>, don't tell me we've got to keep covering *that* ground?) – "Man, I can't believe what Marvel (and/or fill-in-the-blank) is doing/has done," the refrain went. "Yeah, so have you been reducing your *dependence* on them?" "No, but I plan to start real soon, now." Uhh, sorry guys, but it's nearly too late – *this* is what comes from "politeness at all costs," from "we've got to be nice to them,": you've got a small elm tree sticking out of your rear end. *Any* publisher could go out of business tomorrow, and I'll still be standing. How many of *you* can say the same thing? Yeah, that's what I thought.

We're *far* more important to the publishers/ distributors than they are to us. *Never* forget this, 'cuz the second you do, you've got foreign parts lodged in your sphincter.

But, as I said toward the top, just because companies are inherently evil and soul-destroying entities, that doesn't mean the individuals in power are bad people. Hell, there are people at Marvel that I *love dearly* – I'd invite them for dinner at my house in a second, and I'd let them use my bathroom without checking to make sure that they didn't raid the medicine cabinet. However, Marvel, itself, will never get that same invite – I'm too afraid they'll steal the towels. I like most everyone who works at DC, but I wouldn't, for one teeny, tiny second think that Time Warner has anything even *resembling* my best interests at heart. The problem that I believe most people make is thinking that the individuals are the company. No. They work for the company, they may even guide the company, but that's the best you'll ever get. I tend to suspect that Paul Levitz is a really good boss: it sure looks like he'll give you enough rope to either hang yourself or go bungee-jumping, depending on your inclinations. At the least, he's put together a reasonably solid management team that can do their jobs reasonably correctly. What happens (God forbid) the day that Paul gets hit by a bus, though? And Time Warner puts some suit who couldn't give a rat's ass about at least trying to put out good and diverse material, and sacks half of the staff (the good half)? That day *will* come. And while it might not be for 20 more years, that's the day we'll all find out that it's not the company, but the people behind it that are the "good" ones. This goes for *all* companies. There's no percentage, *ever*, in thinking a company is your friend or ally.

I'll be "nice" or "polite" or "friendly" to individuals. But to a company? Hah! Don't fool yourself, or you'll learn the hard way. You are inevitably in a subordinate position when you deal with a company. No matter what you're promised or told, in the end you can be nothing more than a lackey, because, no matter who you are, and no matter what you do, *you can be replaced*.

So, what does that leave us with, you ask? I've long believed that our real future, our real *hope* is with the self-publishers, and creator-control. It's not that the self-publishers don't screw up, or lie to us, or do any of the things I'm constantly ragging about, but when they do, it's *their* ass on the line. If DC screws up on a title, well, DC keeps going on. However, if James Owen screws up on *Starchild*, it's not like he has 47 other projects to fall back on. The self-publishers and creators in-control have something clearly and easily defined on the line: their honor and their financial health. One person "in control" means one person to fix the problem, and one person to reap the penalties if things don't happen. These days, you can find dozens and dozens of examples of creator-controlled projects, and that's where I'm going to put my bank. If *Sin City* doesn't come out on time, or is promoted poorly – it's Frank Miller's fault, not Dark Horse's. After all, Frank made the decision of who to work with, and how, and, while his instructions may not be followed to a "t", creator control *implies* creator-responsibility.

•   •   •   •   •

On a slightly similar tack, Larry Marder (all hail the Nexus!), Rick Vietch (the Rarebit fiend), and I came up with a new term at the Cap City show (and mucho thanks *must* go to Carol & Sonny Denbow of Starclipper in St. Louis for not only doing a self-publisher event in their store prior to the show, but for sponsoring the self-publisher suite during the show, so we had a place to come up with this stuff. Huzzah to the Starclippers!): Self-retailers.

Think about it a second.

Self-retailers.

If you've just got one store, and you're there, behind the counter day in, and day out, fighting directly on the front-lines, you're a self-retailer. If you know your customers by name ("NNNNOOOORRRRRMMMMM!"), and you know what they like, and they trust *you* to steer them in the right direction in their quest for quality entertainment, then you're a self-retailer.

And, you know what? I think self-retailers are inherently superior than other retailers (ooooh, big shock that, eh?), because you've got a lot more at stake: it's *your* honor on the line, and when something goes wrong, it's *your* responsibility (not unlike the creator-control issue above).

Roll that around in your head for a little while, and lemme know what you think.

•   •   •   •   •

Believe it or not, this all fits quite neatly into one world-view. Everything revolves around *responsibility*, both to yourself, your customers, and your peers. Frankly, I look forward to the day that I don't *have* to write this column anymore (what? You don't think I do it for *fun* do you? Hah!) – that's the day that the problems have all been solved, and there's no more windmills to tilt against. While my detractors may think I'm out to grind an ax, or fill an agenda, I do this job because of my deep and *passionate* love for it, and because I deeply believe that we have an *obligation* to make this industry a better place.

As I walked around the Cap City show I was struck by how many retailers were there not to learn; not to strive, not to add something to our industry; but to get some free stuff, to get *autographs* signed! "Wow," I overheard, "I got a Platinum Superman!" "I got an 'ashcan' signed – I can sell this!" Yuck. I think it's obvious that far too few of the retailers there, far too few of the people reading these words, are anything even resembling professionals.

The weekend before, I attended Pro/Con, the comic book professionals con, held in conjunction with WonderCon in Oakland. About 7 retailers came to this convention – and not one came to get autographs signed or to kiss up to anyone; we came because we felt it important to show that retailers are just as much professionals in this business as creators, or anyone else. My original thought for this column was to exhort you to attend the *next* Pro/Con – to make an effort to show that the retail community wasn't as bass-ackwards as our reputation. But Comic Relief's Rory Root cautioned me: "If they throw the doors open to any retailer, invite them all to come, there'll be a lot of people attending who don't *deserve* to, who will turn this con from something positive, to just another comics convention," and, after the Cap City show, I'm not sure I disagree. (A slight digression, to clear the record once and for all: a lot of people out there seem to think that Rory and I are enemies of some kind. Nothing could be further from the truth. Rory's second store is located about 8 blocks away from mine, and we have nothing but the greatest respect for each others operations. If I don't have a comic, there's one place we automatically recommend, and that's Comic Relief –

they do they same for us. *That* is a professional relationship! No feuding, no back-biting, but mutual respect, instead.) I *want* retailers to be better represented at this type of event – to participate in making this industry better for us all. But I watch our collective behavior, our overall attitudes, and I fully understand why elements of the creative community are less than sanguine about inviting us into their sanctuary.

So tell me: are you wholly professional? Or are you just talking the talk? Do you attend conventions and trade shows because you want to make this business a better one, or are you trying to line your own pockets (and, not coincidentally, perpetuating the same elements that I've watched you rail against) with free books and autographed items? Are you a pro, or are you a con?

Well, if it's "con," then I seriously don't know why you still bother to read this column – there's nothing I can say to you. But if it's a "pro," then I urge you to begin making plans now to attend Pro/Con 3, next April, in Oakland. It's time to stop messing around – it's time to declare your loyalties and allegiances because, if there's anything the last year has taught us is how fragile we all are – how elements out of our control can throw us out of business in a second.

Where do you stand? It's time to decide. Now.

Tilting at Windmills #28
(Originally ran in Comics Retailer #29)

One of the biggest problems in writing a column like this is the time delay. I'm writing this on May 30th for it to appear in the August issue of Comics Retailer.

What this means, of course, is that if I've got something timely to talk about, like this month, you won't be reading about it until it's become history. This is sometimes frustrating. Most times, I attempt to couch my statements in such a way to be universal and timeless, but every once in awhile it's imperative to discuss something that is, to you, the past.

The issue this month is one of missolicitation.

There are a lot of ways for a comic to be missolicited: different creative teams; erroneous catalog descriptions; format or price changes; incorrect shipping dates. But all of these things are covered clearly in the distributor's terms, and we, the retailers, are covered from publisher malfeasance, because missolicited items are fully returnable. However, as of late, we've discovered a new problem – one that isn't specifically spelled out: sequence.

I don't think I'm alone in believing that sequence is as important an issue in sell-through as creative team, description, format, price, or ship dates. We don't want customers, particularly in today's glutted market, to be given any reason to drop a book, and material shipping out of the sequence it was solicited in is as clear an invitation for the customer to reconsider their purchase as anything else. Particularly because we're dealing with serial fiction, and habitual entertainment, where the regular steady fix is what the customer is looking for.

There were two recent attempts to subvert the sequence issue that leap immediately to my mind: Continuity Comics' *Valeria the She-Bat*, which attempted to completely skip the two Spawn crossover issues; and Marvel's *Starblast* crossover, where a number of the crossover issues shipped long before the book they were meant to be crossing into. In both cases, these sequence-errors got rightly shut down by the distributors, and the affected titles were made fully returnable. At the time, I placed several calls to Diamond suggesting that they write into their trade terms a "sequence clause", so that these problems won't arise again, costing everyone more money (in phone calls and employee time, not only in identifying the problem, but in packaging and shipping returns), avoiding "case by case determination." My reasoning was that if these things were clearly stated ahead of time, then the publishers might think twice before soliciting an item if there is any question of it arriving in proper sequence.

Of course, the distributors did not create such a policy, which brings us neatly to the item *du jour*: *Spawn* #21.

We're all aware at this point that Image has announced that *Spawn* #19 & 20 were running behind schedule enough that those issues would've been returnable under the distributors new 30-days policies. #21, however, was for some reason done, and ready to go, and could be shipped "on time" in the month it was solicited for. Rather than be responsible and either ship #19 & 20 late (having to take returns), renumber #21 to #19 (having to take returns) or resolicit the material (meaning there wouldn't be a *Spawn* on the market for 4 months), it was decided to ship #21 out of sequence, non-returnably, resoliciting the late issues #19 & 20 at some later date, sticking us with the ramifications of Todd McFarlane's inability to produce the material when he promised.

And the distributors went for it.

They went for it. Can you believe that?

Now, even ignoring the very very real possibility of customers dropping *Spawn*, losing us long-term dollars at a time where so few of us can afford that kind of loss, there is the inevitable and incessant phone calls we're all going to receive. When things have shipped out of sequence in the past, I generally receive two to three times the number of phone calls asking me to explain it as I have any expectation of selling of the items in question. Some customers will call every store in town looking for the "missing" issues, although it's been carefully explained to them several times that those titles weren't even produced yet - they seem to assume that the retailers are holding the comic back in their storerooms, although no one in town has ever even received the book. I logged at least a dozen calls each on *Starblast* and *Valeria*, and I was selling less than five copies of those books. I can't even begin to guess how many calls I'm going to be fielding on a good-selling book like Spawn. Each and every phone call you take on these issues is costing you money, not only in time that could be better put towards keeping your store running efficiently, but also in potential loss of real customers who aren't going to be able to get through to you.

And we *are* going to lose some sales – it might only be one copy per store, but I know consumers: when faced with something confusing, a certain percentage will go away. And for us, that not only reduces our potential profit all the way down the line, but it leaves us with merchandise that we have no surety of selling, for at least the next three months, until we can adjust our orders again. .

However, Todd, Image, and the distributors are all protected with a non-returnable #21: they have no unsold inventory, and we're stuck paying for their decision – a decision that we not only had no say in, but no culpability for as well! And that's not right nor fair.

Of course, I think we can all guess why *Spawn* is being allowed to get away this, while others are not: *Spawn* is one of the best-selling books in this industry. Doing the right thing will cost Image and the distributors many thousands of dollars. But who should bear that cost? McFarlane, who made the promise he was unable to keep? Image, for allowing solicitation on an item they had no reasonable expectation of being able to ship on time? The distributors, who seem more concerned about their suppliers than their customers? Or the retailers, who ordered in good faith, playing by the rules, then were told those rules no longer apply?

This is not only a financial crime, but a precedent setting one, as well. If the distributors allow *Spawn* to take blatant advantage of what is a loophole at best, then they have to allow other publishers and other titles to do the same.

By the time you read this, you've had *Spawn* #21 for at least six weeks. If you have unsold, and unsalable inventory on this issue, send it back.

That's right: send it back, and strike that amount from your next bill. That's the only way they'll learn they can't do this to us.

I am unwilling (and unable) to pay for Todd McFarlane's and Image's negligence. I am unwilling to support a distributor who perpetuates this kind of crass manipulation of the marketplace. By remaining silent, by eating #21, you are, in fact, condoning this action – "political action" is your only recourse. Did I ever tell my story about the "Gold" *Venom* #1? You remember that, right? It showed up, outta the blue, with no orders placed for it, and some really expensive net price attached to it...$17.50 is what I think Diamond was asking for it. I recognized that this too was a dangerous precedent: you simply can't ship things that were unasked for, then expect us to pay for them! And they had the unmitigated gall to bill this as a "thank you" for supporting the first *Venom* mini-series! So I took the copy they sent me, neatly cut it in half with a pair of scissors, and sent it back with a note saying that I expected a credit to appear on my next bill, or I'd take it off myself. If you don't stand up for what you believe, for what's important, then you can't complain as they take your livelihood away, inch by inch.

So, I urge each and every one of you to return your unsold merchandise to your distributor, along with a polite note explaining why you are doing so. If you can include secondary information, like your cycles sheets, or the number (and length!) of the phone calls you received, that will make the point that much more clearly. I would also suggest you write a note to both Todd and Image, as well, expressing your displeasure with this action.

If we take this action together, they'll have no choice but to take the book back, and to learn they can't play this kind of numeric semantics with us again. We'll all stand together, or we'll fall separately. Do the right thing.

Tilting at Windmills #29
(Originally ran in Comics Retailer #30)

Even in the best of circumstances, ordering comics is more of an art than a science – we're asked to make decisions, sight unseen, three months in advance on some 600 different items, each of which is in some way dependent on the items around it. Even with the best tools we can muster (like, say, cycle sheets and a subscription program), we're still essentially guessing what books will have what sales.

And the publishers seem dead set to make it less scientific each month, and more whimsical.

In the last two months, we're had three major publishers screw mightily with our ability to confidently predict where our sales will be: DC, Image, and Marvel.

With DC, it is, of course, *Zero Hour/*Zero Month.

By the time you read this, the first of the "zero" issues have shipped, and we'll know whether or not we guessed right – a source at DC suggested to me that orders came in well over 20% higher than "baseline" numbers. Can we actually move that many more DC titles? Who knows? But, it's rather frustrating to have to order five issues of a crossover mini-series, and 40 #0's in a two-month period without any concrete way to determine whether our orders are sound or not.

Of course, with "Zero Month" we do have at least a "baseline" to work from. I personally went from between one and five copies higher on each book, on the assumption that some people at least are going to want to sample the "new" DC. But since I've placed my order, I've heard grumbles from many long-time DC fans that *Zero Hour* is where they're going to step *off* rather than on. Will readers be converted from other lines, other publishers? Will they magically find more money in their pockets? Will DC dabblers start buying more titles? We hope for the best, but the point is none of us know what the results might be. We're forced to *guess*, albeit with a base to extrapolate from.

Much more difficult to figure is Image.

Image, as you well know, has announced "X month", where we're asked to order five Founding Image titles, each by "An Image Founder" – but we don't know who is doing which book.

We. Don't. Know. Who. Is. Doing. Which. Book.

There are many factors that go into a books sales level - not the least of which is creative team. Let's face it, the Image Founders don't sell comics equally. Todd McFarlane has a demonstrably different level from Jim Valentino. I know that I'm going to sell significantly more copies of *Shadowhawk* if Jim Lee is drawing it, just as I'm going to sell significantly less copies of *Spawn* if Rob Liefeld draws it (your mileage might vary). It's wholly self-evident that creators make a huge difference in sell-though. And to not tell us who is drawing which book is an unconscionable act.

"It's Fun!" the ads proclaim. And, I will happily concede, for the consumers, it may well be. But for retailers, it's an ordering nightmare.

At Comix Experience, here's what we're typically selling:

Cyberforce:	19
Shadowhawk:	6
Spawn:	100
Wildcats:	43
Youngblood:	15

Given this set of numbers, how do you order "X Month", besides "badly?" No matter which book Todd is doing, there's *no* way to order enough copies of it from baseline. Similarly, whichever book Valentino is doing, it's clear we'll have too many copies.

The only way, the *only* way this promotion can make fiscal sense to a retailer is if it's the *character* that sells the audience, *not* the creator. That is, it's *Spawn* selling 90 of my 100 copies, not Todd McFarlane. And, if that's true, then Image may as well be Marvel, as that's always been their argument. I thought we were striving for something better than that.

Dave Sim and I were joking that this was the "Ringo ploy" – like how every Beatles album had the Obligatory Ringo Song, so that he could make some money, as well. The net effect of this promotion is likely to be the jacking up of all the numbers to near or equal each other, so that no matter which book "Ringo" is doing, he makes some lucre.

We'll see, I guess. Perhaps the numbers have even been released by the time this sees print. For myself, I did the only thing that I could do, given the circumstances: I limited the books to subscription only.

Yeah, that's right, I knowingly cut myself out of potential sales. And for one simple reason: I'm not in the business of selling raffle tickets. Let's face facts: whichever book Todd does will skyrocket in price on the secondary market. It doesn't matter what the *reasons* are (and I wholly believe when Image declares that this is "fun"), but the *net effects* must be taken into account. Just like the "limited to 20% of the print run" special covers the Jim Lee books have sported recently *created* a collectible item. You may disagree, but I'm not in business to sell "collectibles." What I sell is Habitual Periodical Serial Fiction. And I'm *certainly* not in comics to sell *artificially created* "collectibles."

Make no bones about it: I *want* to participate in the "fun" of "X Month" – as a reader, I'm sure I'd get a kick out of this experiment – but, it is wholly unjust to ask retailers to take the ordering burden in determining what the audience for these books might be! How do you order it? I don't know, and preliminary conversations say that most of you aren't sure either.

How do you order it? How do you order it? It's not like it's a first issue of something, so you can depend on the following issues to absorb a minor amount of over-ordering, and it's not like you have something else to compare it to, to find the right ballpark. It's a complete shot in the dark.

And what about Marvel? Surely they are without sin? Nope, they ain't.

Marvel is now soliciting for two different versions of the "X" books. Each title has a "deluxe" format (better paper, $1.95), and a "regular" version (newsprint, and $1.50) - my suspicion is that the "regular" version is the newsstand copies, but that's pure hearsay. The idea, in and of itself isn't so bad, until you realize that the "regular" version of these books doesn't ship until two weeks later! Remember: we're in the business of selling Habitual Periodical Serial Fiction. This means that most of our consumers are a little...fanatical about their purchases. Wait two weeks? You must be nuts! The most frugal, or on limited budgets, might be willing to wait two weeks, but most regular customers are going to buy the first one you put in front of them.

The little, evil suspicious part of me whispers that evidently Marvel needs to increase profitability, and standard marketing practices are no longer working for them. By raising the price by nearly 1/3 on their best selling franchise, they are clearly trying to raise the bottom line. If the market rejects the higher price, they still have the cheaper ones to fall back on, and if (much, much more likely) the market can't wait for their "fix," they can discontinue the $1.50 titles, pointing towards our buying habits as "justification." Bravo! A Master Stroke of Misdirection!

My prediction is that the more expensive versions will get substantially higher orders, and each "family" will get the split format rolled out, before a year passes, and once they're all converted, the "regular" versions will get phased out.

Again, we're posed with an ordering quandary. Who will wait? How many people won't accept the price hike? What percentage can we reasonably expect on each permutation, and will they even be close from book to book? Is it not possible that the *Cable* readers will wait, but *Uncanny X-Men* ones won't? What makes this even more hinky to guess is that several of the books, if the consumers are willing to wait for the "cheaper" version, will get *price decreases* (but only, of course, if we, collectively, are willing to stock the "two weeks late" version).

Is it any wonder, with programs like these that our orders are more and more and more conservative? How do you order any of this stuff? And (this is the big question), *why are we being asked to take all of the risk in publishers' experiments?*

Oh, sure, the publishers all have their platitudes: DC says it's "re-energizing our Universe," Image says it's "bringing fun back to comics," and Marvel is "giving the customer a choice of better quality," – these are all reasonable assessments, I guess, perhaps even laudable ones, but it's we, the retailers, with the most to lose and the least information to work from, who are being asked to subsidize these programs, at a time all evidence says we can least afford to do so!

It's time to seriously discuss returnability again (and it has been for *months*) - if not across the board (which I still think is the wisest course), then, at least, in cases like these, where all of our information is thrown right out the window.

My proposal (first mentioned, what, a year ago?) is that we be allowed to return a fixed percentage of our orders – say 20% — with minimum and maximum quantities possible – say 3 and 20. In order to pay for this privilege, we'd be charged a small sum per title – say 15 or 20 cents – which would be split between distributor and publisher. The important bit is to cover the distributor's costs in handling the returns. The rallying call of the anti-returns faction is that returns will inevitably lower our discounts. Well, damn it! They don't *have* to! If we cover their expenses, there's no reason to adjust the discount structure.

Right now our marketplace is very unhealthy – I don't know one retailer that isn't struggling to stay on top of it. It's a stone-cold bitch to order comics today, and you would think that publishers would be more cognizant of that fact. I think we're going to continue to be a marginal business unless and until we have either an external market change (like returnability), or an internal one (like publishers increasing quality, reducing quantity and halting their collective dependence on hype to sell comics).

Hopefully, one or the other will happen soon, but until then, the least you can do is make your dissatisfaction with these effectively anti-retailer experiments known. Retailers don't have a voice until we all speak up, in unison.

Heh.

Tilting at Windmills #30
(Originally ran in Comics Retailer #31)

It has been suggested to me that I've been less than even-handed in this column's focus. "You," it has been said, "focus exclusively on publisher and distributor screw-ups, but you never ever talk about the retailer's culpability in the market."

Fair enough.

The simple fact of the matter (and I thought it most self-evident) is that the bulk of retailers are sub-moronic twits who wouldn't know how to run a real business if their lives depended on it.

Let's start at the beginning, though.

The number one strength of our industry is also our number one failing: we exist through fandom. Up until a couple of years ago, it was far, far too easy to open up a comic book shop. A solid collection of back issues, and a couple of thousand dollars, and boom! you were in business. You didn't *need* to do any real marketing, because comic fans were always on the look-out for another source of material. You didn't *need* prime retail space, because comics were a destination business (that is: the customers come looking for you – you didn't need to depend on new foot traffic). You didn't *need* a cash register, or fancy racks, partly because many of the customers didn't care, and partly because the business was small enough that sophistication was almost overkill. You didn't *need* a growing customer base, because costs were low, and besides, one of the main reasons for opening a comic book shop was for the retailer to get his comics cheap. And you didn't *need* to do cycle sheets, or tight inventory controls, because *anything* **would** sell *eventually*, and, besides, it was all so cheap, that it took a *lot* of comics to amass any serious debt.

Any fan could open a comic shop, with a little elbow grease, and a little money. And it was fine, because we were a tiny little marketplace.

That was then.

Somewhere in the middle of the Eighties things started changing. After nearly a decade and a half of price guides, the idea became ingrained in the consumers minds that comics inevitably rose in price, as the years went by. Suddenly we were seeing people buying comics *because* of the value. While there had been speculative-driven product before (*Shazam* #1, *Howard the Duck* #1), we had never before seen the industry-wide feeding frenzy that the black & white glut produced. For a couple of months there, *any* black & white title (though often with the "adjective-adjective-adjective-noun" pattern), no matter how amateur or goofy (like, say, *Reagan's Raiders*) was getting big orders while we all cast around blindly for "The Next Turtles."

While that market eventually crashed (they *always* do, kids), it taught the mainstream publishers a few lessons. Namely, that the marketplace didn't have much problem supporting material that was higher-priced, but smaller in print run; that, as long as there was a perception of "heat," quality only marginally mattered; Retailers were gullible enough to buy into "get rich quick" scams, and would happily convince their customers to buy into the same mentality, making "heat" a relatively easy thing to generate.

We all started to make a lot more money, without looking at the long-term consequences of our actions (a problem, I should add in the interest of fairness, which was indicative of American culture in general, and hardly a problem specific to the comics market), and the publishers, in general, got a lot more sophisticated in what and how they sold to our consumers. Time ticks on and on, and we get Wizard, and the Image phenomenon, and movie deal after movie deal, and wider and wider civilian understanding of the potential of comics, and all of a sudden, we're a big business, with big money realizing the potential to profit enormously. Marvel goes public, Acclaim purchases Valiant, investment bankers buy Kitchen Sink (!), etc. etc. Suddenly, we're "legit."

Well, the publishers are, at least.

The retailers, on the other hand are still mired in the dark ages. As near as anyone can tell, less than a quarter of us use cycle sheets at all. Without any cogent ability to predict our sales, we, as a whole, rely on "feelings," and "eyeballing" the rack as our major tool in making our orders.

You don't have to be fanatic in keeping records – lord knows that I'm only cycling about 90% of what comes through the doors, but to not keep regular and active counts of the monthly ongoing titles at least? That dumbfounds me.

We're also, overall, less than professional in our projection to the public. My good friend Bruce Costa likes to admonish you to keep your bathrooms clean, but I'm talking even more basic than that. I can't count the number of stores that I've gone in that are poorly lit, with boxes strewn all over the floor, with actively hostile counter-people working out of cigar boxes for change. I'm about as big as a comic fan/geek as you're likely to find...I'm also a big slob, but these stores turn even me completely off!

And let's not even begin to talk about pricing! I've got a catalog from one of the bigger retailers in the business where they list common, in-print items at up to ten times cover price! I've got stock lists from several publishers, and when you compare their in-stock, available-at-wholesale lists to catalog prices, or prices you can find advertised, say, in *CBG*, it becomes readily apparent that we're infected by a virtual plague of low-level hustlers and grifters, trying to make a profit at the expense of their customers', and their own, ignorance.

It's nearly a criminal shame, the sheer number of poorly run, inefficient, badly focused, price gouging retailers out there. One would hope that if you've learned anything by reading the commentary from me and my fellow columnists over the last few years, is that it's damn bloody time for us to get our acts together!

I hate publishers, right? And I hate distributors, even more, right? In my estimation the vast majority run their businesses in ways that are antithetical to our continued health and well being, as well as to that of the creators. Well, let's look at it square on – it's mostly *our* fault. No, no, not the 100 or so of you who understand the way this market works, and what our responsibilities are to keep it healthy and sane — the rest of you. The ones who, with your orders, forced upon us this festering pile of garbage that we're limited to selling; who said, "oh, yes, please polybag everything," "oh, yes, we'd rather sell the shiny covered version, at a 50% higher price, and not even give our customers the *choice* of the 'regular' version;" who encouraged your customers to buy geared based on collection and value, rather than joy and entertainment. To all of you I say: get your damn act together.

As long as you continue to play into the old, outmoded methods of doing business, methods that have brought nothing but a glutted market, a confused and growingly disinterested customer base, we're going to be trapped at the mercy of the *rest* of the shams and grifters, and ones who have a whole helluva lot more money than you. If you can't play in the big leagues, and most of you hardly have the wherewithal to do that, you're gonna get run over...and take the rest of us with you.

I think it's time for a change, because we can hardly hold up the publishers and distributors to a standard that we can't match ourselves, now can we?

Next month I'll go back to yelling at everyone else, but it's time to clean up our own backyards! We're all counting on *you*....

Tilting at Windmills #31
(Originally ran in Comics Retailer #32)

So how many of you are actually using cycle sheets, Hmm?

The reason I ask is that I've been looking at the sell-through data Diamond is reporting, and extrapolating from that, I can't imagine it's very high.

Either that, or we all suck miserably at our jobs.

And I don't know which concept scares me more.

I don't know dick about your specific store. Maybe you're one of those places that pretty much only carries the top 100 titles (Capital City's charts seem to indicate that the Top 100 account for more than half of all the sales in this business). Perhaps you're thinking to yourself, "Self, I'm not stocking a full line of comics...heck, we only carry 125 titles...so why should we bother doing all that counting, and writing, and extra work? I can eyeball the racks just fine to determine my sales!" Those thoughts are mostly wrong.

Sure, if you're small, and behind your counter every day, and you only stock a finite number of items, you probably won't go out of business by eyeballing, but I betcha a buck that you're taking greater losses than you *need* to be. Even a couple of unsold books each month begin to add up real fast, and it's taking money out of your pockets that could go to better things.

Now, I don't *totally* trust the Diamond sell-through figures. They've made some fairly dopey math errors on occasion (If *Supreme* #12 sold-in roughly half of *Amazing Spider-Man* #390, by the Diamond charts, then I find it very unlikely that "average number of copies ordered" of *Supreme* is five, while *ASM* did 29 [the 7/6 report]; or the listing on 7/13 with *Prime* #12 selling-through 112.2% of orders), and I question strongly the basis of the numbers (Diamond pools "50 retailers from 10 different geographical regions of the world. Five retailers from each region represent three large stores, one medium store, and one small store. All information is based on standard discount plateaus." – I really don't think that 60% of the retailers in this business could be defined as "large"), and they've only just started (two weeks ago, at this writing) listing the overall week's sell-through. But, even with these flaws, this is a great first step in determining what it's *really* like out there, regardless of distributor or publisher hype.

And it looks pretty scary.

Comic book store consultant Mel Thompson suggests that any overall sell-through greater than 70% is profitable, but that we should be aiming for 90%+. For myself, with my particular expenses, I need approximately a 78% sell-through to start earning profit, and it wouldn't surprise me if many of you 40%-off accounts need well in excess of 80%, given that you need a 60% sell-through just to cover the costs of the merchandise (with no other expenses, like rent, or salary thrown in)! You're the only one who can determine your exact needs.

Doing a little "reverse-engineering" on the first nine weeks of reporting, I came up with these inexact figures for over-all sell-through:

The Week of:		
	5/10/94	76.26%
	5/17/94	80.22
	5/24/94	83.47
	5/30/94	79.79
	6/06/94	81.34
	6/13/94	82.84
	6/20/94	81.87
	6/27/94	79.86
	7/04/94	82.29
	7/11/94	78.00
	7/18/94	77.05

What potentially disturbs me the most about these numbers is that, as far as I can tell, Diamond's "Retail Advisory Board" was self-selecting. That is, for the most part, Diamond didn't approach the participating retailers, but they issued an "open call", and had us offer our services to them. I think it's reasonable to assume that the retailers motivated to submit their sales data would also tend to be more sophisticated in their record keeping, and, potentially, better at accurately determining their orders. There's no way to be sure, but my instincts tell me that the reported data will be slightly more rosy then if it were a wholly random sampling.

As near as I can tell (extrapolating from books that I've got nearly exact figures on), *Amazing Spider-Man* is currently selling something like 180,000 copies each month. Diamond lists #391 as having a 76.85% sell-through, #392 as 85.5%, and #393 as 81.77%. If these numbers have any validity whatsoever, then there are some 41,000 copies (!) of #391 floating around the marketplace unsold! Along with 26,000 of #392, and nearly 33,000 copies of #393! Think about it for a second: in a three-month period, we're talking about *one hundred thousand* unsold copies of *one* title! What a flabbergasting level of waste!

Or try this one on for size: the month of June averages out to an 81.47% overall sell-through. The total "order-index" of June's top 100 Diamond books (how the sales relate to *ASM*) is 8111.5%. Again, if *ASM* is selling 180,000 currently, then the Top 100 books sell-in approximately 14 million units, altogether. If June's sell-through is accurate at 81.47%, then we're looking at **two-point-seven million** unsold comics sitting around in our back rooms in the month of June!

I'll admit we're working from several not-altogether provable assumptions (such as *ASM*'s actual sales, and the specific industry-wide overall sell-through), so if it makes you feel any better, cut that number in half (though you just as likely might *double* it!) – we're still looking at more than a million unsold comic books! In one month! With an average cover price of slightly over $2 (the Top 100 tends to skew slightly lower than the overall charts), we're looking at somewhere between twenty-four (to be optimistic) and ninety-six (if we're feeling completely pessimistic) million dollars a year in unsold merchandise sitting in direct market stores! If there are 5000 DM stores these days, then that's somewhere between $5-20,000 dollars that each store (on loose, broad-based average) is taking it in the shorts on unsold material.

I'm very curious to see where these Diamond listings go in three months or so. At that point we should begin to see if some of the member stores have never cycle-sheeted in the past. The percentages *should* begin to creep up, as the stores figure out what they're ordering too many copies of. In the meantime, all of you out there should be taking a very close look at your inventory control systems.

It doesn't have to be fancy computer systems and the like, y'know. I'm still on a paper-based system, after all. But if you don't have a tight handle on what is flowing through your stores, you're cheating yourself...and more importantly, to my mind, you're cheating the rest of the marketplace.

Publishers respond to our orders, so every time you over-order (or under order, for that matter), you're not only hurting yourself, but the rest of the industry, as we send the wrong messages about what the market can and will support.

Think about it, O.K.?

Tilting at Windmills #32
(Originally ran in Comics Retailer #33)

"Small Store Strategy"

So, this *Comics Retailer* "Y month" was all my idea, right? I thought, "Well, that'll be clever: we can all riff on each other's columns, and have a fun change of pace." Since I suggested the idea, I figured I'd get my choice of columns...and I was all set to wail on Costa (14 solid paragraphs of "Clean your bathroom," over and over again). But, of course, the best laid plans, and all that, and I get randomly selected to write Preston's bit. D'oh!

In terms of lampooning, Preston might have the easiest column (after mine!) to do, so I sat down, and did my research, and read all 25 of Preston's published columns in one marathon reading (I'm a trained professional, kids, *don't* try this at home!). I think something might've snapped. Not only didn't I find a hook with which to hang Preston upon (dismissing the far too obvious Telephone jokes), I actually found myself agreeing with 90% of what he wrote. Horrors upon horrors! Preston Sweet and Brian Hibbs actually agree on most subjects (with a minor quibble here and there)? Who woulda thunk it?!?!?

Preston's POV can be summarized like this: it's your store, what *you* want to do with it is more important than anything, and, while we all desire to make money, you *can* do that sufficiently, without necessarily getting larger than you already are. I can't debate that at all.

How's about I tell you a story of my own experiences? Good, I'm glad you agree. When I first opened in 1989, my business plan assumed that by 1994, we'd be making solid plans to open a second location. Bigger is better, yes? Nope. Neil Gaiman said to me, "Brian, if you don't keep growing, there will be a perception that you are standing still, or, worse still, moving backwards." Five years ago, I agreed with that assessment, but, about a year ago, I realized that I'd be trading the enjoyment I receive from day-to-day interaction with the customers for, essentially, a desk job, where my knowledge would be handed to me from effectively middle management. It's hard enough to keep a handle on customer desires and patterns with one store, when you're behind the counter half of the hours the store is open. How much more difficult would it become when you double those hours? Especially given that doubling the hours adds about another 25% of work in the form of paperwork and such.

Even when you're blessed with the greatest employees of all time, like I am, each person *adds* work to your plate, not takes away. Once you start growing, it becomes harder and harder to maintain a status quo in cash flow. For example, the first year we were open, when I worked six days a week, with five hours of help, we had to spend about $1.25 to make $2. Now, that I've got about 60 hours of employee time each week, it takes us spending about $1.60 to make the same $2. This is the law of diminishing returns. While, in theory, employees give you more "free time," that time gets rapidly eaten up with federal and state paperwork, communication, and the like, and you're working that much harder to stay in the same place.

I believe what separates a great store from an O.K. one are the intangibles, like customer service. But, part of being able to offer that service is being in contact with your customers – knowing their likes and dislikes; where they stand on particular issues; what kinds of material they do like and what kinds they *might* like. And the further you get away from one-owner, one-store, the further you drift from understanding exactly what customer service is appropriate to your particular store. In today's market, I'm firmly convinced that being a "self-retailer" is the way to go.

I'm not a "small store" anymore (loosely defined as under $100k in business a year) – I'd call myself "medium-sized" (roughly a quarter of a million gross sales each year), and my platform, in *Tilting at Windmills*, has always to expose the hypocrisy, and greed at play in this marketplace; to fight for what's moral, and correct, and to never lose sight of the fact that although we *are* business-people, *who* we are and *how* we do our job is nearly as important as the financial results of these actions. But that's not the purpose of Small Store Strategy. Rather, the goal here is to provide the "little guy's" perspective, as well as to give suggestions and aid that *other* small stores have implemented to success. Overriding this is the implication that "Do what Thou Wilt shall be the Whole of the Law." Bearing that in mind, let's talk about one area of customer service where you can easily "compete" with the "big guy": subscription services.

Most "subscription" programs (also known as "Pull and Hold," "Saver Boxes," "Folders," and a host of other names) work off the assumption that it's better for your ordering if you have a solid commitment in ordering information from your regular customers, rather than depending solely on rack sales. Unfortunately, most of them are implemented in such a way to make this a little difficult in practical application, because they work off a "standing order" policy.

The problem with standing orders (customers fill out a form one time, and you continually pull from that) is that, these days, they're hardly comprehensive. Looking at the most recent Diamond catalog, we have the following number of items that would "fall through the cracks" on a standing system: 38 brand new titles, seven TPB reprint collections, and seven variant editions. Note that I'm *only* counting Marvel, DC, Dark Horse, Image, Valiant, and Malibu (the "big six"), this doesn't even take into account items from other, smaller publishers – from whom, might I add, you can get your best guaranteed sales from consumers. That's 52 titles that a standing order system will have a hard time dealing with! That also doesn't count the half a dozen or so cancelled items, which you will have to eventually remove from your standing order lists.

Additionally, you can get stuck with material in the time lag between shipping and pick-up with a standing order system. If Jimmy decides he doesn't want *Snotman* anymore, and he's signed up for it, you've got at least two months of orders outstanding before you can even begin to adjust your pull orders to reflect the new reality.

In the old days, this wasn't *so* bad – there were only 150 or so items shipping from the major publishers, and prices were still cheap enough that Jimmy wasn't changing his mind nearly as much each month as to which comics he was going to buy. Not any more!

For nearly a decade, I've worked on a monthly-driven order form (I created the system at another store I was working at before I opened my own). With this system, you create a new form every month, with specific issues and variants listed. That is, Jimmy is ordering *Snotman* #436 in June, #437 in July, #438 in August, rather than merely ordering *Snotman* in perpetuity.

The advantages of this type of system should be clear: you get an immediate, month-to-month feedback of what your customers are wanting, even if they don't verbally communicate this to you. You get a lower default rate, because Jimmy has to be specific when he starts and stops a title, and you can also see, at a glance, whether he's overbudgeted for the month ("Uhhh...Jimmy, are you *sure* you want the $4.95 prestige version of all these books – your order is gonna come to over $100 this month..."), as well as reducing misunderstandings about when a title is added or dropped. And I find that it helps immeasurably when you're writing *your* monthly order.

The down side is, of course, more work for you. Not only do you have to prepare a form once a month (more on that in a mo), and do it *quickly* (the faster the customers get it, the faster you get it back); but you also have to collate that data each and every time a book ships. Back before we got a computer to do this for us, it would take very roughly about an hour and a half to process 100 customers: writing on a sheet of paper the books that are shipping this week, then going through the forms, one at a time, writing the individual customer's names under the appropriate title, so you have an accurate list with which to pull from. Depending on your own skills, that time could be reduced to as little as an hour, or increased to three hours or more. A master list tally sheet (with just quantities, no individual names listed) takes about the same amount of time for the entire month. Adding in the time to create the form, it's somewhere around ten to fourteen hours of additional labor each month (which, needless to say, doesn't *have* to be done behind the counter) to maintain the system. You can calculate your own value of that, but I would say that if you're generating $100 more in sales, or avoiding $100 in losses, because of a more complete data picture, it's probably worth the time.

There are several ways to generate such a form, depending on your level of commitment, and free time to spend. The simplest, of course, is to use your distributor's monthly catalog. The downside to this is three-fold: first, you have to spend x amount of money each month on the catalogs themselves (Diamond charges $1.10 if you order less than 100 copies – I can photocopy my form for something in the neighborhood of 25 cents each); the second is that you're abrogating control of presentation to the distributors (personally, I think it's worth the effort to create your *own* spotlights and focuses that speak to the specific tenor and character of your store); while the third is the sheer unwieldiness of coordinating 56 pages, and some 1300 line-items.

The second method is to take a pair of scissors to the order form, cutting out the columns of titles, issue numbers, and prices, and pasting together your own form. Generally speaking, it's a good idea to try and get everything you choose to list onto one double-sided page. We use a piece of legal-sized paper, folded lengthwise, to create an 8 1/2 by 7" booklet. The benefit to this tack is being able to control the presentation, while the downside is that, unless you're good at cut and paste (unlike me), this can look less than professional. You may also need to do a little reduction photo-copying to get the spacing exact for your format.

When we were using this method, it took me about two hours to generate the form each month.

The third method (and, sorry, this one only works for Diamond accounts, as far as I know) is to get a computer disk from the distributor. The monthly Previews on Disk has the entire month's order in a "comma-delineated" text format. It is a snap to import this to a spreadsheet program, then edit out the columns/titles you have no use for. You then cut and paste as above. When we switched to this method, it would take me less than an hour to generate the form.

The final method (that I've used, at least) is to create a master list of titles shipping, then each month do minor maintenance in adjusting issue numbers, deleting one-shot or discontinued items, and adding new titles. While it's a bear to input all that data initially (took me about eight hours), monthly maintenance can be done in less than half an hour. Of course, like method #3, you need a computer to do his effectively.

While the third and fourth methods can be cut and pasted the low-tech way to create your form, once you've got the data computerized, you can import it into a desktop publishing program to create a very professional looking final product. We use MicroSoft Publisher, and I'm confident that there are several other programs that could suit you.

If there is space to run it, you should find a sample of our efforts somewhere on this page.

You also might want to create a monthly newsletter (or a "tip sheet") to go with your form. Since we use a booklet format, our tip sheet goes inside the form (we vary the color of the paper each month, so we can immediately identify which month is which), and describes, in depth, what our staff thinks of this month's offerings. Whether or not you do a subscription program, you should look very strongly at doing a one-page newsletter: it's one of your best tools to communicate directly to your customers, and establishes a store's character clearly. And it's something the big guy down the block can not easily copy.

I'd go on, but the little word count buzzer has started screaming at me (actually, it started about 5 paragraphs back...), so I must away. Come back to this space next issue when Preston returns, and, with any luck, he won't

laugh at my suggestions to you. Next issue, I'll be firmly ensconced again at the TaW ranch, taking indiscriminate pot-shots at what ever target dares to show its head...be there, won't you?

This is a strange and fucked up "column," mostly because it was one of J.J.'s "gimmicks" for *CR*.

CR, at the time, had four columnists: Me, Bob Gray, Preston Sweet, and Bruce Costa (Bruce still writes for *CR* to this day). The premise of the stunt would be that we would be asked two or three questions by *CR*, each would answer, then we'd "pass our column to the left" and, say, I would comment on Preston's comments while he commented on Bob's. We swapped twice each, I think.

It sorta made for interesting reading, but it's pure hell for reprinting like this.

Anyway, I've only included the bits listed under the "*Tilting*" portion of the stunt – although there are another 1500 words of mine floating around this issue (#34) of *CR*.

One other note: I don't even have the original file for this anywhere – since it was done in several parts. Ended up scanning it and running it through an OCR module. Damn, I love technology!

Tilting at Windmills #33
(Originally Ran in Comics Retailer #34)

Comics Retailer: *It's time for the comics industry's end-of-the-year check-up. Give it to us straight, doc. How many years have we got left? Is this a cyclical recession, or is it indication that something's wrong with the system?*

Brian Hibbs: 1994 was pretty weird year for the direct market. After the "heady days" of 1993, we hit a pretty hard slump. The reasons for this are many-fold, but they can be summed up fairly well in one word: *speculation*. For a little while there, comics looked like a way to make easy money – nearly every company had a "hot" comic, and it appeared that new launches could do no wrong. We were struck by a boom the likes of which we've never seen, and product line after product line, at ever-escalating prices, were foisted upon us unsuspecting retailers, each scrambling to find the next "big book" that we could make a killing on.

And then it ended.

Sales started dropping like flies as the consumers finally realized that they were (and still are, to a large extent!) paying far too much for far too little entertainment value. We have, in large part, moved away from being a truly affordable medium – the average comic book now costs more than a video rental for the night!

We've seen this type of boom and bust before in the black-and-white glut of the 1980s, and we made it through it then. I suspect (desperately want to believe) that we'll make it through again. The difference between the two times is this: when the black-and-white market crashed, it dragged most of the worst offenders down with it, because they were poorly managed and had poor cash flow. However, this time the largest predators were the largest publishers, most of whom, while certainly feeling some pain now, are well-capitalized enough to comfortably weather this storm. This means that the rapacious bastards who saddled us with the poor-selling, low-quality material that precipitated this crisis are the "industry leaders" through the fallow parts. I think it's clear, that although we've gone through one of the biggest rough patches we've ever seen, Marvel, as one example, still hasn't learned the lessons...

So I think we can make it through this if the publishers begin to wise up and ignore the ephemeral lure of "collectibility," and if we, as retailers, take to heart the two lessons we've now sat through on the Evils of the Quick Buck. I don't think we're going to get a third chance.

Having said that, I want to observe that I think we're not completely through the bust yet. After all, summertime, which is traditionally our best selling period (kids not at school and all that) has been, industry-wide, pretty mediocre. Once we get past the November slide and the Post-Christmas Blues, I think we'll have a significantly clearer picture of the real health of the industry. I expect moderate casualties all the way through to next spring.

Comics Retailer: *You've pointed out various threats to the industry before. Which one do you feel poses the **most danger** while being **most overlooked** by the most people?*

Hibbs: I suspect the biggest pitfall facing us in the next year is much like a rose: its alluring charms mask the fact that it's covered in thorns. I'm speaking, of course, of Big Money Entering the Direct Market.

For years we've been asking for attention from the rest of the world – "Oh, if only Mr. and Mrs. John Q. Public were aware of comics! Think about how much better that would be for all of us here! Movie deals. Licensing arrangements. Comics Characters emblazoned on every kid in America's sneakers!" Well, there's an old proverb (Chinese?) that says, "Beware what you ask for. You just might get it."

The thing is, when we were "small and unnoticed," most of the people were here because of *love* of the medium. The people who see dollar signs couldn't really care less about comics – it's just another commodity to them. And, if they strip-mine our land and make in uninhabitable for future generations, they don't much care, because they got what they wanted.

Be watchful against short-term thinking. If a hungry tiger lives in a castle filled with resplendent gems and treasures beyond ken, don't get blinded by avarice. The tiger can eat you just like he eats anyone else who steps within his domain. And please don't say, "Well, he's not going to eat *me*. I'm smarter and quicker than *that*," because you're not.

Bruce Costa: I agree with Brian's analysis, if only to say that it's like looking at a photo album and wishing the "old days" were here again. I'd like to suggest some steps for addressing the new days, to make sure you don't end up as food in a tiger's belly.

It's simple, really, and it's a concept with which every gamer is familiar. Just role-play the part of the larger retailer. Let's pretend you were looking to place a large, well-capitalized comics shop somewhere in your city. Where, would you put it? There are probably several appropriate locations, and I doubt that they'd be stand-alone stores. Then, simply imagine that the store is already there. With some time, and a careful analysis of your mailing list (there's no end to the usefulness of a thorough mailing list.) you can probably figure out, with a small margin of error, how much of your business would be lost in each scenario.

After losses are figured, develop a plan of action for each situation. How can you be different? How can you complement a high-end store, thereby giving your customers reason to shop at your store anyway? What can you offer that they don't, or won't? And don't say a friendly staff and a clean environment. Those are lowest common denominators. You've got to come up with something exciting and not easily duplicated, like a special service, product line or premium. Force yourself to develop 20 such ideas and you'll find that one or two are worth doing. Do your planning in writing, and file it away for an emergency. You might even choose to put some of the ideas into effect right away.

By the way, would that hypothetical large chain store prefer your spot to any other in town? If the answer is no, you might want to figure out why you should move to the locations you've targeted, as opposed to focusing on why you're not there.

Hibbs: A minor note that "friendly staff and a clean environment" are not *yet* the lowest common denominator in this business. Would that it were so.

I'll also note, for new or first-time retailers reading this that there are sometimes practical reasons for not getting the most "prime" retail space. In San Francisco, for example, if I were eight blocks up, on the commercial corridor of Haight Street, my rent would be at least twice as high, with the necessity of having greater overhead costs (more staff to adequately manage the increased customer counts, higher insurance premiums, *etc.*). My calculations show me that I make a greater profit with my slightly-off-the-path location than I would on the local commercial drag. Always remember: gross sales are reasonably meaningless, in and of themselves – profitability is what counts.

Comics Retailer: *It's nearly 1995. What are the topics/rallying cries/buzzwords that you think are least helpful to the resolution of this industry's real problems?*

Hibbs: My first choice would be "hot." It's meaningless and is the Huckster's tool. I'd also get rid of "enhancements," if only because they're usually not.

I just want to note that this was published in February of '95. All of you cats who are singing about TPs now? Pft! I'm half a decade in front of you!

Tilting at Windmills #34
(Originally ran in Comics Retailer #35)

I feel like I've been gone forever. From your point of view, you've had month after month of rampaging hippie spewing forth his opinions, but from my side this is the first real *Tilting* I've written in a couple of months – we took time out for "Y month" (and, hey! I think it worked!), and the first draft of the roundtable was done concurrently, so it might take me a little while to get back into the scheme of things here, after a two-month "vacation."

Since I last wrote this thing, the market has gotten significantly worse, not better. I'm writing this December 3rd, and early indications are that '94 will go down in comics history as not only "The Year Without a Summer"... but *also* "The Year Without a Christmas Time." I understand from a fair number of my brethren that *Magic* (the card game) has been keeping the market afloat, to a great extent, but as far as I can tell, *Magic* stopped flowing into the stores long before Thanksgiving. We're coming up to what are historically the worst selling months of the year (January and February), so I think that as we move toward summer '95 things are going to get a lot worse before they get any better.

Without the benefit of any clear cash-cow (*Mr. Punch could* have been that for Comix Experience, but a heavy allocation with no reorder availability cut that one off at the knees), I wonder how a lot of stores are going to make it to April, because the evidence is that most of us are still relying on this week's comics to pay next week's bills...hardly a healthy situation for a retailer to be in. "Industry Experts" claim that we've lost around 1000 stores over 1994. I'm gonna go out on a limb and suggest that we might be losing *another* 1000 stores because of the first quarter of 1995.

All this month I've been reading things in the industry press that say things like, "Well, we're finally down to the *actual* readership, with no speculators left." Sorry, folks, I don't think we're there quite yet. The Speculators have just mutated slightly – we're still infested with a preponderance of low-level grifters and hustlers...they're just at flea markets now, rather than standing in our stores. There are, sad to say, people who still believe that comics retailing can make you rich. Hah! It *can* provide you with a comfortable life-style, but rich? Nah...

We've got another 6 months to a year to slog through before I believe we'll have any meaningful, or significant recovery, but that timing is going to depend completely on what *we* do. That ol' cowpoke, Beau Smith, posted a message on CompuServe recently to the effect of, "Hey, stop whining – we all know the market is screwed! Let's start suggesting *solutions*." So, with the little voice of Beau in the back of my heard (now, *that* is a scary thought!), and in the spirit of the (to me) impending holiday season steering my hand, allow me to make a few suggestions on ways we can fix this market:

For Retailers: *Stop abrogating your decision making processes to the distributors and publishers!*

It continually surprises me how often I hear, "I let my customers decide what I order." The market has changed to the point where I believe you can no longer be reactive in the way you represent your stores – you must be proactive. When the apex of your promotional energy goes into tallying up distributor catalog orders, or listening to what your customers say after reading *Wizard*, then you've given up your control. To use a fairly clumsy analogy, it's still your car, you've just given someone else the keys. It's kind of stupid to whine about how bad their driving is – just kick them out of the front seat!

Try this experiment: block out one day this week to study your stock. Take this seriously! Give instructions to your staff, to your family, to your friends, to treat this as though you're on vacation, and completely unreachable except in the most dire of dire emergencies (like "the store is burning down", not, "Hey, boss, there is a Golden Age collection for sale.") Pull one each of this week's new comics (even if you only have one copy!) from the shelves, and start reading. You should have at least 50 comics, and eight hours of blocked-out time. If you have less than 50 titles from this week's batch, supplement with other titles from last week, or the week before.

As you read, try to not to let sales hype or your sales figures affect the way you approach the material. This is a difficult thing to do sometimes, but it's an important element in this experiment. As you finish each title, put it in one of three piles: "Wow! Excellent! *This* is *why* I read and sell comics," "O.K., but not brilliant," and "Yeesh! That *sucks*!" You have permission to not go past page six, on titles that fall into the "sucks" category (if it's bad, you'll know by page six...). Don't add "ifs..." or any qualifications to your separating out books. What's important here is how you *personally* feel about the material.

After you've divided the titles, hopefully you'll have at least two titles in your "excellent" pile. *Now* look at your sales figures. Are the books that *you* think are the highest quality, the most engaging and entertaining, your *best* selling titles (in your store's Top Ten)? If so, then you're excused from the rest of this section – your tastes closely mirror your customers, and you've just been completely validated in your approach. But, if your personal favorites don't match with your sales patterns...well, my friend, you've got a *focus*, and a *goal* to achieve.

Unless you've burned your customers, they should be looking towards you as a source of guidance and news. *Use* this ability to affect your sales – set yourself modest goals to start ("I'm going to raise this by five copies this month"), and dedicate yourself to achieving them. Give your "excellent" books the best rack placement in your store; create a rack of their own to help spotlight them; write up a one-page review you can xerox and hand out to your customers; offer a money-back guarantee on the material; be creative and innovative, and, above all else, let your enthusiasm shine through. If you believe in a title, you can't *help* but infect your customers with that same joy.

In order to help you pay for the greater stock, and greater attention paid (but again – *be modest*...don't think you can double a book's sales in a month...go for small quantities, steadily applied), save money by reducing orders on the material that was in your "sucks" pile. Don't keep backstock on material you don't believe in, material that doesn't reflect what you think your store should be.

The core of this is determining, *for yourself*, what kind of store you want to be, what type of material you want to stock. You'll probably find that quite often that the distributor catalogs, or *Wizard* magazine, don't completely mesh with *your* vision of what you should be selling. And that's O.K. In fact, that's better, significantly better, because it's the first step to creating a unique voice for your store, that *no one* can copy or mimic — it's the first step toward being truly independent from the rise and fall of what others do.

Ask yourself: what are you promoting in June, 1995? "Uhhh...," most retailers will say, "...what's being solicited that month?" This, I believe, is a very short-sighted attitude. It's not that you *won't* want to push some "new this month" item, just that you don't *have* to be tied to a publisher or distributor's push. If you think, for example, that *Flash* is a really swellegent comic, you don't *need* a high-profile story arc, or a foil-stamped cover for *you* to push it...in fact, I think those are often the *worst* times to push something, because your customers are likely to believe at first that you're handing them a line.

But no matter who you are, where you're located, what your customer base is, sincere, honest passion and belief about what you're selling is *always* a strong component of sales. Use your power! Don't hand it off to others!

I also think publishers should do this, as well, even if they're more hamstrung with, "I have a personal relationship with Joe Penciller," or "As a company, we want Franchise A to succeed."

For Publishers: *Think small, and steady, and always in the long term*

There's only so much product that customers can, or *want to,* absorb. For long-time health, it's far better to under-supply want, rather than over-supply it. I'm of the opinion that no character, franchise, or linked imprint should have more than one book per week shipping. And only then, in the most significant and unusual of circumstances. *Superman, Batman, Spider-Man,* and *X-Men* – these are all strong enough to handle four title lines, but I can't think of another that deserves more than two titles...and even then, that's probably one too many. Why are there three *Justice League* books? Three (plus innumerable one-shots and specials) *Punisher* titles? Hell – why are there some 14 titles that are identified as *Spider-Man?* I wrote about this before – less is more. You make a franchise too unwieldy for a consumer to *afford* to get involved, and you'll just end up cannibalizing your *own* sales.

For "universes" like Valiant, or Ultraverse, where the individual titles don't *necessarily* have anything to do with one another, I look at it in terms of end dollars – more than $5 or $6 a week is too much to ask for from most consumers. This translates into three $2 titles, or two $2.50 titles. More than that, and, again, you start to cannibalize your own sales.

My final piece of advice for publishers (though this has even a smaller chance of being implemented) is that I don't believe any periodical is worth publishing anymore if it's not *intended* to be paperbacked down the line, unless it's part of a franchise that's been running since the beginning of time. I think all new titles should be looked at with that criteria in mind: When you start a new book, do you intend to collect each arc, a year or so after it's initial publication? If not, why are you clogging up the shelves, the catalogs, the traffic flow in your offices with some-thing you evidently don't believe has any real long-term commercial potential? As a retailer, I'm far more likely to support the serialization of a Sandman, or a Cerebus, or a Sin City, because I know that it doesn't just mean a sale today – I'll be able to sell these titles in perpetuity, and I'm making a long-term commitment to the health of my store, and the industry as a whole.

Well, those are my suggestions, such as they are. Next month, we'll see The Year in Review. I know *I* can't wait. In the meantime, take a close look at the way you do business. Are you working toward creating something strong, and vital, and singular, for yourself? Or are you just playing Business as Usual, futilely hoping the rest of the market will fix itself to suit you?

It's your choice.

Ah, 1995. The Year That Fucked It All.

Here in 2002 we're still playing out the ramifications of '95. We will be for years to come.

Estimates say that perhaps as many as half of all comic book shops went away in '95. Think about **that** for a few moments, will ya?

I got the scenario about half right, I think – and the other half was much much worse than I ever could have imagined.

Tilting at Windmills #35
(Originally ran in Comics Retailer #36)

I was going to write one of those dopey Year-in-Review type columns this time, but thank the Lord that on Christmas Eve word came through of the biggest news story of the year – a story that, frankly, makes the rest of the year look like no great shakes; a story that threatens to fundamentally change the way that we look upon the business – I'm talking, of course, of the Marvel Entertainment Group (MEG) buy-out of Heroes World Distribution Co. (HWDC).

Before I go on: *This column is the sole and singular opinion of Brian Hibbs! It contains some conjecture, as well as rumor...and any datum that is not clearly noted as fact should be taken with a grain of salt! You should in no way, shape, or form interpret these opinions as necessarily having any basis in fact, or reflecting any "inside information!" Nor should you believe that these opinions are in any way endorsed by* Comics Retailer, *Krause Publications, or any employee or owner of Krause – they just give me the space...I fill it up! No animals were harmed in the writing of this column!* Tilting at Windmills *is filmed in front of a live studio audience!*

There. That should satisfy the lawyers.

As we all should know by now, as of December 28th, it was officially announced that MEG bought HWDC. How is this going to affect us?

The first thing to figure out is: Why would a publisher buy a distributor? I can identify three likely reasons: #1) You want to "bail out" a failing company, to continue an atmosphere of competition. I suspect we can write this concept off the list – my understanding was that HWDC was in a sufficiently O.K. position to weather 1995, simply because they didn't expand in 1994 like most other distributors. #2) You want to create a new profit center. Not *completely* beyond the realms of possibility, but given the retail climate as we end 1994, I judge this to be unlikely – the market is collapsing (sorry, there's no other word for it...), and it's likely to get worse throughout the first half of 1995, long before it gets any better. Especially given that HWDC controlled what appears to be around 8% of a 600 million dollar industry – that makes their share something on the order of 48 million dollars...with what I assume to be a minimum purchase price of 10 million dollars. That makes HWDC a long-term investment, and I think it's fair to say that such a purchase doesn't exactly fit in with the typical MEG acquisition.

This makes the third option the most likely one: You want to control your own distribution. As it has been relayed to me by more than one reputable source, MEG has trimester-based contracts with its distributors, and said contracts expire in either April or May. So I expect MEG to simply not renew these contracts when they come back up. Effectively making HWDC their *sole* distributor.

"Far fetched!" you say? "HWDC can't be geared up to handle that kind of volume!" you cry? "They don't have regional warehouses!" you exclaim? To which I reply..."So?"

If MEG and HWDC were to switch to a set of what are in effect Street Dates, they wouldn't need to have more than one shipping warehouse, with a *large* bank of telephones.

Here's how I see it working: HWDC would have nearly 'round the clock workers pulling and processing orders. They would ship out the West coast on, say, Monday; the Midwest on Wednesday; and the East Coast on Friday. All shipments would go out through one shipping company (let's assume UPS), and they'd be COD. The vast majority of retailers would receive their books by the following Monday from the start of shipping. Anyone who didn't could be minorly adjusted to make the arrival. If you received your order before Monday, you'd be asked to hold it until then. Failure to do so would result in your future shipments being cut off. If you didn't know, this is more or less the book- and record-store paradigm, so it has a precedent.

One would no longer go to the local warehouse to pick your own reorders – it would be handled by a phone call on a FIFO (first in, first out) basis. All reorders would be shipped with your next scheduled shipment.

None of this would be especially revolutionary...and I expect it to be more efficient, on some levels (reorders, for example, would not need to spend a week in distributor compiling limbo), but it's got a couple of downsides, as well. Primarily among those would be the presumed COD shipping. I think it's fairly safe to say that MEG doesn't have a lot of account info at their fingertips – they may know who and where we are, but it's unlikely that they'll have data like our credit levels and payment history. For the first several months of such a plan, it is extremely likely that they'll start us from "scratch," with no credit extended. Now, for a lot of us, this isn't much of an issue: as far as I've been told, most accounts are COD anyway, right now. And the majority of those with terms are "net seven." But for those of us with terms (I personally have been on "net 30" for *years*), this could provide a hard short-term cash-flow pill to swallow.

Another possible problem area could be discounts. As above, I expect HWDC to eliminate (at least initially) the concept of discount plateaus, for simple expediency's sake. Now, given that the numerical majority (though not, I think, in terms of buying power) of retailers are buying at a relatively low discount (50% or less), I'm going to assume that this discount is more likely to be lower than higher. On this point, at least, I'm willing to admit I could be wrong – if HWDC offered 60% on all MEG product, they'd still likely be more profitable than they are now (we're talking something on the order of three to five points), but I suspect, with the need to look at the bottom line at MEG, it's more realistic to assume a flat 50% discount (or perhaps net pricing in the same place...) UPS COD, free freight as an economically viable package.

Again, this deal comes out looking a lot more attractive to the smallest of stores. But to the upper level of the retail community, this would represent a severe hit to the bottom line.

Of course, the "benefit to small stores" assumes there isn't some sort of minimum purchases required – either in terms of quantities (how about you need to buy books in increments of ten?), in terms of a percentage of line (what if you need to order at least 50% of their entire output to qualify?), or, perhaps even both. If a minimum purchase is required on this scale, I suspect that current distributors won't be *completely* cut out of the loop — they'll end up working essentially as sub-distributors, buying at that same flat 50% discount, and reselling to us at 40%.

Implicit in MEG being exclusive to HWDC is the assumption that other publishers would want to pull out from HWDC. If you were DC would you want MEG to be receiving between 5 and 25% of your cover price? But, honestly, I don't think HWDC will *want* to distribute other publishers.

For distributors, this is quite nearly a death sentence. MEG represents something like 40% of Diamond and Capital's income (with Malibu factored in). Distributor margins are fairly tight on MEG product, because they're distributing so darn much of it, so that type of a loss could be quite catastrophic for them. Two solutions exist:

Looking for a publisher to buy *them* out.

Downsizing.

I hope for the latter, because the former would break the comics market into armed camps, but either solution will make for drastic changes in the way we do business.

Within a year, I predict, we'll be *forced* to do business with two or more distributors – and even if the unilateral power of MEG doesn't cut your discount, meeting extant distributor plateaus probably will. For example, if I lost the MEG portion of my business through Diamond, I'd drop from 55 to 52.5%. Those two and a half points represent a large portion of my profit, at my current size. Certainly, one could adjust to the new world order, but the short-term impact could be fairly drastic.

In addition to greater costs of doing business, I'm deeply concerned about the loss of advocacy. As much as I feel current distributors don't work to the retailer's best advantage in most cases, they've always been a good "buffer" between retailers and publishers. They have the ability to set some policies in the ways product is handled, and they lend a certain amount of clout to retailer complaints. But, a publisher-controlled distributor has no such concerns. For example, we could have a scenario where MEG decided to go back to the old "it's not returnable until it's *90* days late" rule. Or, they could take offense at something you write in an industry trade magazine, and cut you off from receiving MEG product, altogether (hey, hey, folks, let's not forget what happened to poor Walter Wang and Comics Unlimited...). They are now in a position where they can dictate terms to us that we will have no choice to but follow.

A couple of other thoughts: historically distributors have acted as the "banks" of the industry, extending (or adding) credit when retailers were cash-poor; releasing even partial shipments when payments got behind, to keep the cash flowing through our doors. Although I'm proud to say I've never had to avail myself of this service, I know a lot of you have. If shipments are arriving off the back of the UPS truck, the UPS man ain't gonna accept partial payment, the truck driver ain't gonna extend you terms. If you come up a little short, you may be going without merchandise that week. Or if you accidently bounce a check, you may face your product flow being permanently cut off.

I think it's safe to say that before a year has passed on the HWDC deal, we'll be looking at a vastly different way we do business, and we'll more than likely be less profitable, as a result. This business has been, and will continue to be, difficult for retailers: the uncertainty of having to order product sight unseen months before it arrives is enormously large. And I'm very afraid that the hassles in dealing with more than one distributor, with having less distributor accountability and competition, with the myriad of problems this acquisition will cause us all...it's just going to get more and more difficult at a time when we desperately need relief more than anything.

In the meantime you should be taking a hard look at your store, and the various options you're going to have when the changes start a flyin'. The only practical suggestion I can have for you is to not be foolish enough to instantly kneejerk your business away from MEG to another publisher. Take it from someone who knows: it takes between six months to two years to change the minds and patterns of your customers. Sure thing, work towards that day, but don't expect it to happen overnight.

Take care of yourselves out there – the streets just got a whole lot rougher. I hope we're all still here, able to talk, a year from now. Maybe then I'll finally write one of those dumb Year-in-Review things...

Tilting at Windmills #36
(Originally ran in Comics Retailer #37)

Retailing comics is a difficult job in the best of circumstances.

And, of course, the last year has not been the best of circumstances.

So why on earth do publishers insist on making it harder and harder for us to sell comics?

In this week's shipment (2/1), for example we received three *Batman* titles, four *Elfquest* books, two issues of *Ultraverse Premiere* (that's the nearly double-priced flipbook), four *Spider-Man* titles, three different *Star Trek* comics, and a staggering 14 Image titles! And this is not an exceptional circumstance! Most weeks we have some sort of stacked shipping.

Is it just that publishers are idiots who have no one with recent retail experience? Or is there an easier explanation, like they're too busy to pay attention to such minor details?

Two issues ago, I suggested that most franchises should be smaller, simply because the consumers don't have the money anymore, and when you ask them to make choices, you give them the option to choose to leave. This bears repeating (probably every month!), but if you insist on having large, unwieldy franchises, at least accept the responsibility of evening your shipments throughout the month! By stack-shipping, you make it even harder for retailers to sell your wares. Can't you see that? The customer isn't going to "come back next week" to pick up the titles they can't afford – next week there's a whole 'nother passel of new comics vying for their attention!

Figure it out!

Look at the way our marketplace has been collapsing (and as much of a happy face as distributors try and put on it, that's the cold fact: it's collapsing) – I'll certainly grant you that retailers are not as savvy or capitalized as they perhaps should be, but I think there's an equal measure of responsibility in making sure they have the basic tools needed to sell your material – especially in this market, in this climate.

Part of this is, as I said, is making sure your material is salable, whether that includes breadth of line, or timely (and logical!) shipping. Pricing is another component — in the April shipping catalogs (still new, as I write this), all the DC books go up 25 cents or more. Ouch! The bar of entry level price points has now been raised to $1.75...and within a year it will likely be $1.95 – where does it stop? It's no longer uncommon for a book to be priced at $2.95. When we cross that $3 barrier on a regular basis, we're going to be screwed. Who has that kind of money anymore? Price resistance has already set in around $2.00 for most books – my customers are buying fewer and fewer titles, and I bet the same is true for you – they can no longer justify the expense! Who is going to buy *Darkstars* or *Anima* for $2.25 (plus sales tax, at least in California, that's $2.44!). And these titles' sales are already poor enough.

We're no longer competitive with other entertainment forms, and that's simply got to change if we expect to continue into the 21st Century!

With what are likely to be the same effects, though in a more subtle manner, is Valiant's bi-weekly shipping schedule – where customers were being asked to spend $2.50 to follow a character each month, they're now being asked to pony up $5. Am I the only one who sees a problem with this experiment?

C'mon folks, "Bigger! Better! Faster! More!" is not our best technique for survival in the marketplace. Retailers have been falling left and right, and more are failing every day. B!B!F!M! has sent a swath of destruction right down the middle of this business, and everyone left is hanging on for dear life! Help us out here – don't just try and force your latest pogrom down our throat.

And don't try to pretend to support us, while actually giving nothing. It makes my blood boil when I see "deals" like Marvel's "Blockbuster Bonus Plan" (April 1995's *Sales To Astonish*): "Buy 100 copies of the red-hot *Tales of the Marvels: Blockbuster*, and you get FOR FREE: one copy of the award-winning *Marvels* TPB!" Can you believe it? $600 dollars worth of comics, and you get a $20 paperback (which probably cost Marvel far less than $5 to manufacture)! How cheap can you be? Besides that's not much of an incentive – if you consider that the last *Marvels* spin-off, *Strange Tales*, sold something on the order of 75,000 copies.

(Digression: if you can get one solid number, you can figure out backwards what a title's sales are. Neil Gaiman tells me that *Angela* #1 (on the same order form as *Strange Tales*) sold roughly 225,000 copies – this would mean that each point on the Diamond sales chart [*Angela* came in at 181.2] was worth roughly

1250 copies sold (I get 1241.72, but lets be kind). Neil also informed me that *Angela #2* did around 160,000 [placing with an OIN of 144.3]. This means for the January books, one OIN point equals something like 1115 copies sold [1108.8 according to the calculator] – about an 11% drop...in one month! There is no question the market is collapsing! *Sandman #50* sold nearly 250,000 copies, and placed #50 on the Diamond list – that means 49 comics sold more than a quarter of a million copies that month! As I said, *Angela #1* sold 225k, and placed #5 – that means, almost a year and a half later, less than four comics sold more than a quarter mil! If that's not collapsing, what is? End Digression)

If you figure there are roughly 4000 comics shops, this means the average comic shop sold well less than 20 copies of *Strange Tales* (18.75, on the calculator) – given the diminishing market and diminishing returns on similar projects, we could be looking at well below 15 copies per average store. Given this kind of average sale, how many retailers will be buying 100 copies? The largest 5%? Less? I don't work for Marvel (no duh!), so I don't know what their goal is, but doesn't it make more sense to do sales incentives that most retailers could make? Maybe in 20 or 25 copies increments? Few retailers I know are going to order more than five to ten copies to meet an incentive plan. 4000 retailers each ordering two copies more than they would have to meet a 20-unit incentive will do a lot more for the bottom line than 200 retailers each ordering ten copies to meet a 100-unit incentive.

And let's not even get into Marvel's attempts to sell us promotional material! You want me to sell your books? Well, you damn well better give the tools I need to do that.

Is it just me? None of this is exactly rocket science, folks! We're pissing off the older reader, and we're pricing ourselves out of the hands of the younger readers! Can't anyone see this? Every month I look at the order form, and I shake my head with sadness – comics are seldom sold as mere entertainment anymore. No, they're "events," or "sagas." My customers don't want it anymore. Hell, nobody's customers do! Look at the sales figures!

A lot of publishers bitch (rightfully so!) about how the retailers let down their side of the game, but can't you people see how screwed we are right now? I haven't been hurt nearly as bad as some of my brethren, this last year, but even I start getting scared when I see that January of 1995 was my lowest grossing month since April, 1991 (!) Since you can't fix our problems, the least you can do is not make them worse: ship the books in a sensible pattern (all the time, not just most of the time!); don't overload your franchises; keep prices affordable (even with paper cost increases! This time you have to eat that cost); help us grow with reasonable incentives; and give us the tools we need to sell your material.

It's not that hard, is it?

Tilting at Windmills #37
(Originally ran in Comics Retailer #38)

How I learned to love the bomb

There are days it just doesn't pay to be a columnist.

Take today for example. I asked John Miller to hold my deadline to the last possible moment this month, because I would be (or, probably, more accurately, I am) at DC's fourth annual Retailer Representative Program's meeting in Nashville. I was kinda hoping, since they paid to get some 60 or so of the most influential retailers in one room, that they'd give us some sort of announcement as to what the status of distribution might be.

The best laid plans of mice and men.

So, I'm sitting in my hotel room, waiting for check-out time (two and a half hours from now. D'oh!), trying to bang out these words so John won't have to rip out his hair at the prospect of a blank page. But I don't have a lot to say.

No, that's not precisely accurate. I simply don't have any *news*. As I said, the best laid plans....

But I do still have *opinions*. Hell, the day I don't have opinions is the day I throw in the towel. And I'm not prepared to do that quite yet.

Now, it's entirely possible that when you see this column three weeks from now that DC will have made the final announcement of their distribution plans, and that, as a result, other publishers have made their plans (I don't think it's any state secret that Dark Horse and Image, at least, are essentially waiting to hear what DC does before they make their final decisions), but as of the minute I'm writing this, such things are still up in the air.

However, it's not impossible to speculate on their motives and their likely moves. I think it's safe to say, based as much on what they didn't say as what they did, that the likely plan right now is for DC to arrange an exclusive distribution deal, probably with Diamond.

As near as I can gather, the primary reason for this action will be to "fix" some of the problems that we're facing: namely, in the short term, to keep retailer's discount structures more or less intact, and over the longer haul, to overhaul the reorder system so that we can get more reasonable fill rates, reducing, in essence, our exposure to, and risk in, ordering the volume of merchandise we do, sight unseen.

While these are, of course, noble goals, I strongly question the ultimate value of a unilateral system of "my way, or the highway." Naturally, when one distributor becomes the sole choice in getting a given publisher's wares, we lose most factors of competition – particularly the ones that matter the most: advocacy and free movement. We've enjoyed a circumstance over the better part of the last decade where if one distributor didn't give us the service we wanted or needed, we could use their competition as a cudgel to get better service. Either you give us what we want, or we walk. Exclusivity will punch a gaping hole a mile wide and six miles deep in our individual abilities to have and receive advocacy. And, as such, I think it's a fairly horrible model to base our businesses upon. Capitalism, and a free market, depend upon strong and healthy competition, to avoid devolving into WeSaySo.

So, if we're to lose our free market on a distribution level, what does that leave us with? Well, as long as you're willing to work for it, we're unlikely, in the short term, to lose the free market of publishers and product.

If DC does as they claim, and preserves the discounting structure (or perhaps, more accurately, adjusts the discount structure so that our current levels stay intact, no matter how many sources we may end up using), then they just bought us enough time to get our own shit together. They are not the Great White Hope by any means whatsoever, but they're buying us the breathing room we need right now.

Oh, let's not be too optimistic: sometime in the next twelve months, our overall discounts will almost certainly drop by 5%, or perhaps more. But, instead of that happening in July, when Marvel pulls out (coitus interruptus, don'cha know?), it might now happen in December or later (just watch, though: DC won't be able to do the deal the way they want, we keep the old system, in the new order, and all our discounts plummet. Retailers take to the streets, pitchforks and torches in tow, demanding my blood for being wrong – another damn reason I sometimes hate writing these things, even with my shortened deadlines. A fortune teller I'm not!) What this means is that we've got us a grace period, in which to change, transform, and survive.

Who would've thought that Paul Levitz and Dave Sim would ever think alike about our marketplace (don't worry, folks, this may seem like a digression, but actually, it's well on the point)? I mean, both men are smart and passionate about our medium, but their background, focus, and directions within the industry could not be more diametrically opposed. But both have said recently something that could be paraphrased thusly: "As a retailer you make a lot of choices in what and how you stock your store. But, historically (at least, as much as the recent market could be said to have a 'history'), few retailers have been clearly focused on what kind of store they want to run. The day of the 'full-service comic shop' is gone, if it ever really was here, and what you choose not to stock is nearly as important as what you do. There are products on the marketplace, even ones from, and this is the important bit, my company, that not all retailers should try to stock. Because if you do try to carry it all, that increases the chance that you're going to marginalize your cash flow and rate of return until you go out of business." Although, being a comics retailer, I can see that it's not quite as easy as they seem to believe to pinpoint with brilliant intensity the kind of store you want to be, I think they're right that, as an industry, we've barely begun to take the first baby steps towards deciding what exactly it is we want to be when we grow up.

You don't have to carry a full line of Marvels, unless you're a Marvel Store. You don't have to carry a full line of DCs, unless you're a DC store. Hell, you don't have to a full line of Vertigos, unless you're a Vertigo store. And, you know what? Even if you do decide to align yourself with one company or another, even then, you don't have to support the entire line! I don't think I'm alone in believing that *Blackwulf*, or *Gunfire*, or *Kid Eternity*, to pick three recent examples from each faction named above, have "Dog" written all over them, but still most of us signed off on each of these, to some extent, because we see ourselves as "Marvel stores" or "DC stores" or "Vertigo stores." But we're *not*! (However much we may choose to fervently believe that.) Moreover, we *shouldn't be*! What we should be is on the cover of this magazine: Comics Retailers. The questions you need to ask yourself right now is "what are my strengths?", and "What kind of a store do I want to be?" But you should never (or at least nearly never) align yourself around publishers. Genres, yes. Creators, yes. Characters, even, yes. But not *publishers*. Publishers aren't (and shouldn't *ever* be) what you sell. You sell *comics*. And if there is one lesson the last five years have hopefully taught us, it is that not all Marvel comics are good, and not all DC comics are bad, as well as the reverse of that. And that's a lesson we need to re-acknowledge every month when we fill out those order forms.

So that's where we have our freedom of movement, and the power we can wield – not in what the mechanism of delivering product is (which should be merely a logistical problem), but what material we carry and stock, and why. We've got a little breathing room to make these choices, and I'm sure the next year will find more than a few of us making the wrong choices, but I hope the wheels have at least started gearing up in your head to how you're going to face the coming revolution. And always remember, it doesn't have to be a "Marvelution," or a "Dcution," but the revolution is on it's way, whether you want it to or not.

Marvel may have invaded Poland, but DC holds the Atom bomb. And like any good "weapon of peace", that bomb forces us to re-evaluate we view the world, and our place in it. The power to choose for you has always been in your hands. It's time to use it.

a   r   t   i   c   l   e

3 8

Tilting at Windmills #38
(Originally ran in Comics Retailer #39)

So, I'm a little pissed.

O.K., that's not a big surprise, I 'spose.

I'm going after Marvel this month, and Marvel alone, so let's get this disclaimer stuff outta the way: these are my opinions, and mine alone. They don't necessarily reflect those of Krause Publications, or any employee thereof. Anything not specifically marked as fact should be considered conjecture! If you're the kind of cry-baby that can't take a little ragging, well do something to me, not Krause. I've been asked to not just dun any one organization, but I'm breaking that request of my own volition. John never tells me what to write (nor does he censor me), and your wrath should be aimed at me, not him, Maggie or Greg.

There. That wasn't so hard, was it?

I wanted originally to call this column "Do The Math," with an emphasis on analyzing your Marvel purchases with a hard eye at what your bottom line would be. But after a few moments of reflection, I realized that all I could tell you is how to determine what your discount would have been, not what it is going to be.

Oh sure, we've got a handy little chart of Marvel's projected discount, and the various "incentives," but they don't really tell you one damn thing – in the end, you don't have any idea of what your discount is going to be in, say, December.

That's the insidious bit of this New World Order – you can't plan for it, you can only react.

Oh, sure, you can, more or less, determine what your basic discount is going to be – assuming Marvel doesn't decide to "move the goalposts" every quarter, at least. But you're gonna have no idea if you can meet their incentives or not! Don't believe me? Well, how are the incentives determined? The "full line support" bonus is determined by, well, full-line support. If you don't know what the full-line is, how can you know if you're going to be able to support it? What if (a purely hypothetical) Marvel decides to create three spin-offs of, say, *Fantastic Force*. Will you (can you) be able to support them all? What if they decide in September to produce eight TPBs a week? Matt Ragone, at the San Francisco Marvelution meeting stated that TPBs would be included for the purpose of supporting full-line. Will you (can you) support them all?

Or what about the "Sales growth" bonus – Marvel has stated that "sales growth" will be a function of the product mix that month gauged against a "base month" – but they get to determine how you should be performing. Your "incentive discount" exists at, shall we say, their suffrage. Their numbers will not be based upon (if *Sales to Astonish* is any indication) where we are, but rather where Marvel thinks we should be – dissimilar numbers to be sure. But the real point is, you won't know what that incentive level is until you get the catalog for the month.

Even the "dealer loaders" become problematic – what if they decide one month that the loaders should be 25 copies each of *Barbie Fashion*, *Ravage 2099*, *Fantastic Force*, and *Dr. Who magazine*. Will you meet those minimums (can you)?

How this effects you is in your ability to walk into a bank and ask for a loan – most financial institutions are going to ask you for a business plan, with your projected cash flow for at least a year. But, if Marvel is any significant portion of your business, you've now lost the ability to do this.

Or how about Marvel underwriting the expansion of chains, and buying you out? The quickest way to "grow" your business is not roll-up-your-sleeves hard work and dedication – it's buying up smaller businesses (Marvel sure knows this lesson – hasn't the majority of their growth in the last 18 months come from purchasing other companies as opposed to growing their own business?) Let's say I'm a twelve-store chain that does a million dollars a month in Marvel retail business. I want the 2% growth bonus, but my sales are declining. 2% of my sales are $20k. If I go to Joe's Comics Hole, and offer him $19k to get out, take his bills with him, and give me his storefront and customer base (and I think most of the "Joe's" of the world would take the deal in a heartbeat), I've just made $1000 of Marvel's money for doing nothing! Even if the-store-formerly-known-as Joe's Comics Hole goes out of business next month, I've still made a profit!

Sure, there's a point of diminishing returns, where the growth bonus gained offsets the short-term purchase of a store – but where is that? 50 stores? 100?

Terry Stewart said at the SF meeting, perhaps apocryphally, that he had over 20 retailers, on the first four tour stops alone, offer to sell their stores to Marvel.

Look at all that statistical information at the end of the Heroes World credit application – note that nowhere does it state or suggest that this data is proprietary. What's to stop them from giving this data to your competition? To the future chain builder? After all, they're already underwriting him buying you out!

The question becomes, how much do you trust Marvel to look after you and yours? This is not a dollars and cents equation. From a little straw polling, about half of you expect your discount to lower between two and six points. The other half expect them to rise an equivalent amount, predicated on the "incentive bonuses." So how long do you trust them to keep giving you those "incentives?" Ask yourself: what if they throw a Marvelution, and nobody comes? What if their sales don't rise to their targeted levels? What will they do then? I'll tell you what they are likely to do: take away or cut back upon those incentives.

And in the meantime, you're paying them to underwrite your own inevitable destruction.

At Comix Experience, only two non-X-Men Marvel titles sell over 20 copies. I believe this is solely a function of the editorial quality (or lack thereof) on the Marvel line. I'm currently receiving a 55% discount from Diamond. Based on Marvel's published terms, I'm going to receive an average of a 49.5% discount (taken from my last twelve months of Marvel and Malibu sales). It is generally acknowledged that you must achieve a 90% sell-through before an individual title starts making a profit for you. A 55% discount on a 90% sell-through nets me the same profit as a 49.5% discount with 100% sell-through! We've decided that we have no recourse but to go subscription copies only on any Marvel title we're not confident could sell 20 copies or more (a 90% sell-through on 20 copies only leaves us two copies "wiggle room"). This leaves us with Hulk, FF, and the X-Men family as the only comics we will rack anymore.

This may not be your best decision – pull out your last 13 months of Marvel and Malibu orders. Note your total dollars, so you can determine your base discount. This is the only number you can count on, for sure!

Try to determine whether you qualify for the "full-line support" bonus. This is a fairly complex piece of math. First, count the number of titles solicited, then count the number that are under their plateau (as of this writing, it's stated as five copies – at the meeting, however, they suggested this might drop as low as two copies) – this will tell you what percentage of full-line you're at (again, at the meeting, they suggested 75%, but it might rise to 95% to qualify). Then figure out the least number of titles each month you'd need to get to Marvel's bonus – if, for example, Marvel and Malibu published 80 titles, at 95%/2 copies you want to look at no more than four titles selling less than two copies. At 75%/5, you want to make sure no more than 20 titles are selling less than five copies. If your number is greater than these, then you want to add up the cheapest number of copies, and their total cost that it would take you to get to Marvel's minimums. Then multiple your total cost, plus the amount you'd over-order to get to Marvel's minimums, by 2%, and compare that what it would cost to meet the minimums. If your cost is lower, then you could get the extra discount, and just give away the unsalable comics – but if it's higher, then you probably won't qualify.

Under the 75%/5 plan, it would, on average, cost Comix Experience twice as much to match the incentive as we'd benefit!

The last thing to do is compare your totals on a month-to-month basis – if you're not getting an annual 10% growth, or better, I would hazard a guess that you won't gain the growth bonuses, on any dependable schedule.

This is a lot of calculations to do – some of them fairly complicated. And you're going to need to do this every single month to arrive at what your final discount will be. And the formulae will change each month! This is almost the least of the extra work you'll need to do in order to deal with a second primary distributor.

It's time for you to take a hard look at your product mix and how important each part is to your overall business health. Even a 2% loss of discount could easily put a lot of us out of business.

I also point to several secondary signs that Marvel is expecting more than we can, or would want to, deliver: The June Maximum Clonage co-op ad says, "You'll find all six issues of this amazing Spider-Man saga (and multiple copies of each) at..." – is this not an exhortation to speculate? How about this tip on *Pocahontas* in "A View From The Field" in the June *Mega-Business:* "Multiply what you think you can sell in one month by six, that's your order." Ouch! Why isn't the publisher pledging reorder availability for six months rather than asking us to foot the holding costs? Or how about this statement in the solicitation for *Spider-Man 2099* #34 (also in the June information): "You should order this title based on #'s for *Amazing Spider-Man.*" Do any of these statements sound like they're coming from a publisher that has any understanding of actual sales reality or long-term planning?

I decided that I don't trust Marvel, that they're going to cost me the equivalent to two month's rent a year in lost profits – because of the decisions that they have made, not my own – and that they don't have my best interests at heart. Is it any wonder that I can't, in good conscience, support their titles in my store any more?

What's your decision?

This column was written before the Great Water Pipe Explosion which completely razed CE to the ground. Below that, even. We don't use Long Whites as Sub dumps anymore. In fact, when I think just how much we've changed the look of the store in the time I've been writing Tilting, I nearly get freaked out.

This one's bleak. But man, if you weren't a comics retailer in 1995, no one can really explain to you how fucking **hard** it was.

This was Ground Zero, and we were standing right in it.

Tilting at Windmills #39
(Originally ran in Comics Retailer #40)

There's more information, and misinformation and rumor and innuendo and gossip and whatever other words I don't feel like looking up in the thesaurus right now, floating around this industry then ever before (well, duh, Bri!). We keep trying to get a handle on the scope of our situations, and what the impact will be for each microcosm of the industry (our stores), and it's just too big – your brain can't possibly wrap around all the facets of our shifting and transforming marketplace, because we're no longer a single (or singular) type of demographic. I mean, just try to describe an "average" comic book shop.

Oh, sure, one can take an average (mean, mode, median, whatever) sales level, based on whatever (woefully inadequate) information exists, and come up with some sort of a number, but that doesn't tell you much of anything about the store. And there are a lot of stereotypes about comic retailers, some of which I plead guilty to continuing to perpetuate (gasp! It's the new kinder, gentler, *Tilting at Windmills*!), but it's all just wrong – retailing is an individual task.

Let me try to make an odd example to illuminate this point. Mimi Cruz runs Night Flight in Salt Lake City, right? She's in a mall, it's extremely friggin' clean (I mean, she's showing me pictures of signings with 100 people in line, and in the background you can see that every single rack is perfectly straightened! How in God's name she manages to accomplish that, I'll never know, but suffice it to say that the store is pristine), and she offers full-on service-with-a-smile, the-customer-is-always-right attention to her clientele.

Now I, on the other hand, am in San Francisco, with a street location almost, but not quite, off the beaten path, our neatness sometimes wavers on the fringes (Just ask Ann Ivan about the broken-in long whites I use to hold the subs!), and we're not wholly above being ever so surly (but in a loving way!) with our customers.

Now, if we had a dimension-hopping machine like the one in *Sliders*, and we went to a parallel universe where Mimi and I were switched at birth (yoikes!), and she opened Night Flight at my location in San Francisco, I opened Comix Experience in her mall in Salt Lake City, our sales would still reflect our personalities. That is to say, the books that Mimi can sell 50 copies of, and I can only sell five (or vice versa), would sell 50 copies in San Francisco if Mimi were behind the counter. Certainly, location and customer base do play a significant role in how far your customers are willing to follow the directions you lead, but I think that personal passion (or dispassion, for that matter) for individual works is the greatest single component of what sells in which store. Nearly every day I'll talk to a retailer who will astound and amaze me with their sales on a favorite title, or genre, but it's because the passion of the leadership of the store (whether it be owner, manager, or even, quite frequently, a single employee) is a tangible, shining thing that the customers can't help but be affected by.

Do you see? You can't generalize about retailers, except in the most shallow of terms, because we're like snowflakes – no two are truly alike upon inspection. (We're also like 1000 cats, but that's not my story...).

And, like the retailers, you can't truly generalize about distributors or publishers either. Diamond is not Capital is not Friendly Frank's is not Hobby Game, and Kitchen Sink is not Dark Horse is not DC is not Aardvark-Vanaheim. Nor should they be. Our strength is in our diversity, and, just like in Diamond's slogan (though I'll be charitable and spare them a paragraph questioning how closely their definition of "diversity" follows mine. I mean *Beavis and Butt-head* is hardly diversity, folks. Ah, but onward!), we need to celebrate diversity.

To get back to the original train of thought, the distribution changes that have been happening are, I believe, nearly impossible for any single person to fully process. Why? Because you can't work out all the intangibles. What exactly their effect on me will be will be different than their effect upon Mimi, or upon Rory

Root, or Carol Denbow, or Bob's Comic Hole in Pigsuck, Arkansas. And any plan that doesn't take into account these differences (not geographic or cultural or architectural or whatever else you choose to throw around – but differences, instead, in personality) is a plan that's going to hurt and confuse an already shaky and gun-shy market-place.

And that's the last thing we can afford right now.

I know a lot about this industry, right? I work hard every day to try and learn the business from every side. I try to stay plugged in (BBS services like CompuServe are great for this), and keep educated about publisher concerns, distribution concerns, creator concerns, what have you – because the more I know about all corners, the better I'll be able to service my customers, and my store's best interests. If I understand how the distribution channels work, then I can explain why a title didn't show up this week; if I understand how publishing works, then I can explain to my customers why the book they really like got canceled, or why price increases happen, etc. None of this is necessary to keep my doors open, but I figure it allows me to better service all of my customers concerns – because, just like us, there is no such thing as an average customer, either. I get lots of comments from lots of people of what a great job I'm doing (the recent Pro/Con was a most excellent stroke-fest for me), but I'll say this much loud and clear: my education hasn't even started.

I can be one helluvan opinionated bastard at times (you can hear the sounds of nodding heads coast-to-coast on that one), and I eat, breathe, and sleep comic books. Hell, I nearly sweat the damn things from my pores. If I've got a life out-side of this industry, it's news to me – 12 to 16-hour days don't give you a lot of time to pursue anything but your calling. I'm often hailed as an "industry insider," or a "top retailer," or whatever the hell you want to call it, but the things I don't know, the parts I don't understand outnumber what I do understand ten-to-one (ah, screw that! It's a hundred-to-one!). I'm man enough to admit it. Which is why I find it the height of arrogance, the height of ignorance, when anyone stands up and says they're doing X, Y, or Z to help or support this marketplace, and not their own perceived "best interests."

D'you see where I'm going with this? Paul Levitz and Terry Stewart (or Steve Geppi, or John Davis and Milton Griep, or the Snyder family, or...) may well be bright and caring individuals who are dedicated solely to the future of our medium – I dunno, I don't hang out socially with these folks. But I do know that however well educated they may well be about the aspects of the business outside of their purview, it's nowhere near enough, at least to enact the kinds of sweeping and broad-based changes these folks have unleashed upon us all. Oh, they can prolly individually debate the "big picture" better than every contributor to this magazine rolled into one, but, time and time again, they seem to forget that the big picture is made up of thousands upon thousands of "small pictures." Kinda not seeing the trees for the forest, as it were.

As we try to reconstruct the puzzle of the comic book industry after the mailed fists of this industry have come crashing down upon the table, scattering things to and fro, a lot of the "small pictures" are never going to fit back in again. It's simple to reason that not everyone is going to receive the information they need to survive (No? As I write this, it's less than three weeks before our July orders are due – both Marvel and DC [!] reps are telling me they're getting phone calls from guys asking "so what about these rumors about Marvel and Heroes World?" Hell, Marvel hasn't even given us the damn order form yet – if that's not the simplest part of the distribution process, I dunno what is! And DC expects Diamond to hook up every Cap City, Friendly Franks, Styx, Multi-book, etc., etc., ad nauseum, client in ten weeks? Pull the other one, folks!) And each one of our "small pictures" is made up of hundreds of even "smaller pictures" – our customers! When a shop closes down (any shop), $x\%$ of customers go away, too. Our market is shrinking for any number of reasons (quality, price point, availability, etc.) – to throw what amount to Machiavellian political reasons upon that as well is...irresponsible, to say the least.

Ladies and gentlemen, the direct market is dead. If there was any question of it, it's gone now that DC has announced their deal. I don't know what exactly it is that we'll end up replacing the direct market with, but what's more important (and infinitely more sad), neither do the architects of its assassination. I sincerely hope we're still all here in a year to toss back a cold one, and reminisce on when this game was still relatively simple. Until then, I beg all of you to watch your backs, and be safe out there – the cold streets just got a lot colder.

"And the three men I admired most, the Father, Son, and the Holy Ghost, they took the last train for the coast...the day the music died."
–Don McLean, American Pie

Tilting at Windmills #40
(Originally ran in Comics Retailer #41)

As some of you may have heard, I'm the newest board member of the Comic Book Legal Defense Fund (CBLDF), so, this month I'm gonna use my space to do a little proselytizing. Don't tune out – you never know what tidbits I might plunk down in the middle of the column!

First off, what is the CBLDF anyway, and why is it important to our businesses? Here, let me quote from the literature – the CBLDF is "A non-profit tax-exempt organization dedicated to defending first amendment rights in the comics industry." The first amendment is, of course, Our Right to Free Expression.

Part of the problem in writing about Our Right to Free Expression is it's difficult to talk about it without using the language of the censors. I've tried writing this opening three or four times now, and I keep erasing my words, so let me try it this way: I'm proud to be an American. Oh, not the global-political entity in and of itself, but the America that I was taught about in school – the America that may not have ever existed except in the textbooks and our collective unconsciousness.

The Right to Self-Determination. The Right of Freedom from Oppression. The Right of Self-Expression.

I sure as hell hold those truths to be self-evident.

They're not just words. They may be interpreted in many different ways, but I think it ultimately boils down to one word: Freedom. If I want to, let's say, shave my head, paint my face blue, and walk down the streets singing show-tunes, I can. To another extreme, if I want to go on Oprah and espouse the philosophy that Jews are the lowest form of life, then that also is my freedom. In point of fact, I can just about to do whatever it is I please, as long as it's not harmful to myself or others.

But that's where it gets sticky. What *is* "harmful to myself or others?" There are some, for example, who would claim going on that fictional Oprah show is "harmful to others" because by being exposed to that hateful philosophy others could embrace it. To them I say this: all rights *must* be absolute – otherwise they're not rights at all, they're largesse from the state. Say that back with me: all rights must be absolute.

Especially when we're talking about thought or communication. I give you a for example: artist Mike Diana did a comic called "Boiled Angel." I've seen it, and you've probably seen at least portions of it in trade coverage of his obscenity bust. Allow me be the first to say it: Diana's art is ugly, crude, anti-religious, violent, gory, obnoxious, and just about any denouncement you might care to attach to it. It doesn't appeal to me in any way, shape, or form. But do I want it *banned*? Do I want Diana not to be allowed to *draw* for three years? Do I want him to not be *allowed* to be *near* children? Screw that! *Whether or not you agree with something's merit, you should not be allowed to suppress it!*

So, you see, we're right back in the censors domain. All debates about Freedom ultimately come down to "how far do we go" – in this case, do we allow things that don't fit our generally accepted world-view as "decent" to exist? A man named Martin Niemoller said this:

> *In Germany they came for the Communists, and I didn't speak up because I wasn't a communist.*
> *Then they came for the Jews, and I didn't speak up because I wasn't a Jew.*
> *Then they came for the Trade Unionists, and I didn't speak up because I wasn't a Trade Unionist.*
> *Then they came for the Catholics, and I didn't speak up because I was a Protestant.*
> *Then they came for me, and by that time no one was left to speak up.*

Even if you disagree with the subject matter a creator like Diana portrays, you *have* to let it exist. We're thinking, reasoning people. We can just as easily *not* look at something if it offends our sensibilities. *Any* erosion of our fundamental rights harms *each* of us in countless and unshakable ways.

(Let me take a quick digression and say this: if personal preference were the sole issue, my own predilections would call the arched-back, stuck-out-tits, pouty-lips, pseudo-pornfests that pass for super-hero comics these days more harmful to people that ten Mike Dianas. We all *know* that thousands of boys are furtively masturbating to Image comics, right? Ain't *no one* doing that with Diana! [Especially since he only did *300* copies, anyway!])

But first amendment rights are not *always* about "obscene" material.

For example, artist Paul Mavrides is currently fighting with the California Board of Equalization (BOE) over whether or not comic book original art has the same literary status as an author's manuscript. The BOE want Mavrides to collect sales tax for his royalties. Their argument is essentially that the sale of the reproduction rights to his original art (i.e., so a publisher can print the comic!) is manifestly different than a writer selling the reproduction rights to his prose. In all states (to the best of my knowledge) the only time an artist has to collect sales tax is when they're creating one-time work that is meant to be commercially reproduced. In other words, if I paint a painting, and you make postcards out of it, I have to collect sales tax on the money you pay me. This is because I'm essentially selling you "tangible goods or service." On the other hand, if I'm a writer, and I give you my novel to publish, I collect no sales tax because writing (and by extension, creativity) is an "intangible" thing (i.e., it's not the words on the paper themselves that matter, it's the "creative act" itself).

Comics are, one could construe, a "gray area" – you are indeed selling the specific reproduction rights (the lettered, inked board), but anyone who knows anything about comics can tell you that the creative process between writing prose fiction and writing and drawing comics fiction are not wholly different. It's the base creativity – an "intangible," whether wrought in tangible *form* or not, that is at stake.

Now I can hear you saying out there, "how does this affect me? I can't even follow this debate, let alone understand it – what's my position?" Well, it's fairly simple – increased costs to the publisher (which is from whom the artists must collect this sales tax) inevitably translate into increased costs for you and me. *Inevitably.* "Yeah but, this is just about Mavrides, the Freak Brothers, and Rip Off Press – none of these matter to my store." Hello?!?! Pay attention, kid – this is the *California* BOE we're talking about! If they win against a California creator dealing with a California publisher, who do they go after next? C'mon, think about it. Yeah, that's right, Image. If you're in the industry norms, that's about 15-20% of your sales, right there.

And, guess what? In case you haven't noticed, most states are *hungry* for funds these days. If California passes this through, how long before other states start to look upon it as a valid revenue source? Yeah, *today* it's just Mavrides, Freak Brothers, and Rip Off Press, but they're the "Communists" in the Niemoller quote.

"O.K., O.K.," you say, "I've heard you ramble on about supporting our rights for the last 1200 words, Bri – what do you *want* from me?" Well, that's friggin' easy. *Support.*

There are two forms this can take (both are recommended): direct donation or ideas. Direct donation first. If *everyone* reading this can take five minutes to write a $10 check to the CBLDF, that would help the fund run for another year. I mean *everyone*, too. Oh, I know you guys on the publisher or distributor payroll, for whom it's "required reading" to read Comics Retailer cover-to-cover. "Oh! I read your column every month!" Yeah, fine – go get your checkbook right now, and write a check. Ten bucks, what can it hurt?

Send it to this address: Comic Book Legal Defense Fund c/o PO Box 693, Northampton, MA, 01061.

Your money can *really* make a difference. Just between you and the wall, the CBLDF didn't have the best '94 – positive cashflow was like four-figures (and very, very low ones, at that), and without dipping, seriously, into the money from Dave Sim's issue of *Spawn* from '93, it would never have seen that.

And, you, retailer guy, don't think I'm not looking at you! I saw you at the DC & Diamond "New Dynamic" tour (the paltry few of you that went) – cheap mothers, not even trying *token* bids for the CBLDF auction stuff. In San Francisco we had maybe 10 guys, tops, out of 60 even bidding. Pathetic to watch.

The fund needs money, and it needs it now. We're looking at mid six-figures in outstanding legal fees, and, with every new case that increases.

And we're successful, kids! Half of 1994's case-load has been dismissed, thanks to the fund, and we've shut down another three cases before they started.

I've got one goal in being a CBLDF member – to make '95 & '96 the best years the fund has every seen. To generate enough money so we never *have* to come to you for direct donations again.

So, I said there were two forms your help you take. *In addition to direct donation* (not as a weasel around it!), the CBLDF can use your brainpower. Like I say, I want the next year to be the best it can be – the best way to secure that is *not* direct donations (though they *really* will help) – it's ideas for low to no-cost fund-raising. For example: beyond organizing the San Francisco stop of the Neil Gaiman lecture tour, I want to organize "be in the comic" raffles, and a "celebrity pool toss" (what would *you* pay to be able to throw Todd McFarlane or Gary Groth in a pool?). I want to hear *your* ideas, no matter how wonky they may be. If'n we can't use them, maybe we can adapt them for use instead. The best resources are personal resources – i.e. blood, sweat, tears, and labor. At the very least, you could put a donation jar on your store's counter

We need your help. Really we do. Think of it as a vote for your future. That's the only thing we have.

Before I go, Kurt Busiek posted me this quote that's too good to ditch: Abraham Lincoln, in a letter to Joshua F. Speed, on August 24, 1855: "I am not a Know-Nothing ... How could I be? How can anyone who abhors the oppression of Negroes be in favor of degrading classes of white people? Our progress in degeneracy appears to me to be pretty rapid. As a nation we began by declaring that "all men are created equal." We now practically read it "all men are created equal, except Negroes." When the Know-Nothings get control, it will read "all men are created equal, except Negroes and foreigners and Catholics." When it comes to this, I shall prefer emigrating to some country where they make no pretense of loving liberty – to Russia, for instance, where despotism can be taken pure, and without the base alloy of hypocrisy."

And, just so we don't wholly ditch all "industry reportage" this month — I like the new DC terms. Very much. Free reorders and advance reorders are much to be desired.

Tilting at Windmills #41
(Originally ran in Comics Retailer #42)

Seeing that I'm tired of writing (and you, chances are, are tired of reading...) about the "big issues" that effect us (distribution, etc.), this month's column gleefully abandons all that to talk about another kind of issue – back issues, to be precise.

I'm starting to hate them.

Well, actually, maybe that's not the best place to begin. Let's try a minor historical lesson, instead.

Now, look, I've been a comics retailer as long as I can remember (started at 16, and I'm *<gasp>* 28 now), but I certainly wasn't there at the beginning, but as close as I can determine, comic book stores exist because of the back issue market. Stores started popping up that dealt primarily in older comics, and, after a period of time, the direct market started to form around this nucleus (Hey! I said this was a *minor* historical lesson!). These earliest stores were buying new material from the newsstand distributors, and existed primarily from sales of "vintage" material. When I started in this business, a decade ago, the store I worked for did roughly a third of its volume in back issues. When I opened Comix Experience, six short years ago, the percentage was hovering around 20%, but today, in 1995, that percentage rarely cracks 7%.

(Sure, I only have the one store, so I don't exactly have a statistically viable base to determine if this is usual for the rest of you, but in casual conversation, it certainly appears to be the case.)

The scary bit about back issues occupying a shrinking portion of our sales is that they are continuously growing in quantity ever week. Six to eight hundred new comics a month yields 150 to 200 new "back issues" thirty days after these titles are released. Just *one* copy held back of every title the direct market receives gives two to three new long boxes a month for our back issue bins – that's maybe 32 long whites a year!! Yoikes! Go back ten issues to the November '94 issue, and read my article on sell-through. To refresh your memory, because industry averages are something like only 80% overall sell-through, we're looking at somewhere between $24 and $96 million dollars a year in unsold merchandise sitting in our back issue boxes!

Managing a back issue inventory has become one of the most critical tasks a comics retailer has to face. And that is because the *nature* of back issue consumers has diametrically changed in the last few years. It used to be that we'd get five or six people in a day with little lists of all the titles they were looking for – these guys were *readers*, for the most part, mind you – now if I get five a *month* I consider myself lucky. It used to be that most regular customers would, once hooked into a title, jump all over the back issues, trying to get "caught up" – this, too, has become a rarity.

I believe there are three key reasons why the "back issue customer" has started to become an endangered species of sorts:

1: The proliferation of new material. Ah, the "good old days" – when 100 different new comics was considered a *flood* – you're looking for something to read, so you buy four or five new comics, as well as a back issue or two, just so you get your RDA of reading material. But today – today 100 new titles is *puny* – there are more choices than the customer could really ever *want*, let alone be *able* to read in a given week.

1.5: This is really a subset of #1, so we can't count it as its own point – event-driven marketing and cross-pollination of titles has created a more focused consumer. In a world of "Family Groups," we've lost a fair amount of sampling. If you like, say, X-Men and Batman, there's something not unlike five or six comics a week right there, in those *two* groups!

2: Increasing cover prices. Though this works in tandem with #1, this point can *not* be understated – $10, five years ago, could buy (if you shopped wisely) 13, maybe 14 comics. A couple of those were bound to be back issues. Today, you won't get half of that – probably less than a third. This leaves little extra discretionary income to buy back issues.

3: Speculators turning back issues from entertainment to commodity. I've watched as heavy back issues buyers get depressed because the market caters to buying for value – driving up prices on titles they wanted. Some of them tried to play the game as well, but most of those got burned, and dropped out, too. By association all back issue collecting got smeared with the speculative paint brush.

In early winter of 1993 I suddenly woke up and realized that the amount of floor space my back issues were taking up was *way* out of line with the money they generated. Back issue sales were declining, while stock was mounting faster than we could sell it. So, we did a massive declining discount sale: we started at 30%, and each week dropped the discount another 10%, ending up at 90% the week of Christmas. I want to note that, at the time, we probably had the widest array of back issues within San Francisco – some 24,000 *different* titles. We excluded about 20% of the stock from the sale – stuff we thought didn't *need* to be discounted to move. We sold $40,000 "worth" of back issues for about $8000, and counted ourselves lucky. And, even after all that, we still had about a third of our original stock left.

After that I started color-coding stock. Anything that went into the boxes got a blue tag, instead of the white ones we used the first four years. About three months later, I switched to green, then yellow, orange, and today I use red, tying to switch every three months or so. When we switched to yellow, we started discounting the remaining white tags 25%. When we went to orange, the whites went to 60%, and the blues switched to 25% off. When we went to red, white tags got dumped in the quarter box, blue went to 60%, and yellow became 25% off. I'm sure you can figure out what happens when I go off red. Basically, when this means is we give a book a year at "full-price", and another six months a various discount levels, then we yank it.

Based on the full cycles we've done so far, it becomes clear that back issues are dead. Bereft of life, it rests in peace. It's rung down the curtain, and joined the choir invisible. This is an ex-market.

O.K., O.K., all stealing from *Monty Python* aside, there are, of course, some exceptions – maybe, possibly, 10% of the stock sells steadily (At CE, that would be *Spawn*, *X-Men*, some Vertigo titles, *Daredevil*, maybe half-a-dozen other books. And, of course, whatever 20 or so comics *Wizard* is currently focusing on as "hot"); while another 20-25% sells sporadically (it at least appears to be tied to the presence of out-of-town visitors, here) – maybe we'll sell a copy or two a year. But that other two-thirds just sits and sits and sits.

This is recent-ish comics we're talking about, by the way – say last 20 years. You certainly can build a business in Silver and Gold which is relatively bullet-proof, but that takes a fairly large capital investment, and requires a lot of scrounging around to get going in any significant manner.

As far as I'm aware, we're still the only store in town that buys from consumers every hour we're open. We also never cherry pick collections – we'll buy every comic in your collection. But we only pay salvage rates – two to ten cents a piece, depending on the "quality" of the stuff (JLA and FF might get you seven cents, but Arak and Arion are two cents). We switched to this policy six months ago after I saw the early results of our color-coding. I understand some retailers use a by-the-pound method to similar effect. The reason for this is really simple: we don't especially need any more back issues. We're down to 6000 different titles – but that's still probably 5000 too many, based on how often they turn over, and the floor space they consume.

The funny thing is, our purchasing of back issues hasn't decreased in any substantial way. What we've found is that the vast majority of back issue sellers will take what they can get – very few people sell back issues because they want to – but they *have* to. They're moving, or they need room, or they need a couple of bucks for rent money, or something. They want to get rid of them fast and easy.

Now, I can hear some of you saying, "Wait a minute, are you advocating ripping people off because they're in a rush, Hibbs?" No, no, no. The other important bit is to "read people their rights" – we make a point of telling people to shop around; we attempt to point out specific items that other stores might pay more for; we explain that why these policies are in place; we suggest donating the material to a charitable organization, and getting a tax write-off (or just a good feeling) etc., etc. And 95% of the sellers listen to all that, and say, "Fine, we'll take it, anyway."

Right now I've learned enough about the state of sales, in this store at least, to start seriously thinking about eliminating back issues altogether (or, at least, all but three long boxes up on the counter) – that floor space can be more profitably given over to merchandise that has a faster turn-rate, and a higher price point. It's a hard step to make though, because there is certainly an element of customer service in carrying a wide array of back issues. I certainly don't want to alienate *any* customer, but we're talking about less than 2% of my base – it's a hard call, but I'm thinking about it.

Honestly, the thing that's really holding me back is the sticky question of what to with the left-over "new comics" once they ain't new no mo'. I mean, eventually, they're gonna land in the dollar box, or quarter box, but I can't put them there straight from the rack – that's just gonna devalue the cover price of the comics (not that comics aren't, for the most part, over-priced) – I feel you need at least a six month gap between the two. Our sell-through is getting tight enough so that this is less than a short box a week, but it's still somewhat of a potential cash-flow concern.

One way that we *have* found to quickly turn over back issues is packaging them in cheap sets – ten issues of *New Mutants* for $5 (an aside: I have come to the conclusion that *every* collection I've seen from a ten year or more collector, selling over a long box, comes with a complete, or almost so, run of *New Mutants*! Number one to somewhere in the 80s, usually. It's a pretty ridiculous phenomenon); or *JLA* #1-10 for $9 – basically any contiguous run packaged for a cheap, cheap price will sell better than the individual issues, even at that same cheap price!

My eyes were *pried* open when we went to color-coding. Things that I *believed* sold well actually barely trickled – there's, say, 365+ issues of *Avengers*, after all – you *could* be selling an *Avengers* a day, but still only be moving any individual issue once a year! This is, of course, an extreme example, but it should convey the chasm between belief in salability, and actual results. Whatever you *do* with the information, I strongly urge you to start color-coding, just so you have the essential data!

Tilting at Windmills #42
(Originally ran in Comics Retailer #43)

O.K., it's time to get back to talking about the distributor shakeups again.

As I write this, it's a week after the San Diego ComicCon – all the big news hit there: Dark Horse, Image, and Acclaim with Diamond, Kitchen Sink with Capital City. Something like 75% of the marketplace is now exclusive to one distributor or another. If things go as I expect, by the time this column sees print, we'll have the majority of the rest of the top 20 publishers aligned with either Capital City or Diamond.

The two real critical paths facing our industry in the next quarter are 1) will we have a viable second distributor to ensure an open capitalistic industry distributor relationship, and 2) can we create a fair and *realistic* pricing structure for the "alternative" segment of the marketplace – any publisher with a, say, 7% or less market share? Like all good numbered points go, let's deal with these in order:

Viable second distributor?

I'm quite deliberate in my usage of the word "second" in the question. To be perfectly blunt, I think Marvel/Heroes World has made itself utterly irrelevant for two reasons: a) their fortunes and business is completely divorced from the rest of the publisher/distribution portion of the industry. What Diamond, Cap, DC, Image, or any one else does now only has indirect effects on the MEG empire. They are dependent on no one but themselves, but, being divorced from the rest of the business mechanisms, they have to do a significantly *better* job than they used to need to do, in order to claim the *same* attention. This brings us neatly to b) they've made a huge cock-up of it so far, and this marketplace (hell, this culture) has a notoriously small attention span. As of 7/31 I've still yet to receive a single *advance* reorder – you know, those things we send in *before* the print-run is set? But I've been billed for some of them. At *cover price* (*no* discount), no less! But billing errors, those are my problems – it's the no-reorders-for-the-first-month, which is Marvel's big problem. The customer can't get this month's installment of three of the Spidey books? That creates a good chance (maybe up to 50/50) that they'll give up the Spidey "habit" altogether. The customers will find something to spend their money on, whether it's in the store or not. Every Marvel book not on the stands, not in the sub boxes, is one more reader who may quit it altogether (and maybe *all* comics, too – if their dander is up enough). I'm not even going to get into the other fundamental problems MEG/HWD has (being put on hold for 20 minutes at a time, no conclusive answers, horrible problems with billing/credit, ridiculous waste in shipping costs [there's a whole column by itself – like the second day UPS package I got that weighed five pounds, but only contained a single promo poster – for a title I'm ordering a single copy of!], etc.). I believe that in the time it's going to take them to fix these systemic problems, coupled with their reduced visibility in most venues, Marvel will have only succeeded in making themselves irrelevant to the short-term survival of this marketplace.

In fact (he said, making a new paragraph for those of you who just skim these things) on the week of 7/27, when we received our books on Thursday, rather than Wednesday (usually a sales killer), we had our single-best non-event day in the six years we've been opened – *without any Marvel titles besides Hulk and X-Men!* Yes, that's right, with 90% of my Marvel comics sales subscription-only, my sales have gone *up!*

While Marvel may certainly have a much-greater importance to your store, I believe my experience shows that MEG/HWD is going to become more irrelevant to the overall marketplace as time goes on.

So, the question becomes, "will there be another viable distributor now that Diamond has locked up a third or better of the marketplace while CCD only holds about .05%?" The question of viability is not only one of straight market percentages, but the question of whether a "second-class" distributor can make ordering *possible* for a large enough base of stores.

For example: my beloved fellow columnist, Preston Sweet has more than once addressed the concern of unrealistic minimum orders on the distribution level. Let's say that CCD gets the publishers I expect and/or hear good rumor on them getting: besides Kitchen, this might be Viz, Antarctic, WaRP, and the non-MEG part of Planet studios (I must stress that none of this is from any solid source, but a compendium of "word on the street," which might well be all or in part wrong) – I still don't think I can make current CCD minimum orders. Or if I do, it'll be at a crap pricing structure. These five publishers comprise less than 3% of the overall marketplace. How many retailers are going to be motivated to fill out a *third* order-form, with the *sixth* separate discount structure, for 3% of the market? I personally suspect it will be very few.

I certainly *want* another viable distributor – as much as Diamond has cleaned up their act (I *used* to say that if I ran my store like DCD ran their business, I'd've been out of business in six months, but my opinion has turned 180-degrees around – they have become extremely conscientious for this retailer, at least. While not being exactly what I want, they are at least close enough to call it hand-grenades), I don't want them being the sole player in the game. Let us not forget Diamond comics, at one point, refused to distribute any "adults only" titles. If, let's say, Geppi decides to run for Governor (I've never even *been* to Maryland, but he sure seems primed from this side of the counter), it sure would be a political liability for him to be opened up to the label of "porn-merchant." What's to stop Diamond, in a world where they're the only viable national distributor, to go back to the "safe-only" policy of the past? Hell, to be able to set up a comics rating system (think about it: the distributor becomes the only one with the authority to make it stick)? Whether or not they abuse it, Diamond is in a position to wield an *enormous* and unprecedented amount of power over the future of a lot of people.

Something to think about, huh?

Pricing Structures?

Finally we're in a real solid position to address the inequities of a multi-tier nationwide-based discount structure.

Just because I like to bitch, let's consider Marvel first. I had a very good April with MEG titles – disproportionately good, in fact, what with the $3.95 *X-Men Omega*, the $3.95 *X-Men Chronicles*, and the two double-sized *Spidey* issues. Because I supported them so well in April, I'm getting penalized for the rest of the year, with the net effect that Preston Sweet (who runs a store about half my size) is getting a better discount than I do, *even if* I didn't just order for subscription customers (I've run the numbers both ways) I mean, good for Preston, of course, but why have I been screwed? I'm well aware of any other stores like mine – penalized for supporting Marvel's biggest push of the year.

In another way, I get dicked on the small press every single month. Let's consider *Stray Bullets* for a second – we're at the point where we sell 70 copies of this title in the first four weeks, with a shelf-life that probably will double that again over the year. I get 45% off *Stray Bullets*. Of the 16 total Acclaim books shipping in September, I'm ordering a *total* of 52 copies (!) On these titles I'm getting 52.5%. Why is that? Not only "why does my discount suck on *Stray Bullets*?" but "why are they giving me such a good discount on Acclaim titles?"

The only time I think these overall-dollar-volume discounts make *any* sense at all is when you're talking about titles that are interrelated on an editorial level, and only then when there are, say, 30 or more of them. That leaves us with Marvel, DC, and Image as the only companies that can pull them off – not coincidentally, the only three publishers with greater than 10% market share (6%, really, but ten *sounds* so much better) – because they're not selling the individual books, but rather the line identity. Everyone else, in my oh-so-humble opinion, needs to switch to *quantity-based* performance system.

When you query a distributor about the discount structure on any given item, they usually give you some rigmarole about "it's a very complex formula weighed with publisher's prices to us, as well as the number of copies we have" – actually, it's not rigmarole, that's sound business, but, naturally, you can never pin the distributor down on the specifics of the formulae. I have found many, many cases where the distributor price was *way* out of line to the publisher's provided discount to them – where they're making 20% of the cover price, on a project that sells decently.

It's not like they're *evil* – but sometimes they can be pretty damn stupid and/or slow to react. But, really, I do understand the economic underpinnings of distribution – there are titles where the "handling" costs of distribution make them unprofitable, or so marginally profitable that they drag down your efficiency rate. DCD and CCD carry a whole lot of dead weight along to give us "open access" to the market place – I acknowledge that, and even thank them for it – but retailers have every financial incentive in the world to *not* succeed with small press books. At my discount level, if I sell one copy, or if I sell 100 copies, I'll get the same discount – typically 40 or 45% – though sometimes it's a measly 35%. Where is my incentive to grow my sales? Why on earth would I "celebrate diversity," no matter how "certified cool" something is, when I profit more from promoting where the discount lives?

What I think is fair, what I think gives retailers a *reason* to grow their sales, is *per-title* quantity-based pricing. It would run something like this:

1-5 copies	40% off
6-10 copies	45% off
11-24	50% off
25 copies or more	55% off

To try and put these numbers in perspective, if there are 6000 DM retailers, 25 copies sold by each would be 150,000. As near as I can tell, there are top 20 titles that don't sell 150k! Five copies at each comic shop would be 30,000 – which is a strong independent book (there are Marvel and DC titles that don't sell 30k!).

Of course, the specific numbers might be a little wrong in one direction, or another. Maybe it's seven copies that can make the distributors point on 45%, maybe it's three – I don't know, because I don't have their hard numbers. And, naturally, these numbers assume a 60% or better distributor discount. As near as I can determine, though, that's darn near industry average, so it's not too obtuse to insist on that for all comic product, as a condition of distribution. If publishers are hesitant, the distributors can just indicate those publishers to us, and we can petition them to change their policies.

In fact, I think this type of plan could be very well adapted to DC, Marvel and Image books, as well – sure a lot of stores will qualify for 55% on *Superman* or *Batman*, but only the largest will qualify for more than 45% on *Damage*, or *Darkstars*. Even a medium sized store like mine would get only 40% on those titles, because we're doing a lousy job of selling them (not that we have much to work with...) Of course, they might want to add levels of 56% and 57% – maybe 200, and 400 copies would be those platforms?

In this way, we apportion good discounts to those stores that earn them – but without any particular "hoops" to jump through. You get what you *earn*. No more, no less. Eminently fair, balanced, and reasonable.

Obviously, trade paperbacks, or special items, or reorders would have to have a different kind of scale attached to them – maybe the same type of scale, but the numbers are three, five, seven, ten – if you're selling ten copies of a TPB, or if you're moving a dozen Sandman statues, you should be getting 55%, as well. A dozen $135 dollars statues is $1620 retail – equivalent to 648 $2.50 comics!!!

That's what I would do if I were king.

One last thing before I go – my prediction if we stay wedded to overall-dollar-volume based platforms is that the typical retail operation will polarize even more than we have so far – there will be "Marvel & Image" stores, there will be "DC & Dark Horse" stores, and dozens of other permutations with all the other publishers as well. Call me old fashioned, but I think it's in our entire industry's best interest to encourage the "full-line" (defined these days as "top-20 to 50 publishers, or so") store viable – cross-pollination between different readerships brings strength; closed systems breed stagnation.

Tilting at Windmills #43
(Originally ran in Comics Retailer #44)

One of the joys of retailing (as well as one of the biggest headaches) is that it is perpetually a learning experience. The retail environment both must and does continually change. The challenge is to stay current with these changes, and never let the forces of history hold you back from reaching your store's full potential.

While we lived in a world of great stability for the longest time, the comics market has transformed tremendously around us (duh!). Some of these changes were of retailers' making (i.e. price manipulation on the part of the majority of the marketplace has lead to price-consciousness on the part of the consumers), while others have been thrust upon us, without any ability on our part to change or deflect them (i.e. the lowered editorial standards most of the publishers appear to now hold) – either way, the world we once knew is gone, and we have to be quick on our feet to react and change.

Now, I'll admit that I don't hold out a lot of hope for the greater mass of retailers, because we've been locked into doing business in *one* particular way for so long (i.e. anything from a major publisher will always, as a result of being from that major publisher, even if it's as a back issue, sell – but this hasn't been true for at least a year, if not more). But if you do – hell, if you *can* – change your worldview, then great things can happen.

The problem is, this is not an "overnight solution" kinda thing – I've been learning what kind of store my customers and myself want to have for *years* – and, although I think I've found several solutions that work for me, it is, as I said, an on-going educational experience.

Let's take my most recent learning experience as an example, shall we? You'll remember how several months ago I announced that we were going to cut the vast bulk of our Marvel orders to subscription-only, in response to their new pricing structures? To quickly recap, we had a disproportionately strong Marvel April largely due to *X-Men: Omega*. So much so that, because Marvel chose that as their "base month" for their "incentive plan," there was *no* way we'd be able to get any of the "bonus" discount points. We were looking at a 5-6% drop in discount, simply because our store skews slightly older than industry "norms." So, in looking at this move as financially stupid for me, and potentially disastrous to the marketplace (and just *look* at the chaos that has been created!), we opted to cut our rack orders to the 10% or so of their titles that either 1) sold really, really well (like the X-books), or 2) we personally believed in (Like *Akira*, or *Untold Tales of Spider-Man*). That's the quick recap.

So, what would you expect were the results?

Honestly, what's your gut feeling? 'Cause I'm telling you what *I*, in my heart of hearts, thought would happen is that we'd take a dip in sales (prolly slightly greater than the percentage of "lost" Marvel sales, as we would have a small number of customers decide they wanted to find a store that racked the Marvel books). That's what you would think, too, right?

Well, we were both wrong!

What *happened* is that our sales rocketed up by nearly 20%! (The end of the month tally gives me 19.68%, to be exact.) Who'da thunk it?

My initial feelings on this (though this could be proven or disproven over the course of time – say a year or more) are that the customers appreciate *you* being selective *for* them. That is to say that the customers are looking for entertainment in comics form, but *what* that entertainment consists of is largely up to *you*.

The funny thing here is that Marvel was right – almost. When they launched the exclusive distribution by Heroes World deal, they emphasized that their research revealed that there was too much clutter on the rack, and that consumers were overwhelmed by the volume of material available. This much was and is correct. They also advanced the position that the wisest course of action would be to focus your store by genre (as well as the natural subset of "family" groups) racking, and to de-emphasize those titles which don't play to your strengths (I am liberally paraphrasing, and giving quite the benefit of the doubt, please realize). While at first I resisted this concept, I've come to understand that this is actually a brilliant marketing tool. But we'll get back to that soon enough…

I said "almost" a moment ago, because Marvel, as any publisher would, simultaneously advanced the position that *their* comics were the best, and the ones that should be emphasized, *because* they published them! This, my friends, is called a syllogism – "Only humans kill things with guns. Ghandi is a human. Therefore Ghandi killed things with guns." Patently false!

I'm starting to come up with a "Grand Unification" theory of comics retailing – it still glimmers and shifts if I look at it too long, but I've learned these truths, at least: the comics market has become such that "hand-selling" material ("Hey! Have you seen this? It's good because x, y, and z") is the most viable manner to shift material. But, most retailers have a limited amount of titles they can promote – humans have physical limitations in enthusiasm-maintenance. A well-run store might be able to juggle a dozen titles they are "in-your-face" behind, but not much more than that. And customers aren't money machines – they can't even begin to afford (for the most part) what they already buy, let alone all the "Gems" and "Pick Hits" we put in front of them. As a corollary of that, line-extensions (adding title after title to popular characters, *because* they are popular) need to be watched, because just one more title can turn a customer off the entire line, and cripple a retailer's cash flow for months to come. Furthermore, the structure of risk in this business is untenable – retailers must be part huckster and part seer, and those two things don't mix all that well.

Because of these things, I believe it becomes important to judge material on its aesthetic value, and what it adds to you and your store, rather than its label or its "family." That is to say that you shouldn't stock a Marvel comic *just* because it's a Marvel comic – you should stock a Marvel (or any publisher's) comic because it *adds something to your store.*

I've been having an ongoing telephone debate with Dave Sim over this very issue: how much control should a retailer put over their stock, and how much should they let it be dictated to by the whims of the overall marketplace? My position on this has changed over the last few months – at one point I strongly believed that it was a retailer's responsibility to stock *anything* under the sun that the consumers might want. But I've come to realize that the customer has a measure of responsibility, as well – if they want a book you don't have faith in, that you don't feel *adds* to your store, then they must be willing to commit to it in advance, just like we do.

If they're unwilling to do that, then they must accept the consequences (i.e. not seeing that title in your store).

We come from a background where we're *expected* to be "all things to all people," but that's no longer financially possible for the bulk of shops, as much as we'd like it to be.

As I said before, I thought my sales would suffer when we removed the Marvel titles from general stock. They didn't. From this, the natural conclusion is that your customers like you playing "daddy" for them – making some basic decisions of the material you present to them, *before* you present it to them. The trick, and the place where most retailers fail, is that these decisions have to be based on merit, rather than raw sales, in and of themselves. For example, most of your new comics sales are prolly in "traditional" hero/spandex titles. But, you cannot just blithely add hero title after hero title after hero title, and expect them all to move – there is a point of diminishing returns. I personally saw it on the Spider-Man "group" of comics – once they got past critical mass for that "family" (somewhere between four and eight titles), individual sales started plummeting ("less is more").

The secret appears to be first diversifying, bit by bit, and, as you see titles gain interest and grow, and start to be able to "walk on their own," to start pruning from the bottom, and removing the "weeds" (I know, I know, I'm mixing my metaphors – but retailing is as much like parenting as it is gardening). By removing the casual choice of Spider-Man from my store (though the customers will certainly get those books, if they're willing to make a commitment, in advance), I've "forced" them to focus on other material that will entertain them just as much, but that we'll both "feel better" about ("feel better" in the context of not straining their wallets, or their credulity). I'd rather sell one issue of *Starman* to a customer than four issues of Spider-Man. Why? Because we found it *much* easier get 80 people willing to make a one-book commitment, rather than 20 people making a four-book commitment.

It is, I believe, the retailer's job to act as a conduit between creator and consumer – in this equation, the publisher is irrelevant, if not counter-productive. Marvel and DC, in particular, have lost the largest part of their fan base over the last few years because of their insistence on marketing the company over the work – look at all the crossovers and gimmicks they've used to try and focus attention, rather than the merit of the work. In an "ideal" store, a publishers name holds very little weight – that's not what you should be selling. Just as when you go to buy a video, you seldom look at whether Warner Brothers or Paramount released the movie – you, as the consumer, are just looking for a good movie that will entertain you. Comics should be no different.

I guess what I'm asking of you is to not make value judgments based on anything that's not *between* the covers. I've had many retailers say to me that they support a publisher because that publisher has the best sales. This is a logical trap. Part of this may well come from the fact that most participants in the business end of our industry (retailers and publishers alike) seem to have no strong opinions on what *is* quality – their faith and belief in the medium, in the form, went away many a year ago, and they are far more concerned about wringing the maximum amount of money from their customers than they are about helping them be entertained. And, if we want to move this business forward, we need to get past that attitude.

Do you believe in what you're selling? I don't just mean do you think you can continue to have a positive cash flow, but do you really believe that what you carry in your store represents the best of the medium – do you feel *proud* when you look at the stock in your store? I try not to make value judgments of other people's decisions – while I like, say, *Eightball* and *Stray Bullets*, that doesn't mean it's not valid that your absolutely favorite comic is *Amazing Spider-Man*. The question is do you have *faith* in what you've stocked your store with, or have you, instead, made stocking decisions based on some mythical "average customer"?

See, my experience shows that, if you're honest, open, and direct with your customers, you will attract those who share your vision. Every time you stock material you have no faith in, trying to please anyone but yourself, you water down your "vision." And without vision, you'll never be *anything*, never go anywhere.

I'll digress slightly to note that I think it's more intelligent to focus on niches that other people aren't already exploiting. While certainly an argument can be made that pushing, say, *X-Men*, gives you a "built-in recognition factor," I believe that if you choose to do so, you damn well better be the very very best *X-Men* salesperson in your area – because of it's "name value," *anyone* can sell *X-Men*. You can spend a whole lotta effort getting consumer awareness up, then lose all your customers to the guy down the block with bigger pockets. Conversely, when you promote books that are outside the "average," that fit into your personal vision, it is extremely difficult for anyone to take that away!

Here's the drill: become intimately aware of your stock – read those comics, talk to your customers, find out what it is that you sell that strikes *your* chord. Diversify, a little at a time, bringing in new material that you've never stocked, and examine that, as well. Once you've found your path (and it's different for everyone), then start following it – start downplaying the material you don't believe in, and promoting the stuff you do. But don't expect a transformation to happen overnight – you have to be a little patient.

Look, as near as I can tell, I'm the first comic shop in America that went from the former industry standards of 60% of gross sales being Marvel comics, to carrying less than 10% of their line – and, I repeat again, our sales are up! "Pfft," you say, "you're in Frisco – I couldn't do that here in South Dakota." Nonsense! If you're dedicated, if you're dynamic, if you're focused, if you're excited, your customers will lead *anywhere* that you follow – they can sense your passion – they can feel it coming off you in waves.

Cherry-pick your store – it's good for you, and it's good for your customers!

Tilting at Windmills #44
(Originally ran in Comics Retailer #45)

The announcement of the "DC versus Marvel" crossover has created a cascade of thought within me. (I'll admit that this time I've cheated a little – most of this column is a rewrite and reinterpret of things I've said on CompuServe's Comics and Animation board. I figure if Mark Evanier can get away with it, well, so can I!) Let me start off with this much: "DCvM" will likely make a lot of money for a lot of people, at a time where it's prolly gonna be another slow Christmas. But I'm particularly concerned about the message this sends to the industry about what our prospects are.

In fact, I find this ineffably sad.

Have the "big two" finally reached the point where there are no longer any new creative ideas left?

It strikes me that as little as three years ago, this would've been an utterly unthinkable move – have sales fallen that far, that fast, that they're desperate enough to finally take this tack?

Year after year DC and Marvel have moved farther and farther away from the basic strengths that made them great: solid, self-contained storytelling that made us care about the characters and situations. But these days, it's like a game of one-upsmanship: "We're doing two covers on one comic," "O.K., we'll do *five*," "Fine, we'll do five, where each have a different eight pages in them," "Sure, but we've got three enhanced covers," "Good for you – we have three enhanced covers, and one bagged with trading cards," "Pfft, that's nothing! We have eight enhanced covers, all bagged with trading cards, and we're doing a cross-promotion with Mickey D's," "We're doing a big crossover – twenty comics," "Ours is bigger – it ties in twenty-five titles, and it's weekly," "Oh yeah, well, we're doing a *thirty* title crossover," "We can do *forty*," "Our *whole line* for *two* months." Etc.

When a publisher competes on any factor except the value of what's between the pages, they're destined to inevitably lose. DC and Marvel have now done virtually every promotion and gimmick under the sun – now they're trying to top them all, in one fell swoop. Oh, sure, it'll work – for those four months, at least – because these things almost always work for the duration of the push, but, as Steve Gerber once wrote, "What do you do the Day After you've Saved the Universe?"

One would think that after taking the serious pummeling the mainstream publishers have taken in sales volume over the last *n* months, someone up there would realize they've always been the architects of their own defeat. That the market vanished into thin air isn't any big mystery – the customers were driven away by deforesting them (as it were); where is the "replanting project?" When an audience gets hooked on adrenaline and speed, they've got to be given more and More and MORE and *MORE* and **MORE** and **MORE** adrenaline and speed, or they're gonna crash and kick. But, paradoxically, if you keep feeding them adrenaline, eventually their hearts are gonna give out anyway...

The rule is nearly universal that while you'll nearly always get a boost out of "event marketing," sell-through, post-event, is usually lower than it was pre-event. Every "jumping-on" point is a "jumping-off" point as well, and mainstream customers are actively looking for points to jump off.

So, there's little doubt in my mind that this will prolly be the most successful series of the last *n* months – I'll take a stab at an easy half a million copies ordered (though if it's not a slow news day when it gets released, that will prolly be far more than there are customers for it), but what happens the month after? I see two likely possibilities, both tied to editorial content:

1) The crossover kicks ass, up and down, so customers decide to re-sample books left and right (or new customers decide to check them out). What will they find? Well, standards may well change between now and spring, but it's more likely that they'll find the very elements that turned them off in the first place – still not only present, but pervasive – and after a brief flurry in sales, they will all drift off once again.

2) The crossover is mediocre (or good, but doesn't live up to what I can only imagine will be omnipresent hype), so nobody feels any need to sample new titles, and, in fact, eliminates some of their "hanging by a thread" comics.

I'll lay my money on #2, if only because we have the weight (and lessons) of history behind us.

And, so, what will they do next? What can they do next? Both Marvel and DC are editorially treading water (certainly *Underworld* has had only negligible impact on day-to-day sales), and by the time "DCvM" comes out we'll have a largely diluted interest in crossovers (*Spidey/Batman*, *Darkseid/Galactus*, and *GL/Surfer* will all be fresh in peoples minds – let alone other "lesser" lights such as the MEG/Malibu crossover, *Shi/Cyblade*, or even intra-company events like *Underworld*, or even *Zero Hour*) events.

Maybe I'm slow, but I just don't get it.

In a way, I'm sorta glad that it's finally gone this far – option #2, as I said, is the far more likely one – this will prolly be the thing that finally sends my customers screaming from universe-spanning books, into the arms of one vision/one book. Of course, only time will tell, but I think that this is the death knell of a marketing method that took its first Baby Steps with *Man of Steel* #1, peaked with the Death of same, and is on its knees by the time we get to "DcvM."

I really wish I had the balls to Just Say No to this event, but I'm not stupid enough to think I can suppress the last dying vines of fanboy interest – and that makes me a hypocrite, I guess. But, at the least, I can raise my voice in protest that we let it get this far.

Oh, you're back to saying, "But where's the harm? We're all gonna make some money! And it will probably be fun!"

I think the harm is that this is yet another symptom of the systematic short-term thinking that plagues the publishers. I can only suspect that a project of this magnitude takes/is taking/has taken a massive expenditure of time and effort on behalf of DC and Marvel management. But is that expenditure building anything, is it moving us anywhere? Or are we simply creating the shortest of short-term fixes (four months) that utterly ignores the long-term problem?

I'm not trying to be a pessimist – really, I'm not! If the tale is well executed and entertaining, I hope to God it sells for all it's worth. But history has shown us that putting all effort into this kind of massive event has seldom produced results beyond watering down an increasingly smaller customer base.

And that's the last thing we need, right now.

Listen, four months of fun, four months of entertainment, four months of cosmic all-out action and excitement is all well and fine – but what happens in month five, or seven, or twelve? If the basic fundamental quality of the material isn't fixed by March, if the publishers can't solidify their message and enunciate a path or direction they're heading, four months of fun will count for nothing.

We do not need any more short-term pogroms to get this market marching again – we need long-term vision and focus. And while I'm sure that both publishers would claim they have a long-term vision, every second that they've spent/will spend on this frippery is a second that could've been spent addressing the underlying, fundamental problems with the system we've all created.

There are those that will argue that we need to take these short term steps in order to assure that we'll have a comics market left in two years. But I can't be that pessimistic – I believe the market can fairly easily save itself – all it takes is looking past our assumptions and striking a fresh path. While we had a year of freefall at Comix Experience, just like all other retailers, once I redefined my attitude towards my stock, my sales have gone up 20% in the last three months.

Yes, yes, yes, I'm the "weird" retailer: "San Francisco, and your segment of it, is so different from the rest of the world, that your experiences are unrepresentative." Christ, I don't know how many times I've heard that!

But – I see stores, I hear from stores, every single day that are transforming their business from "same old" to "something fresh." That is where the retail community will re-win the hearts and minds of our consumers – from honest, open communication of what we really believe is good and worthwhile material.

While (again) I have no doubt whatsoever that this project is going to make a lot of money for a lot of people, I fundamentally believe that it's just feeding the "old" system – a system that we have to acknowledge does not work anymore.

See – and I think this might be the center of it – I don't particularly think the fortunes of Marvel's, DC's, and (let's call this straight) Image's universes are especially tied to either the fortunes of the medium of comics in general, or of comics retailers and talent in particular!

Yeah, they've enjoyed a good long run in the sun, but the time for "event marketing" (and what is a specifically "shared universe" but a smaller subset of "event marketing"?) is long ago over – what this industry wants, what the consumers are responding to, is title/creator specific marketing that has the weight of an honest opinion behind it.

Nobody needs "the DC universe" (and nobody especially wants it, either). What they need and want is *Starman,*or *Power of Shazam* or *Impulse* or *Batman Adventures* – books that may well take place in a specific milieu, but in which next to nothing from other titles significantly impacts their unfolding in any real way!

Titles. Not universes. That's what our customers want.

Retailers everywhere, every day are changing the dynamic with which they work, are changing their preconceptions of the market. You're doing it too – you're reading this magazine, and ideas are viral.

The lesson we've learned (even if it's hard to admit sometimes) is that the "industry" is not Marvel and DC and Image! The "industry" is Neil Gaiman and Frank Miller and Dave Sim and David Lapham and Todd McFarlane and Terry Moore and dozens upon dozens of other talented creators; and us, the retailers who sell those comics. Everyone else is just a to-market mechanism.

But the problem is neither talent nor retailer can effect those things outside of their own hands. I can't change a publisher's reliance on "event" marketing – all I can do is try to identify the books or publishers that attempt to bring substance, bring true value for the money that they ask, and try and promote those things within my store. I can't initiate nation-wide promotion and advertising campaigns that bring wide cross-sections of "civilians" into stores. All I can do is "convert" them one-by-one, "hand-selling" them on the merits of the form.

The apologists say, for example, that "events" like *Zero Hour*, or the "Breaking of Batman" or "Changing the X-Universe" will bring new customers pouring through our doors. They say big blockbuster movies featuring comics characters will get them running our way. And we've had year after year after year of these things, and where are we now? Sales are as low as they've been in the direct market. And confidence is even lower. The "mass market" is an illusion, because we give them nothing substantive to come back for.

Not to mention that we lost a generation of readers because of the virtual disappearance of comics presence on the newsstands. When I was buying my first comics in 1976, they were all over the newsstands – I wouldn't own a store today if I hadn't had my interest sparked as a child. Comics stopped being cool to kids, and have become an insignificant factor in children's lives.

If we really want to be a "mass-market" business, then we need to target the 4 to 6-year olds and their parents (as well as having something other than comics for only boys), and make the next generation comics-literate.

To keep a long-term business, I think we need to acknowledge that we've got to hold on (for ten to twenty years) to the older reader – and to grow from the ground up, the next generation of consumer who can't envision a world without comics.

The direct market can keep the older readers, but we need more viable publishers who will buck the trend of "let's piss off the long-time customers while we vainly hope for a way to real in the Image crowd, most of which have discovered girls and don't read comics anymore, anyway." The direct market will never adequately service the honest-to-God children we need to grow, because of limited resources, and limited geographic coverage – but we're really, really good at holding onto the adults as they grow older.

The general "all kids read comics" that was true of my generation appears to no longer exist anymore. The buying public is aging, and we have few "fresh recruits" coming in – unless we change something pretty darn fast (in content, in placement, in promoting, in advertising) we're gonna be in big trouble in twenty years when all our thirty- and forty- year-old customers start to die...

It is said that the direct market "saved" the industry, but I tend to think that it's proved to be no more than a stay of execution. The DM should satisfy the dedicated, sophisticated, and older customer – but there are nowhere near enough of us to significantly "replant" the market, even if we had the skill or inclination to do so.

Rather than having a "battle of the century," if I were in the big publishers' position, I'd be teaming up to do "Marvel & DC Adventures" – a co-published book aimed at creating new readers, with concise, well-told short stories, with both groups of heroes – like the shorts in *Superman & Batman* magazine, or some of the stuff in *Disney Adventures*, but all comics material, no text articles about how cool spiders are, y'know? Digest-sized, so it can be racked compactly, and a real low price for a thick package – maybe 96 pages for $1.95? Rather than wasting hundreds of man-hours putting together a deal that will yield 4 months or less worth of business, I'd spend those hundreds of hours using the combined might of Marvel and DC to recreate and reinvent the newsstand market.

That (or something much like it) is how we'll get the market started again – not by wasting time or limited resources frantically doing short-term projects. Marvel and DC spent countless money (in man hours and legal fees) to set up wholly different distribution systems. Then what do they do? Spend countless money (in man hours and legal fees) to set up a crossover between these two systems?

Is it just me? Doesn't this seem fundamentally insane?

Why not put that same effort into solving the underlying problems?

Now, I like to think I can count on DC holding its end of the bargain in promotion and delivery (both of initial orders, and quick and steady reorders) – a glance at *Superman* #75 shows that. But MEG/HWD? There's a whole 'nother can of worms. Their reorder fulfillment is positively lackluster, and, because they pack a week in advance of shipping, in most cases turnaround will be no better than two weeks, even if they do manage to print enough copies. So, #1 & 4 will be plentiful, but #2 & 3 might be hard to come by for the casual consumer.

That's not even to get into the reasonably flawed conception of this comic. By allowing "voting" on the results of the battles, they're likely to alienate half of the readership – most of my heavy DC customers don't like Marvel, and vice versa. What happens when you've just spent $16 to see all "your" heroes lose?

This is too damn long already so I'll end it with this point: no matter what the fan mail might say, the best "Marvel vs. DC" takes place in each fan's individual head. My "perfect" "DC vs. Marvel" is different from yours. Or his, hers, or theirs. Putting it down on paper cheapens this particular dream.

Hopefully we'll be able to learn. We need to soon.

See ya next month.

Tilting at Windmills #45
(Originally ran in Comics Retailer #46)

Interview with the Hibbs-pire

This issue's special feature is interviews by regular *Comics Retailer* columnists with industry figures. It's a fine idea, but I didn't know who to do. It would be fairly predictable if I had interviewed a person like Sim or Groth (besides, Bob and Bruce already grabbed onto those), so the next option is to go mainstream. But, while I considered briefly people such as Paul Levitz or Jerry Calabrese, I'm not so slow as to be oblivious to the fact that it's prolly unlikely that such people would be "unguarded" in conversation (especially with *me*!) – and I, for one, am not particularly interested in providing a space for the company line. Oh sure, I could try to be confrontational, but then this would be the smallest column this month (i.e., BRIAN: So, Jerry, how does it feel to be in essence a corporate whore who seems unable to lead your company anywhere but where others have blazed the trail? JERRY: This interview is over *<click>*).

Besides, while I enjoy the hell outta doing interviews, I friggin' *hate* transcription – an hour of work for every ten minutes of talk isn't *my* idea of a good time.

So, in a transparent attempt to hold onto my status as comic's biggest loud-mouth and iconoclast, I decided to take the revolutionary tack of interviewing *myself*!

These conversations took place on Wednesday, September 27, 1995 and Monday, October 6, 1995, and are presented in "raw" form – any editing done is by Boy Editor J.J. Miller. Hopefully you'll find these conversations as fascinating and involving of a look into the mind that some call "The Most Dangerous Man in Comics" (and others call "That Damn Pesky Hibbs") as I do.

Brian: ....just get this tape recorder started, then we'll begin...

Hibbs: Fine, fine...but the clock's ticking, O.K., kid?

Brian: Sure. Testing, testing. Alright, it seems like it's working now...Let's start with a "softball" question, O.K.? <Ahem> "Why don't you tell the audience a little about your background and history?"

Hibbs: What do you mean? In comics, or...

Brian: Well, let's start with the easy biographical stuff, and you can go from there, O.K.?

Hibbs: Sure. Well, let's see, I was born in Boone County, Missouri in June of sixty-seven.

Brian: 1967? Jeez, you're just a baby!

Hibbs: No shit, Sherlock.

Brian: And you're from the sticks?

Hibbs: Listen, d'you want me to answer the question, or not? Let me do this in my own way.

Brian: ....sorry...

Hibbs: S'alright. Yeah, I was born in the "Summer of Love" to a pair of wanna-be hippies, as a backwoods hick. Boone County. Can you believe it?

Brian: I guess we could call it "Out in the Boonies", huh?

Hibbs: Yeah, whatever. Anyway, we lived in Missouri for maybe six months, then my parents packed up and moved to New York. We lived in the 'burbs for a year or two – Long Island, I think it was – before we moved into Brooklyn. We spent maybe a decade there, then my parents split up. My dad got custody, moved us (including my stepmom) to San Francisco, where I've stayed ever since.

Brian: So you spent the majority of your childhood as a New Yorker?

Hibbs: Yeah. I don't have great memories of that time, either – as I said my parents were splitting up, I was an only child, and, since the neighborhood we lived in bordered a heavily Puerto Rican neighborhood, and I was a little blond-headed mouthy kid, I remember getting the shit kicked outta me all the time.

Brian: Doesn't sound like fun.

Hibbs: I think childhood is seldom fun – when you look at it through the patina of time, it appears to be the best time of your life, but I'm convinced that *now* is always the best time of your life. At least, it is, when you let it be.

Brian: I guess that's true. Do you think growing up the way you did creating your character?

Hibbs: How can it not? I'm a New Yorker in my heart – brusque, brash, insensitive, with a layer of Missouri below that: "show Me," y'know?

Brian: Sure.

Hibbs: But, in my soul, I'm from The City.

Brian: "The City?"

Hibbs: San Francisco. Jesus, they don't breed you interviewers too smart, do they? It's called The City, because it *is* The City. Once you've lived here, you'll prolly find you can't live anywhere else; it's got everything a city should have, but it still feels like a small town. San Francisco is a city of coincidences, of happenstance – there are few people you'll encounter who don't know of you, or, at least one of your friends. I think that's the essence of a small town: you know your neighbors, and they know you. There's a community feeling here that I can't live without. Yet...yet it's not so homespun that you're not a block from the corner store, y'know?

Anyway, I'm a "New York Dick," but a "Sensitive San Franciscan" as well.

Brian: Making you, what? A Sensitive Dick?

Hibbs: That's about right.

Brian: How about your involvement with comics?

Hibbs: Well, I was sixteen, and hanging out on Haight St. – Haight was the center of the original "hippie" movement in the 60s, and, while becoming a bombed-out, junky-filled area throughout the 70s, started to resurge in the mid-80s, at least partly based on a generation who wanted some of what their parents claimed they had, and tried to rebuild it again (though with even poorer results) – Haight is Love, right? Anyway, the Haight was going through a small renaissance, and a comic shop opened there. They had just opened, and I was in one of those right-place, right-time kind of scenarios. I'm a snot-nosed punk, but I can smell a good thing, even then – what 16-year old wouldn't give his left ball to work in a comic book store? Within a year I was managing the place, and I started to figure out a) what I was doing, and b) that I couldn't do it much longer for the guy I was working for – he *didn't* know what the game was, beside the "collectibles" scam portion of it.

Actually, maybe I'm misremembering – that patina of time I was talking about before – if it hadn't been for the owner's mismanagement (he lost two of his three stores) I might still be working there today. See, he also had a store in Berkeley, but it got shut down because he didn't pay his rent – he fired all of that staff, and told them, point-blank, he wasn't going to pay them. I couldn't countenance that, told him so, and he promptly fired me as well. Shit, he stills owes me $600 for my last paycheck.

The staff of the Berkeley store went on to open Comic Relief there, while "my" people helped me open Comix Experience.

Brian: Let me get the timing on this straight – how old were you when these events happened?

Hibbs: Lessee – it was like 16 to...19? that I worked for them. I worked for Capital City Distributors for a year or so right afterwards, and spent another couple of months working for a start-up comics shop that failed pretty quickly because the owner tried to open a second location far too soon, and killed them both. Two months before my 22nd birthday in 1989 I opened CE, and the rest, as they say, is history.

Working at CCD taught me sympathy and understanding of the distribution side (and that I didn't particularly care to give them my business – I recall the one time John and Milton came through the warehouse on "tour," and they treated us "grunts" like shit – like we didn't matter *at all*), while my retail experience gave me a head start on that side – *always* be friends with your landlord, *never* make promises you can't keep, and don't let your reach exceed your grasp.

Brian: But, why your own store? I mean, there you are, 21 years old – no higher education, and very little money – why did you think you'd make a go of it?

Hibbs: There are two reasons: one is that I've always been a fast learner – I dropped out of college at 17 because I didn't feel they could teach me more efficiently than "life" could; and the other is the "spark" – when something *sings* to you, *begging* to be done, invading and coloring both your dreams and your waking thoughts – well, it's pretty dumb to ignore that, don'cha think?

Brian: I guess – but if it hadn't worked you'd still be in debt today, slaving away at a job you probably didn't like, owned by someone who likely cared less than you – weren't you scared?

Hibbs: A little. But I felt then, as I do now, that it's better to have loved and lost than never to have loved at all. What did I have to lose? If I didn't *try* I'd still be in that dead-end job being profoundly unhappy. As long as I had my wife Tzipora by my side, fear could never outstrip ambition.

Brian: Why don't you tell us a little about Tzipora?

Hibbs: A little – O.K., I guess. She and I are best friends in the whole wide world, but she's into film as I am into comics. She doesn't care about comics one whit, but she cares about me with the energy of a sun.

We lead radically different lives, and only barely orbit each other – I think that's our secret – we've been together for ten years now, and we haven't had even one serious fight that I can think about. We respect each other fiercely, and the only thing we take for granted is that we love to wake up and see each other in the morning – it's my favorite thing in the whole wide world.

I suspect if Tzipi liked comics, we'd get on each others backs – but since she has her life, and I have mine, there is no friction.

Tzipi and I – well, it was Love at First Sight. We met on a public bus coming back from City College, if you can believe such a thing, and, in the ten years since, I don't believe we've spent more than 24 hours apart, aside from the occasional convention, or the like. She's my anchor, my stability, and, if there's anything in the world I care about more than comics, well, it's her.

Brian: That's really sweet.

Let me change the tape, and we can continue.

<click>

So, let's talk about your methodology and reactions to the business of comics.

Hibbs: Sure – my favorite subject!

Brian: One of the criticisms you frequently encounter relates to the old homily, "you can attract more flies with honey than vinegar." How would you respond to the charges that you're sometimes too strident in your criticism?

Hibbs: *<pause>*

Well, that's not a simple question, as I'm sure you're aware.

<pause>

I think the circumstances as well as the intent have to be measured as much as the message itself – the context is almost as important as the content. Sure, I can hold some strong opinions, but I think if you look at them in the context they were written, they're not as above and beyond as they *could* have been.

Having said that, I think a certain amount of righteous anger is O.K., if you've got something to be honestly cheesed about. I think a lot of retailers are pissed off, *because* they have something to be pissed off about. For example, look at the scenarios with *Spawn* shipping out of order, or with the now-defunct Continuity being unable to keep a single promise, or with our being forced into distributor relationships that we have no interest in, or love for. I could easily go on, but what it comes down to is that when someone does something *so* stupid as to start taking money out of my pocket, *when I played by the rules of their game*, then I've got a legitimate right to be steamed.

Brian: I think you're dodging the question...

Hibbs: Maybe. Part of it is, and I'm not trying to paint myself as any saint, O.K...?

Brian: Sure.

Hibbs: ...but, part of it is that my readers don't see the "behind the scenes" stuff, right? I mean, a LOT of the time, I'm trying to "fix" the problem before I write a column, if a "fix" is indeed possible.

Brian: Not that I doubt you, but do you want to give an example?

Hibbs: Yeah, happily. Let's take a fresh example – the redesign of *Previews*, and Diamond's willingness to let their suppliers design their own sections without any semblance of a "style guide." I found the new formats to be extremely unreadable – I made several phone calls to Diamond, and several to the most egregious "offenders," to see if a solution could be come up with without an embarrassing public spectacle.

Brian: You'll forgive me here, but aren't you a little arrogant?

Hibbs: In what way?

Brian: Well, in this assumption you seem to have that if *you* think an idea is right or wrong, then *all* other retailers will share that same opinion? That is to say, just because you feel a "style guide," as you put it, is important, doesn't mean that other retailers hold the same view!

Hibbs: <*pause*>
Yeah, maybe.

Brian: <*pause*>
So you have no "defense?"

Hibbs: Well, what can I say, really? Yeah, I *am* an arrogant S.O.B. – I know what works for me, and I extrapolate it back out to the rest of the world. What else can I do? I attempt to keep other frames of reference in mind when I form my position, but *nothing* is ever good for *everyone*, right?

Brian: So you're admitting...

Hibbs: Let me finish. What I'm saying is: what else do you expect me to do? You want arrogance? How 'bout this, kid – I'm currently running one of the very few profitable comic shops in this country. I'm told by distributors that roughly 17% of all self-defined comic shops went out of business in the last six months. I speak with *many* retailers directly, and many of them are desperately trying to backfill the debt they accumulated in '93 and '94 – and they're not doing the best job of it. Those that *are* succeeding tend to follow my general model (make your store what *you* want, not what "*they*" want). I'm one of less than half-a-dozen regular retail columnists in the field. And, it sure appears that I ride a few months ahead of the overall philosophical trends. As I said, I'm from Missouri: if I'm wrong, then "show me." I'm happy enough to admit I was wrong, if it's proven.

Brian: But that's what I'm saying: you assume you're right, unless you're "proven" wrong – that's hubris! You argue in terms of black and right, when the world is really grey; you seem not to accept any other viewpoint as valid, unless you generate it; You declare that merely *because* you happen to have a column, you're opinion is *automatically* more valid than anothers...

Hibbs: But what else would you have me do? The world *is* essentially black & white – in *most* cases those who claim that it's "grey" are trying to protect their own interests. Let's go back to the *Previews* example. It was suggested to me that perhaps many retailers would find the redesign more useful as a consumer sales tool – that's supposedly the "grey" area. But I don't think it is: the relationship between *Previews* as a consumer sales tool, and as a retailer ordering tool is irrelevant in terms of the discussion of the ordering tool!

Brian: What do you mean? I think that's a valid concern.

Hibbs: I didn't say it was "invalid," merely "irrelevant."

Brian: But, obviously, it's not, to Diamond – who pays for a second version?

Hibbs: Look, what I'm saying is that the question of "is *Previews* a good sales tool?" and "is Previews a good ordering tool?" are wholly different questions, and any attempt to "grey" the space between them is self-serving in terms of Diamond trying to save a little money. Why are they separate questions? Because one is voluntary, and one is compulsory! Whether or not I use the "sales tool" element of *Previews* is a decision that *I* make. On the other hand, I *must* use *Previews* if I want to continue ordering product for my racks. The little guy who lives in my brain and orders the comics has different needs than the little guy who is selling-through that same material to the consumer. And any poorly thought out attempt to satisfy the both of them is doomed to produce poor results for either.

Brian: I still don't think you see what I'm saying...

Hibbs: Of *course* I do! Do you think we'd even be having this dialogue if I didn't? But, you know just as well as I do that one can "grey" any concept to the point of meaningless.

Brian: Be that as it may, I don't think we're gonna change each other's minds in this forum.

Let's switch gears a little, and get your impressions on some of the "key players" in the new game.

Hibbs: Fine.

Brian: Marvel.

Hibbs: Irrelevant. And what's worse, they *made* themselves that way! By removing themselves from the mainstream of the marketplace, they made it a little difficult to care about them anymore. They also made a couple of horrible missteps in their six months, that, even if they solve, will color retailer's perceptions for years. They're gonna have to learn that they need to convert us back one-by-one – mass selling tools don't work any more because retailers have lost their faith in corporate messages.

Brian: Capital City.

Hibbs: Oooh! Hard call! If they can lock just a few more solid exclusives, and they carefully modulate their message, then they could actually prosper very well in the new climate. They generally have better pricing, and, if they can make themselves indispensable to the "quality retailer" by having more than a dozen comics you can only purchase from them, then their future looks good. The biggest thing working against them right now is their "pity us, please," message – If they could've locked DC, or Image, or Dark Horse in, they certainly would have – and this "monopolies are bad" screed of theirs, while certainly correct, stinks of sour grapes.

Brian: Diamond.

Hibbs: Another hard call. They traded off a lot of their profit in the largest publishers in order to lock those publishers with them – the money is going to have to come from somewhere. Where they used to make up to a 22% profit margin from, say, DC, they're now locked at 7% or so. Plus, as I understand it, they gave up a lot of their advertising revenue, as well, for their exclusives. Given that the publishers they've locked are not exactly seeing rising sales, I'll be curious to see on whose back they make their margins up. Since they can't do it with their exclusive publishers, that makes it more likely that it will come at the retailer's expense, I should think.

Brian: DC.

Hibbs: Schizophrenic. They make some of the greatest efforts to legitimately expand the frontiers of the market, but then they barely support those efforts. Actually, all in all, I would say DC's reach exceeded their grasp, on a regular basis. They hold the most promise for leadership in this market, then they squander most of those resources in inappropriate or dead-end directions. With dynamic leadership, DC *could* be the publishing leader of the 21st Century, but, as with all top-heavy corporations, they seem more interested in reacting to the market, rather than leading it in a healthy direction.

Brian: Image.

Hibbs: In deep trouble. From the outside, it appears that the company is structured to produce almost nothing but mega-hits, but the bulk of their line seems to have dipped down to pathetic sales levels. None of the Image founders, I would say, truly understand today's marketplace, and how "hot" never stays that way. They only seem to have a limited repertoire of tricks in their bag, and they have to learn that once "innovators" stop innovating they lose most of their audience. I don't much think Image will wholly collapse, but they're still playing by the old rules – the ones that put us in the position we face now. There is a *lot* of potential there, though – they just need to "grow up," and fast. Their *complete* dependence on the action genre, for example, is a wretched Achilles heel.

Brian: Dark Horse.

Hibbs: The company I worry about the least, actually. They're diverse, and they're relatively low to the ground. The biggest problems I see is their ambitious licensing program, which, if not managed *very* carefully can backfire; and their sometimes erratic editorial balance – months with three or more *Aliens* projects running concurrently, followed by months with none. But, both of these are relatively minor problems. They don't have as much to lose as an Image or a Marvel, because they never had that much to begin with, so I'm confident that a decade from now Dark Horse will still exist in some form, while I'm not sure the same could be said for Image, Marvel, or even DC.

Brian: The "small press."

Hibbs: Hard to answer, definitively, because there is *such* a range of product and personalities involved. If you keep your promises, if you deliver quality material, and if you don't blindly follow where others have led, then you can prolly make a go of it in the direct market. It's that "promise" thing that hurts them the most, I think. Don't say you're gonna be bi-monthly if all you can handle is quarterly, y'know? I've wasted more resources, proportionately, promoting the small press than the "big guys" ever directly cost me. It's frustrating getting behind a wonderful book like, say, *Tyrant*, then have it fizzle out after three issues – two of which were late! It's unpleasant trying to build, say, a *Starchild*, when the publisher can't keep a single scheduled initial shipdate.

Keeping promises may not be *easy*, but it sure is *important*.

Roughly half of my "want" list is now back in print in 2003. Half down, half to go!

Tilting at Windmills #46
(Originally ran in Comics Retailer #47)

Whether you want to admit it or not, the paradigm under which we do business has transformed in the last 18 months. Sales are dropping faster than they can be adjusted for, and the industry "spin" is more concerned with putting a bright face on a collapsing economy than with bold and dynamic leadership that can bring us out of the hole.

(Example: the introduction to the December sales charts in Diamond Dialogue reads as such: "While overall retailing forecasts for the 1995 holiday season predicted flat or slightly higher sales compared to last year, comic book specialty shops stood poised to wrap up the year on a more upbeat note, thanks to the collision of several familiar characters who have captured the attention of fans and the public-at-large for generations." A nice piece of positive writing, to be sure – but completely untrue for the industry as a whole. Sell-in to retailers is significantly down from Christmas 1994. We're not "poised" to do anything except fall off a cliff. And, while I suppose it could be argued that it is not in a distributor's best interest to panic its customers, the least I believe they should do is not out and out fib to us...)

I don't think it is any surprise to you, gentle reader, that I believe the time of the universe-spanning continuity driven super-hero is coming to an end. We had a great ride for a while, but it's over now. But, lest I be accused of over-arching negativity, let me observe that it doesn't have to be the end of what we know as the direct market, if only we can retool our industry into provide us with more long-term substance.

It is no secret that I believe our future lies in a paradigm more like that of a bookstore than of a magazine rack.

I heard a frightening statistic the other day – one which (as of press-time) I haven't been able to confirm. What I've been told is that less than half of the retailers in this business have *ever* ordered backstock from the Star System.

Whoa.

Frankly, I don't believe you should be allowed to call yourself a comic book store unless you have, at least, one copy each of these five TPBs in stock at all times: *Dark Knight Returns*, *Maus*, one *Sandman* volume (prolly *Doll's House*), *Understanding Comics*, and *Watchmen*. That's less than $50, your cost, and it represents the basic beginnings of a permanent stock section in your store.

At Comix Experience, we have more than 750 "permanent stock items." When a new comics Wednesday rolls around where there is barely enough salable material available to really bother to throw the doors open (mid-November had several such weeks), it is this permanent stock that allows us to maintain our cash flow.

Not only that, but it is this permanent stock that draws the "civilian" in – they don't want flimsy pamphlets that contain 5% of a story! They want a book that has a beginning, a middle, and an end.

The more permanent stock that retailers have effective access to (and effective is defined as systems like the Star System and Hyperlink where a regular pipeline is quickly available for little or no retailer carrying costs), the stronger this industry can become.

Given that (as I write this) Christmas is a little over two weeks away, allow me to present my Holiday Wish List – material that has gone out of print, or out of easy availability, but should be brought back. Material that the "civilian" might be interested in. Material that can provide a foundation for us to build from.

One quick note: some of this material might be sitting in a warehouse somewhere or another, waiting to be sold (I'm thinking, in particular, of titles formerly published by Eclipse) – but it does none of us any good unless this material is listed on Star and/or Hyperlink. I'm also aware that some of this material is available in Europe – but there is no homegrown source for it that I'm aware of.

In no particular order, here is my Top 25 Wish List:

1. *Blood* by JM DeMatties and Kent Williams
2. Garth Ennis' "Irish trilogy" (*True Faith, Troubled Souls, For a Few Troubles More*)
3. *A1* (the original anthology series, not the Marvel/Epic second [failed] try)
4. *Stig's Inferno* by Ty Templeton
5. Anne Rice's *Vampire Lestat, Master of Rampling Gate, Interview with a Vampire*, and (if it can be finished) *Queen of the Damned*
6. *Daredevil: Born Again* by Miller and Mazzuchelli
7. P. Craig Russell's adaptation of *The Magic Flute*
8. *Lone Wolf and Cub*!
9. The *Moebius* series of GNs – Marvel had, what, almost 20 of these at one point?
10. The *Groo* reprints – Sergio Aragonnes is one of the few comics artists which almost every person in America is familiar with
11. Jon J Muth's adaptation of *M*
12. *Mage*!
13. The Alan Moore *2000ad* library – *Halo Jones, Skizz, Dr & Quinch*, and the two short story books.
14. Grant Morrison's *Zenith*
15. Dan Brereton and James Hudnall's *Black Terror* and *Psycho*
16. The *Marvel Masterworks* series
17. *Miracleman*!
18. Mike Allred's early work: *Dead Air*, and *Citizen Nocturne* were the two trades, but there is still plenty of *Grafik Musik/Graphique Musique* material left
19. The Comico *Grendels*!
20. *Signal to Noise*. That we can't get this Gaiman/McKean masterpiece in the US is a crime
21. Miller's Elektra work – *Elektra: Assassin* (with Bill Sienkiewicz), and *Elektra Lives Again*
22. Old *Classics Illustrated*, in collected form. This could be a monster hit
23. A TPB of *Moonshadow*
24. *Stray Toasters*, by Bill Sienkiewicz
25. Simon Bisley's *Slaine*

What books would you like to see back in print?

I haven't got the foggiest notion why this is "#46.5". In fact, I don't even see that it ran in *Comics Retailer* at all. I've transferred all of the pre-#50 columns from my old computer (get this: they were in ASCII text format!), but there's no notes, or useful "date of creation" notations, or anything, really.

It's not especially objectionable, and no *CR* from #45-51 has two columns in it... so maybe I wrote this for someone else?

Oh, wait, maybe this ran in the *CBG* instead? As a "Guest Editorial"? I reference that in #50.

Well, either way, here it is.

Tilting at Windmills #46.5

At sixteen, sitting at her operator's desk, watching the lighted windows of Taggart trains roll past, Dagny had thought that she had entered her kind of world. In the years since, she learned that she hadn't. The adversary she found herself forced to fight was not worth matching or beating; it was not a superior ability which she could have found honor in challenging; it was ineptitude — a gray spread of cotton that seemed soft and shapeless, that could offer no resistance to anything or anybody, yet managed to be a barrier in her way. She stood, disarmed, before the riddle of what made this possible. She could find no answer.

– Ayn Rand, Atlas Shrugged, 1957

O.K., let's admit it, the direct market is nearly dead.

Now, I don't want to be pessimist (honestly! – I want to sell funny books for the rest of my life!), but we've got to call a spade a spade: overall national circulation is way off – maybe by as much as two-thirds (where one point on the Diamond "order index" used to regularly represent 2,500 comic books ordered, it now [November shipping] apparently represents a meager 850 comic books ordered. and, even scarier, average sell-through percentages reported by Diamond have dropped from averaging in the 80% range to averaging in the 70% range!).

We're past simply "collapsing" – the market is imploding. And this at Christmas time – the easiest time in the entire year to sell merchandise (unless you're on a college campus, where all the students go home...). Come the slow parts of the year (January to March) it's going to get even worse. When April 15th rolls around, most retailers are not going to have the cash flow remaining to pay their taxes. May, June, and July (the first traditionally strong period for selling comics in a fiscal year) are going to have a lot more retailers going out of business as their bills turn into "interruption of service" notices.

The strong and pervasive rumors of Marvel licensing off their titles to other publishers, if true, represents endgame for universe driven superhero concepts – to extend Dave Sim's Chess metaphor, it's like we thought we were playing Bobby Fischer, but it turned out we were actually playing Bobby Brady. Less than a year after MEG "shifted the blame" to the mechanism of delivery of comics, they are apparently realizing that this analysis was, in fact, incorrect (duh!) – it's what is between the covers that the consumer cares about. While the distribution aspect of the market did need an overhaul (and, in fact, still does, in some respects), it was never the root cause of comics' declining market. The content, and pricing, was.

MEG's abandonment of their paradigm not only is a matter of "too little, too late," but it is a clear sign, to this observer, at least, that the "Exclusives War" was a complete and utter waste of the resources of all the participants. DC, in particular, holds a massive responsibility for the position we find ourselves in – if they had just held out for a few more months, MEG would have shot themselves in the foot, and DC could have looked like the real white knight. Rather than concerning themselves with solving the problems, the "exclusive" publishers bought into MEG's party line: "It's not us, it's them." As I said then, I say again now – that paradigm is the old paradigm, and has no basis on selling funnybooks to the consumer.

It is not too late to rewrite the rules to suit the game we're actually playing, but the participants must recognize that the board has changed.

The retailers (as well as the consumers) are sick and tired of being treated as pawns. One of the underlying reasons that the market has imploded as fast as it has is that we (consumer and retailer) aren't willing to stand it anymore – we've lost our faith, we've lost our spark, and we've lost the dream – all because we were repeatedly told that we didn't matter. Well, here is a lesson for you, Mr. Publisher Man – we do matter, more than you ever thought. Retailer and consumer backlash has created a scenario where the major publishers can not win — we've lost all faith, and, so, we're not willing to accept just whatever is handed to us, anymore.

The implosion will continue to accelerate, until all we're left with is the vendors, the retailers, who are actually serious about this market. My guess is that this is something like 2000 retail stores – not enough of a base, in my mind, to continue playing the universe game.

Look, for the last three years I've been "Chicken Little" in the pages of *Comics Retailer*. I said that speculation would lead to bad ends. But publishers, distributors, retailers, creators, and even consumers refused to get off that train until it ran into a wall. I said that long-term planning, of building a perennial-based support system to equalize industry cash flow, was the essential key to having a future, but, to a man, the major publishers, as well as the distributors and retailers, decided that short-term profits were what we wanted to pursue. I said that the race to "exclusives" would backfire, but still the publishers chased after that plan as if it were the Holy Grail. So maybe, maybe, will you listen to me now? I'm not the brightest guy in this industry, but I've been right all the way across the board on our long-term prognosis and health.

I'll also note that I've tried my best to offer solutions as the problems came up – sales dropping because of retailer confidence? Institute partial returns to get no-risk material in the hands of those floundering without a direction. Can't write discount terms without screwing someone? Institute per-title discounts that reward retailers based on specific effort, rather than over-all, non-focused support. Yeah, I'll happily admit I'm a little full of myself, but I never stop thinking of ways to make this industry stronger and healthier. This is our responsibility to this industry we all hold dear.

I don't want to sound like I'm only beating up on the publishers – every other segment of our industry has its own measure of responsibility in how we got to where we are. Retailers chased the short-term dollar as much as anyone else, and sent the wrong messages to the publishers. Distributors exacerbated this situation by promoting the "sure thing" to the detriment of the "long-term thing." Consumers' buying patterns reinforced the idea that the only thing that mattered was a little glitz, a little glitter, and a whole new range of new first issues each and every month. Creators dogged it for a buck, trying to get their piece of the pie. And the trade press put their "stamp of approval" on the whole mess. But publishers have to be ones to take the first step of dynamic leadership, because they're the only ones in a position to generate and/or finance the projects that can lead us out of the mire.

A retailer has the ability to say, "I'll order more copies of title *x*," or, "I decline to stock item *y*," but if I want to have more material like *Sandman* or *Stray Bullets* or *Optic Nerve* – well, I have no ability to generate more. A creator can come up with a dynamic, long-term new project, but if no publisher will accept it, it's far more difficult to get that material to market (self-publishing is only a real option for a small percentage). It falls to the publisher to create a long-range direction for the market to head.

Were I a major publisher, here is what I would do:

1) Forget about the first half of '96. Get your house in order first, before you try to launch new products and concepts into this market. I predict that no new title launched by a major publisher in January to June will "stick" – this is not a market which is willing to take chances anymore. Sales are going to continue to decline, and retail outlets are going to continue to go away. Start making plans right now for Christmas '96 – and for God's sake, involve the "leading retailers" in those plans.

2) Forget all about cross-line continuity. Don't cross titles into one another, focus on self-contained stories that give a significant value for the dollar.

3) All new launches must have a focused marketing and promotional plan behind them, that is sustained throughout six months to a year. One of the greatest sins that all publishers commit is only having a promotional campaign that predates a book's launch. Once the title arrives in a store, it is left to sink or swim on its own (because there is another new launch coming in right behind it). In much the same way, if a periodical title is launched, trade paperback collections must be part of the first year plan. The first arc (or natural trade break if the work is largely self-contained) should be on the market approximately three to six months after the final chapter has shipped – this gives you a long-term base to work from, and the ability to achieve

the all too necessary "critical mass" that a title must achieve to survive. Look to *Sandman*, look to *Sin City*, look to *Cerebus* as the proper model on which to build a title.

4) In conjunction with #3, create ongoing promotional efforts that don't become useless 30 days later. What retailers need are sales tools that don't expire. Where are the modular displays that can be redesigned as needed? Where were (for this year's Christmas) the promo items that promote the backstock, as a focused line?

5) Forget about unnatural line-extension when a success is built, and strip away the current lines until they reach the core. It is mad to have months where ten or more (for example) "Batman-line" titles are shipping. The consumer can't afford it, the retailer can not take any significant stocking position, and the publisher can not sustain it (either editorially, or from marketing) – two Spider-Man comics are a lot more effective than fourteen. Less is more. Titles, not Universes.

6) Forget about the bulk of the current sales force (i.e. the retailers). This may sound a little funny coming from a retailer, but one of the traditional problems publishers have to face is how do you tailor the marketing messages so they are appropriate for 6,000 different retailers, many of whom may not have a strong grasp of business principles (I'm being polite...). That is: it's not terribly cost-effective to print 6,000 promotional items if only 600 (or 60) retailers are going to use them. Publisher marketing plans (when they consist of more than "put out some number ones, put out some crossovers") are aimed at the worst retailers in the business, not at the best. I think just the opposite is the way to go: raise the bar. The raw numbers leave very little question: many, if not most, retailers are going to go away in the next six months. It is going to be a terrible tragedy for the livelihoods lost, but it is ultimately just economic Darwinism at work. We've needed to change for years, and we forestalled it as long as we could, but the days of anyone with a comics collection, and a couple of thousand dollars being able to open a comic book store are now gone. Focus on the needs of the top percentiles of retailers – the ones who will still be here next year – not the bottom.

7) Push the talent to be innovative, not repetitive. New ideas are needed, new genres, new approaches. Stop relying on formula, or get off the bus.

8) Don't publish anything that you're unwilling to make a long-term commitment (i.e. TPBs) to. It is a waste of resources to do otherwise. Every dollar spent in editorial should be focused at making ten dollars over the next five years, not three dollars in the next 30 days, and nothing thereafter. Entropy dictates that readership will dwindle, unless they have clear paths to entry into a work. In a focused backstock plan, one sale leads to another, as it is clear where to go. If I, as a retailer, can successfully hand-sell one *Sandman* trade to a customer, other sales naturally follow to the other eight trades. If I hand-sell someone the *Spawn* trade, there is no "next sale" – the gap from issue #5 in the trade to issue #36 on the rack is too great for the average new reader to hunt and chase. Trades should be the goal, not an aberration.

9) As much as the direct market has been a cash cow, it is time to look beyond this base if we want to have a market in the 21st Century. We, as an industry, lost an entire generation of children, as we depended upon the direct market as our primary revenue source. The direct market, while perhaps adequate at servicing children, creating the long-term reader, is actually geared towards serving the older, and more sophisticated consumer. And we certainly are poor at creating the

new child reader. Why is this an important consideration? Because you need to "start them young" in order to generate new readers who are comics-literate. I, and probably most of you, got my first comic when I was six or seven, purchased off the newsstand. That started a love affair with the form. But newsstand presence is greatly diminished in 1996 – where you could find comic books in virtually every "corner store" in 1972, this is a rarity today.

We need a "feeder market" to generate new customers – customers that might not buy their first comic with their own money for another half a decade, perhaps – but they'll be the new crop of twelve-year-olds in 2001. And if we don't get that crop in 2001, then we can forget all about any hope of comics being more than an anachronism. To believe that the direct market can support the medium without a feeder system is like believing that record stores would be successful without the radio or MTV.

There is more (there always is), but we'll start with that. Note that this, once you strip away all the permutations breaks down to one phrase: Think long term. Build a future, don't strip mine the present.

That same advice applies to retailers – we have to be in building mode. In the next six months, your permanent stock should continue to become a more significant amount of your floor space. Don't promote that which you haven't faith in – if you don't burn, you can't earn! Don't support projects or publishers that don't show you long-term plans. Your cash flow isn't strong enough to be the sole promotional source for a title. Your cash flow isn't strong enough to build the necessary critical mass a title needs to "break out." The books we can build at Comix Experience are the books that have an open supply line that is both regular and steady – the *Stray Bullet*s, the *Strangers in Paradise*s, the *Sin City*s, the *Sandman*s. Don't commit your resources, your time, your money to suppliers that can't assure a strong and steady line. An army moves on its stomach. Retailing is no different. You control what comes into your stores, how it is sold, and too whom – don't abrogate that responsibility to lines that haven't your best interests at heart.

I recall a thread in one of Asimov's *Foundation* books where a choice had to be made that would lead to either a hundred years of "Dark Ages" throughout the galaxy, or a thousand. The shorter option required hard painful action that would make things worse for the time being, but presented a quicker recovery. But if the choice was made to take the short-term easy path, then the recovery would be that much further off. This is the scenario we face now: do we continue to focus on the short-term to the detriment of the long, or vice versa?

That's it. It's not too hard. Make a choice.

When Dagny left the Board room and walked through the clean, cold air of the streets, she heard two words repeated clearly, insistently in the numbed emptiness of her mind: Get out...Get out...Get out.

She listened, aghast. The thought of leaving Taggart Transcontinental did not belong among the things she could hold as conceivable. She felt terror, not at the thought, but at the question of what had made her think it. She shook her head angrily; she told herself that Taggart Transcontinental would need her more than ever.

— Ibid.

Tilting at Windmills #47
(Originally ran in Comics Retailer #48)

Do I get to say "I told you so" yet?

The Marvelcution. The DCD Implosion. It didn't take a prophet to see these coming. In the short-term, our prognosis is grim – coming into the slowest months of the year (late January to early April) is not the time *I* would have chosen to rewrite the distribution system and create a product bottleneck, but I guess that's why I'm just a struggling retailer and not a highly-paid comics executive.

You're reading this at or around the middle of February. Comics retailing is coming out of the second slow Christmas season in a row. Cash flow is at its worst, and you're busy trying to learn a whole new set of rules to the retailing game. Happy New Year, and welcome to the next level!

Here's the deal: your costs, after going up for the last six months, are going to go up again. A lot. I certainly expect my freight charges to double. Especially given that I'll be paying *separate* freight for reorders.

I think it's inevitable that the relative ease of service you're accustomed to will diminish – with a local warehouse you're more likely to have a particular employee who dealt with your idiosyncratic operation in the way you expected to be dealt with. But, in a national model, that "hands-on" customer service is bound to diminish.

Ordering will become more problematic as, now that we finally got the reorder systems work with a modicum of effectiveness, the associated freight costs will hamper our ability to place small and steady increases.

These increased costs of doing business (not even especially monetary – my paperwork has nearly tripled since July – that's a lot of man hours) coupled with still declining sales on many lines is going to put a lot more retail operations out of business.

By trying to service their 5000 (+/-) accounts by UPS exclusively, with no particular experience doing so, I predict a long "shaking-out" period before service is adequate. Even if they have a "problem rate" of only $1/10^{th}$ of 1% each week, that's still five retailers a week who might get late or damaged or partial shipments *through no fault of their own*. That doesn't sound like much, I'll admit, but it can be life or death if you're one of those five stores that week.

The product bottleneck that Marvel has been seeing (they are the number one publisher for late-shipping product, currently) is likely only going to get worse as fewer editorial personnel (with shaky morale) try and finish jobs they didn't begin.

But, then, you know all this, don't you?

Actually, I'm starting to get a little tired of being negative. Oh, it was all well and fine when I was the only retailer in the business who was willing to call the bad stuff out – but now all of you sound like *me* when I talk to you...it's a little depressing, y'know?

So, let's try to find some good points in all of this, O.K.? The general implosion of this market is more likely to create a "level playing field" than all the "open access" promises a publisher or distributor makes. The room on the shelf that has been/is being freed up in the wake of the collapse of the super-hero stranglehold must be filled by something. It is as likely to be filled with a comic that reflects a personal vision as that of a corporate one, and, further, it is likely to be less dependent on a single genre than ever before.

There are two ways to rack your store: by merit/consistency, or by the cost associated with a product. The best retailers take both into account. Merit/consistency relates to selling material by the quality involved, not the logo on the cover. I look to fill my store with the best comics available – comics that give me and my customers good entertainment value for my dollar. The important bit to remember is that you really do have control over what you stock – while you need to keep consumer patterns in mind, your customers will largely follow where you lead, if you have faith in the material. The company logo doesn't matter, unless you *make* it matter. Giving rack space to a vendor is a *privilege* for them – always remember this. That rack space is *yours*, you *owe* it to *no* publisher, large or small. They have to *earn* it by putting out material that *you* feel belongs there. Once you recognize and affirm this (as you will *have* to, to come out the other side), you'll soon see that distribution-driven catalog space and profile is often out of line with the merit of the material presented. What this means is that the forward thinking comics retailer "skims the cream" from a variety of publishers.

Because many of the advantages a large publisher has (subsidizing costs with the savings from volume printing, or being the only party with distributor recognition, to name but two) are diminishing in our new climate, I fully expect to see a renaissance in passionate, creator-driven visions from a wider variety of publishers. I'd love to see six to eight publishers, each with a different focus, and all with about a 10% market share. As the super-hero market as we know it continues to shrink, this only creates new opportunities for visionary entrepreneurs. I stress the word "visionary," though. We've had some commendable stabs in one direction or another, but we've yet to see any measure of the sustained effort all start-ups require.

The other factor in racking your store is by the associated costs. For example, a store spends $5000 and gets 52% on Marvel (plus some possible, but less likely, "incentive bonuses") at Heroes World, 55% on DC and Image (as of this writing!), 50% on Dark Horse, and most "essential publishers" (please note this is not an endorsement for what I find to be a horrible and biased layout for Diamond's *Previews*. It is merely the quickest way to illustrate a point), and 45% on almost every other publisher from Diamond, or (in almost all cases) 50% on all titles not DCD-exclusive or Marvel at Capital City.

In this example the store gets the best margin on DC and Image, then Marvel, then everyone else, especially if they use both Diamond and Capital. Now I know someone out there is sharpening their pencil (Preston?) to rightly point out that a retailer's purchasing power is not as 1:1 interchangeable as I posit. A $5000 purchasing budget is not going to be spent 100% at any of these distributors, if you even slightly resemble a comic book shop. Maybe only $1000 of that budget goes to HWD – that's only 46% on Marvel. Maybe it's $2500 – that's 49% on Marvel. $1000 on DC is 50%, and $2500 it's 52.5%. $1500 total at DCD gets you 45% on everyone but DC and Image, but even $5 gives you 50% on most every comic CCD carries.

The point of all this harrowing and confusing math and chart checking is to look at where your costs are, from *each* distributor. Especially if you're a small store – you might find that the flat pricing Capital City offers gives you an equal or greater margin (*Cerebus* is 55% to *everyone*!) on many self-published and small-press titles than you might get from most of the major publishers at DCD or HWD! Generally speaking, it is wise to focus your efforts on the titles that give you the best profit margin. Remember: a 5% difference in discount is a 10% difference in profit! With a higher margin, your risk is lower, too, so you can take stronger and more confident stocking levels. You might find out that some publishers are performing very differently than your time and effort in racking and display.

But you'll never know if you don't do the math.

I think having a clear vision of kind of store you want to be, paying close attention to margins and sell-through, having a wide (but not deep) selection of perennial merchandise, and focusing on the comics you *love* to sell are the four keys for success in comic book retailing in the new millennium.

We've got a lot of challenges in front of us – no doubt about it – and we've got a lot of wrinkles to figure out and smooth, but the smart retailers will find a path through the storm. Let's hope you're one of them, too!

Tilting at Windmills #48
(Originally ran in Comics Retailer #49)

Boy Editor J.J. Miller made the astute observation that, excluding San Diego, we've lost all other retailer trade shows as the debris from The Upheaval continues to settle. Distributor-driven trade shows are apparently a thing of the past, and the few regional conventions that held such things have seemingly abandoned them.

What's ironic about this is that this is the *very* time most retailers need more information about running a more professional business and juggling more paperwork! Business is seldom easy, and The Upheaval has only made it more difficult for comic book retailers to survive, let alone prosper.

My largest concern is the lack of communication between the various levels of the industry. My feeling over the last few months is that while some publishers have gotten more focused and professional in presenting their marketing messages, the underlying plans are not created in consultation with the retailers – the ones who, at the end of the day, are taking the greatest risk and responsibility with the product.

Now, some may accuse me of hubris in this matter, but I firmly believe that retailers are better able to determine what is workable and salable in a publishing and marketing plan than nearly any publisher employee. That's not to say that there are not many dedicated, and wildly intelligent, people working at the publisher level – there most certainly are – but they don't look the customer in the eye when they come up to the counter with their purchase.

This, I think, is the key – the publisher, the distributor, they're "insulated" from the actual purchase of the product. Unlike other kinds of retailing, comics have always been fan-oriented. We've only got a limited number of consumers purchasing our product, with little mass market penetration. Customers are leaving the field, and it takes months for that information to get back to the publisher level. I was having a conversation with a creator who used to work for one of the former Big Five. He told me that, eighteen months ago, as the decline started, the publisher kept insisting that the sales figures had dropped as far as they could. Then, a month later, when the new, lower figures would come in, the same statement would be made. This continued as long as this creator kept working for the company, and I presume it is still occurring today. The very nature of the direct market encourages thinking focused on the wrong elements on the publishing level.

The nice thing about retailer input is that it is "free." I've yet to meet a single retailer who didn't have hard-won opinions on what and why are problems are. They're happy to share and process this information, because they're the first ones at risk of going out of business from bad publisher decisions. An enormously large pool of information is there, waiting to be tapped by the intelligent publisher or distributor.

What we need to avoid is the "dog and pony show" mentality that has colored previous industry functions. Most "trade shows" appeared to be designed to sell more material to us, rather than working with us to sell more product. This may sound like an exercise in semantics to you, but I learned early in my short life that there are two kinds of power relationships – power-over, and power-with. Power-over can be as blatant as "do what we tell you, and no one will get hurt," or as subtle as "do what we tell you, because we know better." Power-with, on the other hand takes the form of "We think this is what you should do, but we're happy to be proven wrong, and to find a better way." Most relationships between the points on the direct market triangle are one form or another of power-over. By example: Diamond has announced they're setting a "comic shop locater service" (a worthwhile goal, by the way) – this service was set up by Diamond, with input from the largest publishers. Retailers are being asked to fund this program, but, as near as I can tell, no retailer has any input into how this program will be run, or how resources will be allocated. While, as I said, I think it's a noble goal to set up this program, I'm not sure that I'm willing to give the distributor $x a month for a program that neither I (or any other retailer) has oversight or decision-making input in. Diamond may well believe that they are working for the best interests of all participants – and I have no doubt that they'll *try* – but the "power" in this transaction flows from them, rather than being mutual and shared. Diamond has had, for the last two years, a "retailer advisory board" – I know this because I "sat" on it this whole time – but not once in that time did they ask us for any input in such a program, whether it being in starting it up, or organizing and running it. I mean, here you have a group of fifty retailers who have *volunteered* time from their busy schedules to do work for *free*, and they never once utilized this resource in any substantive manner.

The marketplace is dying. Now, more than ever, we need to fundamentally alter and transform the relationships of communication in this business. Were I a publisher, I'd have at least one employee whose job is to be on the road organizing small pockets of retailer communication. Not the "Fall Fling" model, where the very act of bringing together fifty or more retailers causes the whole act to degenerate into a free-for-all bitch-fest – no, I mean targeted "focus groups" where half-a-dozen retailers are put together to discuss specific, practical agendas. Promotions, organization, marketing plans – these things simply cannot be discussed in "open sessions."

Publishers will say, if asked, that they'll happily attend such things, but only if we take the initiative, and set them up. Witness the DLG meeting in January. While it is very useful for retailers to be able to determine an agenda that suits their needs, I also feel that the publishers need to bring to us where and why they're going. A small example: I thought almost all in-store promotional elements of Marvel vs DC were garish, badly designed, and inappropriate. A retailer-driven agenda is not going to touch the specifics of upcoming in-store promotion, if only because we have no idea what these things are going to be. I cannot plan title-specific promotions more than three months in advance, if only because I don't know what titles are coming when, and what tools I'll be provided with to promote those titles. I can only speak for myself, but I want to start planning for the fall *today*. Not set-in-stone plans that aren't flexible, but at least a solid outline of what my options are.

Retailers don't organize, don't utilize the power that we have, because we've been trained to think we have none – few retailers will spontaneously organize, because we believe it will do little good. CBRI lasted a few years, then fizzled under it's own weight. The DLG announced ambitious plans, then apparently had no follow-through for two years. PACER seems to accomplish nothing. We're talking about a long history of retailer's groups that can't even publish the simplest position paper! I'd love to be proven wrong, but it appears to this observer than comic book retailers are like the (soon to be?) proverbial 1000 cats. Heck, I *tried* to start my own organization, but it quickly became apparent that if *I* didn't do *everything*, then *nothing* would happen. That's not to fault anyone – hell, we're all working enormously hard just trying to keep our stores running – but if publishers and distributors want to stop the free-fall, want to halt the distrust, want to restore our faith, then they need to come to us. I used to joke after the Defiant fiasco that Jim Shooter would have to visit every comic shop in America personally, and hand us a $100 bill, in order for us to trust him again. But it's not just Jim any more. It's virtually all of you.

I don't have the resources, or the time, to set up a focus group locally. It's not a cop-out, it's the truth. I can't do it, nor can most retailers. But DC can. Marvel can. Image can. Dark Horse can. Diamond can. Capital City probably can. Let's make something happen, folks. Because you've lost our faith.

Tilting at Windmills #49
(Originally ran in Comics Retailer #50)

Happy May, everyone. Sure, it's still March when I'm writing this, but as you're reading this, summer is nearly upon us. The first real convention of the year (WonderCon in late April) has just happened, and with it Comix Experience's seventh anniversary.

Compared to some of you, I'm still a kid at retailing comics, but seven years feels like a fairly significant watershed to me. As we go into "Lucky Seven," CE has actually gotten healthier, as we redefine and refocus our goals. Those goals are to be the kind of comic shop that *I* would want to shop in, and to sell the *best* in comics, regardless of "name value" (publisher, creator, or distributor exclusives) attached. If only this were as easy as it sounds.

It's actually *starting* to look like the publishers are getting their act together editorially – that's good. But it's costing retailers more money to stock that material, now. In first quarter 1995, I received 55% off on several hundred different titles. Now, I only qualify for that with two publishers – DC and Aardvark-Vanaheim. In first quarter 1995, I had free shipping (via Diamond). Now, my shipping bills are somewhere around $60 a week! (I expect that to be higher any moment now, too, as I expect Diamond's "freight subsidy" will evaporate almost immediately. Any company that has the *nerve* to ask $5 a week to fax you an invoice [which, even in worst case scenario, assuming overwhelmingly penurious phone bills, couldn't possibly cost more than $3] is unlikely to continue to show such stated "benevolence"). Our marginal costs continue to accelerate, and in a field where (evidently) the majority of storefronts depend solely on day-to-day cash flow to keep the doors open, that's gonna kill a lot of people. In fact, I've heard about more stores closing in the first two months of 1996 than I *ever* have before. Though I admit that this is certainly not empirical evidence of the actual state of our nebulously defined market, I find it an unsettling omen of the shape of things to come.

As comic book retailers we're actually given very few tools (and inadequate ones at that) with which we can shape our destinies. I'm talking about the ability to do long-term planning, because of the secrecy of the solicitation process, or to do short-term planning because of the uncertainty of shipping schedules, things like that. Historically, I think, we were largely unconcerned about this because our profit margin was wide enough to absorb this inconvenience. Let us also not forget that, historically, comics have been a very inexpensive medium with a supremely dedicated fan base. It was not until the excesses of the 90s that we destroyed both of these paradigms. The financial impact of the loss of the true fan base sent the shockwaves that brought the distribution system low, and we're left with what's left of the non-retailer part of the market trying to maintain their profit margins at our expense. Of course, that's just *more* strip-mining, and I think we know where that leads by now.

And now that we have to face the price of these actions – some self-inflicted, and others not – the cost remains the same. Ironically, those without the weight of historical patterns of comics retailing upon them are more likely to find the smart path to whatever the new paradigm turns out to be. I submit the likely path to be the "bookstore model," but I'm just as likely to be surprised by something new. In the meantime, it's the path I'm walking, so forgive me if I commit the sin of universalizing my experiences to believe you can find success in focusing your store, too.

The first thing we did was completely re-rack the store away from a periodical focus. We've always had some amount of genre racking at Comix Experience – even the week the store opened we had a separate Underground section, as well as loosely themed graphic novel section. In the early days, I would have given you *such* a pinch if you would even *suggest* racking by company for regular superhero comics! Back when Marvel was 80% of the market place, it was bad for diversity to segregate, but today, now that no publisher seems to be able to manage more than 1/3 of the market, single-handedly, it allows you to clearly focus and target your sales message.

Prior to February 29th (Superman's Birthday!), the left hand side of the store was all graphic novels, books, etc., while the right hand side was the last 30-60 days worth of periodicals, in mostly A-Z (we had a few exceptions, like Manga or Alternative, that we pulled out, but it was pretty firmly alphabetical). In the Big Change, we broke everything into genre-like categories. We're only a week old at doing this, but the first blush results look promising. We created plastic sign-holders for each shelf so we can quickly change and rearrange categories with little or no fuss. We have roughly 1300 "facings" available to us (though we tend to run a little tighter than that with spine-up titles, as well). In the first round, we've divided the store into the following sections:

Adult/European	Industry/Genre Magazines
Alan Moore	Kids
Alternative	Licensed Comics
Anthologies	Manga
Art Instruction	Marvel Universe
"Bad Girls"	Miscellaneous
Batman	Neil Gaiman
Caliber	Other Hero Comics
Crime/Mystery	"Recommended Reading"
DC Universe	Self-published
EC & other classics	Star Trek
Fantasy	Star Wars
General Science-Fiction	Superman
Horror	Tekno/Valiant
Image/Extreme	Underground
Image/WildStorm	Vertigo
Image/Other	X-Men

I offer this to hopefully spur your mind into thinking about how *you'd* break *your* racks out. The nice thing about this kind of set-up is that, for example, on the Batman rack you have both periodicals and trade paperbacks intermingled, heightening sales between both. Some of these "genres" occupy multiple shelves, while others barely take a shelf alone. I fully expect these divisions to mutate significantly, over time.

You'll note that I use "genre" loosely – splitting the superhero companies into "brands." One of the reasons for this is the distribution of space. One of the problems with strictly "genre" racking (as opposed to "family" racking) is that the superhero genre comprises the bulk of the comics available to us, significantly reducing the value of stock separation. The question is what kind of public perception of your store do you want to create? Most regular customers are already well keyed into superhero style comics, and, it can be argued, that's really about all they want, unless you work to change their natural inclinations. But the "civilian" – well, they're simply not interested in this type of material, as a general rule. If you want to attract a new class and type of clientele, then you need to present them with a vision that doesn't contradict their sensibilities.

Roughly 25-33%% of our floor space is devoted to superhero-style comics, but by dividing the hero publishers into "camps," and dispersing them along the sales floor, rather than keeping the hero books in one clump, I've created the illusion that the presence of hero comics is far less than it actually is. The point is that this type of material is there, accessible, for those who want it, but the overall "color" of Comix Experience presents another feeling altogether.

Another advantage to breaking your racks into closely defined groupings is it will help your perspective of what items sell to what people. As I said earlier, comic book retailers have few and inadequate tools to determine proper stocking quantities – chief among these tools is our friend, the cycle sheet. Cycle sheets *are* an incredibly useful tool for analysis of what sells, and when – but that information tends to live in its own vacuum, without relationship to other data. By this I mean that my cycle sheets may tell me that I sell no more than five copies each of, say, *Youngblood* and *Blood Pool,* but this data is separately wildly by the alphabet. I have a general benchmark to work from in terms of knowing that, for example, sales of ten copies is modest, 25 is decent, 50 is strong, and 75 is a hit, but my comparisons are limited to book to general benchmark: how does *Youngblood* compare, how does *Blood Pool* compare?

This type of analysis, while not *un-useful,* doesn't give you a lot of qualitative data to work from. By abandoning straight ABC, even in something as simple as organizing cycle sheet flow, you can quickly see the relationships between titles. Now that my cycle sheets are categorized by "genre," just like my racks, I can get better data about the relationships between titles, without having to *hunt* for it. So, now that all Image/Extreme books are lumped together, to continue the example, I can now *quickly* see that I'm not selling more than five copies of *any* of them. No longer am I comparing specific book to general benchmark (five copies of *Youngblood,* to 25 copies of overall "decent seller"), but rather I'm comparing specific book to specific benchmark (five copies of *Youngblood* to average sales of five each on Image/Extreme) and *then* to the general benchmark. This has caused my perceptions of various lines to change, and allows me to *quickly* see which lines are "pulling their own weight."

I think the difference in seeing relationships between titles and *lines* is an important one for the retailer to acknowledge. Given that rack space is finite, and product offered is (at least *relatively*) infinite, you don't want to think about sales only in terms of the vacuum of your racking system. By having a tool available to show me that I sell an average of five copies each on the "Image/Extreme" shelf, but an average of 50 copies each on the "crime/mystery" shelf, I now have the ability to make an *informed* modification in my "behavior." Maybe I want to fold Image/Extreme into Image/Other, maybe I want to reposition Image/Extreme on my shelves, or maybe I want to make that line of comics available only through advance subscription orders. I've *always* had this data, but I wasn't getting the "signal" through the "noise" of a straight alphabetical system. This is not unlike the epiphany retailers who didn't cycle sheet get when they've done their first batch – "Jeez! I *thought Youngblood* was selling 15 copies a month, because when I eyeballed the shelves, it didn't seem like the stack was too high – but I'm only selling *ten* copies each month! Whoa!" – I *thought* Image/Extreme was selling better as a whole than it really was, because I was letting my *eyes* do the work that is better suited for *data.*

There is a hew and a cry across the land for retailers to "clean up their acts," to "act more professionally," and while it is true that we could stand some improvement, I think the truth is that *we're doing the best that we can within the limitations as we understand them.* An important thing to keep in mind, for those critical parties, is just how much comics retailing has changed over the last half-decade: previously our margin was fat, our cost of goods low, and our customer base large. This created a large amount of complacency is *how* you run a comic book store. I don't suppose that most of you are much different than me – I've got only two part-time employees, and while I make enough money to keep a roof over my store and my home, I don't have a thick excess of time or money to do all the things I might think I *should* do. For example, I *know* it would probably be wise to get a point-of-sale system that can create these kinds of reports at the push of a button – but the initial cash-outlay for the system, as well as the mountain of data-entry we'd have to do, daunts me. Sure, it would *probably* increase my cash flow so that a new system would pay for itself, but I'd rather try and find a low-tech solution that accomplishes the same goals than spend the money.

Low-tech is a fine way to go, because you can tailor the path to *your* inclinations. It doesn't add any appreciable time for me to change colors on the back issues tags once a quarter. But to type every back issue I have into my computer, and have it spit out custom bar-codes, so I can get a quarterly report on what items aren't pulling their weight, is likely to cost me an hour a day, if not more. The low-tech color-coded method accomplishes (effectively) the same general task as the high-tech POS system, but it doesn't significantly increase my workload. In much the same way, simply changing your racking and paper-work system away from the *most* obvious system (alphabetical) to a slightly more arcane system (by "genre"), you can achieve a much larger knowledge about the minutia of your business without significantly adding to your work load.

You *need* this type of information to keep your profitability high, as the rest of the industry tries to take that margin away from you.

Tilting at Windmills #50
(Originally ran in Comics Retailer #51)

Welcome to the 50th installment of *Tilting at Windmills*, the column that makes you glad you're not me!

This is actually the fifty-first *Comics Retailer*, and I've had an article in each, but the first installment was a reprint from the *Comic Buyer's Guide*, so it doesn't count towards the "official" totals. There are also three pieces I count as "1/2" issues – things that got written for *TaW*, but ended up running somewhere else (the Neal Adams bit that ran as a letter, the *CBG* "guest editorial" from a few months back, and the "*TaW plus*" from K.C.'s days as editorial slave), as well as an article or two for the now defunct Tundra's *Title Waves*, and the two bits that were meant to run in *WAP!*, the freelancers magazine – but on the official tally sheet, this is #50 – a must-have, double-bag collector's edition! Only ten to go, and I can do the "Tilting at Windmills: the First Five Years" TPB I've been thinking about (the annotations will be the best bit).

So, for the big five-oh, let's tackle publisher discounts, and what's wrong with them.

Most publishers/distributors give us a discount based upon overall volume – whether that's in the case of a line (such as Marvel, DC, or Image's charts) or volume through a particular distributor (Diamond, Acclaim, and Dark Horse). The problem is, this is a model that doesn't work very well anymore.

Historically I believe such structures were created because the vast bulk of retailers worked exclusively with one distributor or another – I, for example, was a Diamond guy – and such a program made a measure of sense, because your overall sales drove your overall discount, and your value as an account (and the rewards you earned for that value) was clear. I was just told by a distributor representative that it costs (on average) one dollar to handle (pull, pack, invoice, etc.) one line-Item on your invoice. This (no need to tell me, Preston) is not an accurate statistic for any individual account, but I'll accept it as an overall calculation – I do much the same when I think about Earnings-Per-Square-Foot of Rack Space, for example. The appropriateness of a tiered chart can be understood to operate in terms of lowering the distributor's marginal costs in servicing your order – if you can generate, for example, an average of $20 per line-Item, you'll deserve a bigger discount than if you can generate $10 per.

However (and you knew there had to be a however, there, right? 'Twouldn't be a *TaW* without one!) the value of this calculation drops substantially in the New World Order. Why? Because the numerical value of my order through any given distributor is no longer representative of my value as an account to that distributor.

The old system didn't work great, I think we *all* know, but at least the economic calculations made a modicum of sense. Whether or not the distributors were raking the money in from other fronts, or from not passing benefits onto the retail community, it was not *unreasonable* to pay based upon volume, because there was at the very least, a logical basis for such: you're paying for the marginal costs of distribution, and your expenses reduce in relationship to those costs.

Those relationships no longer exist. Under the exclusive arrangements that Diamond negotiated, they work from a fixed percentage of cover price. Unless they were incompetent in the extreme in those negotiations, such a fixed price should more than cover base operating expenses.

What value does a tiered system hold to a brokered publisher? Remember, please, that their marginal costs have not increased (I know of no brokered publisher who hired someone new to deal as "Distributor liaison" – positions were created by shifting people internally), and in fact, should *decrease* because they're now dealing with *one* system, rather than seven or more. There are two things I can see:

1) To line their pockets while the market is in a free-fall. Publishers historically gave between 60 and 65% discount to distributor. But, in a brokered arrangement, it's a flat percentage. Let's say it is 7% (which I understand is on the high side). If the "average" retailer gets 50%, then the brokered publisher is giving a 57% discount on that product – a gain of potentially 8% of cover price (or, my calculator tells me, a gain of more than 18% from their gross margins – from 35% to 43%) – with *no* increase in their expenses between a 40% account and a 58% one. Sure, one could make a case that they're making a slightly lower percentage from the very largest stores, but I'll assume that the lowered advertising costs, and streamlined procedures more than make up for this.

Now, that's not to say that it is heinous to try and make up in margin what you've lost in volume (remember, too, that the brokered publishers have seen the largest hits from the Fallout) – in fact it's a sound business practice. But we can't let it hide under the banner of corporate benevolence, when, clearly, the brokered publishers are the number one beneficiary of the brokered deals. Any benefits retailers may see (and we've been promised many) are purely coincidental, and only occur when they don't impact the bottom line (c.f. the reduction or elimination of reorder fees – it doesn't cost the brokered publishers any more money to service reorders, therefore, they're happy to let them flow cheaper).

2) The other aspect is the "carrot and the stick." The idea is that by having tiered systems, you will be able to drive sales as retailers try to achieve the next tier. On the face of it, this is a viable strategy, but when you look at the specifics of it, this begins to fall apart.

Wait. Let me backtrack a bit. As I said, I suspect that originally tiered systems were set up as a relationship to the marginal costs associated in dealing with an individual. That it *also* had some carrot and stick function often worked as a benefit to the retailer – if you were *right* on the edge of a plateau, you could pump your discount a little by ordering a few more comics – but since you had such a vast palette to choose from, you could generally get potentially salable material: the stuff you were "iffy" about. Still the number of retailers who tended to be "on the edge" from one plateau to another was likely statistically small.

Back to today. The carrot and stick doesn't especially work in today's market. Comics, while *being* a product, are not *merely* products. If I ran a hardware store, and a manufacturer said to me, "I'll give you a better price if you buy eleven pounds of screws, rather than ten," I might do it – screws will sell eventually, and the sales of screws are not dictated by which worker machined the individual screw. Comics, on the other hand, are an ephemeral art form – sales are limited to a very particular window of time (usually in relationship to the next delivery), and sales are dictated by the consumer's impression of the individual creator(s). "I don't like the art this issue – I'm gonna skip it." On our cycle sheets, and on the publisher's balance sheet, *Amazing Mucus Lad* #67 look remarkably similar to *AML* #66 and *AML* #68 – but to the consumer, there is a higher relationship informing their decision to purchase. The effect of this idiosyncrasy is that determining discount by dollar volume is problematic. All comics are *not* created equal. My decisions to purchase are driven as much by my understanding of my customer base's *aesthetics* as it is by their buying habits.

To put this into more practical terms, if I do my order form, and I come out with $1100 worth of Marvel comics, my cost will be $605, because I'll get (currently) a 45% discount. However, at $1200, I get 50%, for a cost of $600 – so I might as well go for it, seeing that I get $100 worth of comics "for free," *and* I saved five bucks. However, if I'm like most comic book retailers, if I want $1100 worth of Marvels, it means I think I can sell $1100 worth of Marvel comics. Now it's not impossible I could sell $1200, but, odds are, I'm far more likely to only sell $1000. If you don't sell that "extra" stock, you incur needless costs: original shipping to you, increasing your tax liability by increasing your inventory, and the costs of inventorying and warehousing.

Ask Preston Sweet. He'd tried playing that game, and ended up no better off at all.

Having more copies of *Spider-Man* doesn't mean you'll sell more copies of *Spider-Man*. When your only choices for "extra" merchandise come from a limited subset that a publisher offers, you're unlikely to reap any benefits if you are even marginally aware of your store. The market has changed to the point where the carrot and stick no longer has much practical value.

Even if it *did* have a real-world effect, do the charts as constituted make any sense? Not really. First off, they're (oddly enough) in reverse order by cost-of-goods. What do I mean by that? Check it out: the first chart is (for May 1996 shipping) the average price-point for the three term-setting publishers (calculated by dividing the number of offered titles by the total cost to buy one of each title – only comics books and TPBs are considered, and front-list only, at that.); while the second chart is how much you have to spend to get a particular discount.

(Chart #1 – average price point)

Publisher	Total cost	# of books	Av price point
DC	$232.84	81	$2.87
Image	$136.39	42	$3.25
Marvel	$126.84	55	$2.31

(Chart #2 — Discount plateaus)

$	DC	Image	Marvel
$.00	40%	45%	
$300.00		35%	
$600.00	50%		
$601.00	50%		
$800.00		45%	
$1,001.00		53%	
$1,200.00		50%	
$2,000.00	52.5%		
$2,001.00		55%	
$2,500.00		53%	
$3,000.00	55%		
$4,000.00		54%	
$5,001.00		56%	
$7,000.00		55%	
$10,001.00		57%	
$15,000.00	56%	56%	
$20,001.00		57.5%	
$30,000.00	57%	57%	
$75,000.00		58%	
$100,000.00	57.5%		
$100,001.00		58.5%	
$125,000.00		59%	

Weird, huh? Marvel has the cheapest price-points, but you have to buy the most dollar volume to "earn" discount (at least until you get to the higher ends of the chart). Image has the highest price-points, but the "easiest" chart to match.

It's worth noting again that not all titles, not all lines, not all publishers, are created equal – because all stores don't have equivalent sales patterns. I can't get my "expected" discount on Image and Marvel because my volume skews low for those publishers, and I know more than one retailer with some variation on this theme. Our discounts align around the "kind" of store we are, which creates a self-fulfilling prophecy – if you get a better discount on Image, you'll tend to push Image, at the expense of Marvel or DC. So rather than having the intended effect, it has the direct opposite instead!

(What I really don't understand is why Marvel would want to make it so difficult for a store to keystone [to double the money you invest in an item] their merchandise? Without keystoning, it's much more difficult for a business to profit – wouldn't you want the *strongest* and *healthiest* customer base you could muster?)

While these discount calculations confound me, I'm even more bugged by exclusive publishers who either opted not to set their own terms, or worse yet, decided to roll through Diamond's chart. Yuck! You can get a 50% discount on DC and Image if you buy $1201 (combined) worth of comics, but to get 50% on Dark Horse or Acclaim at Diamond, you've got to spend at least $2500! At 55% that's $5001 versus $11500! Talk about your second-class citizens!!! Why would any publisher sign a deal that virtually ensured a worse discount than their competitors?

My margins are down substantially, from almost all publishers. Evidence suggests yours are too. Where are the all the "benefits" exclusivity was supposed to bring? All I see is a system that works worse than it ever did before (if such a thing is actually possible), where those of us in the front lines have a greater amount of expenses, at a lower margin.

What have we wrought?

Tilting at Windmills #51
(Originally ran in Comics Retailer #52)

Industry conferences are an odd thing.

You've probably not been to one, actually, so this column may well be of only limited use to you, but stick with me for a few minutes here, and I'll tell you not only why they're a waste of time, as well as why they're absolutely necessary to our forward progression as an industry.

A conference is a different beast than a convention, a trade show, or a presentation. We have all these things in our industry, and each one serves a different function. I suspect the first thing to do is to draw the distinctions between these forms.

A convention, at least so far as we use the term in comics, is a gathering primarily designed for the consumer. There is a wide palette within this term – everything from six dealers with a dozen tables of long whites in a church basement to the pageantry and spectacle of the San Diego ComicCon (Whoops! Sorry! That's "ComicCon International: San Diego!") to twenty or thirty creators banding together for a Spirits of Independence stop – the *goal*, whether expressed, or not, is commerce. *Most* professionals (named widely, with retailers, creators, and manufacturers all counted) go to sell themselves, or their work, or their products to the general public, or other professionals. Hundreds if not thousands of conventions are held every year. You've, in all likelihood, been to several of these.

A trade show is just that: a show for the *trade*. This is just as sales-oriented for the exhibitors, but this tends to take broader forms, because without the presence of the "fans," it's a "freeer" environment in which to talk pure business. Very few creators attend these functions in any capacity other than publicity tool. In direct market 1996, I believe we are left with exactly one trade show: the San Diego Expo. I've no hard figures, but empirical evidence suggests that far less than half the retailers in this business have ever been to a trade show.

A presentation is what I call the road shows we got last year from DC and Marvel – open invites to all retailers, (almost) no creators, where the point is: here is what we're doing, what do you think? Narrowly targeted, the largest function of these is as a bitch session, no matter how the organizers present it. I'll guess that a large majority of retailers have made it to one or more of these.

Finally, a conference is a forum where people involved in an industry come to debate and discuss cogently the various issues that face them. 99% panels and presentations, designed to inform the participants of underlying causes, meanings, or principles in their chosen field. We've got exactly *one* of these: Pro/Con. And virtually no retailers are aware they're even *invited*. In point of fact, I can only recall six of us attending one: me, Rory Root, Mimi Cruz, Joe Field, Bill Liebowitz, and Steve Milo. I'm forgetting someone, I know, but even if we double this, it's still just a dozen.

To be fair, Pro/Con is not designed with the retailer specifically in mind. Which gives me the perfect segue to tell you what exactly Pro/Con is. P/C was first suggested by Peter David in the 8/14/92 installment of his *But I Digress* column over in the *CBG* (it's also in the TPB, for those of you who are interested). To sum up, Peter observed that nearly all fields have conferences where leaders in that field get together to discuss techniques, changes in technology, philosophies and approach. No one is trying to sell much of anything to each other – they're trying to help educate one another. Peter's original suggestion was a conference for creators only, which is rather close to what transpired at the first P/C in April of 1993, but the difference between comics and many other fields is that creativity and technique go hand-in-hand with commerce. We do not yet work in a field egalitarian enough so that any comer may achieve the same level of success and market penetration as a established player, so it becomes very important to have a line of programming that involves the publishers, distributors, and retailers. As good as a creator's talent may be, they need to understand the economic underpinnings of the marketplace in order to make their way.

After the first P/C, the organizers threw the description of "professional" open from "working creator," to "anyone who makes their living from comics" – openly inviting retailers, publishers, distributors, printing reps, etc., to attend. This is different than what Peter envisioned, but in my particular world-view, a much more effective gathering, because all levels of this business can learn much from each other. In fact, I'd go so far as to say that the second P/C was of immeasurable value to most of the participants.

The fourth P/C has just come and gone, and somewhere a turn was taken for the worse. Perhaps it's just a reflection of the turmoil and strife that faces the market itself in 1996, but P/C 4 gave virtually no value for attendees' time or money. Panel sessions turned into rambling bitch-fests, confidence was nowhere to be seen, and the split between the various levels of the industry was laid open like a festering wound. Perhaps worst of all, Pro/Con was attended primarily by the "Usual Suspects" – the same 30-50 people who go to *every* industry function, so you can recite their opinions by rote (like me!).

Our industry doesn't need very much new blood. Really! We have one of the most fertile confluences of intelligence, perception, and passion that any field has ever seen. But most of us stay silent. Why is that? You, reading this magazine, most likely face one of the most difficult jobs, in one of the most difficult fields, in one of the most difficult time periods this field has ever seen, and yet chances are you've got your shit together. You're not getting rich, but you're keeping all the balls in the air because you believe in what you're doing, and making money is just a bonus at that point. Yeah, sure, the industry as a whole is a lumbering dinosaur, barely aware of what it's doing, where it's going – but the fact that you're reading this magazine means you understand that information is power. And that, sir, is half the battle.

Most of you will never write *Comic Retailer*'s letter column, or that of the *CBG* or the *Journal*, or *Wizard*, or whatever else – but you read everyone of them. Most of you, if you *are* online, are content to "lurk" rather than participate. Most of you have decided it's more important to tend to your own backyard than that of your neighbors. And, all of you, I salute you! Not all of us are suited to be extroverts, and not all of us need a soapbox to be happy. It's just...well...your opinion matters, damn it!

I get letters from you people, y'know. You people are friggin' *brilliant*! You know your market, you understand your business, and no matter how many times you get kicked in the teeth for simply *doing your job*, you get up, dust yourself off, and get on with the job, because you know it's a job worth doing. So many people in this industry denigrate retailers at the slightest opportunity, and – hell yes! – we have a significant portion of visible fuck-ups, but that's not most of you!

As much as it is against your character, in 1996 and 1997 you have to get visible. Our industry sorely needs leadership, and that's *you*.

Really.

This has been a vast digression from my main point, but, hell!, we both know you really do need the pep-talk – make plans *now* to travel in 1997. At bare minimum you should hit one big show (Chicago and San Diego would seem to be the viable options), one regional show (it's Wonder-Con, out here), and one trade show/conference (either the San Diego expo, or the 5th Pro/Con, barring something East Coast or Centrally organized between then and now). You don't have to commit to the idea of doing this regularly – just in '97. Hype notwithstanding, the overall market is clearly still declining, as of this writing in March of '96. We're still in the process of shaking out the card-vestites, the weekend warriors, the people who aren't actually serious, the people who don't *burn* like you or I. Yes, you'll lose a combination of two weeks behind your counter if you follow this advice, but think of it as an investment in your future, as you involve yourself in what's left of the "meta-industry" – I promise you that by next year's convention season, they're going to *need* your passion, your commitment, your industry. You *will* be listened to this time, because you'll be the last, best hope.

And, so, back to the main point.

We *need* a Pro/Con. Information is power. And we *all* need a measure of both. But, we needn't *any* Pro/Con – but a *damn* good one. P/C 4 was *so* excruciating that unless #5 is *kick-ass*, there probably won't *be* a #6, y'know? So, in a continuing effort to not merely bitch, but to suggest solutions as well, here's my list of this that could be improved for the next one:

• There need to be at least two tracks of programming: one purely creative-interest oriented and one purely business-interest oriented. Anything less and you end up alienating half the attendees.

• Rather than have a few long, unanswerable panels (like an hour-and-a-half "women and comics" panel), have fewer, specifically-focused panels (like three half-hour panels – say, "advertising to women," "creating comics for women," and "successful extra-market outreach," or something along those lines).

• Get moderators who are willing to be hardcore about mic time. The simultaneously best and worst panel this year was Mel Thompson's "Industry experts identify key problems," or some such – the information given was phenomenal, but seven panelists reading to us their written proposals (that were handed out to all comers!) was excruciating. I suggest a minute egg-timer for all commentary – audience or panelist (O.K., maybe two minutes...).

• Set up sections of time that are designated "bitch-time" – obviously people are bringing their agendas to such an event. A forum where these agendas are not merely tolerated but encouraged would be beneficial for not only keeping focus, but for understanding each other's personal situations. Whether it's publisher-specific, or the industry in general, a lot of people need to vent before they can be rational about the real causes and effects of our decisions.

• Such a conference *has* to be self-sustaining. Accepting revenue from publishers in exchange for what amounts to advertising time taints the openness of such an event.

• Make sure people *know* they're invited. How many retailers out there knew they could attend the last three Pro/Cons if they wanted to? See? Less than 20 hands. I suspect much the same is true in the creative community – whole segments were virtually unrepresented, in part, I believe, because word of mouth seems to be the driving advertising vehicle.

• And, personally, I'd cut the ties to WonderCon, folks. I recognize the pragmatic desire to keep it up, but I think it's hard to keep such an event serious with a typical consumer show directly following.

Pro/Con 4 was a waste of nearly every attendee's time, I'm sorry to say. (That's not to say, in a perhaps futile attempt to stave off the nasty letters from the P/C Board of Directors, that there wasn't a modicum of value somewhere in the program for some people. I only know that if I didn't live a mere 15 minute BART ride from the event, there is exactly a zero chance that I'd go again.) But five can be alive, because we need this event. We don't have a way to come together as a community besides this path. I hope the P/C organizers get their act together in time for next year, and, if they do, I further hope that every one of you, gentle readers, show up to help move this industry forward to the 21st Century.

While we all hope, your homework is to write me a letter (and CC: it to *Comics Retailer*!) and let me know what *you* would like to see as programming at an industry conference. Who knows? Maybe someone will even listen to us.

Keep the faith.

Tilting at Windmills #52
(Originally ran in Comics Retailer #53)

Ch-ch-ch-changes!

As I write this, it's old news for you, but fresh off my fax machine this week are four pretty big pieces of news – Crusade has decided to go non-exclusive, DC announces new sales terms, Top Cow is breaking off from Image (as well as exclusivity), and Marvel is "consolidating" their shipping operations. Hey, when you're short on time (if I don't write, edit, and e-mail this column in the next twelve hours, I will be the first *Comics Retailer* columnist *ever* to break a deadline!), any port in a storm!

One at a time, then?

1. Crusade was the first "small" publisher to sign an exclusive with Diamond. I can only presume (and the press release appears to back me up) that at the time, Crusade *believed* that exclusivity would knock Capital City from the game, and so signing with Diamond made good sense, if only to "beat the rush" (as it were). While there is a teeny-weeny nugget of sense in this approach, it is only efficient *if* CCD went under. If CCD does *not* go under, then not have you cut yourself off

from *x*% of your customers, but you've also put yourself in a clear competitive disadvantage – CCD would be very likely to give Crusade a cover feature, for example, because Crusade is one of the largest of "small publishers," but you'll never, ever, ever, *never* get a cover feature at DCD, unless you're DC, Dark Horse, Image, or Acclaim.

(Tangentially, what a great deal Acclaim got! I mean, here they are, clearly a "small publisher" in sales terms [Crusade is often two to three places above them in publisher rankings] – they seldom manage to crack the Top 100 in sales! And yet, there they are listed before Dark Horse, DC, and Image! How'd the heck they manage that, and where can *I* get hold of whatever the DCD executive team was smoking that day?!?!)

It was a dumb agreement to make in the first place. I don't know spit about publishing, and even I could tell that! But, still, congratulations, and a big ol' "thank you" from retailers everywhere to reinstating a little more Freedom to the Free Market! Hopefully the other "small exclusive" will soon also see the wisdom of this choice. When the first to join is the first to leave...

2. Anyway, speaking of Freedom, let's talk about DC's sales terms for a mo'. Now, obviously circulations have dropped quite a bit, so one can't *blame* them for wanted to preserve their margin by trimming a little for ours. And I suppose we have to applaud them for taking that margin from the top and the bottom, preserving all of us in the middle – unless, of course, *it's you on the top or the bottom!* Still, I figure Preston is going to discuss this either this column or next, so I'll leave the vitriol to him on that issue. B-U-T, why the hell aren't you concerned about the premise that they can audit you, if you go over a certain sales plateau?!?!

And I'm told you *asked* for it! "Oh, poor us – subdistributors allow stores that don't 'earn' it to receive a large enough discount that they can compete with us," you cry. "Please, please pity us! Flea market discounters take away some of our customers," you moan. Bah! Buncha whiners – that's what y'all are!

Listen to me: in a free market, *there is no such thing as "unfair competition!"* One can compete on price, one can compete on quality, or one can compete on service. Your customers are probably sensitive to these factors in a variety of measures. Yes, *of course*! you will lose some measure of customers to a discounter, because they are more price-sensitive than service-sensitive — but the discounter isn't "unfair" – you could discount too. Now, you're smart enough *not* to do that, knowing how much it will cost you, but possible competition on price is a factor of business.

It's up to *you* to deal with this. *Not a publisher.*

It's never a good idea to hand the keys to the chicken coop to a fox. It doesn't matter if the fox is currently well fed and domesticated – 'cuz the fox's kids may not be. If you say to a publisher, even a publisher that we all currently respect and trust, "go ahead, we want you to determine who and who is not a 'bona fide' retailer – here's access to our books," then some day he might decide that you are the one who isn't "bona fide."

Paranoia? Perhaps. But so few corporate entities keep the same personality over the decades, and I fully expect that some day, (though God, please, let it not be within my lifetime!) DC will be run by soulless accountants who don't know or love comics. I don't want these people access to any comic shops' books!

Right now we're all nodding our heads at the presumption that DC has our best interests at heart, so giving over the right to comb large retailers' books looking for (horrors!) them selling comics to another retailer doesn't seem like so much to give up – but some day it may well be. "Hey, you've been O.K. with this for over a hundred consecutive order forms – you've lost your right to bitch," the Time Warner lawyers will say.

And they'll be right.

I publicly vow today that I give *no* publisher the inherent right to inspect my books now or at any other time in the future.

And if I were you, I'd do the same – even if (hell, especially if!) you think this will never apply to you.

3. What's next on the agenda? Oh, yeah – Top Cow leaving Image. I suppose we all knew it was inevitable. I kinda thought Todd would be the first to go, but what's life without a few surprises?

The press release was vague on reasons, but it seems to me from the outside that Silvestri has a smooth enough operation going that moving away from Image will not be a significant detriment to him. Top Cow has been the *only* Image studio to promise and deliver on specific sales dates, and hopefully this won't change. By itself, this gives Top Cow a significant leg-up on other "small" publishers.

Top Cow also moves non-exclusive, which is another positive step for the free market. All in all I salute this maneuver, as well!

As for Image itself, this is another step in the weakening of the Image brand name. Commercially most Image books have become relatively mediocre sellers, and the "i" is no longer enough in and of itself to push big sales. It wouldn't surprise me a bit if over the next few years the dissolution continues. Certainly Rob and Jim each see the value of creating multiple pots to keep their fingers in. I doubt that Image, itself, would ever cease to exist, by the way – only that I expect to see at least one more "defection" before too long...

4. The last piece of news is Marvel's "consolidation" of warehouses. At least that's how it was presented (and you gotta admit that's *world-class* spin! Ten points to the architect of that one!). But my understanding of it is very different. What I hear is HWD is going to an outside source for the physical distribution of the product. Customer service, and order collation will still be handled by HWD (Gee, the two jobs they did best!), but pulling, packing, and shipping will be handled by a newsstand distributor by the name of Donnelly. As I understand it, Donnelly, while very good at handling newsstand pulls, doesn't have any experience doing the kind of precision shipping the direct market requires. What will happen next is anyone's guess, but I sure wish they hadn't picked the week of the San Diego con, when many many people are away from their desks for the inevitable first week problems...

Anyway, like I say, there's no way to tell what will happen here, but I think it's beginning to be time for the major manufacturers to more seriously consider street dates. Inconsistent shipping has dire effects on the cash-flow dependent Direct Market retailer.

5. That's about all I have for this month – oh, wait! There's one more thing! For those of you who like charts, and overall pictures of what the market is doing, here's a good one for you. Diamond, as you all know, is gracious enough to print

a relative sales chart every month. Using a figure known as "OIN" (Order Index Number), you can see the relative strength of a book. *Batman* is 100, so *Supreme*, with a OIN of 26.6 in June, sold 26.6% of *Batman*. The nice thing about this ranking is that if you have a hard figure for two positions, you can figure out any other on the chart with an excellent degree of accuracy, and, if you've got a calculator, and some free time, you can make some wonderful deductions about the state of the marketplace.

This round, let's talk about overall sales for the first half of 1996.

Before I bring on the chart, a couple caveats, if I may: first, the charts I extrapolate from are for Diamond comics only. Sales through any other distributor are not counted. Second, sales are for pre-orders only, for comic books only. No trade paperbacks, no advance reorders, no reorders, no back-orders, not counting that call you made the day after the order form was due, doubling your order on *Kingdom Come*! Third, I can only work with the data I'm given; i.e., Garbage In, Garbage Out!

	Top 100 OIN	Ttl 1-300 OIN	1 OIN=	Top 100 Circ.	Ttl 1-300 Circ.
Jan '96	6100.7	8053.2	796	4856157	6410347
Feb '96	5854.9	7441.7	775	4537548	5767318
Mar '96	7132.3	8796.7	768	5477606	6755866
Apr '96	6469.2	8595.9	750	4851900	6446925
May '96	6472.6	8570.1	767	4964484	6573267
Jun '96	5839.1	7503.6	805	4700476	6040398

The first two columns are summary totals for OIN – top 100, and 1-300. I added the OIN for each title in that range to one another. The middle column tells you what one OIN point is equal to in real circulation, while the last two columns translate that real circulation to a hard combined circulation number.

Again, this is for only a portion of the market. Conservatively, you should be able to add at least 60% to these figures to account for other distributors, non-Diamond publishers, overprints, and reorders. Still, it appears that the stabilization trend might've been a plateau – coming into the first month of summer with that low a number is a bit scary!

See you next month, presumably with San Diego observations.

Tilting at Windmills #53
(Originally ran in Comics Retailer #54)

Let's start off with my absolutely favorite story from the San Diego ComicCon Expo:

So, I'm doing booth time at the Krause publications table – I'm meant to be signing autographs, I guess (like *anyone* would want my autograph by dint of me being a loudmouth!), and it's dead enough that I don't really have much to do but eavesdrop on Greg Loescher's conversations. I mean, even though I felt that the level of attention, passion, commitment, enthusiasm, and optimism was as *high* as I've ever seen at a SD Expo, attendance was sparse. At points it certainly seemed that *exhibitors* and their staff well outnumbered the *retailers*.

Anyway, Terry Stewart approaches Greg, to ask some questions about the record collecting magazines that Krause publishes – as I understand it, Terry is a huge record collector, with a very impressive vinyl blues collection (right on!) – various small talk ensues, and Greg says to Terry, "Not a great turnout this year, huh?" Terry looks back, with absolute sincerity in his eyes, and replies, "Well, you know, a lot of retailers went out of business this year."

A. Lot. Of. Retailers. Went. Out. Of. Business. This. Year.

I'm telling you with all sincerity that it took every ounce of self-control that I possessed to not leap across the table, grab Terry by the name of his t-shirt and *scream*, "And just whose fault was that?"

Is it just me?

•   •   •   •   •

Welcome to San Diego.

I don't know about you, but I hate San Diego. It's painfully, deathly hot; disgusting humid; absolutely characterless; and thoroughly ugly. I can't, for the life of me, understand why anyone would *choose* to live there, let alone spend the meager leisure time that most people possess visiting the darn place.

But they throw a great con.

If only they'd throw it in a civilized city, it'd be the most perfect show on earth, but even with the beastly, oppressive heat the middle of summer brings, there's nothing quite like a San Diego ComicCon for sheer volume, for spectacle, for density, for breadth.

As I noted, the retailer Expo proceeding the Con itself was dead (because a lot of retailers went out of business this year, don't forget), but those who attended were there to work. In previous years, the Expo has sometimes slipped into "bitch mode" – last year, in particular, people were depressed, and they carried it with them like a badge of honor, wanting to spread it to someone else, too, so they weren't all alone in their misery. Fair enough – I did it too, because it looked liked our industry's number was up.

This year, however, I could *smell* the enthusiasm.

We've lived through the worst of the Long Night, and while Dawn won't be hear for a little while yet, and there are still sorties yet to fight, and brush fires yet to put out, those of us who are still standing understand what a joy it is to be alive – that which didn't kill us has made us stronger.

1996 will be my *best* year yet. Sales are up 25%, and we've got some projects in the works that are going to rock everyone's world. Your mileage may vary, but I think it's a safe bet that if you're reading TAW #53, you're still going to be here for TAW #100.

Hope is in the air, and while the overall market is unlikely to recover by this Christmas (the publishers still have a way to go on their editorial schedules), I think the upbeat tenor of the Expo signals that we're ready to roll up our sleeves, and finally get to work.

Good for us.

•　　•　　•　　•　　•

Meanwhile, the Legend Of Hibbs continues to grow.

Even when it has *no* basis in fact.

On Tuesday evening, Comics Retailer had their annual "Punchline Live!" panel following Frank Miller's excellent Keynote Address. This year the professors from Rutgers presented their survey data to a panel of representatives from Capital City, DC, Diamond, Image, and Marvel. After a brief statement from each representative, Costa, Gray, and I were to ask questions of this panel, more or less alternating our own questions with those collected from the audience. The panel wasn't exactly well organized (true of nearly every panel that I attended in my three days in San Diego, in J.J.'s defense), and I had a scheduling conflict with the Comic Book Legal Defense Fund's Board of Directors meeting which started basically at the same time as the Q&A was meant to commence, so it ended up that I had the time to ask a single question, then I had to run like the wind to the Doubletree hotel in order to fill both my obligations.

Since Bob and Bruce had the harder job of collecting the questions and making sense of them, it was ultimately decided that I would lead off with the first question, so they'd have time to do their jobs (this is, in no small part, my fault – Bruce wanted to have a meeting earlier in the day to discuss strategy, and I blew it off with a "let's play it by ear." But once I was in the room, it was clear that wouldn't work. *Organization* now is my watchword for Panels '97, and I apologize, Bruce, for blowing ya off this time!) I decided to ask something that could be broad enough that any and all panelists could answer it, and yet focused enough that it could give us a clear picture of the thought processes involved: "Given that sales patterns are still flat or declining (see the chart in last months TAW), and that even the best results on the Rutgers survey (DC's showing of at or around 4.5 overall on a seven point scale) clearly show that most retailers frown upon the distribution moves that have occurred, would you do it again, knowing what you know today?" Jerry Calabrese took the first shot at the question (because, as he said [paraphrasing], "we started it"), and I quibbled with his expressed motivation (I believe "vaguely paternalistic" was the phrase I used), and then immediately realized that if we had the debate on a live mic, *I* would eat the entire 20 minutes we had left for *everybody's* questions.

So, I handed the mic to my fellows, looked at my watch as Chuck Parker assayed the issue, and signaled J.J. that I had to jet to the CBLDF Board meeting. And did.

Imagine my surprise when I reached the Expo floor the next morning and was told that I had fought with Calabrese, *flipped him the bird*, and stormed out in a huff! Wow!

Even people with a little more perception then that congratulated me on "nailing Calabrese." "Nailing Calabrese?" Excuse me? Read the question again, kids. It's loaded, I'll give you that, but you give me credit for a more Machiavellian intent than I actually possess! In fact, I would say that I was, perhaps more interested in Image, DC, and Capital City's responses than I was of Marvel's. You know, however wrong-headed the decision was, at least Marvel *acted*. Everyone else *reacted*, and that's what really caused the worst damage, from my perspective.

Another one of the panelists approached me the next evening, and made some comments that suggested I somehow pissed Calabrese off enough that I should somehow be prepared for physical violence. What the heck did I do? Is my "reputation" that far out of whack that it precedes me, and twists the listener's hearing of my words? Wake up, kids! I don't "hate" Marvel – I may dislike the majority of decisions that have been made there, beginning with the one to take the company public, but it's my responsibility as a participant in the system to challenge things that could harm the Body Politic. But "hate" them? "Have an axe to grind?" Want "revenge" on them? *Get real!*

Marvel is around 8% of my business. I'd *welcome* them to become a greater part of that, if I thought their policies and programs were such that they'd mesh with where *I* want to take *my* business. Listen, we're doing a signing with Jim Lee for *FF* #1, because I respect the possibilities of this particular project. The question is not, "who do I hate?" but "who is doing work that fits with the image that *I* want to project?"

Don't you get it yet? I've written 53+ of these damn things, and the message in each of them is *you* control what is done in *your* store. *You* control what titles are stocked, and in what quantities, *you* control the message of what gets promoted, and what does not, *you* control how your customer buys, and why, because *you* are the authority on the medium, and *you* have the commitment, passion, and energy to get the job done!

Anything less is *excuses*.

So to you who think I spoke in anger, and left with it, too, I say, "get with the damn program already." There's no room for hate anymore. It is said "there is no room for sentiment in business." Once I would have said, "untrue," but today I understand that it's true in that you have to check your *feuds* at the door – bring your joy, your passion, your energy, but ditch the ire.

And to Jerry, himself – if I pissed you off, personally, I apologize. Give me a call, and we can talk about it, 'kay?

(Much to Jerry's credit, his answer to "would you do it again?" boiled down to "maybe not," which I feel is about the closest one could ever get to "no" in a public panel in front of hundreds of retailers and press, from someone in his position.)

•　　•　　•　　•　　•

In other Marvel news, they've announced a program to do TV advertising in selected test-markets, to see what happens.

Digression: both Matt Ragone and Bruce Bristow expressed to me that the exclusive publishers didn't feel they had the *ability* to try many kinds of programs under the old system. Exclusivity, they feel, gives them ability to try things they've wanted to do forever. Matt gave me the image of a list with a hundred items on it, and now that the short-term flurries have settled down, they're starting to go down the list, checking 'em off with a "That works. That didn't."

I, not being privy to backstage dealings, feel that this assessment of not being able to do things is, in fact, wrong. The problem was that the publishers didn't want to organize retailers, because organization eventually leads to empowerment, and on the path they thought they were walking, empowerment was the last thing they wanted to give us. But the rules of the game reverted back, overnight, to the rules they *should* have been all along: retailers hold the *power of free choice* in the equation, even if we're just now waking up to that fact, and they have to work *with* us, rather than dictate *to* us. Like a dinosaur, it takes a long time for the message from the "tail" of the sales floor to travel up to the "brain" of the publishers, but I find it ironic that the very situation they were trying to avoid became their only chance for survival.

See, I believe that if they wanted to do these programs, and were somehow stymied by distribution, they should have come to *us*, and had us put pressure on the distributors from the other side as well. But they took the hard road, hacking away the retailers who were marginal, or weren't serious, and they're left in the same position if they had just asked in the first place, with a considerably weaker base to support them.

But back to Marvel's TV commercials.

I don't have the press release in front of me, but they're advertising several specific issues of specific books in specific markets. *X-Men* #55, instead of all X-Men titles, for example. As Ragone explained it to me, local retailers would be double-shipped (?), for free those specific issues, to see what the impact was. I caught one of the commercials in San Diego (one of the five test-markets), and it was slick, well-produced, and ended with a generic "check your local comic shop."

I applaud the concept. I mean *wildly applaud*.

But I'm concerned about the *application*. My major concern is that if Matt is checking off his metaphorical list, and this doesn't fly, that will be it for ever seeing TV commercials from Marvel again.

And I'm concerned because I don't think it *can* fly.

I've a couple of issues, but the major one is that I bet you five bucks that *X-Men* #55, and the other half-a-dozen titles will not be comics with *a self-contained beginning, middle, and end*. When you're selling to civilians, that's what you have to give them – the question isn't really how many copies of *X-Men* #55 are sold, but how many copies of *X-Men* #58 sell. Money can be spent on a one-time influx of consumers, and have decent results, but keeping them coming back is where the real payoff lies. I don't believe that the multiple title serial nature of the X-Men line can generate new "raw civilian" customers.

Another issue is that promoting a periodical of serial fiction, a package which the greater buying public has not been wildly exposed to, is inherently flawed. I've found that often the greatest impact from advertising comes months after the promotion has run its course. I think it's much wiser to promote a *perennial* package (like, say, the *Dark Phoenix Saga* TPB) than it is something that is *designed* to be *ephemeral*.

My final concern is that it didn't appear to me that the stores have a great deal of notification in order to properly prepare themselves, or create proper displays and signage. I feel target marketing *has* to be done with the awareness and participation of the targeted market.

I hope it works – hell, I *pray* it works, because I'd like to see more projects like this occurring, just a little better thought out.

•   •   •   •   •

Still speaking of Marvel, I just about crapped my pants when I wandered into their booth looking for Matt, and the Voice of God came over the speakers announcing "Brian Hibbs is in the Marvel Booth." I didn't realize Marvel had their own exclusive set of speakers in their booth, and it was that wacky funster John Dokes playing with my head! Here I am thinking there is a lookout in the rafters of the Convention Center, spreading the news across the entire floor! I'll *get* you Dokes, if it's the last thing I do!

•   •   •   •   •

Paul Levitz expressed to me that he thought that DC had to make a move, because the loss of *x%* of the then extant-distributors' Marvel business would have crippled those distributors irreparably, and we'd be left with no one. I think the survival of Capital City calls this premise into question. Furthermore, I suspect that the loss of margin Diamond has experienced by working from 7%, instead of their former 10-20%, has likely put them in a more precarious position, because volume is/has decreased from when they cut those deals. They are *forced* to distribute titles that my running of the math says are solidly unprofitable.

What do *you* think? Without knowing the specifics of the distributors cash flow position, do you think there were alternative solutions that could have been assayed?

•   •   •   •   •

Finally (if I don't end soon, J.J. will kill me), allow me to make some observations on cards. This is part of a thread I participated in on CompuServe, and I wanted to fly it past y'all, as well.

It strikes me, a guy who doesn't carry cards, that gaming and entertainment and sports cards are all significantly different and distinct markets, and that while a teeny tiny space can do sports just fine, gaming and entertainment customers are very likely to be equally desiring "value added" services as much as price/selection. By "value added" I mean things like forming relationships with local gaming clubs; providing in-store gaming, or trading networks; whatever promotions you might do that appeal *directly* to that kind of customer.

The little I know of sports cards, customers, and buying habits makes me think that it's just not worth it, unless you're going into memorabilia as well. If a competitor suddenly opens a low-rent, small square-footage space, they can likely potentially sell for less, because expenses are lower, and without *another* magnet (signed baseballs, magazines, general sports memorabilia, etc.) for that class of customer, you can easily lose on price sensitivity. At least with entertainment cards, you prolly *already* have other "magnets" – I'd guess at least half of the entertainment releases have a comics analogue.

I don't like cards, because I've always thought of them as "change absorbers" – we carried dozens of lines back when we could sell packs for $0.99 or less, because it was the impulse buy for the consumer. But at SRPs of $2 and up, and with the lousy and inconsistent collation, and distribution of individual cards (which, personally, I believe are manipulated by manufacturers to make it much much harder for you to assemble the complete set, meaning you'll [in theory, if not in practice] buy more cards), I just can't waste my resources on something with such a lousy margin. I mean, we're looking at two products both having a similar price point, and one offers you maybe eight images, tops, that, since you don't have them all, have very little coherency, or intellectual link; while the other offers, hopefully, a complete thought, with at least 22 story pages, figure a minimum of 70 "images per unit." The former gives you a discount in range of 35%, the latter I'm almost always at 50% or better. The latter you can micro-manage your draws to virtually assure adequate sell-through (if you've a brain for that work), while the former insists that you buy in multiples of 24 or more. Imagine if Marvel or DC said, "if you want to *buy [insert title here]* from us, you have to buy them in lots of 20, and we're only gonna give you 40% off, unless you buy in lots of 300, in which case we'll be giving you 42%?" Well I bet a million bucks that you'll not be long carrying as large of a selection of affected titles at that point. In fact, comics might not be profitable any more!

The key, or so I think, to be successful in (non-gaming) cards is volume, volume, volume, as well as the morally questionable cherry-picking rare singles, and marking them through the roof. If each of those twenty packs of comics I posited had a single variant cover, and 19 regular editions, pretty much the only way to stay profitable is to immediately mark that single "special" copy up by 500% or more to cover your inevitable dead inventory for unmatched sell-through.

Or am I wrong?

•　　　•　　　•　　　•　　　•

I leave it there, my friends, with the admonition to continue to think, continue to find the passion within you, and continue to push your store in the direction *you* want it to go.

That way lies success.

Tilting at Windmills #54
(Originally ran in Comics Retailer #55)

More than one industry wag said to me in the last 48, "well, we've given you what you asked for – you wanted to order from just one distributor, and now you've got it." Naturally, this missed the gist, which was "we want to *choose* which distributor we order from," but hey! I guess it's our own fault for not being clear enough.

Just goes to prove: be careful what you ask for, you might just get it.

•   •   •   •   •

Welcome to direct market 2000, where you've got one choice, and its name is Geppi! All hail Geppi! (Next question, then: Is it "Sir," or is it "Master?")

(Aw, hell, that's not fair. But let me get a *little* of the cattiness out of my system, will ya?)

Actually, I sorta feel sorry for Diamond some days. Look at it this way: they're now in a lose-lose position. If they make certain financial movements which are, quite likely, necessary for their continued *survival*, they're gonna piss a bunch of people off; but, if they don't take certain steps, they run the risk of destroying their own business.

"What's he talking about," you wail, "Diamond is the anti-Christ!" Nah. Think about this: Diamond signed deals with DC, Dark Horse, and Image that are very likely to be only marginally profitable (if not, in some cases, wildly unprofitable) – DCD seems to need to work on a 10-15% margin to support the level of service they provide – yet the brokered publishers are apparently locked into long-term deals that only gives the DCD a percentage somewhere near 7%. Some brokered titles are selling at or around 5k, nationwide – that's pretty sad.

But, if some (many?) brokered titles are unprofitable, and Diamond is in no position to renegotiate such deals in a declining marketplace, where can they make up their cash-flow?

By and large, the future of the direct market lies in the hope that Geppi was smart enough to salt money away during the good days, to get us through these bad days intact.

Is this a reasonable hope?

As I said, Diamond currently is in a lose-lose position – if they move to protect their profitability, there are only a few places they can take the money from. Most notably, from small publishers and the retail community. However, if they resist this easy temptation, then they run the risk of marginalizing their business until they're not here to distribute *anyone*. Do the needs of the many outweigh the needs of the few, or is it vice versa? This, perhaps, is the key question facing us as we rush headlong towards the 21st Century.

Because Diamond is the only game in town, there is very little they can do that won't piss *somebody* off. You couldn't pay me enough money to be in this position.

And, no matter where your loyalties lie, we'll all be more reasonable if we bear this untenable position in mind.

•   •   •   •   •

However, far be it for me to be a Diamond apologist – they've got people who they pay oodles of money to take *that* role.

So let's talk about some of the potential positives of our new reality, look carefully at where the negatives might come from, and discuss some possibilities that Diamond can implement in order to help our struggling retail sector.

The key positive is one of financial stability for publishers. I'm told that DCD has been regular as clockwork in payment, and there is no reason to think this won't continue into the future. Assuming it does, this hopefully will provide a solid enough base for many manufacturers to properly make the transitions the market is dictating.

Additionally, there may be a small savings in time and shipping costs in streamlining operations to DCD-only for retailers.

But, where I hope to really see the biggest positive change is in putting distribution as the *focus* of the industry's time and attention behind us. Ever since December of 1994, when Marvel launched the shot that destroyed a nation, we've poured immeasurable resources into obsessing about the *distribution* of the product over the *content* of the product. Hopefully we'll now be able to collectively direct our energies into more productive ventures.

•   •   •   •   •

But, while monopolistic distribution brings stability (Il Duce made the trains run on time), it also brings along a lot of potential problems.

Competition fosters a climate where either you give 100%, or you marginalize yourself. Without competition, however, you tend to engender a system which quickly becomes stagnant and unresponsive to its clients.

For example: DCD's "TRU" system appears to have been a direct response to the success of Capital City's Hyperlink system. It's hard to "prove" such things, but it strikes me that DCD wouldn't have implemented such a system without the free market breathing hard down its neck.

Without that healthy competition, a monopoly has less impetus to try "radical" new ideas.

Lack of competition can also create a scenario where DCD is now free to dictate terms in any manner they choose. While it is certainly past history, let us not forget that DCD was the distributor that had made decisions such as refusing to carry adults-only material. They're also the organization that originally didn't want to carry ground-breaking work like *Yummy Fur*. They're also the organization that decided not to carry *Puma Blues* in retaliation to Dave Sim's choice of selling *Cerebus* trade paperbacks direct. It only takes a few minutes to come up with a pretty wide and varied selection of material for which DCD made irresponsible choices. These choices were largely reversed because of the existence of a strong competitor who provided another choice for this product – the threat of losing volume on *all* other product lines is a pretty strong economic cudgel.

As I said, most of these decisions are past history, and should be judged as only a barometer of the times in which they occurred, but those who forget history have a tendency to repeat it...

DCD now has unprecedented power is determining whether or not a comic is even *presented* for sale to retailers. Without distribution by Diamond, a publisher has virtually no chance of success. When I hear the (perhaps apocryphal) stories that *Bone* sold less than 600 copies of the 4th issue, before launching into the tens of thousands it does today, this notion gives me pause.

If DCD were to decide tomorrow that they were withdrawing all credit terms, and that we only were to get a 35% discount on non-brokered lines, there's really not much we could do about it. Now, they probably won't make any such an industry-destroying call, but the possibility now exists where it never did before. And this notion gives me pause as well.

The last eighteen months have brought us to a place where we're forced to depend on the good will of an extremely small number of people. I don't know the exact number, but it's prolly somewhere less than a dozen. Sure, we're in a position where most of these people are men of good conscience, but I don't believe that we can assume that men of good will *always* be the ones with their "fingers on the button." In practicality, those we count upon to give good fortune are but a single heartbeat away from being replaced by another. With human nature being what it is, the likelihood of this other being someone without the aesthetic passion for the medium itself is extremely high.

The finite number of people in whom the true power of this industry is concentrated means that "politics," your relationship with these people, suddenly becomes an incredibly important part of your business.

I don't like having to *depend* on the good will of another for my survival, but as of 7/27/96 that's the reality to which we're currently consigned.

•   •   •   •   •

So now that Diamond has all this power, doesn't it follow that they therefore have some more *responsibilities*? Uncle Ben's death taught us all that!

Here are some things I think DCD can do that will bring some greater stability to the market. With any luck, all of these things are being worked up as we speak, but if you agree with any or all of these ideas, throw down this magazine and write them a letter! It's all well and fine when a lobbyist like me makes a public pitch in a regular column, but it's up to a groundswell of support from the thousands of you out there to make them a reality.

I'm deadly serious about this – you don't have any right to bitch about industry leadership unless you're clearly communicating your needs *to* that leadership. Too few retailers seem to understand that change can't and won't come unless they make their needs clearly known. Most distributors and publishers haven't any idea of what the day-to-day realities of retailers are, because that experience is *so* far afield from their own. Lord know I get letter's from y,all saying, "yeah, I agree with ya, Hibbs," and that's pretty nice for my ego, but it don't do *jack* for getting anything *changed* – *I'm* not the one you have to be telling these things!

Anyway, with that in mind, here's my initial list (feel free to add to it!):

1) The most obvious thing is that **Previews needs a major overhaul and redesign**. I mean, it's freaking ugly! It's very very difficult to use, because publishers aren't in alphabetical order, and the use of color on every single page is distracting in the extreme. *Advance Comics* – now there was a catalog with a strong yet simple layout.

2) A little less obvious, but even needed more is **that there needs to be a responsibility taken by Diamond towards proper shipping**. By this I mean, if *they* make an error, they need to make restitution. And this needs to be a formal procedure. An example: the shipment of the latest *Nexus #2* got water-damaged en route to the Los Angeles DCD warehouse. Retailers serviced by this warehouse only received a percentage of this comic – I believe it was just under half of what we ordered. Now, just how I am to sell #3 and #4 of this mini-series, when I received less than half of the #2s that I ordered? The answer is "not very well." My local customer service guy tells me "we'll work something out," which is certainly appreciated, but I can't be alone in thinking that there needs to be a formal procedure to address such situation.

In much the same way, we have a "uniform release date," but what happens when DCD blows getting you your shipment on that date? Or even worse: if everyone else in your area gets those books, and you don't? The damage done to the individual retailer is incalculable, but S.O.P. amounts to "well, that's life."

I'm not going to sit here and dictate exactly *what* should be the compensation, but there needs to be one: returnability on the affected items, a couple of extra discount points rebated to the account, maybe extra terms to pay. *What* this penalty might be is less important than the recognition by DCD that they have an *obligation* to deliver the material precisely to our order, unless it's stated before the order is turned in that we should have a different expectation.

3) **Free 3-day freight needs to be reinstituted on backlist** ("Star") items over a certain dollar amount. Prior to Marvel leaving the direct market, DCD used to offer this as a matter of course. The economic base of backlist was not appreciably affected by MEG's departure (MEG had the worst backlist program of any major publisher), and DCD's infrastructure costs were significantly lowered by the consolidation of most backlist stock into one central facility, rather than twenty-something individual distribution warehouses.

Of the increased costs I'll incur with CCD's demise, free three-day shipping is the one I find the most burdensome. Book distributors offer free three-day freight, and give returnability to boot. The former is far more important to me than the latter.

With the addition of CCD's supposedly impressive backlist sales to DCD's, with virtually no new costs associated, this is a no-brainer which should be immediately implemented.

4) **DCD needs to improve its system for handling authorized returns**. CCD was great because they listed the book the week that it came out, so it was clearly flagged to your attention. DCD often lists items as "future returnables," then never actually gets around to putting them on the returns list. I've got a short-box of stuff piled up that was on the CCD return list, but that DCD hasn't acknowledged as of yet.

5) **DCD needs to address discounts**. I still don't find any logic in basing "small press" discounts on your volume of DC and Image comics sold, nor am I particularly enamored with a system which disallows me the possibility of "keystoning" (doubling wholesale costs) certain lines, when, in most cases, discounts *to* the distributor are equivalent. If you're ordering more than 15-20 copies of *any* comic, you should be getting 50% off cover, at least. Many, many, "mainstream" comics don't sell that well for the average retailer.

I favor a plan where discount is determined by individual title quantity, rather than overall volume. 1-5 copies gets you 40%, 6-10 gets you 45%, 11-15 gets you 47%, 15-25 gets you 50%, over that gets you 52-55%, or something along those lines – then those titles which are performing well for the *individual* retailer can compete on a *fair* economic basis.

6) Maybe the most important (which is why I left it for last), Diamond, in my humble opinion, needs to have an outside advisory board to handle the inevitable problems that are bound to come from monopoly.

Until a smaller regional distribution system creates itself, we're relying on the aesthetic judgment of a purchasing department that has only marginally shown itself to possess one. And this will cause problems.

I recall the year ('94?) that Paul Auster and David Mazzuchelli's *City of Glass* came out from Avon, and was nominated for an Eisner award – Diamond did one initial solicitation and promptly ignored the book. I called Schanes to find out why the book wasn't listed as a Star item (I think Jason Lutes' *Jar of Fools* was also affected that year), and he hadn't even *heard* of the title. When you've got a system that doesn't embrace Eisner nominees as a *matter of course*, it's safe to say that new quirky material is likely to fall through the cracks. I've heard tell that several of the Xeric Grant winners need to fight to get in the catalog, and it becomes apparent that there needs to be an outside body that acts to mediate between Diamond and whoever else to provide an extra aesthetic judgment, rather than a purely economic ones.

Disputes are bound to occur, and I believe it is absolutely in Diamond's best interests to have an outside panel, who are not employees of Diamond, to provide as a additional formal sounding board.

Obviously, such a body would be non-binding – ultimately DCD must make its own decisions, but I know I'd feel a lot better knowing someone was consciously looking out for the little guy.

Especially since the little guy has no other choices anymore.

Tilting at Windmills #55

(Originally ran in Comics Retailer #56)

Let's talk about me for a while.

I musta read too many comic books when I was growing up – I got this funny idea that one must strive to empower themselves and their communities, that one must better and enrich the world they find around them.

One part (some say the largest) of the world around *me* is comics.

And some days that world seems to be coming apart.

Lord knows that as an "industry pundit" I am far more likely to cast a cynical eye upon the affairs of our business than I am a cheery and optimistic gaze. But that stems (largely) from the historically unprofessional way we, as an industry, have conducted our affairs.

We brought ourselves to this crossroads because we misunderstood the customer – we *thought* they wanted chromium covers and polybagged books and trading cards and crossovers and spinoffs and investment stock and collectible nonsense – but they never really wanted any of that. They wanted comics.

Comics are a unique and amazing art form. I could wax passionately for hours on the virtues of our form, the majesty of its language, the energy and enthusiasm of our creators, the strange energy that crackles forth from this static medium – *but none of that matters when our audience is walking away.*

All they want is comics. Good ones.

These days, civilian exposure to our form is nearly nil, and long-time readers are walking, or have walked, away in droves. They just want comics.

We give them manufactured "collectibles," but all they want is comics. We give them internecine bickering, but all they want is comics. We give them 18 months of distributor wars, but, listen to me, *all they want is comics!*

The most ironic part of the collapse we engineered (by focusing on everything *except* the comics themselves) is that there are more good comics available today than in the history of our medium. There are comics for nearly *every* taste, in nearly *any* style, and old-style supply/demand problems are largely a thing of the past. I find it quite mad that the industry isn't growing by leaps and bounds: it is easier than ever to run a high-quality comic book store because of the wealth of material available.

I can say this with all honesty because my sales are up 22% from last year.

So we've got all this potential, with scads of quality material to bring to people who would genuinely love it if only they knew it existed — what's the next step?

Comics are poised (and have been for years) to truly break out into the general public consciousness again. The material is there. The knowledgeable and passionate retail work force is there. We have a core base to expand from, and many dedicated voices to join the chorus. Why are we being held back?

I'll tell you: we're being held back by the lack of quality leadership, and by the lack of understanding of what the customer really wants (comics, remember?).

Leadership will find and identify ways to reach out with our superlative product, and understanding will reach out in a way that makes sense.

Let me tell you a secret. Lean in a little, I don't want this getting around. Here goes: in order to sell comics, you have to promote *comics*. Motion pictures of *Batman*, or *The Crow*, or *The Mask* don't sell comics. Tie-ins with themed restaurants or fast food outlets don't sell comics. Toy lines don't sell comics. Video games don't sell comics. T-shirts don't sell comics. Collectible card games don't sell comics. Breakfast cereal promotions don't sell comics. The only thing that sells comics is selling comics. And given that precious resources are seldom allocated intelligently, what we're left with is a small but dedicated retail base 90% reliant on hand-selling as the primary tool.

(Forgive me when I speak in absolutes. Yes, yes, some small amount of new consumers inevitably enter in during any non-directed campaign – but look at the typical consumer life-expectancy in these cases! How many people who wandered in after *Batman Returns* or *Barb Wire* came back again? Why is it so few? Because we're not selling them *comics* – we're selling them the comic-book tie-in to some other property. This can get people in the door, but it almost never keeps them coming back.)

Even when we remember to sell the right thing, we do it in the wrong way. I remember when Malibu launched the Ultraverse – they spent a million bucks promoting that launch. Some of that money was spent here in San Francisco, on "construction site posters" and the like. But did anyone from Malibu ever *call*

San Francisco stores to tell us about this, maybe help us capitalize on the effort? Well, I'm sure you can guess the answer to that one.

It would be difficult to mount a national or regional campaign because of the inherent difficulty of driving consumers to a small-scale network of stores like we have, and local campaigns are impaired by local stores often having contradictory needs and goals in promotion. These, of course, are not *insurmountable* problems, but I think it's clear why outside advertising is seldom tried.

After spending several years thinking about this, I think I've found a solution to some of these issues.

Again, the first thing to consider is that you have to promote the product you want people to buy. And the best way to promote comics is to actually give people *comics*. "The first one is free." Comics are indeed like drugs in this regard. Give 'em a taste – if it is good quality stuff – and they'll be hooked for life.

I caught my real inspiration when I got one of those "PC Mall" catalogs. You've seen these things, right? Big thick catalogs of computer stuff. Well, I was paging through one, and it struck me that the style and tone of each entry was often wildly different than the entries around it – heck, the type face changes in places! What could be the cause of this? I jumped to the conclusion that these pages must be bought as "advertorial" content by the manufacturers.

So, how could this be adapted to my ends? I pondered awhile, and then it hit me – do a catalog where you run *actual sequences from the books* as a teaser for the uninitiated! I crunched a bunch of numbers, rolled the thought around my mind, and realized this was an excellent tool screaming to be used.

So, just before the Christmas selling season begins, Comix Experience is doing a 100,000 print-run 36-page comics-format catalog focusing on eighteen graphic novels or trades well suited for civilians.

Here's how it works: we're doing editorial write-ups of these 18 titles in 18 pages. The other 18 pages were sold to publishers to *reinforce* the editorial message we are providing. For example, we're running a review for *Sin City*, and on the three following pages, there will be one of the short *Sin City* stories, printed in full. The idea is that a new reader reads about a book that sounds interesting to them, then they get a short sample of the work to reinforce this interest.

The idea is to expose people who don't read comics currently to the range of the form. Most of the copies will be inserted in the local free alternative weekly, *The San Francisco Bay Guardian*, with their regular distribution. This gives us a wide readership in several demographics, and reaches them in an economical way.

As I said, we're selling the "comics pages" to the publishers – we took our expenses, and divided them out, and came out to $600 a page – very inexpensive in a media-drenched city like San Francisco. The beauty of this is that every participant's *individual* cost is relatively low, because we're all collectively kicking into a common pool of money. I couldn't begin to afford to do such a thing on my own. Nor could any of the participating publishers – what are their chances of recouping $12-18,000 in expenses in a single city?

I'm not only gratified, but also impressed with the positive reception this project received from the publishers. The participating publishers are Bongo, Cartoon Books, Dark Horse, DC, Fantagraphics, Kitchen Sink, and Marvel comics. I don't think you can assemble a more mixed group of publishers, and certainly few of these would have worked together in such a way independently.

We're covering titles from *Batman* to *Cerebus*, from *Sandman* to *X-Files*, from *Bone* to *Eightball*, from *Star Wars* to the *Complete Crumb Library* – in short we're surveying the range of material available, both "mainstream" and "alternative," trying to show that comics have *something* for *anyone*.

Another thing we'll be doing is collecting some simple demographic information (age, sex, zip code, "did you see this in the catalog?") to try and create a clear picture of who we are able to reach. With luck, we'll then be able to target the next one that much more accurately.

I'm sharing this with you for a couple of reasons: the first is to show you that publishers *are* willing to work with you if you provide them with a plan. All this took was a professionally written letter, a clear goal, and a couple of phone calls, and we were able to put this together. Many of you may be intimidated by doing such things, but seriously, it is dead easy to put together a promotional plan, and takes no special skills besides the *same* instincts you're using every day to stay alive in a hostile market.

The other reason is that eventually we're going to expand the magazine into other markets, involving other retailers, if this is the success I think it will be. I plan to do 2 to 3 issues locally to test the feasibility of this plan, then to slowly expand out to other cities with different "sponsoring stores," hopefully with a quarterly schedule. Obviously, marginal costs decrease with a wider circulation, and I think this can easily become an inexpensive self-sustaining program that can bring enormous benefit to our market.

There are a lot of people out there. Very few of them read comics. Realistically speaking it is in your hands to change this status quo, and there are people out there willing to help you. I've given you my plan. What's *yours*?

Tilting at Windmills #56
(Originally ran in Comics Retailer #57)

I am apparently from an alternate universe from the rest of you.

It appears that the dimensional frequencies our universes vibrate on are awful close, because I seem to be able to get messages through pretty easy – heck, at least once a month the door swings open enough for me to send this column through – and every once in a while, the dimensions become close enough that I can actually step across the border and visit in your world for awhile, a real-life Jay Garrick hanging out with a real-life Barry Allen.

At least, that is what it seemed like at DC's fifth annual RRP meeting in Montreal the last week of September.

(To digress: this is actually number six — DC held a "retailer focus group" prior to officially forming the RRP, and I was there at what I now call meeting number zero.)

Well, wait, let me back up a tad — I know I wrote about meeting #4 (hell, I wrote my column in my hotel room on-site), but I bet most of you have forgotten all about that — memories are notoriously short in this field. DC comics, once a year (or so — this was 18 months after the last) invites the participants of their RRP program to meet with DC execs face-to-face in a "neutral" city to discuss editorial plans, and to talk about how DC can be a better publisher. What does "RRP" stand for? Beats me. I knew once, but I've forgotten since. Retailer

Representative Program, maybe? Irrelevant, in any case. We've had meetings in LA (twice), Nashville, San Antonio, and now Montreal. At these meetings, DC outlines their editorial presentation for the next "year" (but it never seems to be more than six to nine months out), gives presentations on how things work (this year we got walked-through the printing process at Ronalds [do this and you'll be surprised that comics *ever* ship on time! *So* many things can go wrong!], as well as getting a run-down on the manufacturing process for the porcelain statues), and then opens the floor for q&a (effectively a bitch session).

Don't ask me how you can join the RRP — DC has some arcane formula that brings them a reasonably valid cross-section of stores in the industry. They seem to add about a dozen new retailers a year, and the best I can suggest to getting "in" is making buddies with your DC rep: Ann, Nick, Shira, or Vince — maybe they can put in a good word for you. If you don't know any of these people, well, there's a damn fine chance you'll never get invited!

So. Alternate Universes. That's really the only explanation for how I feel when I'm in the middle of the room with a bunch of other retailers.

I mean, sure, I'm nuts, we all know that, but I feel like an alien when I start discussing specific sales figures at dinner, and the other retailers at the table can't believe I've put the hour a month into running the sales charts. Is it just me? Don't you see the value in gauging the health of the industry, or specific books/publishers? The current performance of any given item is an indicator of the long-term benefit to your store. But, apparently being able to recite some facts and figures — like that preorders in pieces for comics from August are only up maybe five percent from January; or that there are fair odds that any color comic that doesn't place in the top 150 on Diamond's charts is likely to not be making a profit — is contrary to your average retailer's thought processes.

Or let's take the *Superman Wedding Album*. I'm talking to stores that went *five to ten times* their regular Superman orders, who are getting upset that "DC didn't push the book more." Oh, please! Do we as a group honestly believe we need publishers to hold our hands when we cross the street? The responsibility for promotion and publicity, like it or not, is ultimately in *our* hands. Think about it this way: *Superman*, according to the Diamond charts, is selling in the 60-70,000 copy range (preorders from the direct market only). If DC printed in the 10x range, let's call that three-quarters of a million copies (being generous). With a $5 cover price, that's a retail gross of $3,750,000. Allowing DC a generous 10% profit margin, we're talking about a profit of $375,000. Well, sure, that sounds like a whole lot of money, seeing that most of our stores don't even gross that much annually, but if you try and turn that money into a national advertising campaign, you're going to get late night cable TV in Dubuque, at best. Oh, sure, they could spring for advertising on *Lois & Clark* itself, but what will $375k buy? 30 seconds? 45 seconds? Do you think it would be wise for DC to spend all of their profit from this book on a single 45-second ad?

Do you even watch the show? Not only does it generally suck, but the wedding episode in particular was awful. The "Wedding Destroyer?" "Mike?" What the hell was that? If there are 50,000 people who don't read comics that saw that episode and would say, "Golly, I'd love to buy the comic book, if only I knew where to find it," I'll be stunned. No — I'll be *flabbergasted*. And if there are 5,000 people who would even consider buying comics ever again, I'll be doubly surprised. Now,

5,000 customers is nothing to sneeze at, to be sure, but given that this yields a little more than one new customer per store, I think these are resources clearly better allocated at the local level. $75 a customer is a steep price for DC to pay, seeing as how they're unlikely to get more than 1/3 of that customer's dollar, but it is not an unreasonable price for the retailer to pay — $50 worth of fliers and a classified ad will probably have as much effect for you (if not more!) than DC would have spending their entire profit margin.

I hate sounding like a DC apologist — me, scourge of the corporation! — but the fact of the matter is that all the things the average retailer gnashes and moans should be done cost a fair piece of money, and certainly a greater amount than the books could be possibly generating in revenue.

Another alternate universe experience is the beliefs about collectibility. Virtually all of us started as "collectors" before we opened our businesses, myself included — but I think there are two kinds of "collectors": "Accumulators," and the hard-core. Accumulators collect something purely because they like it — if the hardcover edition is cooler than the soft, they'll buy it...but they'll probably give up the original comics in the book. What they want is the best, most complete package of the core product, and they'll pick up what strikes their fancy on ancillary merchandise. The cooler, and more affordable it is, the more likely they'll spring. The accumulator has an affinity for a line, but only buys the best products in that line.

The hard-core, conversely, has a mania for a line — and must have every variation thereof in order to feel "whole." My store's manager Rob, one of my best and oldest friends in the world, is a hard-core Star Trek: TNG action figure collector — he has, I don't know, eight or nine different variations of nearly each character, but I know it eats him up that he'll prolly never have a *Tapestry Picard* (only 1701 made!) or the variant Tasha — even if they were ostensibly put out *exactly* for the hard-core collector like Rob.

I've watched hard-core collector after hard-core collector crumble by the wayside once they realize they can't have it all. Oh, sure, some end up as accumulators, but the majority walk away from whatever hobby they once supported with hard feelings.

I'm all for "accumulators" — I accumulate many things in my life, but I think "collectibility" is a mug's game, and is something that we actively have to work against for the continued survival of the market. But for most of you, this places me square into alternate universe territory. I opined that I'd rather not even carry the *Superman Wedding Album*, because the civilian who wants it is more likely to be deformed by the media perception that it is a sure-fire investment, than to have any affinity for the work. So, then, I'll just wait for the inevitable trade paperback, because that's the package I feel comfortable putting in their hands — the package with absolutely no "collectibility" attached to it. This opinion got me some pretty darn funny looks, I'll tell you.

"We must preserve collectibility!" came the screams when the topic switched to the high-end material DC produces (statues, hardcovers, etc.) — "the customer needs to feel their investment is secure." What the hell is *wrong* with you people? The "investment" should be the pride and pleasure of owning something you like, you think is cool — not some nebulous concern about being able to liquefy that purchase down the road! I want DC (and all other publishers, for that matter) to go back to press on an item any time there is a demand — "collectors" be damned. Because if there is *anyone* we *should* be supporting with "collectible" merchandise, it is the accumulators — they are the bulk of the sales potential in this market. I *want* third and fourth printings of the *Sandman* hardcovers (I'll seldom sell a current hardcover to a new accumulator, because they know they can never accumulate three or four of them); I *want* them to go back to press on the statues (I suspect I could be making $4-500 a month on older statues, if only they were available!); and I *want* them to do another run of merchandise like the *Death* watch, or the *Vertigo Tarot*, because I could be selling dozens upon dozens of units every month.

Screw the collector. Let's get the product into the hands of the people who want it the most. And maybe, just maybe, if we do larger and more frequent runs of this stuff, we can get the prices down so even more people can enjoy this stuff.

Being in Montreal was like being in an alternate universe, all by itself. It is North America, and everyone seems to speaks English fluently, yet it is a world all its own. It is very weird going into a Chinese restaurant and finding every sign and menu in French. You end up walking into a place and saying, "I'll have a #3 and a #8" and hoping for the best!

Plus, Montreal is Smoker's World. There is nowhere (that I noticed) that you can't smoke. It is just about the weirdest experience imaginable to go from a major airport like Chicago, where you have to walk 4.2 miles and go outside at six in the morning on a frosty September day to have a butt, to Montreal's airport, Dorval, where, when asked where it is cool to light up a little death, they wave vaguely and say, "ah, just go lean up against the wall over there." Plus, they don't treat you like a rampaging idiot in the Montreal airport. I am frigging sick and tired of being asked in American airports moronic questions like "Did any strangers hand you a package to carry on the airplane for them?" (Excuse me? Do people actually *do* this? Are there actually people *that* mind-numbingly stupid getting on airplanes? Exactly how many flights have gone down, in the *entire history of aviation*, because of someone carrying someone else's bomb on to a plane? Please!); or being forced to show ID before boarding (if I'm smart enough to figure out how to get a ticket billed in another name, doesn't it stand to reason that I can prolly figure out how to get forged paperwork?) — none of that in Montreal. Hell, I even thanked the clerk at the Canadian Mickey D's for not asking "Would you like a drink with that?" Of course I don't want a drink! If I wanted a drink, I'd *ask* for a drink!

I'm just so tired of being treated like a fool, or a baby. Maybe there are lots of Americans who need that kind of "help" — but I can tell you that I resent it. It may well be for my "safety and convenience" that they assume the average Joe is likely to carry a bomb on to a plane, but I'm more than willing to take that risk to minimize the contempt the authorities evidently have for us.

And it ain't just the FAA either. I see this kind of contempt in our business nearly every day. Take for instance Diamond's new position on street dates, revealed at the RRP meeting. Diamond has finally apparently recognized that we honestly do need time to process our shipments beyond when the customer is standing there salivating. However, because, they're "concerned" that some retailers will break it, they're completely unwilling to give it to *everyone*.

Thanks, Dad.

The deal is this (and, I should note for fairness' sake, that this plan was "still under discussion" and not yet a written-in-stone program): they'll give "early" shipping to selected accounts. Said accounts have a number of criteria to meet, such as having a subscription program, but the key error, in my mind at least, is that a store must have a certain dollar volume of sales before they could qualify. Cindy Fournier declared that volume to likely be at least $50,000 a month in retail Diamond orders, if not $100,000.

Excuse me?

Let me get this straight, O.K.? Unless you're (basically) American Entertainment, Westfield, or Mile High, you're not "worthy" of time to accurately do your job, of time to find and fix mistakes, of having some modicum of protection from UPS shipping errors? Unless you're in the top 10% of all stores in the country, you can't be trusted to not break an agreement? Yeah. That sounds fair.

Answer this one, too, please: assuming all other things are even, who is less at risk for economic sanction from breaking street dates? Bob's Comics Shack, who gets 40% off, and sells $200 in comics a week? Or Steve Milo, who is earning top discount, and is certainly in the top *n* for volume of all shops in the world? I know this much: on the rare occasions I see street dates being treated blithely in industries that have them, it is almost always the largest accounts breaking them — places that have enough economic clout that they have no fears of being cut off from the supply of product.

Last point here: let us say that you're in a town with one of these largest of accounts (think about it — if you're buying $50k or better a month from Diamond alone, chances are you're grossing a million or year, or better — I think it is safe to suggest this is the top 5% of stores, or less) — they get their books on Tuesday, to sell on Wednesday. Wednesday morning rolls around, and they play by the rules, and don't release the material early. They're bigger than you, so they've prolly got longer hours, more staff to run it, etc. When they open on Wednesday morning, every book is in its proper place, every sub has been perfectly and precisely filled, and the staff isn't as harried as you naturally are when you're trying to play *Beat the Clock* in a store full of anxious customers. However, UPS never shows up with your comics. Even if UPS is 99.9% accurate in proper shipping, that is still four retailers across the country who don't have their books at the same time as everyone else (or, if you prefer [and this is thanks to that ole' dog Rob Snell] they're "in the barrel"). You're sitting there, and Big Boy Competition has everything gleaming and perfect, and good to go, thanks to them getting their product ahead of you, and you're in the barrel — there is no chance you'll have your books for another day — and you might not have them for *two*, because the distributor's natural response is "let's see if they show up tomorrow" before actually doing anything.

Street dates are meant to *level* the playing field, not stack it so the rich get richer. Bad call, and bad plan, Diamond.

And so this is where I really feel like Alternate Universe Boy: where they can get up in front of a room full of theoretically the best and brightest retail minds in the country, and make it sound like they're doing us a *favor*.

I like living in *my* world a whole lot better.

a   r   t   i   c   l   e
5 7

Tilting at Windmills #57
(Originally ran in Comics Retailer #58)

Tilting #56 was long enough that J.J. split the column in half, running the second quarter or so in *Comics Retailer* #58. In order to "fill out" the page, he asked me to write a sidebar on #58's "theme" which was "The Biggest Mistake I Ever Made". Not exactly a "full" Tilting, this mistake still nearly **killed** me in the early days.

•   •   •   •   •

The Biggest Mistake I Ever Made

Sometimes mistakes are through no fault of your own – sometimes you don't even know you're making a mistake until it is too late to deal with it.

In most cases, you can work around your mistakes, but sometimes you're dealing with someone or something that just has no room for slack.

The IRS is one of those organizations.

See, when I first opened, I had no idea that when you're "self-employed" the Feds expect you to pay your projected taxes in *advance* — I'd never even *heard* of such a thing.

So, as we closed out year two, I hadn't realized that I had to take care of year one's taxes in addition to prepaying year two.

Whoops.

Cash flow was not at all fun for a few months there. And if anything ever had even the slightest chance of putting me out of business, it was that.

The best piece of advice I can give any retailer (especially those starting out) is to have a separate savings account where you regularly "hide" money from yourself, so it is there to pay the Government at the end of the year.

I make twice-weekly deposits to a separate bank account. These deposits include all sales tax we collected in this period, then I drop in an extra amount equivalent to 1% of my yearly tax liability. When the quarterly payments come due, I transfer the money back to checking, and usually end up with a few dollars "extra."

The important thing to remember is: *this money is not yours!* Even if you feel like you need it, you should never "dip" into it – if you think the distributor credit departments are unforgiving, then you've never met the Feds.

Tilting at Windmills #58
(Originally ran in Comics Retailer #4)

As I write this, we're in the final week before Christmas. Comix Experience is having what appears to be its best season ever — in part due to the *Top Shelf Sampler* catalog I told you about a few months back (and, hopefully, next month I'll have a report on the results, what sold best, and demographic information) — but for the industry, as a whole, it looks like another Year Without Christmas.

The advance order charts that Diamond provides show an 11% drop in preorders from November to December, with orders for 12/96 coming in as the *second worst month of the year* (mildly ahead of only February)! That's scary bad, because when we get into the slow months of the early '97, I'm not 100% sure there is enough volume to keep the industry afloat.

Still, I know several retailers who are also posting remarkable sales gains this year, so maybe these figures don't tell the complete picture. I'll hope that this sales drop reflects leaner, smarter inventories, and the shaking out of those stores that didn't add to anything but volume.

'Course it would be *much* easier for retailers to keep themselves afloat if seasonal product actually flowed into the stores when it would do some good. As it is every year, DC gets the big thumbs down in timely delivery. This year I count four significant holiday products which they've dropped the ball on: *the Dark Knight* statue, the *Sandman* bookends, this year's *Batman* HC, and the *Sandman: Wake HC*.

I've just downloaded this week's invoice from the Diamond BBS, for our final Wednesday before Christmas, and I find that I'll only have one of these four projects to sell before the big day, and that is *The Wake*. No statue, no bookends, no *Batman* HC, and what little we *do* get is coming *so* close to Christmas as to be nearly useless.

Let me tell all you production managers and marketing guys a little secret: Christmas buying begins in late November. Really, it does. If you have a product that you think is suited for the holidays, or is very upscale, then make damn sure you can get it to the sales floor with enough time for us to sell it.

I mean, what is wrong with you people? I know we've gone over the whole "ship it when you solicit it" thing a hundred times before, and, in regards to comic books, generally most of you have learned that lesson (except #$@! Image comics, but they're a special case). But when we look at upscale merchandise, everything falls apart. Look, if you say we're going to get a statue in November, then we *better* damn well get it in November. If you can't deliver it until December, then *solicit it as such*. And if you're less than 100% sure about your manufacturing capabilities, then *err on the side of caution in solicitation*. You have no excuse (at least not one any retailer is willing to listen to). And it is *exactly* this kind of sloppy planning that puts the finite and decreasing number of comic book stores into financial jeopardy.

A "rain check" is good, but it is not *good enough*.

Meanwhile, crosstown from we-are-incapable-of-meeting-a-merchandise-ship-date DC comics, the Mighty Marvel is looking more and more anemic every day.

Isn't it time to acknowledge that as long as Heroes World remains the exclusive distributor of Marvel Comics that Marvel has virtually no chance of competing in this market?

The week after Thanksgiving, Marvel decided to get the books to us on Thursday, rather than the usual Wednesday. I received no notification of this, but at least the opening message on the HWD phone number mentioned this, so I didn't have to go into the non-time of waiting on hold to speak to a human.

But then UPS evidently screwed something up — no one on the West Coast received their comics. So I (and a thousand other retailers, presumably) call to find out why we've been made liars in front of our entire customer base, and I'm put on hold.

For more than half an hour.

At their expense.

When I finally get a human on the phone (who tells me that no one on the West Coast has their books), I ask why this information wasn't the first thing we got when we hit the phone. "Gee, that's a good idea, maybe we should do that."

Is it just me?

Or, lets look at the bizarre reorder shipping they've been doing. In the last two weeks we got reorders shipped in a manila envelope (no, not a padded one!), without even a backing board to protect the contents, as well as having two (2) comics shipped in a 300 count box, second-day air. That's right, *the shipping was three to four times the value of the comic books inside*!

Customer service is a ludicrous joke, shipping is done in the least efficient way possible, they apparently don't take returns, even on product that is months late, and they can't even keep the simplest thing like billing straight.

About the only chance that Marvel has anymore is for the stockholders to resist Perleman's plans, file for Chapter 11, and immediately sell Heroes World, and join back up with Diamond.

HWD is simply the single worst distributor I have ever had the misfortune of dealing with, and I don't think it is too far from the truth to suggest that I could do a better job of distributing Marvel out of the back room of my store!

It is time for Marvel to publicly admit that they made a huge honking terrible mistake, and that they're very *very* sorry, and will never do it again. Marvel's relationship with the direct market is not 100% unsalvageable, but every darn day that percentage gets a little closer....

If you ask me what I want for Christmas, as a retailer I ask only two things: 1) the perennial "keep your word!" (and I'm getting a *little* tired of having to ask for this *every* year!), and 2) the immediate and rapid extinction of Heroes World Distribution, and everything associated with it. I'd even recommend finding a priest to exorcise the building. Much bad Juju there.

Here's hoping that '97 grants *all* our wishes.

Tilting at Windmills #59
(Originally ran in Comics Retailer #60)

Koan time: if 300 gallons of hot water fall on a comic shop, and no one is there, does it make a sound?

I've no idea about *that*, but I can tell you with certainty that it sure does make a *mess*

Comix Experience's flood aftermath, January 19, 1997

On New Year's Day a badly fitted pipe in the hotel above Comix Experience ruptured, deluging the store with gallons and gallons and gallons of hot water. The entire middle of the store was scoured clean of comic books, and most of the right side was wiped, as well.

Over $18,000 of product damage was done. Plus, both the floor and the ceiling need to be replaced.

So, you can imagine that I'm a little preoccupied right now.

The good thing is that my credit is immaculate, and Diamond and Heroes World have agreed to extend me the terms that I need to get past this. DC and Dark Horse have also been extraordinarily helpful in sending me promo packages, and supporting me in other ways. The thing of it is that I've been more than savage to these folks in print over the years, so it is really really nice to know that no one is taking it *personal*.

And ain't that what comics are all about?

•   •   •   •   •

It's not like I don't have plenty of other things to talk about this month — things in this industry have been plenty eventful — but I have so little time, so instead of any kind of in depth commentary, we have to do another set of *TaW* Tidbits.

Take the case of Marvel filing for Chapter 11 protection.

I mean, that's prolly at least *two* columns all by itself, but I've got to settle for only this:

Don't tell me you're surprised.

•   •   •   •   •

Am I the only one who is...disturbed might be a neutralish word...that the distributors didn't even get us our comics the day *before* this year's holidays (Christmas and New Years)? Since both holidays fell on a Wednesday, we had to settle for Friday delivery this year. Why is that? Am I alone in thinking that receiving the new comics on Tuesday was not only doable, but would have solidly helped the retailers' currently fragile bottom line?

I cringe when I do my cycle sheets in late shipping weeks – because the cycle is shorter, odds are good that errors will increase in the basic data. I won't be surprised if reorder activity in March is statistically higher than norm, because most retailers' orders are likely lower than they should be because of data creep.

To compound this problem, Marvel books didn't arrive here either week until the following *Monday*! Talk about difficult-to-properly-sell goods!

It bugs me because this is a really basic common-sense thing that the distributors and publishers could have done to *help* them sell more books (I believe that they most definitely have the slack-time in their respective schedules to manage such a task) – the kind of basic, common-sense kinds of things that are being screwed up on a annoyingly regular basis.

•   •   •   •   •

Don't even get me started on the new "electric" Superman.

•   •   •   •   •

Take a minute now to check your insurance situation. Well, actually, for most small business people, the real advice is take a minute now to *get* some coverage.

I don't care how small-time your operation might be, or how big and cocky you might be – you *must* be insured.

I said above that I've been getting a lot of help from publishers and distributors, and I attributed that to my good credit. That's partially true, but it is equally true that the first question out of everyone's mouth was "were you insured?" That I could answer an unequivocal "yes" avoided a large number of hurdles that would have otherwise been there to clear.

When you add the costs of the repairs, restocking, clean-up time, lost sales, and all the miscellaneous expenses associated with a disaster of this nature you're looking at nearly *thirty* thousand dollars in damage. The money that I paid my insurance company over the last seven-and-a-half years is a mere fraction of that sum. If I had any doubts about the value of insurance, they are utterly and completely erased – my insurance company is being utterly reasonable, and accepting the claim without hesitation. We've haggled a little on the true value of the stock, but the number we decided on was completely equitable.

If you don't have insurance – go get some *now*. If you *do* have insurance, review it *right* now to confirm you have enough coverage to start over from scratch, if you need to. CYA. Cover your ass.

•   •   •   •   •

("Look! Up in the Sky! It's a bird! It's a plane! It's...a lightning bolt?")

•   •   •   •   •

I prolly should send this in to Diamond Dateline to get that $25 credit in the "sales tip" section, but I'm such a generous guy that I'll do it for free here. If you want the ability to openly discuss money without anyone but the staff knowing what you're talking about, use a code.

We use "pathfinder," but any ten letter word with no repeating letters would do. See, the first letter, "P" represents $100. "A" would be $200. "T" would be $300. "H" would be $400, and so on. If you want to be clever and more specific, you could use multiple letters: "tap" would be $321, but that's usually overkill. "The Word" is $1000, and if you get two words or more, you're speaking sentences! "Cracking the Word" is always my daily goal, quite unrealistically. We've spoken sentences on maybe 5 occasions.

Credit where credit is due department: this is by no means *my* idea. It predates me to the old BOTW days. I have *no* idea who taught me this – it might have be Ski Ford, it might have been Rory Root, or it might have even been someone else. I can't remember, but credit doesn't belong to me, so I wouldn't deserve that $25 anyway...

•　　•　　•　　•　　•

But the Comic Book Legal Defense Fund sure does!

I said above that I do this column "for free" – that's only mildly accurate. *I* get nothing, but the CBLDF gets the full pay – this being a painless and regular way to support an organization that defends *your* livelihood. Think of the CBLDF as *legal* insurance – and it is even more vital that you contribute, because the CBLDF doesn't make contribution a condition of taking on a client.

With no new caseload (hah!), and steady continuation of current donation patterns, the CBLDF will have all its debts paid in a year or so, but we've got at least 2 potential cases we're currently reviewing, and it seems to me there are another 3 or 4 situations we're monitoring, plus the Planet Comics defense is ongoing – well, it just makes me a little nervous.

That's where *you* come in. Personally, I don't think *any* working professional in our industry should make less than a $25 contribution every year (no, that's not right – I actually think it is $50, but I'm talking to a group of retailers who have mostly gone through yet another crappy year, so I gotta be realistic). Look at the calendar. It is 1997. Since there are damn fine odds that you haven't given to the CBLDF this year, I want you to go over to your checkbook right now (well, after you've gotten off the phone with your insurance agent!) and write a $25 check to the CBLDF: PO Box 693, Northampton, MA, 01061. You could also call 1-800-99-CBLDF (992-2533), if you'd rather use a credit card (but then it *better* be $50!)

If, God forbid, you need legal defense from any first amendment related legal problems, remember that number too: 1-800-99-CBLDF. The Comic Book Legal Defense Fund: support it early, support it often!

•　　•　　•　　•　　•

That's it! Next month, I *swear to God* you'll have the demographic results of the Top Shelf Sampler project. See you then!

Tilting at Windmills #60
(Originally ran in Comics Retailer #61)

Right, so several months ago I told y'all about the *Top Shelf Sampler* that we created. This was a 36-page catalog with a wide variety of comic book collections that we inserted into the *San Francisco Bay Guardian*, a free weekly alternative newspaper with a circulation in excess of 100,000 copies. 18 different projects were featured, running the gamut from the *Simpsons* to *Stuck Rubber Baby*, from *Bone* to *Naughty Bits*, from *Star Wars* to *Sin City*. There was, I believe, something there for every "civilian" who looked at it, and, being a cooperative venture between seven publishers and Comix Experience, was done at a very low cost for each individual.

In most cases a capsule summary and review of each title was followed by an excerpt from that title — usually one page, but in a few cases we featured up to four pages. The idea is that in order to sell comics to the unaware, you have to actually show *comics* — talking about them isn't nearly enough.

So the question we're all wondering about is: did it work?

It depends on your perspective.

One of the participating publishers said to me that he would consider it a success if it generated an equal amount of money as they spent on the advertising — a not unreasonable request on the face of it, but very difficult to achieve. In my experience, advertising almost never directly works in this fashion — the goal in most advertising is not as much creating 1:1 sales (though that sure helps!) as it is to create *awareness* of a product.

We kept records of the sales we generated through the *Sampler*, as well as asking simple demographic (age, sex, zip code, and "did you see this in the catalog?") of each purchaser. And while we weren't flawless in our data gathering (on New Comics day, when lines of customers are at the counter clamoring for their comics, it is difficult to juggle surveying against keeping those lines moving, plus the burst pipe on the first of the year proved enough of a distraction to halt our data gathering), we have enough information to extrapolate some positive conclusions.

During the six weeks we ran this promotion, we sold 373 copies of the 18 featured titles (most of which were series, for a total of 67 SKUs) — historical sales patterns for these titles would normally have yielded around 125 units sold of these same SKUs. That's approximately 250 units sold over and above traditional sales patterns, or a 200% increase.

Comix Experience has a regular customer base of at or around 500 people. We attracted slightly over 150 civilians *who actually bought something listed in the* Sampler. That's a 30% increase from our normal customer base with a one-time sale, and (though this is where we get very unscientific) we estimate that at least 20% of these people have come back again to buy something else. This, to me, was the most important part of this experiment — getting people in the door once is one thing, but getting them to come back, to become part of the regular customer base, well, that's gold.

We were able to bring more than 150 *new* customers into the market (possibly more, as non-*Sampler* items weren't demographically tracked), and perhaps 30 of them are staying. In absolute terms, this is a drop in the bucket, but I can't think of any promotion we've ever done previously that has that kind of drawing and sticking power. By those terms, the *Sampler* was an uncategorical success — the kind of success that should make me jump up and down.

But by other standards, the benefit becomes less clear — the *Sampler* reached 100,000 people, but only .1% responded. In direct mail that is a reasonable percentage, if I recall my marketing books, but I'm not sure if that is healthy for an inserted catalog. Honestly, I have to admit that I was pie-in-the-sky hoping for at least 500 new purchasers, but doubling customer counts maybe wasn't a reasonable goal at all. Economically, this project becomes a little hinky to justify — the combined expenses of the *Sampler* were something like $15,000 and we sold under $4,000 worth of product as a result. Ultimately, I don't think that raw sales count as much in this case as in bringing new blood into the market, particularly because those expenses were apportioned out among the various participants, but I'm not sure that my accountant agrees!

But let's look at the reality of it: even the simplest and most minimal advertisement in San Francisco is going to cost at least $500 (for a display space of about a business card) — you've got to sell 25 $20 graphic novels in order to gross as much as you spent on the advertisement alone. Figure in stock costs, and that number leaps to 50 copies ($500 for the ad, $500 for the 50 copies at whole-sale cost to sell). It is pretty darn unusual that anyone can make that little space sell that many copies of nearly anything. In eight years of advertising in San Francisco, I can only think of *one* occasion where we directly sold an amount of product that offset the expenses occurred.

The real benefit to advertising is in increasing the *awareness* of your product. On that score, I think we succeeded in spades — at least 90,000 people who have never once in their entire life been in a direct market comic book shop have been exposed to a critical sampler of the breadth our market has to offer. But one exposure only brought in 150 purchasers. I don't think it is unfair to assume if 150 people read the *Sampler*, then got in the car and drove to a type of business they knew next to nothing about, and likely didn't even know *existed*, then 1500 read the *Sampler* and thought there might be something they wanted to read, but didn't motivate themselves to leave the house for it. And that 15,000 read the Sampler, and while they didn't see something they *want*, are open to future possibilities. On that scale, I think this money is well spent indeed, *as long as we keep following up.*

The plan is for the *Sampler* to continue — now that we've tried this once, we can reformat it some, and try it again, this time including other San Francisco Bay Area stores. Assuming all goes well with that, we hope to produce a *Sampler* quarterly, and bring it out regionally, and then nationwide — higher print runs, and more stores involved will reduce the costs for everyone, to the point where we have a de facto "Got milk?" kind of campaign, without any one faction contributing a disproportionate share.

So, let's get to the actual data, and see what (if anything) we can learn. What follows is a chart with the sales of *Sampler*-listed material from 11/27/96 to 1/15/97. The first column lists the title and how many volumes are in the series. The second column lists Volume Sales, the sum of all sales within that group. The third column is Average Sales for a book in that group. This allows us to see the relative sales of a line. The third column is the Average Age of a purchaser. The fourth column gives a breakdown by Sex, both as a raw number and a percentage. The fifth column gives the raw number of "Civilian" purchasers for that line, as well as expressing it as a percentage. The final column shows the number of ad pages a line had.

Overall statistics:
Average age of purchaser: 30
30.8% female
58.2% civilian
Average of 1.2 books sold per purchaser

Title Data	V Sales	Av sales	Age	Sex		Civilians	Ads
Batman (3 volumes)	13	4.3	30	8M (89%)	1F (11%)	7 (77%)	0
Big Books (6 volumes)	33	5.5	34	23M(85%)	4F (15%)	26 (96%)	3
Bone (3 volumes)	16	5.3	33	9M (75%)	3F (25%)	3 (33%)	2
Cerebus (9 volumes)	26	2.8	32	22M (85%)	4F (15%)	18 (69%)	0
Crumb Library(9 vols)	9	1	29	2M (33%)	4F (67%)	3 (50%)	1
Eightball(5 volumes)	22	4.4	29	17M (89%)	2F (11%)	13 (68%)	1

Title Data	V Sales	Av sales	Age	Sex	Civilians	Ads
Gaiman/McKean(3 vols)	25	8.3	31	13M (65%) 7F (35%)	12 (60%)	0
Hate (3 volumes)	11	3.6	24	5M (71%) 2F (29%)	3 (43%)	1
Introducing Kafka(1 vol)	25	25	26	16M (67%) 8F (33%)	18 (75%)	1
Marvels (1 volume)	13	13	28	12M (92%) 1F (8%)	6 (46%)	1
Maus (2 volumes)	9	4.5	31	4M (57%) 3F (43%)	4 (57%)	0
Naughty Bits (3 vols)	17	5.6	29	4M (27%) 11F (73%)	10 (67%)	1
Sandman (9 volumes)	93	10.3	30	42M (57%) 32F (43%)	42 (42%)	0
Simpsons (3 volumes)	27	9	22	11M (55%) 9F (45%)	15 (75%)	1
Sin City (3 volumes)	18	6	31	14M (88%) 2F (12%)	7 (44%)	4
Star Wars (2 volumes)	7	3.5	25	5M (83%) 1F (17%)	2 (33%)	0
Stuck Rubber (1 vol)	9	9	35	6M (86%) 1F (14%)	6 (86%)	2
X-Files (1 volume)	0	0	n/a	n/a	0 (0%)	0

So what *can* we learn from these figures?

This is the hard part for me, because these numbers are wholly different than my expectations. For example, the extended ad pages had apparently no effect whatsoever — the relationship between number of pages sampled and sales is virtually non-existent. I assumed that *Sin City* would have the strongest sales of the bunch because it had the longest excerpt sequence. While it is the top half of performers by average sales, it is the lower half of civilian percentages — absolutely contrary to the intention. I also would have never picked *Introducing Kafka* as the break-out hit of the *Sampler.* The single biggest seller by units, and number three by raw number of civilians, it took me wholly by surprise. On the other hand, that the *Crumb Library* is the second worst seller is confounding — all I can guess is that Crumb and Kafka sounded better to people than Crumb by himself.

One can read the sales as being kind to familiarity — the *Guardian*'s audience has heard of Gaiman & *Sandman*, giving it the massive 42 civilian sales, and the *Simpsons* and the Marvel name seem to be good draws too. But how do we account for *zero* sales of *X-Files*? Or the *horrible* civilian sales of *Star Wars*? 33%? I thought that would be 66% or better!

For the next time, we're going to go a smaller — 16 pages is more likely, with six to eight featured books, rather than 18. I also think some sort of incentive, be it a coupon or a giveaway, to draw a larger percentage of those possible readers is in order.

I strongly suspect that as we do more of these, the response rate will increase as well — repetition is one of the keys to successful advertising.

We'll keep you posted on what happens next.

Tilting at Windmills #61
(Originally ran in Comics Retailer #62)

I've extremely mixed feelings about Marvel returning to Diamond. On the one hand, "it will return stability to the market," and help somewhat in lowering retailer's costs with consolidated shipping, and whatnot — blah, blah, blah, you've read the press release — but the whole deal just leaves me cold when I begin to consider the costs.

Dozens of distributor warehouses shut down; hundreds of retailers unable to compete in the new economic reality — either way, hundreds, possibly even *thousands* of jobs lost, scattered to the four winds. The surviving retailers facing the burden of radically increased costs. The combined energies of the finest minds in our industry spent on two wasted years that ultimately amounted to *nothing*.

When Marvel declared the "Marvelution," they promised us a better world — order reductions, guaranteed stock, better discounts. Diamond and DC countered with their "New Dynamics," with much the same promises.

How many of those promises did you see fulfilled?

I used to have a choice of two full-line distributors in my local area — they competed for my business, and I was able to get good service and pricing because of it. While some things were slightly inconsistent (like fill rates on reorders), the multiplicity of sources usually allowed one to get pretty much whatever they needed. With dozens and dozens of distributor warehouses dotting the land, most retailers in most major cities had direct face-to-face contact with their distributor.

The Marvelution and the New Dynamics changed all this. Instead of two competitors locally servicing my needs, I'm forced to have the majority of my goods trucked in from Los Angeles. Instead of being able to restock by tomorrow — walk in, pull the comics off the shelf, go home — I have to order by remote control, and wait at very least a week, and more likely two to three weeks for that restock. Instead of being able to negotiate for a better deal (pricing, delivery costs, how they pack your books, whatever) with someone I knew face-to-face, I'm now stuck calling a stranger, who doesn't actually touch the comics themselves, and hope they have the foggiest notion of what I'm talking about. Instead of having multiple full-line sources for restock, where overlapping independent warehouse orders meant I could usually find what I wanted somewhere, we have a single stocking base which is horribly unwieldy to use and, more often than not, is out of stock on most non-brokered goods.

The publishers told us that the old system just didn't work — it was "inefficient," that distributors were intractable. These changes were being made for our own good, and that, accordingly, everything would be so much better, if only we'd be patient.

And while we waited, Rome burned.

I spent $3500 more in shipping in '96 than I did in '94. My discount on many lines decreased. I was forced to buy from people that I had no desire to support. I incurred nearly countless expenses as my time was wasted while the system tried to figure out if it had any idea *how* to do its job. I wasted money, I wasted time, I wasted brainpower — and so did all of the rest of you. Many couldn't afford the extra time, the extra money, the extra thinking, and so they perished.

Take a moment to think of the fallen hundreds. And the thousands of lives their passing has effected.

Such a waste. A damn tragic waste.

We're left with a monopolistic system. One that does fairly well for its brokered and in-control constituencies (DC, Image, and, we'll presume, Marvel), and anywhere from fairly poor, to downright awful for everyone else. Diamond's annoying rush towards centralization has depersonalized distribution relationships, and resulted in a drastic drop in their ability to restock product from the "big two, soon to be three." I mean, my fill-rates have gone from 80% or better, to maybe 50% at best. This is not only annoying, but directly *disruptive* to sales.

We've talked about how the nature of the marketplace is starting to change — that we're gradually moving towards a "bookstore economy" where backlist is at least as important as frontlist, if not of far greater significance. More and more retailers are realizing this, many of the publishers have realized this — so why is it that our sole national distribution source seems hell-bent to destroy this emerging and growing segment of our market? I placed a Star System order over five weeks ago that is still trickling in the door. Why is that? Recall that Diamond makes a *much* higher percentage of the cover price from a non-brokered publisher's backlist than they do from DC, Dark Horse, or Image. Think about how multiple shipment and multiple week turn-around on backlist fulfillment costs *Diamond* potentially thousands of dollars in sales — I cannot place a Star order until my previous one has arrived, because it is virtually impossible to recall, when looking at a blind list of 3000+ items which have or have not been ordered, which have or have not arrived. By "going to the well" less often, I'm keeping books out of stock that could potentially turned multiple times, costing *everyone* possible sales.

Sure, I could simply buy more books up front, but that almost completely negates a key value of the book economy — being able to run a mile wide, but an inch-deep via "just-in-time" reorder availability provides critical cash flow that every retailer needs to survive.

Diamond needs to focus on the Star System as an absolutely key element to fix if they're actually dedicated to our success (as they are wont to claim) — the list of product itself is so riddled with typos, poor categorization, and bad organization as to be unwieldy and annoying to use. In-stock availability of non-brokered product is very poor (I can always expect at *least* a third of what I want won't be in-stock — and another third will take three weeks or more to actually arrive), making ordering a frustrating shot-in-the-dark experience. And they have to get us those books within a guaranteed window of time. (I also think reorder penalties are evil on products *designed* to be reordered, that the selection is not nearly as comprehensive as it should or could be, and that we shouldn't be charged for shipping if we meet reasonable order minimums, but let us stick to stuff that Diamond is *likely* to do without being forced by an outside body.)

And the scariest part is that this is only likely to get worse. Diamond's system bent slightly once DC cut their deal, and bent a little more with each successive publisher — it twisted *hard* after the buyout of Capital, and I see no reason to believe that it won't *break* with the addition of Marvel.

Oh, sweet Marvel — architect of our predicament. Oh, sure, it was DC that built the foundation, by "picking the survivor," but Marvel's purchase of Heroes World was clearly and without question the domino that set this chain of events into motion.

One of the things that Marvel (and DC) claimed during their little dog-and-pony shows was that the then-current distribution system simply didn't work for them — distributors held too much power in deciding what information got trickled down; what products were available to restock; what services the publishers would be able to offer to retailers.

There *was* indeed an element of truth to this pronouncement — extant distributors were in fact largely acting as a barrier between their two constituents, rather than a conduit. Publishers found it difficult to target opportunities to *specific* retailers through the system; sales incentives were not being directly passed through to retailers; stocking levels seemed a matter of whim rather than reason — well, you can recite the list as well as I.

But, somehow (though it was, in fact, a historical inevitability — once Marvel chose a regional distributor to handle their national business, virtually the only *possible* result was exactly what occurred: the failure of that regional system and the consolidation of the strongest publishers behind one single source, eliminating the economic viability of any competition), rather than reducing the power of the distributor upon the direct market, and increasing the strength of the retailer, *exactly* the opposite occurred — *one* viable national distributor remains, and wields ultimately life or death power over the numerical majority of our field, and retailers are left with *significantly* less power and options in stocking these non-brokered lines.

And Marvel wants to waltz right back the door, whistling a happy tune, like nothing happened? Well, fuck them!

I mean *seriously*, folks! We're having a party, and Marvel suddenly goes psycho, flips over the punch bowl (and *on* to the stereo, no less!), flings handfuls of salsa and chips all over the room, and splits, declaring, "this party sucks! We're going to throw our own across town!" We all sit there, shell-shocked for a few minutes, and start trying to clean up. But the CD player is just ruined, and the radio only picks up a handful of AM stations; the purple stain in the carpet is *never* going to come out; and while we were trying to figure out just *who* was going to scrape the salsa off the walls, guests started leaving by the dozens, because it just wasn't *fun* anymore.

Then, around 1 am, there is a loud knock at the door, and, wonders of wonders, it is *Marvel*, saying, "Hey, dudes, we ran out of beer at the other place, but we rolled a drunk on our way over for this bottle of Thunderbird, so let's party! Woo!"

Now, we're genial folks and all, and, sure everyone deserves a second chance, but I'm quite sure I didn't hear the words "we're sorry" anywhere there.

Now, I'm putting aside that in a sane and rational world, we'd expect Marvel to at *least* rent a steam-cleaner for the carpet, and maybe find someone to repair the CD player. I'm also putting aside that a lot of the people who left the party will never ever come back, relating *our* hospitality to other people's behavior. And I don't really care the guy who actually *instigated* the situation is Pete, and Pete was a little too drunk, and is back at the other place praying to the porcelain god.

We. Deserve. An. Apology.

Repeat after me: "We're sorry. We made a terrible mistake, and we understand that now. We hurt many people, and we feel really awful about that. We're humbly, deeply, and truly sorry, and we'll never, *ever*, try something like that again."

No "but...;" no, "we're doing this for your benefit;" no corporate doublespeak in carefully phrased press releases. Just get down on your damn knees, take out a full page ad in *Comics Retailer*, send us personal letters, and tell us you are sorry. Make us *believe*.

We're cutting you an awful lot of slack as it is anyway — but we've known you since we were kids, and that kind of bond gives you an *inch* of room to get back into our good graces.

Hundreds or thousands of dollars stripped from every retailer in this country. Massive brainpower wasted in chasing an inevitably spiraling hole. Hundreds or thousands of people losing their livelihoods.

Look upon their works, and despair.

Marvel Comics owes the direct market an apology. There are no extenuating circumstances, there is no plausible deniability.

And *if* they deign to do what is right, then maybe, just maybe, we can begin to trust them again. We might be able to hold some hope that they can be a positive force in our industry again. We might feel a little safer, a little less like we have to keep one hand on our wallet, and one eye on our back. I couch this in "maybe" and "might" because we were horribly betrayed, battered and abused by something we thought was our friend. And it will be very very difficult to regain any semblance of that trust again.

You out there who read the press release and smiled ("everything is now back to normal"), you out there who by fate or design are predominately Marvel-based stores, to you I say this: be careful, be very very careful. To hold close to your breast a creature who has shown a historical tendency to bite the hand that feeds it is not the wisest of courses. And if again they do something stupid or evil (depending on your perspective), and you get hurt once more, *this* time there will be no sympathy, no pity. And this is one of the very few cases where I *don't* want to say, "I told you so."

There is no redemption without contrition. And there is no faith without honor.

Marvel Comics: do the right thing.

Tilting at Windmills #62
(Originally ran in Comics Retailer #63)

Short column this month – J.J. says the TSR/WOTC dealhas absorbed all available space (now you gaming guys get a look at the fun of utter upheaval that us comics folks have been trudging through for the last umpty months), which is fine with me because I'm covering all of Rob's hours, while he goes on a (much-deserved!) vacation, the store is just about to have its eighth anniversary gala, we're finishing up the remodel of the store (finally!) after the burst pipe near killed me on the first, and Pro/Con and WonderCon is coming up too. Busy little Brian!

•   •   •   •   •

I (gasp!) owe a public apology – to (gasp!) Diamond. Last month I stated that it took me six weeks to get the entirety of my Star order. While this is true, it was not due to the reasons I ascribed. Cindy Fournier (who is absolutely the most valuable person Diamond has in its employ, and should be given a large raise, gosh darn it!) found out that it wasn't in-stock items that were taking too long to wend their way through the system, as I assumed – instead, despite my requesting (twice! Once written, and once verbally) that no backorders be placed, they were – and this is why it appeared to me that something stupid was happening to the system.

So, sorry Diamond, and thanks, Cindy, for getting to the bottom of the problem. The lesson, boys and girls? Always double check your facts before you yell them in public. If I looked at the right column on the Diamond invoice, then I could have been publicly castigating them for the right thing (placing backorders on my order), rather than something they were innocent of.

• • • • •

While I'm being all publicly aware and stuff, let me clean off a few things from the Big List of Stuff to Write About.

Please let me publicly thank boy editor John Jackson Miller for the fine ongoing job he does putting this magazine together. I want to take special note of the spiffy job he does in writing my headlines. It's a little back-stage thing that you prolly didn't know, but J.J. writes both the headline and sub-head for my columns. I don't know if the rest of the Gang of Four writes their own (I bet Costa does for sure, and maybe Preston, but those aren't Gray's), all I can say is that J.J. never fails to bring a smile to my face with his choices, and usually sets the proper tone, even when I don't figure it out until the fourth paragraph. So, take a bow, Sir – you deserve it.

(Now if only I could get my columns flagged on the cover more....)

• • • • •

Usually I deny that being in San Francisco, in and of itself, gives me any real advantage in being able to run the kind of store that I do – but as of late I've been seeing one place that this is wrong: backlist distribution options. With Cold Cut and Last Gasp right in my backyard, I can quickly and efficiently restock, and do it with people that I have a relationship with. This is a superior system to remote control ordering like the Star System (which doesn't work properly, anyway) – without these two I would be out of business.

Last Gasp in particular should be singled out for having Kristine Anstine come to my store, and acting as a real and actual sales rep – "Here's what we have that you're out of, here's some stuff I think will work with what you're doing, and here are a couple of things that you're gonna take returnable on a flier." Kristine can do this in a way that Diamond can not – even if local rep Dave Hawksworth did this with a Star list, they'd be out of stock on half of what I'd want, negating half the value.

Anyway, Kristine and I have gotten very sympatico – I have to only change three or four items on her first pass "recommended order," which is as good as any human being who is not me is *ever* going to get. And I have to honestly say that this is the single best distributor relationship I've ever had in the history of the store. Kristine, I really appreciate your efforts.

• • • • •

I also owe a belated thanks to Mike Patchen, owner of San Francisco's Comic Relief. Mike closed almost a year ago today, and was my closest "competitor" – eight blocks away, yet the very first place I'd send people if I was out of something. When Mike closed the door he did something very classy – he made a point of directing customers my way. He went so far as to distribute our newsletter to his regular customers, so they'd be right up to speed with how we operate. This was a fundamentally magnanimous gesture that Mike received no benefit whatsoever from, besides knowing that his customers would be in good hands. If they ever had a "good deeds" Eisner award, I'd nominate Mike in a *heartbeat*.

• • • • •

Hmmm, 855 words. I think I can squeeze *one* more item in. And it must be full of spite, because I can't be *Tilting* just on niceness.

I *loathe* Dark Horse renumbering their titles every three or four issues on regular monthly books. It screws up my databases, it screws up my back issue bins, it confuses the customer, and it smells of utter manipulation and desperation. *Star Wars: X-Wing Rogue Squadron – Requiem for a Rogue* isn't a title – it's a headache. Especially when the indicia reads *SWXWRSRFAR* #1 as issue #17 – just put the proper issue number somewhere on the bleeding cover, O.K.? Make our life a little easier, please? I bet a stat geek like J.J. agrees with me on this too, right boss? And he doesn't have to explain it to anyone else....

• • • • •

Outta room, so we'll leave it until next month where I'll tell you some of what happened at Pro/Con – since I know you won't be there. Hey! Go make a reservation for the San Diego Expo right now – knowledge is power, and so is networking.

(Hmm, Marvel didn't apologize yet, did they?)

Tilting at Windmills #63
(Originally ran in Comics Retailer #64)

I hate to use the "H word," but, Lord Almighty, Diamond is getting more and more like Heroes World every day.

I don't know exactly what is going on, but it sure seems like that when Diamond took over Marvel's distribution part of the deal including hiring all the HWD employees that ruined that company. How else can you explain the extremely sharp nosedive in service we've seen over the last two weeks?

Diamond personnel seem utterly unable to read instructions off faxes. If you say "no back orders" you can be sure they will back order any unfillable orders. If you say you want books reshipped (to not pay the satanic shipping charges associated with direct shipping), you can be sure they will be direct shipped. If you say you want current-size bags, you can be sure they will send you Silver Age ones instead. If you get a confirmed order, they're just as likely to lose it.

I'm ready to go postal, and you're damn lucky that Krause don't let me but mildly curse, 'cuz the air'd be turning blue right 'bout now.

First, they lose my April Marvel order that I faxed in, and nobody up there catches that it is missing. I think that is pretty bloody ridiculous — *especially* because this was the first month of the changeover, and one would assume that they'd be extra special vigilant. Gosh, what was I thinking?

Thank god I download my invoice from the BBS! I caught on Tuesday morning that only six Amalgam books were arriving, and that tripped the flag that something was wildly wrong.

Now, let me give Diamond their proper respect due and note that, so far, every problem has been solved and jumped on, usually at an enormous expense to Diamond — this is something that Heroes World never bothered to do. But this brings its own set of problems. In the example above, Diamond (properly) overnighted the books to the store, and I had them for New Comics Day, but we both know that this means that Diamond lost any chance at profit it would have had. That is customer service done right, but if it happened to me, then I know it is happening to a dozen other of you, too. And given that I've personally had at least a half a dozen transactions in the last two weeks where Diamond has (properly) lost money in the name of customer service, and that would seem to indicate that they might be making hundreds of money-losing transactions every week.

Honestly, it is hard to muster a tremendous amount of sympathy (after all, distribution *was* making truly obscene profits just a few years ago before the crash, and they seldom missed an opportunity to take advantage of the system when it suited them), but right this second is not the moment to have Diamond go away suddenly. We need a stronger alternative distribution system in place (I'm not laying odds on *any* of the current choices just yet, thank you very much) before we have either the complete crash and burn, with as many as 80% of the publishers going away due to debts owed; or the buyout by DC & Time Warner, which is at least twice as scary. (picture the darkest future, where Time Warner buys a chopped up Marvel Comics, and completely controls the only viable national new comics distributor. Brrr.)

The problem is, Diamond is likely to be spending so many resources scrambling to *fix* the problems that they'll not be able to *solve* them. When we couple this with the continually failing market (unless my information is wrong, or I've made a calculation mistake, the total sum of the top 300 books distributed by quantity dropped from April to May by a whopping 18%! Good lord! Higher priced goods offered in May might offset this to some degree, but things are not getting better, coming at the height of summer. Yet I, and another dozen stores I know, are having our best years ever [I'm up by 19%]). We better hope Geppi stockpiled *two* vaults full of money during the good days.

I'll also note that while I *have* been getting good fixes on the problems, it took going up the chain. I *fired* my assigned account rep because she was an idiot. Only the supervisors seem to have the ability to properly deal with problems on the fly, which is a frightening turn of events. Hopefully most of you haven't had a bad experience with the new "One Call Does It All" (not) service, but when my rep pronounced "*Schizo*" as "Shiatsu" I knew I was done. I will never speak to her again.

Right, so as I said, as long as they fix it, I could deal with them losing one order, and only for the Marvels, at that. But the fun just begins there. The books are invoiced at a 35% discount. O.K., that can get fixed. Then they lose my April Marvel order, *which was uploaded to their bulletin board system, and given confirmation of being received!* This time, I didn't find out until Friday, costing me money and reputation.

In between I sent a fax order for Star System stuff (which needs a whole separate fix unto itself), and wrote in inch-high letters, underlined, bordered, and with arrows drawn to it "No backorders, reship all items." Last time, with this same notation, all the out of stock items got backordered anyway (even after I reconfirmed this on the phone with my idiot assigned rep), and this time, all items got direct shipped. Why? Because, fool I am, needing some comic bags desperately, I put a note next to my bag order, saying "please direct ship this item, but reship all the other ones." Can't confuse the monkeys pulling the order. Of course, when the bags do come (and that is not until *after* the Star stuff arrives...of course), they're not currents, like I specified, but they're Silver Age. And the Star order, of course, has mistakes — like instead of getting the *Tales From the Crypt Annual* 1 ($8.95) that I ordered, and was billed for, I got sent the *Complete Tales From the Crypt* Boxed Set ($125) instead. Bet that made Bill Schanes happy!

Then there is the six copies of *Starburst* I got instead of six issues of *2000ad* (aw, but they're both British, so what is the difference, really?)

And that is all in the last two weeks. I'm horribly, horribly tired of this.

I never, *ever* want to talk to the distributor. If I'm talking to them, then there is something wrong. And a key component of their job is to make sure nothing goes wrong — *they're just freight forwarders!*

You do a fine job of fixing the problems, Diamond. now it is time to stop them. Cold.

•   •   •   •   •

Bill Townsend at Electric City Comics (1704 Van Vranken Ave, Schenectady, NY 12308) puts out an annual look back at the year just past. This year's edition weighs in at 70 pages, and is a series of devastatingly funny/insightful essays/rants about comics in 1996. I think my favorite section aside from *"Bill Vs Marvel Part IV — Picking on Cripples"* is *"Harvest Time for Rob* (Liefeld) *— Kick him! Kick him when he's down!"* My only complaint is he is way way way too nice to DC who made more then their share of dumb mistakes in 1996. I bring this up because you really want to read this. It is seriously funny. It has got a $2 cover price, so send him....let's say $5 to cover postage, and packing, and doing the good deed of publishing this tome. Tell Bill I sent you, too.

The other reason I bring this up is in Bill's cover letter he observed that too many retailers are getting mad at the wrong people especially in regards to Diamond. When you're speaking to a representative from a company, don't always assume that *they* are the architect of your misery — in point of fact your customer service person at Diamond has literally nothing to do with any physical problem with your order (pulling, packing, shipping) — I don't even believe they're in the same state. You have the utmost right to be angry about your problem because it is costing you money. And you should *always* complain when they make a mistake. But don't let your anger overrule your civility or professionalism. It is hard. I know. I do have a tendency to get hot. But the person on the other end of the phone is almost never directly responsible for your problem, and deserves to be treated like you'd like to be treated. If you don't get immediate satisfaction, ask for that person's supervisor. And don't hesitate to take it up the chain further, if need be. Even if you're a small account, in a remote area, your problems are important, and my experience with most people in this industry is that if you are civil with them, they will work to fix your problem. Be angry. Be righteous. Just don't be rude.

●　　●　　●　　●　　●

As you've noticed Marvel comics has still not publicly apologized for destroying the Direct market (not that I thought they really would), and until then I believe there is no reason for you to ever think they're working with your interest in mind (not that there was to begin with, but some of you need to be hit with a two-by-four). And I was planning to keep up a public campaign of shame every month in this column. But something happened which changed my mind.

Now I actually wasn't in to take the call, so all I have is a detailed message from the wonderfully anal Rob Bennett, but it seems while I was away at Pro/Con Stan Lee called.

Look, we all know Stan no longer has influence or sway over Marvel comics. But for a lot of people, Stan *is* Marvel, no matter who may own the company, or what direction it might head.

So when I read that Stan had read my column about Marvel apologizing I was stoked. Heck, who'd think he'd even read *Comics Retailer?* And when I read that Stan thought I was a good writer, I was primed ('course that's probably just Stan being Stan, right?). But the kicker was to read the words "Stan says, I quote, 'I Apologize.'" That was a gesture of class and dignity and great respect that he didn't have to make. A gesture that I'll note that no single person in Marvel management has tried to broach, even privately.

Do I trust Marvel? Not in the slightest. They'll try to succeed at our expense again, if we let them. But the fact that Stan Lee, figurehead or no, apologized directly for sins that he had nothing whatsoever to do with has convinced me to Let This One Go. In public, at least.

Thanks Stan.

Tilting at Windmills #64
(Originally ran in Comics Retailer #65)

I tell you what *really* pisses me off: when something takes money out of my pocket, and I had nothing to do with it, nor any way to deflect it.

A month ago, your time, but tomorrow by my schedule, Diamond Comics Distributors will not deliver the books on time for Wednesday. Their computer went down for (at least) three days. Whoops!

Now, certainly Diamond's expenses will be fairly enormous in this mess – repairing a crash takes huge amount of manpower, and the backup of data to be entered from reorders almost certainly will be extensive overtime. For all we know there may even be new hardware expenditures. A bunch o' money, to be sure.

But comics retailers get hurt too. My records show that every single time New Comics Day is a day "late" usually due to a holiday or other shipping-related problem, my weekly sales total is always at least 4.5% lower, with a high loss of 17.6%. It averages out in the 10-12% range, and most other retailers I've spoken to tell me their losses are equivalent.

When I've breached this subject with the distributors in the past, very few seemed to truly understand the extent of the problem – they seem to think, reasonably logically, that since we've a (relatively) captive audience, they'll buy the book whenever it is available. There are two problems with this: 1) a significant percentage of comic book retailers' customers have to make a special trip to get to our store. For some it is a long trip on the bus, for others their only time they can make it in is Wednesday afternoon. These people don't come back until the next week, and almost never buy two full weeks worth of material — the "marginal" books are put aside. 2) a significant number of comic retailers' customers are, for lack of a better term, grazers. Comics are not their sole source of purchased entertainment, and they come on Wednesday to buy entertainment. If you don't have it, they'll go to the record store or the video store or the bookstore, or the toy store, or whatever, to find some new entertainment. Also, these customers tend to be the least consistent in their purchases – they'll buy *Superman* for three months, but not buy *Man of Steel*, and then they won't buy either. They always try something new, but they seldom stick with anything. They are the bane of our cycle sheets. Grazers.

This adds up to an average of 10-12% of our weekly sales just evaporated, as we can't produce what we as an industry have trained our customers to expect. That sucks.

This also hurts our reputation. At least with a holiday, the customers may understand – but when you say, "yeah, the distributor's computer went down," they feel like you're screwing with them. Hell, some of our customers still seem to think we print them in the back room!

This, of course, hurts DCD's reputation, as well – but it's not like we have the option to change distributors, now do we?

And what about this loss? DCD can write off their extra costs, because they are tangible – comic retailers can't write off missed sales opportunity (unless your accountant is better than mine!). Which "Service for Your Success" was this one?

Diamond gets paid for the books either way. If Diamond's computers went down for a week, rather than three days, and we got two weeks worth of comics at once, there is nothing in the agreement we sign each month that says that DCD has any responsibility whatsoever.

Well, not a legal one, any way.

But I think they've got a moral one.

This is a month old for you now – so you should have a very solid idea of what this cost you. Calculate that number out, and write a short *polite* letter to Chuck Parker including that figure, and asking how Diamond intends to recompense comic book retailers for this loss. Just because I like making his life hell, also send a copy to J.J. here at *Comics Retailer*, as this'll add a check to the system, to see how widespread this problem is.

Let me tell you something else, too – we *do* have power, we *do* have a voice, but it is only meaningful when we use it collectively. If I'm the only guy who writes a "here is what you cost me" letter, it will be *meaningless*. If twenty of you do it, maybe it will raise an eyebrow, but if every retailer reading this column sends in this calculation, you can be damn sure they'll react.

I get a fair amount of mail, with a lot of praise for what I say, but I always wonder: are you saying it too? Or are you just *thinking* it? If it is the latter, do me a favor, and close down your store today, we don't need you anymore.

Comic retailers are treated as cattle – publishers, distributors, manufacturers push us around, and herd us to an ultimate bolt in the head. And they do that because we *let* them – because we do not explicitly voice our concerns. They can't change in the ways we need them to until we are able to let them hear what our needs *are*. And right now, in direct market 1997, if you're not part of the solution, you *are* the problem, and you're more than welcome to take my place in line at the slaughterhouse.

So, what do *I* think DCD should do about the economic morass they've (however unwittingly) foisted upon a sick and withered marketplace? Short-term, I think they have an absolute obligation to offer at *least* 5% returns for the week of June 12th. This would be, at least, a nice token gesture, and a sign that they understand the depths of their responsibility in delivering the comics when they say. When Steve Geppi sends out press releases about his purchase of two Archie comics for a hundred thousand dollars (more money than almost all retailers will ever possess), I think he can eat a few unsold comics that were *entirely* the fault of his MIS team.

I honestly think DCD *should* have overnight shipped that week's books, because we *could* have had them on-time then.

Long-term, I think they only possible solution is street-dates. In case you hadn't noticed, Diamond has flatly admitted that they could easily get us the comics on Mondays. The reason our shipments don't arrive until Wednesday is because of merchandise, and the packing of reorders. Diamond could have comics on Monday presumably as early as next week, if we asked them to – this could well have given us extra time to absorb Diamond's computer failure. At the very least, we would have had an early "heads-up" – likely early enough to properly warn our customers.

We've trained our customers to expect Wednesday deliver, yet we only get the comics that morning. Surely I can't be the only one to see how tenuous and unrealistic this system is? How it depends on everything going 100% right,. all the way down the chain? How very very few things are ever 100%, and UPS isn't one of them? We need to change this, and change it now.

•   •   •   •   •

Another thing Diamond announced this month (well, last month, for you) was they'd be taking discount calculation off of the *Previews on Disk* program.

Why do I need a computer program if it is not calculating discounts for me? This is the most basic and primal thing it needs to do.

Once again, this is proof positive that Diamond has no idea whatsoever about what retailers do, or how they do it. Will someone up there please wake up? Anyone?

•   •   •   •   •

The last Diamond thing (J.J. wants to hit me about now, I'm guessing – I'm supposed to provide some manner of balance in *Tilting*. If I nail *x* this month, then I'm meant to lay off for a few months, so's no one feels they are persecuted. The problem with this in relationship to Diamond is that they permeate every single aspect of a retailer's day-to-day life – one cannot *not* deal with Diamond and be a comics retailer. Diamond is the single largest external force in all of our survivals. I'm more worried about what they do than I am about an earthquake leveling San Francisco!)

Diamond has announced that, whenever possible, rather than returning late, or missolicited merchandise, we will instead be able to freely adjust our order, with the unstated goal of stopping the merchandise before it reaches the shelf. This is wrong.

Why? Because not all late material is unsalable – some customer segments are more patient than others, and often, we don't know who these segments are until the product arrives. Sometimes you can sell a significant percentage of missolicited or late product. The returnability is there as a safety net, just in case the product doesn't perform the way it "should."

While, on the face of it, there are sound economic reasons to handle it this way, at this point in time I think that dismantling this safety net is absolutely the wrong choice. In these tight economic times for stores, the natural impulse is slash that order to the bone, or eliminate it outright. Anything that lowers your possible sales isn't a good thing. I think it is in *everyone*'s best interest (distributor, publisher, creator, retailer) to have that book out on a shelf in the store's, rather than never printed in the first place, or languishing in the publisher's warehouse.

I also think it has the effect of distancing Diamond for any responsibility whatsoever from the items that they list. If the goal is to reduce the volume of returns, then they need to go to publishers and tell them they will no longer list new solicitations until they are provided with a B&W photocopy of the issue in question. Certainly, for egregious offenders like Comico or Mad Monkey, this would greatly reduce the signal-to-noise ratio, something I think we all long for.

Diamond needs to stand behind the products it solicits, because, whether or not DCD feels this way, they are a series of promises being made to us, and more importantly, as *Previews* is *actually* a consumer publication, to our customers on our behalf. I don't need that kind of "help," unless DCD is willing to stand behind and enforce those promises.

I want late books to be returnable, not (effectively) a second shot at ordering them.

•   •   •   •   •

On to the great positive this month, the light swings around to...Marvel Comics?!?!? What's Bri been drinking?

No, I'm totally serious – Marvel has just introduced the "Guide to the Marvel Universe," a fold-out cover with summaries of the past issue, and who the characters are. This is a *great* idea, and one I hope other publishers pick up on. I'm not as hot as Maggie Thompson for "Done in One," but if we *are* going to play the continuity game, this should be the house rule.

However, the fold needs to be a little closer to the edge of the cover – as flush as is physically possible. It doesn't look quite "right" yet. Plus ditch that "World's Greatest Comics" banner – only the *Fantastic Four* is allowed to use that!

Tilting at Windmills #65
(Originally ran in Comics Retailer #66)

I got charged a fee last week for ordering comics.

I ordered a single copy of *Spectacular Spider-Man* (with a potential gross profit to me of 98 cents), and was told that this transaction would cost me five bucks.

Ouch.

Sure, and you're not surprised that this sent a big red flag flying up the Hibbsian pole. I mean, seriously, why in God's name are we being charged a penalty for ordering more product? Does any other field work this way? I'm trying to make a customer happy; to give the publisher and distributor some more money — and I get charged so that the entire transaction becomes wildly and grossly unprofitable to me.

Well, here's the deal, as I've been able to piece it together. Four publishers (Dark Horse, DC, Image and Marvel) have individual Terms of Sale that override Diamond's. I'm sure you've noticed page after page of sales terms at the front of the catalog each month; odds are pretty good that you've never actually bothered to read them.

These four publishers, to the best of my knowledge, work under a fee-based system (I am unsure about Acclaim, but, then I find them irrelevant in most discussions, anyway) — rather than selling to Diamond at one discount, which Diamond then sells to us at another, these publishers are selling "directly" to us, and Diamond takes a fixed percentage of cover, and, apparently, assesses per-transaction fees.

So, if I were to publish a comic, I might sell it to Diamond at 60% off cover. Diamond then would sell it to the retailers at a discount they control — they might offer 40% off, they might offer 50%, but it is solely at their discretion. Diamond pays for the cost of operations from this margin, but they are assuming some small measure of risk in stocking reorders, etc. Diamond may be receiving anywhere from 7.5-20% of the cover price. I believe this is referred to as a "buy-sell" relationship.

The "brokered" publishers, on the other hand (and please understand that my terminology is my own — I have no specific knowledge of the contractual details, and I may be wholly misunderstanding the specifics of these relationships) are free to set their own discounts. If I buy $600 of comics from DC in a given month, I get 50% off, whereas if I buy $300, I only get 35%. Diamond apparently gets some percentage of this sale. Let's call it 6% for ease of discussion, but while I've been led to believe that it is in the range, I suspect that there are a host of variables that could affect the exact percentage. In this case, Diamond makes that same 6%, regardless of the volume I purchase, but DC stands to make 59% of cover price if I buy $300, or 44% if I buy $600.

What I've just learned is that Diamond apparently also charges a per-transaction fee to these publishers. I have absolutely no idea exactly how said fees are assessed, but I got the impression that every single time a retailer contacts Diamond to order a book, these publishers pay Diamond a small amount for that service. The one thing that I am completely unsure about is whether this transaction fee is per-order, or per-item. That is to say, if I order ten Image titles in one transaction, I am not clear if Image pays ten fees, or just one. Nor do I know if this fee is equal at all times, or based upon volume ordered in the transaction.

If I understand this correctly, here is how it might break down. Let's assume a, I dunno, 25 cent per-transaction fee (this, please let me stress, is a wholly fictional example that may or may not have any basis in reality. If I had publishable facts, I'd give them to you, but this example is 100% ignorant and uninformed, and should not be taken as anything having to do with actual reality!).

So, I order 50 comics from DC in July, that sum to a retail cover price of $300, and I reorder 20 items in two transactions for another $200. The gross retail cover price is $500. I get a 35% discount (discount being assessed by initial orders only), meaning I pay $325. Diamond makes 6% of that $500 ($30), as well as 25-cents per-transaction (another $0.75), for a total of $30.75. DC gets a check for $294.25.

If I order 50 comics from DC that sum to a cover price of $600, and I reorder the same 20 titles for the same $200 in two transactions, we have a gross of $800. I pay $400 (50% discount), Diamond makes $48.75 (6% of $800 [$48], plus the same $0.75 for transactions), and DC makes $351.25.

(A buy/sell publisher under the same relationship [70 items sold for a gross of $800] might be making $320 — they sell to Diamond at, say, 60%, but do not pay per-transaction fees. Diamond might sell these titles to us at 45%, but they'll assess a 3% fee to us on the reorders. We'd pay [{$600 x .55} + {$200 x . 58}] $446 for these comics, so Diamond would make $126, but they would be assuming the per-transactions costs, as well as any risk in stocking reorders).

With this background in mind, you can now flip to the "Order Increases" section of each publisher's terms of sale, and see how each handles this apportionment of costs.

Diamond, as we just noted, has the retailer pay 3% of cover price for the privilege of ordering comics after the monthly order form due-date.

Dark Horse and Marvel give us one order-increase call per week (see below) for free, then charges us $5, unless the order totals over $100 at retail. Marvel, however, assesses a 2.25% fee to the retailer for any order-increase, and Dark Horse charges 2.5%.

DC also gives us one free increase per week, then charges $10, regardless of the amount ordered. DC charges no percentage for these reorders.

Image allows two free increases per week, then charges $10, unless the third one is over $150 retail. Image also charges no percentage.

You will note, however, that "week" is not defined, except for Marvel, which specifically states a seven-day period. This is actually important, because a "week" in Diamond terms is Wednesday to Tuesday. This fact is not stated anywhere in any publishers' terms (we're just supposed to know, I guess).

The reasoning behind this fee is apparently that some retail accounts have in the past not ordered, shall we say, effectively. They'll order one copy of one comic, then call the next day for another, then the next day for another, and so on. Under the brokered terms, this could cost the publishers huge sums of money, possibly outweighing the profit potential of the items being ordered. While I appreciate (and understand!) publishers not wanting to take a potential loss in selling us comics, I have to wonder if this policy is necessary anymore. I would hope that the actual raw numbers of retailers "abusing" the system was on the low side — presumably most of us are organized enough that we don't need to call in reorders more than once a week — and seldom do I think the majority should be penalized for the actions of a few. Presumably since the introduction of this change, those few retailers that were that flighty have learned to minimize the number of calls necessary to doing business, and will not suddenly go back to their old habits now that they've been properly educated.

I suppose one of my biggest concerns with this policy is that it is so arbitrary. I called *Spectacular Spider-Man* in twice in a seven-day period because we got a new subscription customer, and I wanted to confirm the availability of their wants as soon as possible. However, if I had waited 24 hours, I wouldn't've been charged $5 for trying to satisfy my customer. Actually, it was likely less than a five-hour difference — if I had waited until seven pm when the store closed, it would have been nine pm in Baltimore, so the order wouldn't have been entered until the next day anyway! Unless I have a "history" of "abusing" the system, I believe it is completely ridiculous that a 5-24 hour time difference should cost me $5.

I also object to such an enormous penalty when I'm simply trying to make everyone more money. I want to make my customer happy, I want to make the sale for myself, I want Diamond to get their cut, and I want the publisher to be able to sell another comic book. I don't particularly like reorder fees (I shouldn't be penalized for selling *more* comics), but at least I understand the principal behind them — it does indeed cost more to handle an item outside of the "regular" system, and paying a percentage of cover for this "right" is, at the least, not wholly unreasonable. I don't think it helps long-term, but we as an industry are also struggling for short-term survival. However, when such a fee is significantly greater than the profit potential of the item in question ($5 versus $0.98 *gross* profit), I feel like I've just been raped. Where is my incentive to order more comics in any manner than 60+ days before arrival (an outmoded and fundamentally destructive scenario)?

$$\bullet \quad \bullet \quad \bullet \quad \bullet \quad \bullet$$

The terms of sales are also illuminating when we look at returnability of mis-solicited products. As it turns out, when one reads Diamond's TOS one finds that Diamond is not, in any way, shape or form, liable for mis-solicited items (despite the fact that they are the ones who provide this information to us). Certainly Diamond has a *policy* that mis-solicited items will be returnable, but the TOS makes it very very clear that this exists wholly at their suffrage.

It is generally assumed that Diamond will accept returns on a book if it ships during the month following the month following scheduled arrival. That is to say, if a book is scheduled for January, it is "late" (and therefore returnable) if it ships after March 1st. "Ships" is an interesting term, however, because Diamond takes that to mean when it arrives in their warehouses, not when it arrives on our shelves. If you have knowledge of when publishers release titles you quickly see that Diamond often takes anywhere from 5 to 21 days to get "buy/sell" publishers products on our shelves. What this means is that as long as the January product arrives at *Diamond* before March 1st, it is not "late." It is irrelevant when *you* get it.

In any event, this is a "policy," not a rule. Diamond's terms of sales are very clear that this is wholly at their discretion, and that the retailer assumes all risk and responsibility for late shipping product.

In some cases we don't fare much better from the brokered publishers. Dark Horse says that it will "generally" accept returns if a product ships four weeks after the month it was scheduled in. Given that Dark Horse has long given specific ship-weeks (most Diamond "buy/sell" product is listed as a 30-day period), I fell they are being a little too lackadaisical — they should pin that to ship week, not ship month. At least they seemingly acknowledge *some* measure of responsibility. The word "generally" really bothers me, though. Creative or content changes are listed as "without advance notice, to be determined by Dark Horse Comics at its sole discretion," meaning they could legally announce that *I'm* drawing *Sin City* they day before it ships, and not have to take returns.

DC is much better. DC's TOS say that they "shall" make a book returnable if it is more than four weeks after the solicited date. Not the month. Creative and content changes are "as solicited," which, again, is the fairest and most equitable method.

Image is specific that "date from the printer" is the guideline they use (not "date in store"), but they've got until the last day of the next month following the month of solicitation — like Diamond and Dark Horse. Changes to content or creators must be given before original orders are due.

Marvel gives us 30 days after on-sale date (and note that this is "delivered" not "shipped"), and keys content changes to original solicitation. However, just this week I noticed that the issues of *Captain America* and *Avengers* that were done by WildStorm rather than Extreme were only allowed at a 25% return rate. As near as I can tell this is inconsistent with their TOS. If you have more than 25% left over, you should probably return it — the TOS seems to be on your side.

● ● ● ● ●

There are all kinds of things like this in the Terms of Sale you sign every month. Things that are almost certainly not in your best interests. Things that you, as an individual store with only individual buying power, can't possibly affect.

Here's my question: we know that (largely) these terms were written to safeguard both the publishers and distributors, and that very few (if any) retailers had any input or say in them whatsoever. So why is it that we have a national organization for retailers (Pacer) that has, to the best of my knowledge, never tried to negotiate these terms to being more favorable to the retailers that comprise this body?

The only conceivable value I can see in a retailer organization is one of negotiating strength. But we have unfavorable terms of sale that we have next to no choice but to sign, and we have Diamond making fundamental changes like removing discount calculation from the order disk, or disallowing certain forms of returns, and I sure as heck know I've never ever heard one peep out of *any* retailer organization to contest these things. Why is that?

I've got myself a nice little soapbox here, but ultimately I'm depending on the good graces of those who read it to make substantive changes from benevolence. We have no collective bargaining power, because no one has bothered to try.

I've been asked before why I don't join any of the extant retailer organizations out there, and my answer is always the same: when they do something, when they do *anything*, then they'll get my money. But until then? Pfft.

Let's hope that day comes soon.

a r t i c l e
6 6

Tilting at Windmills #66
(Originally ran in Comics Retailer #67)

Lots of small stuff this time out.

• • • • •

Just got back from San Diego. Every year the con seems to this attendee to be more and more distant from the "mainstream" of the comics industry, and this year was certainly no exception.

The first thing that I was stuck by was the number of women in attendance. Without having any solid stats, I'd guess that perhaps 40% of the audience was female. And unlike some previous years, I saw very few who seemed *bored*.

I also saw a lot of children. Lots of them. And lots of pregnant women (at least a dozen) — these could be signs that our future is not in quite as much jeopardy as we have thought.

Or maybe not.

ComicCon International: San Diego is oddly named. First off, it ain't international — heck, it ain't even *national* (throw a con somewhere outside of California, and I'll grant you the name) — but it is less and less of a *comics* convention every year. Video games, card games, anime, film presentations — none of these are comics, and my perceptions (however one-sided) are that every year these "other things" take up a little more floor space every year. This is not bad in and of itself — attendance seems up, and, as I said, was more diverse and more interested, but I wonder if it is not starting to get a little too big for its own good. This year the Con took up every single inch of the convention center — even the tent outside. I had three nights and two days at the convention proper, and I didn't even *begin* to see all the people I wanted to see, or do the business I went there to accomplish. CCI:SD has gone well beyond "comics convention," and is now a *spectacle*, a tribute to pop-culture as a whole.

Ultimately, I guess that I just no longer trust San Diego to be a leading indicator of the comic book industry. It is an indicator of something, to be sure — just not the particular business *I'm* in. And so, while I'm thrilled to see a much more diverse audience attending San Diego, I don't know that this has much if any bearing on the Direct Market.

• • • • •

I'm reminded of something Joe Field said during the Expo — the direct market has fragmented into several distinct types of businesses, and our ability to meet the challenges of the future depends on recognizing that these stores have distinct needs. Joe identified (I think) three types of stores, but I didn't take notes, so the exact wording may be a bit off here. One class of store is the "bookstore." Backlist is a significant portion of business for these stores, and they primarily deal in current comics material. Next there is the "collector's store" where a wide breadth of back issues is their bread and butter, and a significant portion of their frontlist sales are on collectibles (variant covers and the like). Finally, there are the "pop culture" stores that have comics as part of their mix, but primarily focus on whatever is popular at the moment, be it toys, or movie-related items, or whatever.

I'd add to this a category for "hybrids" — usually comics/games, but sometimes comics/books or comics/records (usually in markets that could not support the individual components on their own) — as well as few sub-categories ("pop culture collector's" or "collector's bookstore") for shading, but the principal is absolutely sound.

The point is that the things you need to do to be successful in one type of store are often diametrically opposed to what you have to do for another type. I live in "bookstore" world — variant covers and 1/2 issues are demonstrably harmful to my business, but they're the lifeblood to that little collector's store out on 23rd and Geary St.

Unfortunately retailers are currently looked upon as a single entity — that you are just like me, even though we're not. I believe that unless and until the publishers and Diamond start dealing with these different stores under the terms that the *store* needs, we're not going to progress much further than merely treading water in the direct market.

• • • • •

One of the comments I heard several times at San Diego was that some of you, gentle readers, would like to see more "positivity" in this column. At the same time, I have ten-fold that in e-mail saying, "Yeah baby! Go for the throat!" What's an opinion columnist meant to do?

I'll tell you what *I* think, if it is of any help — I try my damndest to be positive (after all I eat, breathe and sleep this stuff), and I think that if I have a message in *Tilting at Windmills* it goes a little something like this: As a retailer you are The Man (apologies for not have a gender-neutral term to express the same thing). You absolutely rule and control your domain, and you should never give the barest inch of your power unless it is among equals. The vast majority of problems in this market stem from retailers not understanding that they have power, nor realizing that they can express themselves to change things. Publishers and distributors largely do not give us the respect we deserve because collectively we have never asked for it. And if I am sometimes strident (and believe you me, I am), it stems from a frustration that the meekest and/or worst elements of the retailer base are holding us back from reaching our full potential. When publishers and distributors make decisions that are counter-productive to the success of the retail base, it is generally attributable to our worst and meekest. We can't have street dates because some retailers are going to break them; we can take the discounts of the order disks because very few will actually complain.

I know that there are a lot of you out there who won't complain about the service you receive, about the hits you take, because you fear reprisals. *Reprisals*. That you live in that kind of fear, frankly, sickens me. And if, no, *when*, I rage against the machine *that* is what drives me.

M'lud Shakespeare did say it best: "To be, or not to be, that is the question — whether 'tis nobler in the mind to suffer the slings and arrows of outrageous fortune; or to take arms against a sea of troubles, and, by opposing, end them?"

I'll take "to be" for five hundred dollars, please, Wink.

And if that means I have to be *blunt* — and please, gentle reader, try to distinguish between "blunt" and "negative" — then so be it.

What I want to know is why is it that one gets a "reputation" for being "negative" that all the positive things get forgotten? How many times have I urged retailers to pick a pitch and swing (the *Top Shelf Sampler* was the most recent)? How many times have I made an effort to recognize the good things that have happened (Marvel's gatefold's would be the most recent)?

Believe me, I try.

●　　●　　●　　●　　●

I was pretty disconcerted when I read the latest *Retailer* (#65 by my time-line) and I saw that both Preston and Bob are having troubles. Two out of the three retailer columnists are struggling, and I'm upbraided for not being "positive?" Sheesh.

The last time I saw hard data (November), a meager *eight* percent of Diamond's accounts qualified for a 55% discount.

●　　●　　●　　●　　●

I absolutely agree with Preston that you can't sell games *properly* unless you're a gamer.

I find it ironic that all the printed disagreements (#65, again) came from game publishers.

Baby, I've *been* a gamer so I know of whence I speak.

And I'll tell you this, kids, if you ever, *ever* think, "Yikes, the comics customer base is sorta geeky," don't bloody worry. In games it is even *worse*.

•   •   •   •   •

Speaking of games, have you seen the Magic CCG ads airing in *heavy* rotation on (at least) Comedy Central and the Sci-Fi channel? It seems like at least 1 per half-an-hour.

Why is it that Wizards of the Coast can mount such a campaign (and without a focused target like 1-888-Comic-book provides), and neither Marvel comics nor Time Warner can? Good lord, if we can bring these companies together for a series of crossover comics, why can't they enter into joint advertising? This is, I know, a leading question, but it seems valid in light of WOTC's efforts.

•   •   •   •   •

1-888-comic-book only really works for you if you're in a major (and I do mean major) metro area. If your customers drive *any* kind of a distance to reach you, odds are good that they'll be referred to mail order instead of you.

The problem for all ya'll not in cities is that a lot of you have customers who are more than willing to drive an hour to get to you. Sixty miles away from me in San Francisco? Oh, yeah, there is someplace closer for you to go. But sixty miles away in Swampmuck, LA? People travel that kind of distance for shopping every day.

•   •   •   •   •

Speaking of mail order can I give a big Shame on You to all those "1/2" and "0" offers?

Several of my favorite creators and books (Matt Wagner and *Mage* #0, Kurt Busiek and *Astro City* #1/2, Frank Miller and *Sin City* #1/2) have recently made deals to provide an "exclusive" story to an outside-the-retailers venue (*Wizard* or American Entertainment). I understand that these deals are lucrative and attractive to the creators, but I can't help but note that they are detrimental to the long-term health of many dedicated comic book retailers.

Y'know, much of the time a major reason a title does well is because the retailers have gotten behind it — they've ordered it strongly, they've supported it with reorders, they've talked it up, handed it out. It is very painful when, after all this effort, we're told we can't sell our customers part of the story.

"But it will be in the paperback!" Well, that's nice, and certainly better than nothing, but I do have customers who are supporting the regular production (i.e. the periodicals) who not only don't want to deal with mail order, but who I don't want to *send* to mail-order.

I understand and appreciate and *support* mail order in the context of areas without comic shops; people who travel a lot or only have access to stores that *refuse* to order certain material — but if there is a viable and dedicated comic book shop in a local market I can see absolutely no reason whatsoever for a creator or publisher to want to drive a sale out of that venue. Or, worse still, cause a customer to regret that they have supported a series.

Yeah, *Wizard* has a very high circulation, and can help in "creating a buzz," and American Entertainment's catalog and web site has enormous exposure, but, long-term, who is going to do a better job selling your goods? Retailers who display your wares every day of the year, or *Wizard* or AE who are *set-up* to promote *the* hottest, *the* newest stuff?

At least Kurt Busiek came up with a good plan — any retailer on CompuServe (and presumably AOL, and the Usenet) who asked for an *Astro City* #1/2 from him got one. He punched a hole in the top corner to make it easy to display (and to discourage those who might be tempted to immediately sell it) — in this way at least our customers could *read* the comic without having to support mail-order. In the future, I'd hope creators and publishers would see fit to make this type of a plan less self-selecting — any retailer who ordered more than [x] number copies (say 10-25) of the regular periodical version of the exclusive comic automatically should get sent one certified not-mint display and reading copy of the exclusive comic so they don't let their customers down.

•　　•　　•　　•　　•

Finally, now that I've actually *used* a Previews-on-disk without-discount-calculation, please let me complain again.

I gotta say that from a budgeting point of view I have less of an interest in the retail dollars than I do in wholesale costs — that wholesale cost represents the *real* commitment I am making for the month.

I'd say that the disk-without-calculations was worthless, but for the extra weekend it gives to write the order, and the drastic lowering of the chances of incorrect data-entry. But, gosh darn it, that still makes it *next* to worthless!

Please, Diamond, give us back our discount calculations!

Tilting at Windmills #67
(Originally ran in Comics Retailer #68)

Let's start with some nice words.

I think that in the initial stages of the UPS strike, Diamond Comics Distribution worked hard to minimize the effects of the strike. I think that they did a very good job with making a very bad situation better. And I think they should be absolutely applauded for absorbing the significant costs in getting the comics out to drop points.

I actually expect nothing less, but they should be applauded, nonetheless.

Now, one can make a valid argument that the drop points were not a viable alternative for a great number of retailers (predominately more rural ones); or that DCD could have been a little more efficient in contacting people, or dispensing information, but all things considered I think DCD did a good job.

I had a debate with another retailer on Compuserve on this topic – one has to look at the *capabilities* of a system when one tries to find a reasonable course of action that system can take. What I mean by this is that this retailer suggested that DCD should have run a physical truck route out to the door of each retailer. His position was not unreasonable (facing a 3+ hour drive *each* way to get the funny books is not exactly an appealing situation), but was unrealistic to implement.

For example, according the February Diamond Dialogue, there are only 41 customer service representatives – one team leader and four phone reps and one field rep for each of the six distribution centers (Atlanta, Baltimore, Dallas, LA, Plattsburgh, Sparta) and the same without the field for "international." We've no firm statement for distribution personnel, but I think it is safe to assume that the numbers there might be a dozen per – figure there might be at or around 75 warehouse workers domestically.

According to all reports, Diamond services approximately 4000 accounts. If DCD has customer service call every account, each of the 41 reps has to make about 100 phone calls. Assuming a mere five minutes a call, that's eight hours and twenty minutes. Dealing with busy signals, or answering machines, or whatever, plus human needs for rest and food, you have to figure Diamond is doing pretty darn good if they can get in touch with every customer within a day and a half. And I bet there a few accounts that they simply *can't* get in touch with.

How about routes? Let's even go nuts and think that only half of Diamond's accounts need delivery – if each truck can do 20 stops, they'd still need *one hundred trucks* to do the job. Diamond is unlikely to have 100 employees who could legally drive a truck!

Even adding in credit, and management, it is unlikely that much more than 150 people work for DCD that come into direct contact with entering, pulling, or invoicing your comic books. That means that, on average, you have about 1/3 of a person working for you! I think when you look at it in those terms, you can't help but conclude that, actually, it is pretty darn amazing that we ever get comics *at all*, let alone received them during a UPS strike.

So, give them props, people.

The game store down the block from me apparently got *nothing* during the 3 weeks of the strike that they didn't go pick up from their distributors. That's gotta suck. All kinds of businesses were virtually shut down because they didn't have distributors who made and executed a plan.

I think we also need to applaud Diamond for absorbing the costs involved in these drop points. Now, they claim $40k in expenses (and I don't think all of those could be pass-along expenses – I don't recall the number of drop-off points, but I think it was like 20, and that's $2000 a point, which I just can't see). However, we have to acknowledge that it is still a very large amount of money – probably larger than the net profit of any single comic book shop for an entire month.

Further, let's give them a hand for absorbing that cost for the third time, *after* announcing a $3 per box charge! Y'know, sometimes we retailers can be a bit harsh on Diamond, and oftimes for valid reasons, but you gotta admit that it was totally standup for DCD to *reverse a previously announced charge.*

Let's hope (knock wood) that such a thing doesn't happen anytime again, but what could Diamond have done better?

1) Communicate the possibility of a strike, and the reaction to same much sooner.

I happened to know the strike was coming, because I try to be friendly with our UPS driver(s). But Diamond didn't properly flag the strike until we were well into it. Diamond should have had notification about significant possibility of the strike in the Diamond Dateline from the week before, as well as an outline of the options that were available to us. Retailers were not given sufficient notice to warn their Wednesday customers from the previous week, nor were solid plans in our hand until the eleventh hour.

2) Keep new comics day "as scheduled." It was terribly foolish after the first week to hold out for a Monday resolution of the strike before doing drop-off points. Realistically, holding "new comics day" until Thursday past the first week made no real sense – every retailer loses a day of sales, and there was little chance that UPS could have actually made the "right" delivery day.

It is that last point that makes me pig-biting mad.

Because I got stuffed by it.

As I say, Diamond deserves kudos during the strike – they have a realistically small, and relatively inefficient, system that is no longer structured to deal with anything except their standard UPS shipping that somehow managed to transcend its limitations to get the majority of their customers weekly product with a minimum of errors – it is after the strike that they deserve to have their ass kicked.

UPS was backed up. Not only did they have the majority of the material in the system from when the striking workers walked off the job, but the moment the strike ended, shippers dropped huge volumes of material immediately into the system, trying to get themselves back on schedule. Couple that with the natural tendency of people to gear back up slowly, it is very difficult to believe that UPS would be back to full efficiency for something near an equal of amount of time after the strike.

To immediately ship the next week's shipment via UPS was a rookie move. Diamond had the *responsibility* to ensure that their announced shipping plans would work.

To be fair, UPS has supposedly assured DCD of "90%+" capability. But to this pair of jaded eyes what that says is they are at 10% *not-capability*.

That's too much.

Anything less than 99% capacity is not sufficient.

As I understand it, a significant portion of US comics retailers didn't get their delivery on Wednesday, as due. In the Bay Area most retailers got partial shipments on Thursday, and received the balance the next day. This was apparently not an unusual circumstance, though I'm loathe to say much without any statistics. As it was relayed to me, however, 66 retailers did not receive all of their product as of Friday – with the Labor Day holiday that means none of these retailers would get that product until the following *Tuesday*. At the earliest.

I know. I was one of them.

I'm glad to say we finally got the comics today, Wednesday – a full *week* after they were scheduled. Hopefully, so have the rest of the 66.

Why am I mad? During the strike, I've spent a fair amount of time on the phone with DCD suggesting several times that UPS could not possibly be up to speed in time to guarantee shipping – that drop points should be continued where ever feasible.

Diamond was not enamored by the idea. Diamond would not seriously consider it.

I understand this, but I'm just sick of getting caught in the barrel.

I've grown amazingly tired of the fact that the retailer has no recourse, has no power, has no say, and has no ability to change any of this.

There are times I believe with passion and fervor that we can (and do) make substantial changes when we use our voice, but then there are times (like this week) where I feel like it doesn't really matter because the rules of the game are against us from moment one.

If you don't receive your comic shipment by the weekend, you should immediately have as much of it filled as possible by overnight shipping, as well as be fully returnable in a month. Is it reasonable to expect someone to pay full shipping when the product takes days to arrive? These seem to me to be sensible, prudent, and no-brainer ideas, but when one asks about any of these things, the answer always comes back as "we haven't thought about that Yet."

Well, I sure have, and seeing as how some sort of shipping problem must logically happen for at least one retailer a week, I bloody well expect to see policies in place *before* it happens to me. Or you.

Diamond is pretty darn good when it comes to "big picture" issues, like setting smooth drop-points in motion. But it sometime feels as though when it comes to individual decisions ("in what manner do we fix this situation?") they usually bobble the ball.

I wish I knew how to change this. I wish I could find the magic wand to wave and make Diamond and the brokered publishers see how they needed to take into account the individual needs of the individual retailers before they make the decisions that affect me.

But, I fear, that the leading cause of retailer burnout is *not* late books, or bad comics, or too much retail, or whatever – it is the reaction (or lack thereof) of those "powers that be" that causes the burnout. I've never been closer to actually entertaining the notion of "well, screw this – I don't need the headache for the pittance *I* make," than I was in the face of "we'll see what we can do." See this!

Once, just once, I would like to wake up to a phone call of, "We've been tracking your books, and we don't think you're gonna get them, so we've already started pulling you replacements, and you can reduce this week's shipping bill by $50," — or at least something in the same vein. "You *are* important to us, and here is how we're going to *show* you."

Because deeds are more important than words.

Tilting at Windmills #68
(Originally ran in Comics Retailer #69)

(Historical note: written before #66 — this one needed a "few months in the drawer!")
(but I changed almost nothing)

I suppose you've noticed that this column tends to be...a little critical.

Sometimes this gets me into trouble.

Usually this is because the recipients of my "ire" choose not to make a distinction between criticism and disrespect. I've been called once or twice (or thrice, or four times, or...) by a "target" and questioned as to what the *point* of my "attacks" were. "You're too mean," these calls begin, "where is the positivity?"

Well, you know, in most cases, I don't feel much need to play "nice-nice" — usually I'm going after a business relationship that directly *hurts* me or my brethren, and in my mind, I have an obligation to call a spade a spade. When a specific policy does harm, I have found that seldom does my individual voice dealing individually have any impact — but by using a public forum (or semi-public, bearing in mind the limited audience that reads *Comics Retailer*), change has a better chance of occurring.

When I get a red flag, I tend to charge out of the gate without feeling much need to add a preamble. Why? Because we're all adults, and when a subject (distributor, publisher, creator) makes a unilateral decision that affects me, I feel I have not only the obligation to criticize those decisions in a straight-forward, no-apologies manner, but also the absolute right. Further, I find that when I take on institutions, I am (in the vast majority of cases) expressing what is on the mind of most retailers — many of whom feel that their individual voice is so marginalized they no longer bother to speak it.

Your mileage may vary.

However, every once in a while, a situation arises where I see that I need to be the smidgest more polite and political — where I need to make it clear, very very specifically clear, that the target is the *idea* and not the *people* behind the idea. As I'm sure you've guessed by now, this is one of those times.

Because this time I'm compelled to talk about the Will Eisner *Spirit of Comics* Retailing Award (*SOC*).

So, for the record (and *please* be clear about this, folks), in this column I mean absolutely no disrespect — not one tittle, not one jot of disrespect — to any winner, past, present or future of the award; to any judge, past, present or future of the award; to Fae Desmond and the other organizers of the award; and especially, e-s-p-e-c-i-a-l-l-y not to the creator of the award, Mr. Will Eisner.

To drive this home even further, I strongly believe that *every* winner of the *SOC* to date absolutely and 100% deserves the recognition they have received; I strongly believe that *every* judge has been absolutely and 100% fair and correct in the decisions that they made; I strongly believe that Fae Desmond and the SDCC have absolutely and 100% done their best in organizing and administrating the award; and I strongly believe that Will Eisner should be absolutely and 100% commended for conceiving the award. Hell, make that 200% on the last point, for this really goes above and beyond the call of duty, and shows more class and dignity and respect than any fifty creators have shown the comics retailers as a body.

Are we clear? No disrespect intended to any individual involved — more than no disrespect, I want it to be clear as glass that I give props to everyone involved, all the way down the line. This is utterly key to me, because I know that *someone* out there is going to cry "sour grapes" before I reach the end of the column. I'm an utterly arrogant bastard, full of myself and my accomplishments, I know — better people than you have pointed this out, to be most sure — but *this* time this isn't about *me*; it is about the *process*, and I truly hope you don't doubt my sincerity, at least this one time.

(This is one of the reasons I don't like having to "defend" my particular style — 671 words, and we're only just beginning.)

The process that lurks behind the *SOC* award stinks. It sucks. It is, in my opinion, antithetical to the things it is trying to achieve and frustrating to the retailers involved.

There are something like 20 people who have *any* idea whatsoever what I'm talking about, so perhaps a little background is in order.

Let's start with the basics — the *SOC* was created by Will Eisner in 1992 to recognize and reward the unsung of the comics industry: comics retailers. We're on the front lines of the battle to show that comics are a commercially viable medium to the public at large. Mr. Eisner has my utmost in respect that he alone saw the need to recognize and thank comics retailers for their participation in the process that brings aesthetic value to market — it was long overdue, and shows the man is a true visionary. The *SOC* functions (effectively) as a "hall of fame" —

once you win, you can't ever win again. The *SOC* is its own reward — winning one doesn't give you a larger ear at the powers that be; nor does it give you a better discount, or better terms on your comics; nor does it bring in any extra revenue whatsoever — no customer walks into a *SOC* store and buys something because they read about the award. The *SOC* is, in essence, an "attaboy!" for your hard work and dedication, your passion and your commitment.

Once a year a nominating ballot for the award runs in *Comics Retailer*, *CBG*, and *Diamond Dialogue*. I seem to remember also seeing one run in the *Comics Journal*, so there may well be several other venues for getting the word out. Anyone whosoever can send in a ballot — an individual store owner, a customer, a distributor or publisher representative. Oddly enough I understand that at least one store has made up a photocopied stack, with all the info filled in, and asked their customers to send them in — whoever you are, please allow me to say that you are a *moron* — the *volume* of ballots is utterly meaningless in this stage of the process, because it isn't a popularity contest.

The criteria for the award include industry knowledge, a diversity of product stocking, quality of store image and display, and community participation. The ballot asks the submitter to affirm that these criteria are being met, and enters that store's name into competition.

These ballots are gathered, and a judging committee goes through them, determining which stores are eligible for the *SOC* award. The judges pick some dozen-odd stores as finalists.

This group of finalists is then asked to *document* how they fit the criteria, and to me, this is where the process goes completely off the rails.

See, the main thing a nominee is asked to do is produce a video tape, of no more than five minutes in length, where they present their store, their philosophy, their style.

Now, I'm not sure about you, but video production isn't exactly in my skill set. Moreover, I've found that it took me nearly 20 hours to write, shoot, and edit said video, and to create and provide the paper documentation needed to be qualified to win. Twenty hours that I could have been doing things for the good of the store. Twenty hours in which I could have been selling comics. Twenty hours in which I could have been doing the things that, presumably, qualify me for the *SOC* in the first place.

In addition to taking the time away from running my business to gain something that, at best, is a salve for the ego, I don't believe that a video tape can ever *truly* capture the essence of a store — especially not one a mere five minutes in length. I could not even *begin* to tell you *everything* that makes Comix Experience special and unique in *fifty* minutes and we were face-to-face. What I found while preparing my second video (which I ultimately decided not to submit) was that I wasn't showing what I thought — I was showing what I believed the judges wanted to hear.

That made me queasy.

By insisting on a video presentation, by insisting that the retailer *prove* to the judges that he or she is worthy, I believe that the *SOC* becomes less to do with a recognition of the value of a retailer's contribution to the industry, but a testimony to their skills in convincing a body of judges of whose [vaguely vulgar word] is bigger.

That's another part of it as well — how do you compare the incomparable? There are (or there should be) many many differences between my store and your store; between your store and her store; between her store and their store — some of these differences are mild and cosmetic, but most of them are structural and specific to your community and your clientele, and your vision. What you do in your specific city or town (hell, your specific *neighborhood*, or even specific *block*) is different than what you'd have to do somewhere else, even to achieve exactly the same results. And what I might do *under* the exact same circumstances is likely to be wildly different. As it should be.

Rory Root, owner of Comic Relief in Berkeley (a store that I very much admire) is located roughly half an hour away from me — but if a hurricane uplifted both of our stores and transposed them, I suspect very very strongly that Comic Relief would not be a success at 305 Divisadero in San Francisco, just as Comix Experience would not be a success at 2140 University in Berkeley — the markets, the expectations, the clientele, the environment, the perceptions — all of these things are different a mere half an hour away. CR has some mighty strengths, but they also have some towering weaknesses; CE also has some mighty strengths and some towering weaknesses — yet we are both very successful at what we do within our environment. How does one judge which store is "better?" With one set of criteria Rory is the *clear* winner, but with a different set of criteria, I come out first. And we're in culturally compatible venues. How much more difficult when you judge a store in New York City versus a store in, say, Podunk, Iowa?

And a video tape can not confer what these differences are. Can't even *begin* to.

If I'm not skilled at video presentation, my "odds" of "winning" are that much smaller — yet the *SOC* is meant to be a Hall of Fame. I think "competition" is inappropriate. Once an individual store has been "passed" for adherence to the criteria by the judging committee, then I think further store-driven requirements are not just unnecessary, but directly insulting to the stores involved.

Historically, the *SOC* has been awarded to two stores a year (this year they bumped it to three) — if ten percent of the 4000 stores in this country are *SOC*-"worthy," it would take 200 years (or 133 with 3-per-year) to recognize them all!

Were I Comics-God, I'd make the *SOC* a one-step process — ballots are submitted, the judges see who is qualified, and then the award is given. If this results in ten winners in a year, that's a *good* thing — the *SOC* should be a benchmark that the retail base tries to aspire to, not a virtually (mathematically) unachievable standard that odds are ridiculously stacked against you, no matter how hard you try.

That's really it — the *SOC* is most meaningful if *you* have a chance to win it, if you work hard, if you're ethical, if you care. And there are hundreds of you out there. But odds are against you because of the aesthetics of presentation (he who has the best video stands a better chance, and without a video, you stand no chance), and the small pool of winners.

If these structural changes can be made, then I think the *Spirit of Comics* will go a lot further toward achieving its mandate. The *SOC* should be a benchmark, a standard to aspire to, not a contest.

a r t i c l e

6 9

Tilting at Windmills #69
(Originally ran in Comics Retailer #70)

Every once in a while I'm blessed to have a column that writes itself. Something dumb happens, someone says something ineffably stupid, and the clouds part with a golden shaft of light radiating from heaven, illuminating my brow with an effortless writing.

(That don't mean I write *well*, mind you — just easily.)

Welcome, then, to the World According to Griepp.

Comics Retailer #68 featured a (the first?) column by former Capital City Distribution co-owner Milton Griepp. Milton, now a consultant, gives us six suggestions that might help "bring excitement and growth back to comics."

Five are misguided, inconsistent, unworkable, or downright insane.

Easiest if we go one at a time:

1) Stop Selling Crap! Hey, on the surface of it, this one is a no-brainer. The big problem comes from who, or better yet, *what*, is the arbiter of "crap?"

In my world, *X-Men* is pretty crappy — an endless soap opera filled with distorted and unclear artwork, plodding and overwrought writing, and characters who are barely one-dimensional facing inane and convoluted plot twists that wholly abandon the rules of storytelling. But it sure still sells. Even the months where they are *clearly* dogging it.

In a critical world, very few of the comics in the top 20 would still be there — yet most of these comics ride wholly on historical inertia punctuated by big events that will "forever change" the character(s).

At Comix Experience our personal top 20 largely rides and falls on our critical opinion of the material, but if we removed all the "crap" from the store, our sales would drop by 60% or better.

Some customers truly like what *I* call crap, and more important, Sturgeon's Law, as always, applies. 90% of *everything* is crap, in comics as elsewhere.

Certainly I'd like to see less titles of such little value as *Xero* and *Superboy and the Ravers* being greenlit in the first place — we can always use a little more signal and a little less noise — but even eliminating the bottom third of a publisher's line is not going to bring the overall quality of most comic books up significantly.

In comics, "C" performers often are "A" books, and "A" performers are "C" books — the problem is not that the market has to cut the "crap" comics, but that it has to add market presence on the "quality" material!

2) Get out of downmarket channels. No problem here (though Milton's reasoning seems to stem from the "collectible" side of the business rather than the more fundamental "you don't crap where you eat").

3) Shorten the reorder cycle. Milton seems to have smooshed together two different problem areas: availability of product and speed of shipping.

In terms of the former I have no problem, but in terms of the latter Milton seems to be unaware that retailers absolutely do have the option of direct shipping which gets books typically within two to three days. The problem is that in most cases this is economically unviable for anyone in the chain at current volume, because that shipping has to be paid for.

Milton used the example of a store that needs just one more copy of *Iron Man* — but the store can't afford to eat $2+ shipping on his share of the cover price, nor can the distributor or publisher. At least not on that level of volume.

That is the error — most reorders are small, and shipping that first pound is the most expensive. Even when you get into serious weight...well, I'd much rather take the extra few days than give up precious percentages of my margin. When you are working on weight, you're almost always talking about backlist items — and having those as TOS for a week is seldom a business-threatening move.

We all have the option to get the material speedily through "direct ship" — it is just that in most cases the economics of that movement are impractical. I'll address this a bit more in a minute.

4) Release new comics on Thursday and Friday. This, I realize is a very divisive issue among retailers, but I have to tell you that my aggregate sales grew when new comics day was shifted to Wednesday. Certainly new comics day itself dipped a bit, but was more than made up for by the flow throughout the week.

Friday release made the weekend hopping and rocking, and long lines at the till, but customer traffic was nearly non-existent throughout the week. Now I have better overall traffic, and less scheduling conflicts.

5) Underprint occasionally. Ka-boom.

That's the sound of my brain exploding.

That anyone, anywhere, for any reason would suggest to knowingly turn away customers is...is...well, just inconceivable. What a horrendously misguided and destructive idea.

If we want to make comics a mass-accepted product (and I'm not sure that is the sanest idea, really — there is a *lot* to be said for being a niche), then the first thing we have to do is kill all the collectors. Well, the profit-driven ones at least. Comic books are not even slightly intrinsically valuable, and they never have been. Rather than playing to the very thing that allowed our medium to be "short-handed" to ("Look what your comics are worth!"), we should embrace them purely as entertainment.

Never *ever* underprint knowingly. If I ever find out a publisher is underprinting, you can be absolutely sure that publisher will never be carried by Comix Experience ever again.

And I'll tell you what: consciously manipulating a collectibles market is an evil act of the first rank.

6) Change the order cycle to weekly.

Screw you!

This is clearly the idea of one who hasn't run a comic book shop anytime in the 90s.

I spend roughly six to eight hours a month in the ordering process. This time is certainly shorter as a monthly process than it would be in weekly segments because of consolidation. I have not only no interest in weekly ordering, but I simply don't have the time to do so. This would easily add 25% to the time I'm already putting into the system.

Ordering is fundamentally *not* designed for the "external observer," it has to be *purely* at the convenience and schedule of the retailer. And any such move would be catastrophic for most retailers.

O.K. Only a jerk just knocks another's points down without suggesting what can be done. And I am not that jerk. So, even keeping with the theme of this issue, here are ten things that can be done to grow the market. The fundamental premise here is that the market cannot grow unless retailers are better capitalized and supported. While it is true that collectively retailers take the largest percentage of the cover price, it is equally true that we take the majority of the daily risk, and individually tend to be significantly under-capitalized, economically unable to expand our individual markets.

1) Give us street dates! If I'm lucky, I get a whole hour-and-a-half to process some ten boxes of comics each week. This is both unreasonable and purely insane. Every week is a panic, and a hassle, and a headache, and needs to go. Get retailers the comics on Tuesday night, and if you can't do it for 100% of everyone, for God's sake do it for those of us you can!

2) Partial returnability or consistent overshipping. I (as you know) favor return-ability — up to 20% of your order, with minimum and maximum caps, and a small per-book fee to discourage "abuse" by idiots who haven't any clue what to order.

Fundamentally, we need to move more product onto the shelves. There is a very significant percentage of titles which the cost/benefit ratios of racking don't merit *any* extra copies being bought (Milton's twelve *Iron Mans*). But the paradox is that sales on these titles can *never* grow and only shrink, which is certainly in no one's best interest.

Product can't sell if it is not on the shelf.

3) Reasonable discount structures. There should never, ever, be a reorder fee for a title (hello! We're trying to *grow* sales here, right?), and *every* title should have the potential for the average retailer to keystone it (markup by 100%). I favor quantity-based discount structures.

4) Free or greatly reduced shipping for reorders over a certain amount. If I order $1000 worth of backstock, it should be at my door in three days, without charge to me. There has to be a reward for volume, or the market has no incentive to grow. Unfortunately, your frontlist volume dictates your backlist discount, and unless you order through *Previews* (which means no better than monthly restocking), your backlist volume is never taken into consideration. Unless there is a total overhaul of recognizing "qualifying" purchases, the quickest way to fix this conundrum is free shipping at a certain volume.

The big thing no one seems to understand is that quicker shipping means more frequent orders — I'd be ordering backlist weekly if I had *affordable* turnaround on it. As I noted above, I certainly have the *option* of "direct shipping" for three-day turnaround, but the costs are something not unlike 10% of my profit, which makes it unworth it in the extreme.

5) Eliminate "order reduction" on late-shipping books. Not only does this add some amount of time to the processing of these orders (making the books that much later), but this was clearly a cost-saving measure by Diamond. I'm not at all opposed to "order reduction" *in addition to* "standard return policies," but as our only option, it has cost me plenty.

I believe that the goal of *real* order reduction is a good one (where the retailer can stop a slow moving product before it hits the shelf), but that's not what we have right now — right now we have a one-sided scenario designed to benefit the distributor and penalize any retailer who isn't paying 100% attention.

6) Reinstate some form of wholesale shopping, at least in major metro areas. Retailers aren't *that* different from our customers. When I have the opportunity, I buy a lot more on "impulse" than I do by shopping a catalog, or speaking to a salesperson. It is absolutely insane the San Francisco Bay Area doesn't have a Diamond Warehouse.

7) Require storefront photos, business plans and proof of adequate capitalization for all new retailers, and the latter two, plus photocopies from all publishers. Life in the direct market is hard enough without dealing with the vast number of fly-by-night operations.

8) Eliminate all forced collectibility. Comics that are "designed" to be collectible (limited print runs, variant covers, etc.) are counter-productive to our market. We should be in the *entertainment* business — exclusively.

Not only does false collectibility send the completely wrong message to the customer base, but it also plays merry havoc with our basic tool to order properly — cycle sheets. There is no way to determine without sophisticated point-of-sale what relationship raw sales have to number of customers wanting a product.

9) Scheduled ship weeks for all publishers. I'm totally fricking sick of the first week of the month when all the comics that would just be returnable ship. If you can't tell us *when* you're going to ship, then you have no business being a publisher. And if you can't hit within four weeks of that *date*, then you have *no* business being non-returnable.

10) Even shipping weeks for all families. First, I don't think any "family" of titles should ever ship more than three books in one week. And you should shoot for two max whenever possible. But if you do have a mass of books to ship, make darn sure that you ship them evenly throughout the month. If you publish four titles, then we should have one a week, not all four in the first week of the month. If your line has twelve titles, then ship them three a week, not six in one week, three in the second, two in third, and then one lone title in the fourth. This really hurts sales.

Without strong and financially healthy retailers, the ill market cannot heal. I believe that these ten steps would be a good initial movement towards that healthier and stronger market. The market crash partly happened because publishers and distributors took every chance they got to take capitalization away from the retailers — lets start to give some of it back.

Tilting at Windmills #70
(Originally ran in Comics Retailer #71)

Happy holidays, all. I'm writing this a few days before Thanksgiving, although you're probably reading it in the first days of 1998. I'm not much for holidays, but every once in a while I realize that the ideas behind the merchandising are often good ones. In that spirit, I'd like to give some thanks to the staff of Comix Experience.

Getting a good staff is one of the hardest things to do (though I've been blessed with nearly effortless luck in building my own) – there are too few people both skilled at retail (hand-selling, proper customer service, etc.) and knowledgeable about the peculiarities of our product. A good comic (or game) store employee is worth his weight in gold – any chimp can run a cash register, but to be able to rationally discuss the often irrational content of most comics, to be able to assess whether a customer would be interested in Chris Ware or Rob Liefeld or any of the myriad of points in between, or to handle the often (ahem) eccentric personalities that enter our doors every day...well, sir, that's rare indeed.

I'm probably a bad boss in many respects. I don't give kudos often – in fact the first thing I ever tell new employees is "If I'm not complaining, you're doing *great*!"; and I'm often not good at giving direction – I expect my staff to understand what I want with a minimum of explanation. Yet despite this, I have managed to attract and keep what I believe to be the finest comic book shop staff in North America, if not the world.

Being a good comic shop employee is seldom an easy task – most store owners are either psychotic loners who couldn't handle a job in the real world, or desperate extroverts who need the spotlight shone upon them at all times. And in a few terrifying cases, a mixture of both (I'm probably in that latter category.) This isn't fun or easy – when people think "Comix Experience," they think "Brian Hibbs;" when they think "Comic Relief," they think "Rory Root;" when they think "Night Flight," they think "Mimi Cruz" – hell, they never even think of the *partners* involved (I recall Rory lamenting on several occasions that his then-partner Mike Patchen never got any recognition), so, to the "outside world," the staff – the very *heart* of a store – is lower than amoebas. This is not only not fair, but it usually is flatly wrong.

There was a point, indeed, that I ran the store seven days a week (back when I was young and stupid) – but these days I'm on the counter a mere three days a week. When it comes to anything that is not *overall* planning (what's the goal *six months* from now?), I'm probably the *last* person you need to talk to! A good staff has a lot of rope, and almost never hangs themselves. But for this they seldom get more than a paycheck and a small pat on the back.

There are a couple of different approaches towards staff management – and in the real world, staff is usually thought of as interchangeable cogs that are easily replaced. This contributes to the generally poor levels of customer service one receives at most businesses – when a pro-customer plan is in place, it is seldom implemented because the employee thinks it is the good and right thing to do, but rather because it is *policy*. The worst examples of this (in my experience) tend to be those businesses that call you some hooey like a "guest" – they seem to think that by changing a word, your shopping experience is somehow transformed. I've been the "guest" of the local Target stores, and in few places have I seen as many sullen, unhelpful employees. The problem is that it is just a paycheck for these people – they have no stake, no impetus, to do anything but follow "policy."

It is my belief that rather than have "policies," it is better to engender a sense of family; a sense that each member of the staff is an equal and has the freedom to do what they feel is best. I enjoy being with my staff because they are not mere "employees" – they are my friends and my family, and as they succeed or fail, so then do I. I'm not always successful in creating this sense, of course, and every day is a learning process, but I count the CE staff among my dearest friends and my biggest allies. There's little I'd rather do that knock back a few frosty ones with them, and if I didn't live in a condemned three-room apartment with half my stuff packed away in boxes (long story), I'd have them up for dinner once a month. It's not easy telling your family you love them, but love them I do. God bless us, one and all! *sniff*

Look, working retail is no walk in the park – many customers are (let's be honest) idiots who don't know what they want. They're utter slobs; they're rude; and they don't know how to find clearly marked prices on items. Many customers seem to literally believe in the old adage "the customer is always right," without any understanding of what that really means. What the customer *wants* is always right in that you shouldn't sell *Eightball* to the guy who wants *X-Men* (at least in most cases) – but other than that, the customer is almost always *wrong*. You and your staff have to be there every day; you have on-going projects and situations that you must deal with, and you've developed procedures that allow you to do these things in (you hope) an efficient manner, so what a specific customer opines must be balanced against the long-term needs of your body of customers and yourself. Your staff needs to know that they have the freedom to deal with situations on the fly and situation-specifically. This comes back to that idea of family and trust – I don't necessarily *like* everything my (real) family does, but ultimately I trust them never to betray the family because it is against their own interests.

When a staff feels like a family they are far more likely to take responsible actions. They know that it is to their own benefit. When a staff feels like a family there is far less need for "supervision." They are aware of how their actions affect others. And when a staff feels like a family, you'll have very little turnover. They want to stay with the business because they know that it benefits them.

The best part of this approach is that, ultimately, your regular customers become a part of this family with the same beliefs that they want to support the betterment of the family. Further they implicitly trust what you say, because they know you have everyone's best interests at heart. This is the very center of the success of Comix Experience – our regular customers trust our tastes, instincts, and recommendations because they know that our intent is to expose them to the critically best and most diverse comics that are being produced. As long as we use our influence to the betterment of our family, that trust will continue to grow, as will our regular customer base.

This all sounds well and fine to you, I'm sure, but how do you actually *do* it? The rub, of course, is that every family is different, and there is not really a lot I can specifically suggest. In general, though, I can suggest two things:

1) Surround yourself with good people. Hire people that you would like to be a customer of. When I go out and shop, I expect a salesperson to be utterly knowledgeable about any product I ask about, yet not pushing to sell to me, until I am ready for them to. Hire people that you would like to hang around with – would you like to have a beer with them once a week? And hire people that you are willing to deal with on a personal basis. I'm not much interested in anyone's gossip, but if any of my staff ever have a problem, I'm there for them in a second. If you can surround yourself with good people, the customers will find you. If you build it, they will come.

2) Trust your staff implicitly, and give them areas of responsibility. I believe that it is essential to trust that your staff can do the job you hired them to do. The first few weeks, maybe, you need to stand over their shoulders, making small suggestions and corrections, but after that they should be absolutely able to fly solo. Obviously, if they need or want your help, you should be right there, but otherwise only periodic spot-checking should be needed. Further, make sure that they have a direction, and the knowledge that they have authority in this area. While you do, indeed, hold the ultimate veto power, use it very sparingly, if at all. Your staff's voices should carry a great deal of weight.

The simplest and easiest beginning of this (that you could do this very afternoon) is make one of your racks "staff recommendations" and give them the absolute freedom to put any comic that they read and enjoyed on their shelf. If their selection(s) sell-through, be committed to reordering these books and increasing future orders.

I'd like to tell you a bit about my staff and use them to illustrate the Freedom and Trust principle.

Let's start with **Larry Young** (he loves to see his name in print, the bigger, the bolder, the better) – Larry is the newest member of the CE staff, and is our Minister of Propaganda. Larry edits and produces our monthly 12 page (on average) in-store newsletter, *Comix Experience Onomatopoeia*, which is also the mechanism for our sub-

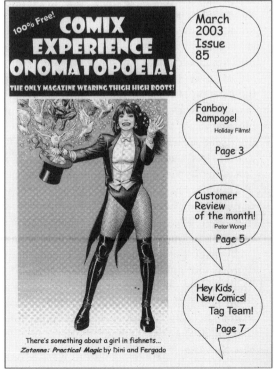

100% Free!

COMIX EXPERIENCE ONOMATOPOEIA!

THE ONLY MAGAZINE WEARING THIGH HIGH BOOTS!

There's something about a girl in fishnets...
Zatanna: Practical Magic by Dini and Fergado

March 2003 Issue 85

Fanboy Rampage! Holiday Films!
Page 3

Customer Review of the month! Peter Wong!
Page 5

Hey Kids, New Comics! Tag Team!
Page 7

scription service. *CEO* contains an interview with a creator (conducted by Larry) every month, commentary from the rest of the staff, and acts as a sort of miniature version of *Previews* discussing the upcoming books. Lar writes all that, as well. In fact, he probably writes 5,000 words or better every month for *CEO*. *CEO* is the leading edge of any publicity or promotion that we do. An interview and favorable write-up by Larry is good for a minimum of twenty more copies sold of any title. In many cases, I can attribute half or more of the sales of any book he features to the verve and passion he brings to the magazine. Larry is also a talented designer – he has created virtually all the signage at Comix Experience, produced the *Top Shelf Sampler* (second issue due in April!), and instigates and manages in-store contests, drawings, and promotions (like the cool pint glasses we did for the Mad Bastards Tour – Garth Ennis, Grant Morrison, Warren Ellis, and, well, the list goes on.)

Larry does virtually all of this without any direct supervision – and does a damn fine job. I often don't see *CEO* until it is time for me to photocopy it, and that's fine because I have the utmost of confidence in Larry to do his job and do it well. Larry has the freedom to feature any creator, any comic that he wants to, and that freedom has paid off in larger sales on his favorite projects. By dint of will and enthusiasm, Larry has got *Transmetropolitan* into our top ten sellers – a massive achievement considering the failure of the rest of the Helix line. Books where we'd be lucky to sell a bare dozen Larry gets up into the fifties. It constantly impresses me, and I believe his success stems from his freedom to promote what he chooses, not what a publisher is trying to push, or a CE company line wants to endorse. The customer can see that the passion is *honest*.

All of our stock is handled by Gary Barger (Zarthanious to you). Gary isn't a scheduled worker on the till, but pitches in when we get rushed, or need a bathroom break, or something. Gary helps me with the count-in of the new product and fills all the subscription orders, as well as tracking when customers need to come in and the like. In addition, Gary single-handedly deals with all the backstock in the store. He processes all new collections bought and bags single issues, but he also handles the creation of back-issue sets. Sets account for 60% or so of our total back-issue sales – ten issues of Fantastic Four for $7, a set of the Hawk & Dove mini for $3, 20 DC first issues for $6, that kind of thing. Gary has complete discretion in not only what sets get made, but also their pricing. This is, of course, simplified because we only buy back issues at a flat rate of 50 cents/pound, but I absolutely trust his pricing sense. He gets us both profit and velocity.

Gary has once more made, because of the discretion I give him, back issues a viable portion of our overall sales. Given how much I despaired in ninety-four and -five of this ever happening again, Gary is an absolute Godsend. Once again, I trust his instincts to do the job and give him the freedom to use those instincts.

Michael Lieberman is our graduate-munchkin. Mike started with us at thirteen years old (!) as gopher and errand-runner and eventually moved up to paid employee when it was legal. Michael is now eighteen and getting ready to move on to college. Almost makes me feel old. I remember when Michael started shopping at CE – little polite kid looking for back issues of *X-Men*; now he is a confirmed alternative-comics head instead buying *Acme Novelty Library* and *Eightball*. Watching the former L'il Mike "become a man" has been a real joy for me, and I give him complete discretion when he runs the store, because he has grown into the role better than any of us. Further, I think the freedom he has been shown has helped instill in him the confidence he shows today – some day he's going to be a senator or congressman, and I'll know that in some small way I helped set him upon that path.

I'll also note that Michael, Larry, and Gary were all CE customers first before we offered them a place at the counter. In fact I've never hired a single person who wasn't first a customer, and, consequently, understood exactly what we are trying to do.

And then there is Rob.

Robert Bennett has worked with me for as long as I can remember – my whole working life. While Gary and Larry take care of pulling and promoting, Rob is the center and soul of the store. He runs the counter more hours than I and consults in almost every ordering decision that is made by the store – he is the absolute anchor of CE.

I'm not good at giving compliments to Rob – we're known each far too long for that, y'know? But I mean it most seriously when I say that I am no longer capable of running the store without the help of Our Man Rob. I could not do it. His influence is so deep, it would be as if I had lost both an arm and a leg. When I say I have confidence in the staff, Rob is the epitome of what I mean. And I hope that someday far in the future Rob and I have chairs next to each other in the Old Funny Book Sellers Home.

If you have faith in your employees and give them freedom to do the job, they'll almost always do better than you expected. Mine always have. And for that, and to them, I give great thanks. I hope they will all always be part of the Comix Experience family, for they've given me more than I could have ever hoped. I hope that you, dear reader, are also blessed with a great staff. If you are, then give them thanks (hey! And a raise!), and if you're not, give them the freedom to become one.

Tilting at Windmills #71
(Originally ran in Comics Retailer #72)

I'm very very incredibly busy right now, and I simply don't have the time to write a new column this month.

So I'm going to pull out an old television trick, and give you the first ever *TaW* flashback. Set the wayback machine to July of 1993. This is the column that I realize still has the most relevance today – a column that I'm *still* telling retailers about, because many of you are *still* making the same mistakes.

This might be more of a Lucas-style special edition, actually, because I went and updated a few of the concepts (sometimes its easy to forget that in '93 $1.25 was an expensive comic book!), so there are a few reasons for you to reread this, even if you were reading *Comics Retailer* four and a half years ago.

"Hey, Mallory, remember that time dad took us fishing?"

(dissolve cut to:)

•   •   •   •   •

Deep discounting never made any sense to me.

When I was in Kansas City visiting a relative, I went into a local store to buy my cousin a copy of the latest Sandman. I was given a 10% discount. I asked why, and the store replied that *every* customer gets a 10% discount, and that regulars do even better. Evidently this is a citywide phenomenon.

I understand in Detroit, discounting *starts* at 20%!

I just don't get it.

Why would anyone give away money, just because a customer happens to walk in your store *once*. I can almost understand giving a discount for someone who *earns* it, but to any Tom, Dick or Harry? No way, Jose!

At Comix Experience, we give used to give a straight 10% discount to any member of our subscription service. Unlike most stores' pull-and-hold services, we put out a new form monthly, so we were able to get (nearly) instant information about our customers likes and dislikes. We thought it was worth giving away that discount in the face of the information we took in. Once I did the math, however, I realized the huge profits I was giving away and switched to a 10% *rebate* system, which costs me 5% at best – it usually comes out to 3.5% or less.

But I'll talk about pull-and-hold systems another day – today the topic is discounting.

Are you aware just how much discounting can cost you? I've prepared the charts below to illuminate my point. First find the chart that corresponds to your discount level (though even stores that get 55% off still have some titles they only make 40% on). I've made four charts, for 55%, 50%, 45%, and 40% discount levels. If you're one of the rarer "odd discount" retailers, I apologize, but hopefully you'll be able to create an appropriate chart with the info I've given here.

Each chart compares six different customer discount levels (none, 10%, 15%, 20%, 25%, and 30%). First you'll see the retail amount a $1.95 comic book sells for at that discount, then the *profit* from that sale. When you give discounts, your *costs* remain the same! Then the chart show how many copies you'd need to sell to make $20 profit. Finally the chart shows how many *more* comics you need to sell to make the same amount of profit. (All numbers are rounded to the next whole number.)

Look at the charts, then we'll talk some more.

Chart #1: $1.95 comic at 55% off — Cost is $.88

Discount Given	None	10%	15%	20%	25%	30%
Retail	$1.95	$1.75	$1.66	$1.56	$1.46	$1.36
Profit	$1.07	$.87	$.78	$.68	$.58	$.48
Number of copies to make $20 profit	19	23	26	29	34	42
% difference from NO discount	—	21%	37%	53%	79%	121%

Chart #2: $1.95 comic at 50% off — Cost is $.98

Discount Given	None	10%	15%	20%	25%	30%
Retail	$1.95	$1.75	$1.66	$1.56	$1.46	$1.36
Profit	$.97	$.77	$.68	$.58	$.48	$.38
Number of copies to make $20 profit	21	26	29	34	42	53
% difference from NO discount	—	24%	38%	62%	100%	152%

Chart #3: $1.95 comic at 45% off — Cost is $1.07

Discount Given	None	10%	15%	20%	25%	30%
Retail	$1.95	$1.75	$1.66	$1.56	$1.46	$1.36
Profit	$.88	$.68	$.59	$.49	$.39	$.29
Number of copies to make $20 profit	23	29	34	41	52	69
% difference from NO discount	—	26%	48%	78%	126%	200%

Chart #4: $1.95 comic at 40% off — Cost is $1.17

Discount Given	None	10%	15%	20%	25%	30%
Retail	$1.95	$1.75	$1.66	$1.56	$1.46	$1.36
Profit	$.78	$.58	$.49	$.39	$.29	$.19
Number of copies to make $20 profit	26	34	41	51	69	105
% difference from NO discount	—	31%	58%	96%	165%	303%

As you can see, discounting eats into your bottom line dramatically! Let's take a couple of examples.

Example #1: You're a 50% discount store that gives a uniform 20% discount to *all* customers (a typical Detroit scenario) – you've got to sell 62% *more* comics to make the exact same amount of money if you didn't discount. To put it another way, if you immediately cut the discount and lost about 40% of your customers, *your profit would remain the same!* You have to sell 34 comics at 20% off to equal the same profit you'd see from selling 21 comics at full retail.

Example #2: You're a small store that gets a 40% discount. You give your customers 10% off. You've got to sell eight more comics to make the same amount if you gave no discount – that's nearly a third! You could lose 25% of your customers, eliminate the discount, and still make the better profit!

Example #3: You're Bob's Mega-comics, and you get 55% off. You give a 30% discount. You've got to sell *more than twice* as many comics to make the same profit as you would with no discount. You could lose more than half your customers and still be just as profitable.

Of course, losing volume could affect your discount from your distributor, so it's not like I'm saying to automatically dump the discount. And, of course, all numbers assume that you've got 100% sell-through (an unlikely event across the board) – the poorer your sell-through, the more you've got to sell to make up for it. For example, you get 100 copies of a $1.95 comic that you buy at 50% off – this costs you $97.50. You sell 90% of those copies. Your gross profit is $78 ([90 copies times $1.95] – $97.50). If you give a 10% discount on all these sales, your gross profit drops to $60.45 ({[90 copies times $1.95] times .9} – $97.50), or a difference of 29%, as opposed to 24% if you had sold 100% of your stock!

I believe that discounting has its place. When someone performs a service for you (like the collection of information from my customers; or the courtesy discount I give to professionals – who supply the material I sell in my shop; or even to other merchants who give you discounts on services for the store), it makes some measure of sense to "reward" them with a discount. But I think it's inane to "give away the store" to any Joe off the street that hasn't even provided customer loyalty to you.

Use the charts to see what you're *losing*. Then make the appropriate decision, based on your store and clientele. But without the basic information, how will you ever know?

Tilting at Windmills #72
(Originally ran in Comics Retailer #73)

Sometimes its funny how everything old is new again. Last month I ran a virtual re-run of an old column, and this month I'm also revisiting a past column (though this is a complete re-write).

I think it was September of 1994 (too lazy to go look it up) when I first suggested the idea of a "Partial Returns Plan" here in *Tilting at Windmills*. Lately this idea was brought forward with a vengeance when if was offered up in *Diamond Dialogue* by the members of BACR (Bay Area Comics Retailers). I am not a member of this group, but was very pleased when they trotted it back out and dusted it off. I don't much care *who* gets the final credit for the idea, as long as we can get it (or some slight modification thereof) going.

Before we talk about the specifics of how it might work, let's talk for a few hundred words about *why* it is so necessary.

I don't think that if you take a good look at the sales charts and have some basic horse sense, you can't figure out pretty quickly that the comics industry is in some hard times right now. Non-returnability, which prevented a slow lingering death on the newsstands, created the workable economic model we call the direct market. Such a model was perfectly viable for the climate in which it was created – a small number of passionate, dedicated stores buying "direct" from the publishers, who, in turn, offered them a small number of products that had a low "investment," is a good recipe for non-returnable products. The retailer orders what he knows he has the clientele for, and, because the buy-in is low, he has an incentive to buy "extras" of this product, to create new readers. From the start of the DM up to about the beginning of the 90s, this scenario not only prospered, but grew at a dizzying pace.

However, a few things happened to change the economic dynamics, and these changes plunged us into a steep and steady drop that ultimately resulted in a marketplace that, for the most part, is unable to have a large and wide enough customer base to be self-sustaining. The first principal change was that we lost the day-to-day enthusiasm and passion of the soldiers of the front line: the retailer. All of us know one or more store owners that have lost the "spark" – oh, sure, they still like comics, maybe even strongly follow one or two, but there are few members of the retail community left who embrace the full spectrum of available material with enthusiasm and joy.

This change was driven, in part, by the second major structural change of the direct market – a steady increase in the volume of products offered. I remember back in the day a typical new-release day might have 20-30 new products coming in. There was only one *X-Men* comic book, but we all loved it – it was our only chance to follow these characters! Today if there aren't three *X*-books in a week, we think it is a small shipment. The rapid growth of the DM spurred extant publishers to expand intra-family lines and to add new titles; as well as encouraging (many!) new publishers to try their hands at it. Let's face it: though publishing is not without some measure of risk, selling non-returnable diminishes that risk significantly in a growing market – the brunt of it was borne by the retailer. Even "back then" a retailer's risk wasn't out-of-hand – with such a small number of titles available, one could take a reasonable long-term stocking position and expect to sell the majority of them in a profitable time-frame. I recall that the small chain I worked for regularly ordered *caseloads* of *X-Men* for the warehouse. "Add 200 copies to the store orders. Wait, Wolverine is on the cover drawn by Barry Smith? Make that 600 copies." How many retailers today order caseloads even for the rack?

Enthusiasm and passion are hard to hold onto in the face of the deluge of product we are faced with. Where once you could ask your local comics retailer about the minutia of the X-Men's private lives (and they knew it, because they cared, they were involved, and they were fans), the retailers who hold that knowledge today are few and far behind.

The third factor is that of price — as title-load increased, piece-counts decreased, and prices rose. Certainly the 80s saw a tremendous rise in the costs of paper as well the costs of attracting and keeping creative talent, and these added to price increases as well. I've been selling comics for nearly 15 years now, and it sure feels like both title-counts and piece-costs have more than quadrupled in that time. And of course, as these things have grown, so shrinks the circulation, sealing the need for further price increases.

I've said it before, and I'm sure I'll say it again: the non-returnable direct market worked like a charm when there were 200 titles that averaged about 60 cents each – even having one unsold copy of each book on the shelf only cost $60. However, today we're facing 800+ titles that average at over $2.50 a throw. Keeping one each of those at wholesale will run you something like $1000!

And therein lies the economic rub.

Go get your copy of the February 1998 sales chart in *Diamond Dialogue*. Use this as your referent: *Batman* #553 had direct market preorders of roughly 51,200 copies. This makes one point on the chart (see how Batman is listed as "100"?) worth roughly 512 copies. Now start doing the math to figure out about how much any given comic sold. I'll write the disclaimer while you're doing this: these figures are based upon a mailer created by Matt High of Antarctic Press. This data can be accessed on the World Wide Web at the following URL: http://lonestar.texas.net/~antarc/salescharts.html. Look for methodology there. I'd guess that these figures are very close to accurate, though, it is, of course, eminently possible that *Batman* #553 preordered at 52,146 instead.

Even these raw charts aren't of total use, because we have no way of knowing exactly how many of the reported 4500 stores ordered each title. That is to say that book #103, *Wetworks* #37, which was ordered at about 21,000 copies, would average out to 4.6 copies per store. Now it is just as possible that there are only 3000 accounts that order *any* copies of *Wetworks* #37, which would mean it had an average sale of 7 copies per store (a significant difference), but we can only work with the data provided.

Wetworks #37 sold an average of 4.6 copies per store. Think about that for a second. Then think about the other 697+ books that sell worse than *that*! Heck, even on the high end it's scary: 138,000 copies of *Uncanny X-Men* #354 (the *number one* book!) – that's only about 31 copies per account!

The underlying economic principles of DM retailing dictate a 90% or better sell-through to remain profitable for the average store. If you're selling 31 copies of a title, you can probably order 34, and not risk yourself overmuch, but copy number 35 or 36 (when you still only sell 31) will eat your profit margin immensely.

And if you're only selling five? (4.6 *Wetworks* #37) That sixth copy is a large risk. It may, in fact, represent your entire profit if it goes unsold.

Yet if you don't carry the sixth copy, the book can't possibly ever grow in circulation, and will, as entropy dictates, shrink as readers leave the book and there is no supply to create new ones.

I think that is exactly it: entropy has taken hold of the Direct Market, and only a entire paradigm shift has any hopes of breaking its grasp.

Once a book drops below ten copies sold, it represents an *enormous* risk for a retailer to build, nurture and grow its audience. An enormous risk and commitment. But I have 800+ choices every month to divide my commitment and resources among, and so many books "fall beneath my radar." This is an important concept for non-retailers to grasp, because it informs and creates the stocking realities each individual retailer operates under. A personal example: I'm said to "hate" Marvel, but the reality is that I don't feel the company has my best interests at heart, and that much of their product doesn't fit in to my store's image. But we easily sold 100 copies of *Avengers* #1 because it fit my aesthetic enough to be something I could tangibly support. Conversely, I am utterly unconvinced that *Marvel Team-up* adds to my store in any significant manner, so I do not rack the book. Is it possible I could be selling two or three rack copies of *MTU*? Certainly so. But my budget is finite, and I'd rather allocate that $2-3 somewhere where I have a stake, interest, or passion about the material. *Avengers* by Kurt Busiek and George Perez is right on the middle of my radar screen. *Marvel Team-up* by I-don't-know and I-don't-care most certainly isn't.

If you're on the radar map, you'll get support, commitment, enthusiasm; if you're not, you'll get bupkis, and entropy-controlled bupkis at that.

All of this is compounded by the inherently fickle nature of the readers. If *X-Men* has a badly designed cover, it can cost me 10% or more of my sales. This leaves me almost no profit margin on the "non-fickle" sales.

I think there is a thought among publishers and other interested parties that says that the constant downward spiral of individual piece-count sales will somehow correct itself. Listen to this now, or regret it later: *the market will **not** correct itself*. The average title's sales in the average comic book store is below the point where it is viable to rack the comic with any support. If my cycle sheets tell me that one month I sold six copies of *Steel*, and the next I sold five, I can guarantee you that, barring personal interest, I'm going to order five of the next issue. I'm not selling a large enough quantity to make it viable to risk the resources to continue, let alone upgrade, the customer base for this title.

These are the economics of the direct market, and a growing number of comic books are falling prey to its clutches. Even stronger books, in many stores, aren't getting the full rack-support that they need and deserve.

Almost every economic incentive currently in place encourages the retailer to order tight going for sell-through over, or to the exclusion of, rack presence. The difference between today and September of 1994 is that now we're in full-scale crisis, and we have to act quickly in order to preserve a future for our industry. Every month most individual titles' orders are dropping 4-6%. Every month. There is only so long that this can continue to happen, for us to still be a viable business. Something must be done to stop the decreasing order cycle that has become our norm, lest we have a business no more.

Further, it is absolutely clear to this observer that the retail base is nowhere near well-capitalized enough to fund the needed expansion, and that we're the only ones who can successfully turn the tide.

Hence, partial returns.

Clearly we have enough evidence that full-returns (as on the newsstand) quite often leads to corruption, and, at least, is absolutely inefficient. Printing five to sell one? Madness!

Further, we need to maintain our margins – if we order correctly we should minimally keystone (double our investment). If we make a mistake, then we should pay a price, but we should not be penalized for doing our job correctly.

Under partial returns, retailers would be able to return a straight percentage of their order (let's use 20% as a working figure), with a minimum of one, and a maximum of, say, ten. If you order one to five, you could return one copy, six to ten could return two, eleven to fifteen could return three, and so on all the way up to 46 and up being able to return a maximum of ten copies.

The biggest costs for returns come from distribution – not only do the books have to processed to come to the retailer, but then returns will have to be handled (with nothing better than interest and cash-flow holding that up) This is a lose-lose situation for a non-returnable distributor. In order to cover the costs of distribution, a per-book fee should be assessed. I don't know what Diamond's hard costs are, but 10-12 cents a book sound right by me, add a small amount as a token payment, and we're talking 15-20 cents a book to return it. Pay as you go.

For $50, I could add 250 pieces to my store with only that $50 risked. Otherwise it would cost me on average $312.50, and I'd be stuck with dead inventory that becomes a tax liability. Adding 250 pieces to my store could result in 100 more sales, but I'll never know under current economic incentives. I can't risk $312.50 on what could be far less profit from the parent books affected.

A few more small things would need to be worked out – we'd need an accounting sheet from our distributors that indicated exactly how many copies of what books we could return each week; returns, of course, would have to be stripped-cover only (the retailer has already paid one set of full-shipping charges after all); and this program has to be entirely self-selected by the retailer (no filling orders at 120%, then saying we can return some), but all such things seem fairly obvious to me, and don't need to be hashed out right now.

I think most retailers will be less conservative in ordering, if they know they have a 20% margin-of-error that is not cost-prohibitive to maintain. I'm willing to risk 20 cents to put more than "subs+1" on the rack for *Steel*, but I am loath to do that at $1.25 a throw.

So that's the plan. It has a damn fine chance of growing rack sales on many many titles, as well as somewhat reducing retailer's current conservatism of rack orders.

I see no positive signs from the market as a whole – we're rapidly reaching a point of unsustainabilty (the best-selling comic only sells 138k?!?!), and something drastic is needed to turn things around. Looks to me that partial returns are the last, best hope we have. At the rate we're going, the best selling comic won't move 100,000 copies by next Christmas. At what point does it become *too late* to fix it, and will we change our paradigm before it gets that far? I only hope so.

7 3

Tilting at Windmills #73
(Originally ran in Comics Retailer #74)

Something changed.

I'm not sure exactly when it happened, but there is a desperation in the industry that's making me feel downright optimistic that the reigns of power have actually started to shift towards the retailer.

My first sense of it came at the beginning of the year when *Diamond Dialogue* printed the BACR proposal for partial returns, and Diamond actually acknowledged that there was something there worth exploring. I caught another sniff when DC (after *years* of asking for it) changed their catalog order to family-order (I saved nearly 20 minutes from the time it takes me to do my first draft of the order form – that's four hours of my existence back over the course of a year! Maybe I can even have a life someday!); and Marvel started putting full listings back into the main catalog.

These are but the smallest steps, but the signs are starting to point toward publishers and distributors realizing that what the retail community wants and needs may well be more important than the way *they* want to do business.

From my perspective as a retailer, this is well overdue, though I really wish it had happened at a time where there was adequate capitalization to ensure that any structural changes to the industry would actually take.

We have lots of problems in this industry, but by far the largest one is lack of adequate capitalization (especially on the retail level) – and the aftermath of the distribution wars did nothing but reduce the capital available to our industry. Certainly my costs of doing business (discounts, shipping, etc.) have done nothing but rise in the last two years, and I expect yours have as well.

Several plans and proposals have begun to circulate through the industry about how to make positive structural changes – but few of these plans take into account the capital-poor nature of most of today's retail base. I got a plan this week that boiled down to "electronic Point-of-Sale systems will help the direct market." It is hard to find fault with this premise, though nowhere in this plan is any mention of where cash-strapped direct market retailers are going to get the multi-thousand dollar investment in hardware and software needed to make such a goal come into reality. Any plan that asks for a deep investment from individual retailers has several strikes against it before it even gets to the plate.

The expansion of the direct market (or even, let's be blunt, the return of the direct market to previous levels) can not and will not happen except at the hands of the retail community – retailers are the only ones with direct face-to-face interaction with the consumer, and retailers are the only one in a position to reach out and bring in new consumers. Publishers and distributors can *help*, to be sure, but unless they're working *in concert* with the retail community such efforts are going to be predominately wasted. The fact of the matter is that unless and until more capitalization is placed in the hands of the retailers, we're going to continue to spiral downwards until we're below enough of a critical mass.

Several months ago I made a list of ten things that could help heal the market. In the interest of keeping these issues in your mind, let me briefly repeat this list for you now:

1) Early release of shipments (nee Street Dates)
2) Partial returns (pay as you go) or consistent, free, overshipping
3) The ability to (at least) "keystone" (double investment) product with reasonable quantities (say 10 or more)
4) Free or greatly reduced shipping on reorders and backlist
5) Elimination of Order Reduction as a *substitute* for regular Return policies
6) More local distribution warehouses and the return of local wholesale shopping
7) Higher standards for new accounts (both retail and publishers)
8) No "forced" collectibility (like multiple covers)
9) Scheduled ship weeks for *all* publishers
10) Even shipping by family within those weeks

Note that none of these suggestions takes increased capital expenditure from the retailer (well, O.K., partial returns would take a little, but for very direct benefits), and most of them would either put more capital into the retailer's hands, or eliminate some of the retailer's cash flow risk.

Several of these don't need much more discussion (4,5, & 8-10, I'd judge), more warehouses is probably a pipe-dream, and we covered partial returns pretty well last month, so that leaves 1, 3, and 7. In reverse order:

One of the things that killed us during the boom was the invasion of the fly-by-night operations. It always has been a little too easy to get into comics; and while this has sometimes served us well, allowing under-capitalized, but full-of-spunk boot-strappers to grow into industry powerhouses, it has more often pushed us down by attracting huge flocks of quick-buck artists and other parasites who ravage the consumer base and sow confusion.

New retailers should be required to submit a business plan and either store-front photos or the number of the landlord with whom they are negotiating, if the store is not yet leased. If the business plan relies purely upon, say, discounting ("we'll steal all the customers if we offer 40% off!"), then the new account should not be allowed. And one of the Diamond field reps should visit the new account six months after they are opened to ensure they are a "real" business (actually, they should visit at least once in that time-frame anyway, if field reps are to be considered valuable to the average retailer). Any legitimate businessman would have no problem meeting a few professional criteria to ensure that only valid retailers get new accounts. When I began my account I had but to show the most perfunctory of "evidence" that my business was "real" – I could have just as well been are store that relied on *stealing away* customers from other retailers, rather than trying to *create new ones*.

Diamond also needs to wield a much heavier hand in purchasing. At *least* 20% of the comics they list could be lost, and *no one* would notice (well, except the publishers) – and probably upwards of half of the merchandise. (Digression: I was amused by the Info Please in the 3/98 *Diamond Dialogue* – they polled about NASCAR merchandise. A staggering 78% of retailers said they carried none. Further an overwhelming 86% said they wouldn't carry NASCAR stuff if more was available in the future from Diamond. In spite of this, Tom Stormonth ends on a quote that runs, "Specialty retailers should carefully consider taking advantage of Diamond's line of NASCAR products to claim some of those profits for themselves." Jeez! *Eighty-six* percent of retailers don't want it, and they end on a sales pitch? End of Digression.) Seriously, a higher creative standard of material in *Previews* would result in it being a significantly greater sales tool.

I'm sure that the executives running Diamond perceive themselves to be in a ticklish position because of Diamond's virtual monopoly. When it started becoming clear what distribution would look like a few years ago, there was a significant concern that Diamond would cut out or eliminate the small press (I held that fear myself), but I think that it is now clear that the reduced volume of the industry means that Diamond needs *every* profitable sale it can get, and that, even with the lower gross sales numbers, significant numbers of "small press" publishers may well be generating better gross dollars than several titles from brokered publishers. With this in mind, I think it is time to start cutting the barnacles from the hull so this ship can move a bit faster.

Even if Diamond got stupid, there is a safety net in the system now – Diamond put together a board of retailers to screen any disputed rejections, and to catch any mistakes. To the best of my knowledge, this board has *never once* thrown back a comic into the system – I believe it was Joe Field who told me a few months ago that "if Diamond rejected it you know it is *really* bad." As long as that safety net is in place, I strongly urge Diamond (and remember, a more small-publisher-friendly retailer than me, you're not likely to find) to start wielding the ax and preventing more clutter from entering the market in the first place.

Once they're in, however, retailers need to have a good chance to being reasonably profitable on them. Look, I order one copy of *Kaboom* from Awesome, and because it is a "D" discount, I get 55% off. Conversely, I order 100 copies of *Hate* from Fantagraphics, but because of the "F" discount, I only get 45%. What's wrong with this picture?

There was a whole column on this, a few years back, but can't Diamond and the publishers figure out a way to competitively price material, so I can make a fair margin on it? I strongly favor a per-quantity discount system – in today's market, if you can sell ten copies of a book you deserve to be able to keystone it (get a 50% discount) – if you can sell more than twenty, you deserve better than that! I love Fantagraphics – not all their books, mind, but several of their titles are solidly in my top twenty overall all-time sellers. Yet every month when I fill out the order form, I have to resist looking over in the "discount" column, else I feel like a knife is twisting in my back.

I don't order with discounts in mind – getting a higher discount doesn't cause me to automatically raise my order, nor does seeing an "F" publisher immediately cause me to order more conservatively. And I really don't think most retailers do. Discount is not "important" in that sense – we order what we think we can sell based on the information we're given. Discount, in and of itself, is but one of many factors that determines an order. However, in the real world, if my resources are going towards inefficient rates-of-return, my ability to grow my business is hampered. The problem is, we're not dealing with interchangeable widgets, we're dealing with individual and idiosyncratic entertainment. Even if I had a mind to maximize revenue by ordering by discount, it would be unlikely if current customers for book *Y* or creator *X* would transfer to book *Z* or creator *W*.

What happens with a low discount is that growth is minimized. When transaction are minimally profitable, or worse, just break even, publishers and distributors are ultimately harmed in the long run because the retailer's ability to move his market forward is dictated to a large degree by the capital available to him. When local markets do not grow, neither does the national market. I won't even begin on major publishers who won't give small accounts but 35-40%. At least Image has a 45% minimum, and should be loudly saluted for that.

More capital needs to be moved forward into the retailer's hands if the market is to prosper, and the *least* thing that should be done is offer a minimal 50% discount on reasonable quantities.

Finally, we should talk about early release of product. Can I tell you something? We made a tactical error ever calling it "street dates." Yes, that is the nearest real-world equivalent to what we are asking for, but the term brings along an implication of "enforcement." And nobody wants to be put in a position where they have to enforce *anything*.

The best statement I've heard yet on this topic came from, of all sources, PACER. I've been waiting for years for PACER to produce a position paper of some kind, and they came through with a good one. Also from the 3/98 Dialogue: "It has never been the PACER position that retailers need distributors, publishers, or any other body to act to 'police' street dates. That is not the function of these entities. Publishers should put out quality books, and distributors should get these books to retailers in a timely manner. Expecting either arm of our industry to "police" retailers is not only inappropriate to their missions; it is insulting to retailers. It is the position of PACER that professional retailers will use street dates as they are intended, to permit the more effective merchandising of products, and not for any short-term, short-sighted profit." Couldn't have said it better myself.

Early release is important for the retail community – we need time to properly rack and process our weekly orders. We need time in the system to cover the system not working correctly. Publishers get months to shepherd their books. Distributors get a week or more. Retailers get an hour or two. All we're asking for is a day (a night even!) with which to do our job.

I don't think this is so very much to ask.

I say again: we must move more capital into the retail market. We must give retailers more confidence in the system, and their place within it. We must bring stability to the market, and the retail community must be the spearhead of that movement. *The market will not heal itself.* It is a fallacy of the first stripe to think it will, and without some economic incentive to deflect it, we're nearing a point where even the publishers and Diamond will not have the resources needed to make the paradigm shift we require to move forward into the 21st Century.

Like I said at the beginning of this column, I'm optimistic that things have been shaken up so far, the powers that make these types of decisions are starting to recognize that changes must be made; that soon we will no longer be able to make any changes. We should have begun re-writing the retailer's position at the beginning of the distribution shake-up – but what we didn't do then we can accomplish now, and quickly before the market eats itself whole.

Bring some portion of the capitalization to me and hundreds of passionate, driven entrepreneurs out there, and we'll build you a business so large all your dreams of avarice pale by comparison. But fail to render unto us what is merely our due, and you will continue to see us struggle into insignificance. We await your decisions.

Tilting at Windmills #74
(Originally ran in Comics Retailer #75)

I just got back from the 7th annual DC Comics RRP meeting, and boy is my brain tired!

Looking back over my previous columns, it looks like I didn't write about the last one, so maybe you've forgotten about this. The RRP (Retailer R-something [Representative?] Program) is a body of a hundred-odd retailers from a wide cross-section of backgrounds, personalities, and locations that DC Comics has assembled to help themselves be guided through the sometimes-contradictory wants and desires of the retail community. The theory is that this mix of big stores and small, of urban stores and rural stores, of single stores and chains will, as a group, accurately reflect the diversity of retailers throughout the country.

Each year DC rents a hotel in some city (we've been to, among other places L.A,, Montreal, and Nashville – this year was Fort Worth) and invites this body to attend. They pay any travel costs over $300, and spring for the hotel rooms and all meals. At these meetings, we spend 2 or 3 days with DC making editorial and product presentations, as well as discussing the pressing issues of the day, and generally learning from one another.

This year, for example, Mark Chiarello and Richard Bruning ran focus groups on DC's covers and trade dress, and Mike Carlin and Bob Wayne discussed what we call "fifth-week" events (like *Tangent* or *New Year's Evil*) – this is in addition to hour-long group sessions where we discussed topics ranging from DC's statue program (eww! William Paquet can't sculpt faces!) to returnability (DC appears willing to examine thought-through plans, but has several "biases" [as Paul Levitz put it] against them).

All the attending retailers learn a lot (this year in particular DC seemed more willing to share knowledge of the general costs, if not specific numbers, of doing various programs), but more importantly, DC walks away learning a lot. DC brought about 20 employees, and each and every one of them walked out of there with pages and pages and pages of tightly-written notes. I'd be surprised if Bob Wayne didn't fill up *two* little notebooks of suggestions. Also in attendance were Cindy Fournier (VP of Operations) and Steve Stoughton (purchasing director of the DCs) from Diamond who *also* walked out with pages of notes.

DC is a large corporation, and, like all such large entities has a hard time changing direction once momentum gets them going in a particular way. I mean, you should see their offices – they are three floors of interconnected mazes and warrens, and you think to yourself, "how can they possibly co-ordinate anything to even produce comic books at all?!?" (The exact opposite of, say, Fantagraphics, which is crammed into a 8 room house in Seattle, where you think, "how do they manage to get out 15 titles a month under these conditions?!?") But the pursuit of knowledge that the DC staff exhibits at these meetings makes one thing crystal clear: *DC listens*. Now, they may not be able to *do* anything, either because of legal reasons (anti-trust makes certain things much harder than you'd imagine), or because of "biases" (though those things can be changed if you supply the right argument), or even that they will do something, but it takes 18 months for them even to begin – but DC listens.

And I cannot begin to tell you how nice that is.

I don't know how one joins the RRP – it is invitation-only – but the first step is to communicate with them. Talk to your DC phone rep: Christine, Fletcher, Vince or Andy; give Ann Ivan or David Vinson a call; speak to Bob Wayne or Paul Levitz (and, honestly, it's not that hard to get Paul on the phone – go on, give it a try!). Tell them your concerns, let them know your problems, offer them suggestions to improve service – in short, let them know that you care, and that you want to help, and maybe they'll want your presence too.

Actually, this isn't exclusively true for DC. We all have a lot of day-to-day problems and concerns and issues with *every* publisher and distributor – how many times have you ever called one up, or written them a letter, or sent them an e-mail? Or were you more likely to tell your customers, but not your suppliers? If the person at a company you contact doesn't seem interested, go up the ladder to their boss. Keep doing that until someone listens, and if they don't, *then* you can write them off. Still and all, I wish more publishers would show the kind of tangible face-to-face support that DC does with the RRP.

Cool projects get launched at these events, too. You know that *Secret Origins* facsimile edition you're selling now? That was because of the RRP meetings. How about that *Transmetropolitan* (which we've, I'd like to add, built into our #2 best-selling regular monthly title – there is a huge potential audience for this book, folks!) overship you're getting? Also because of the RRP. These are not things that would have had any chance of happening without this face-to-face meeting.

But really, the real kudos should come from two RRP announced programs – both designed to bring in the next generation of comic book readers. The first program has already started running: the Cartoon Network promotion giving out free comics to kids who call the Comic Shop Locator Number and come into a direct market comic book shop. DC produced over a *million* copies of this book to be distributed. That is impressive, and directly focused, with a goal to bring people into the direct market. This will not be a panacea for it depends on several things going right: (1) calling the CSLN, 2) there being a direct market comic shop in a relatively small radius, 3) actually going to the DM comic shop, which is often hard for children), but it is an amazingly positive first step towards addressing our generational problem.

The second program you may not have heard about yet: the US Postal Service wants to get kids collecting stamps, so they've started a program where they are targeting public schools. In conjunction with DC, they are producing six comic books starring Superman, Batman, Wonder Woman, et. al. that give the history of our country, and double as a stamp album. The first one of these is going out to "every" public school in America – some *nine million* copies are being produced. Yes, I said *nine* million – a nine and six zeros! The five follow-ups to this program need to be sponsored by local school boards, or PTAs, but the initial one is meant to go out to every child in public school!

Now, there is nothing in this program that leads these kids to the direct market (it is far more likely it will lead them to the USPS to become stamp collectors), but it achieves the goal of getting comics and their characters into the hands of our soon-to-be potential customers. The hope, I believe, is to encourage kids to consider comics to be "cool" (I was about to say "a valid medium" – but kids don't know squat about that kind of thing), and I think it has an adequate chance of working. If we can teach them when they're young to understand how a comic book works, it raises the odds significantly that they will be open to them as they get older.

As the five follow-ups need to be sponsored, you may want to contact both your local school board and DC to see if you can help sponsor these efforts yourself.

These type of generational programs will have little-to-no short-term effect on our market, but the long-term possibilities are *enormous*! And it really does take a company the size of DC (or Marvel!) to muscle them through. We should applaud DC for these efforts and do what we can to make them even more successful, to encourage them to *continue* to do programs like these.

DC has *many* problems in the direct market (like how it would be nice if they would knock off the crossovers between good and poor selling titles – our current customers are tired of them), but they're trying, and they're listening, and they're making positive changes that will ultimately benefit us all. I wish I could believe that these attitudes would have still occurred in a flush market (sorry, I'm cynical that way), or that they would work faster, or more efficiently, but they are indeed the best example of what a publisher can and should do. As you know, I'm not the most generous with praise; and I don't think we should lower our guards, lest Paul Levitz gets (knock wood) hit by a bus (or, eep! DC buys out Diamond!), but we could not do worse if more publishers followed DC's lead in thinking, communicating, and trying long-term programs.

If *every* publisher did the things that DC, does the market *might* not be better, but we'd have more potential, and I think more retailers would feel better about the business we've found ourselves in. Take this as a challenge – you may not have their deep pockets, but listening, communicating and responding doesn't always have a direct cost as such. Follow their lead, and listen, and maybe some enthusiasm will return to the market.

It sure can't hurt.

7 5

Tilting at Windmills #75
(Originally ran in Comics Retailer #76)

It's not that often that I use *TaW* to have a dialogue with someone else (I think the last time was when Lou Bank came to work at Comix Experience for a week), but I recently got some e-mail that I'd like to share. My long-time friend Bob Shreck (international bon vivant and publisher of Oni Press) sent me some comments on my column on partial returnability. Bob is one of the few people in comics whose opinions I can't easily dismiss – he's been doing this for far too long and really knows most every side of the marketplace. Oni Press has had (I feel) the most promising start of a new publisher in recent memory – balancing creatively exciting work with a solid commercial sensibility – and absolutely demands our respect. Let's see what Bob has to say:

The most interesting part of your previous article is the point where you end one paragraph with the rally for retailers to take a stand and act upon making a change in the current marketplace. You then begin the next paragraph with that act being one that can only come from distributors and publishers, which is for the two entities to agree to allow for limited returns of product they either manufacture or distribute. Essentially, you don't ask retailers to do anything in this equation other than to request and push for their distributors and publishers to implement a partial return program. I was hoping that there might have been something more concrete that you were building toward, rather than

putting the burden of saving the industry in the hands of everyone but the retailers.
Your entire view of what risks are taken in the process of financing, creating, producing,
marketing, distributing, and retailing comics almost completely ignores the enormous risk
publishers take each and every month. I would be more amenable to pursuing your partial
returnability program if I saw a thriving newsstand/returnable program to compare it to.
The ID market is all but dead, and has been only a vehicle for advertising revenues for those
that can afford the initial expense of overprinting for years.

Most importantly, the more financial risks a publisher has to take, over and above the
already staggering risks that they are expected to incur, will undoubtedly lead to less
risk-taking when it comes to choosing what editorial content the publisher will want to invest
in. Believe me, I know you are a staunch supporter of creators and their rights, and it is my
strong belief that a partial return program will only make it harder for the art form to
continue to grow, and will greatly diminish a creator's ability to see their vision onto the
printed page, unaffected by squeamish financial and editorial decisions made by publishers.

It is hard to rally 4000 independent retailers to do much of anything, and, individually, each retailer has about as much voice and power as a mosquito. The bite is annoying, yes, but no one really pays close attention to it.

Honestly, I would not be happier if any retailer reading these words could go to a publisher or distributor with a plan or proposal, and have that entity say, "you are a valued account whose strength and continued success allows us to exist, so we will closely analyze your proposal, get back to you immediately with the results, and work with you to ensure implementation is amicable to all parties involved." However, that's about as likely to occur as a monkey flying out of my butt.

And even when there *is* clearly wide and broad-based support for a plan, the retailer can do little if anything to implement it. Heck, at the last RRP meeting Paul Levitz said something that could well be paraphrased thusly: "DC comics can not negotiate with any of you; none of you represent enough of a consensus to represent retailers collectively. DC comics can not negotiate with retailers unless and until a clear majority of retailers cede negotiating power to a single arbiter." This is a logical position, with anti-trust laws being what they are, but it is a frustrating one to have to live with.

The reality is that the best any one retailer can do (and I'd agree that this is also essentially true for the non-exclusive publishers as well) is *lobby*. We depend on the good will and kindness of strangers to arrange the cards in a manner not unfavorable to us. Our only other choice is to walk from the table.

The systemic problems of the direct market (not the symptoms, mind – but the underlying structural flaws that ultimately define the market) are absolutely outside of the control of any retailer. I can proclaim loudly how the underpinning economic biases of direct market retailing favor, in numerous ways, consistently shrinking your market; I can rail against a system that does not reward success in any meaningful way and fosters mediocrity and stunt-making; but there is no tangible thing that I, nor any other retailer, can do to change that system. The retailer can influence what gets supported within the system but none of us can change the system itself.

Let's talk about risk, then. Obviously, I'm not a publisher – my understanding of the costs involved is extremely limited – but it seems to me that the biases against growth put upon the retail community can and will only inhibit growth for the publishing community as well. No publisher can sell a product if that product is not available on the racks. I would argue that the largest risk that publishers today face is that the retail community will under-order their wares. All of those expenses in financing, creating, producing, and marketing comics will all go to naught if the retailer does not deign to support them.

The problem for all of us is getting products to market. The retailer has little economic incentive to grow a title – the reward often has no bearing on the effort (if I increase my DC sales by 20% I earn no greater discount; if I sell 20% more Oni Press comics than *that*, I still get a lower discount than I would on DC) – and every incentive to minimize buy-in; initial quantities on most titles for most retailers have dropped so low that there is no margin for error, and the collapse of the back-issue market has cost us our best method for covering our mistakes.

I'm not sure if publishers realize how much month-to-month variation there is in most title's sales – even long-standing regular ones with significant history. Very few books are actually stable – on most, we're either trying to beat the decline curve so we're not losing money on a per-title basis, or we're facing unmet demand because of ordering conservatism and low initial quantities. This is not something that I believe any publisher can perceive from the numbers they have, because each retailer is screwing up on different sets of books, or is at different stages of the ping-pong cycle of over-order/under-order at different times.

This is the world we live in. I don't believe it will spontaneously correct itself. In fact, I think that odds are that the market will continue to constrict and decline.

Is there more risk for the publisher in partial returns? Sure. But I think that what will actually happen is that retailers will feel they can get slightly more liberal in their ordering policies, and that this will pay off in greater dividends for *all* of us. We need to break the lock of ordering conservatism, we need to bring more product to market – and the publishers need this as much, if not more, than the retailers do. I honestly judge (though only having an incomplete understanding of publisher economics) that the reward that partial returns will bring from greater potential rack exposure wildly out-weigh the risks of having those comics come back. Especially for small or mid-size publishers like Oni.

Finally, I don't think that comparing the ID market to any of the variations of partial returns floating about is apt. The ID is a corrupt and inefficient system that is servicing a market that really couldn't care less about comics or what they have to offer. The goal of partial returns is to retain as much as possible from the current direct market, while mitigating waste to the largest degree possible (hence the word "partial"). We want to encourage accurate ordering, but give the retailer some form of a safety net.

Let's hand it back to Bob for a last thought:

No one said that getting anything done was easy. Here's some constructive, pro-active suggestions I would like to make to retailers who would like to work towards creating a more stable and profitable marketplace.

Sell your product line. I don't know of one retailer that actually sells an X-Men, Spider-Man, *or* Spawn *book. As I see it, they order what they know will move, open the case when it arrives, put it out on the rack, and it is bought. If a retailer (Like Brian Hibbs with his* Sandman *success) actually, aggressively, sells his products to his customers there is no reason why every store across the country shouldn't be able to sell 10 copies of any moderate quality comic, or 80 copies of a good one. Watch who's buying what, suggest other similar titles to the person who comes in only looking for* Hate. *Offer a free read that they can return if they don't like it. Give away a back issue that's sitting collecting dust, of a book still hitting the stands, to someone who might jump on board if they only knew it existed.*

If a retailer wants to attract more readers, then stop jacking up the prices of every book that shows any modicum of consumer interest. When new readers hear by the fourth issue of a given series that there is something being published that they may want to read, and then they are faced with the prospect of making an investment of anywhere between $15 to $40.00 just to get on the bus, they will not buy the ticket. Stop scaring away the average citizen. This doesn't happen at B. Dalton, and while they do get to return a percentage of what they order, B. Dalton certainly doesn't get a 50% discount.

It's clear that you don't have an inkling as to the expenses involved in publishing a comic book. Trust me, they are much higher than that incurred by Ballantine or Doubleday for the average paperback. You also suggest that the direct sales market is a supreme state of heavenly bliss, without corruption, populated by people who care. You forget all the now-deceased trading card turned comics shop retailers that our market co-dependented into and out of existence during the insane speculator craze that has helped to put us where we are today. Were they servicing a market they cared about? Were we? Well, some of us were. And some of us still are. Several years ago, then Editor-in-Chief at Marvel, Tom DeFalco, took umbrage at my using the My Lai incident as an example of what the direct sales market did to its loyal customers and unsuspecting speculators. You know what I always say, "If the war-crime fits... wear it."

Meanwhile, your overall proposal seems to allow for even looser margins for retailers to work within, when I believe that this is a time for us all to get leaner and stronger. Cut away the chaff and get on with the tough decisions at hand. As my favorite songwriter, Ian Anderson, once wrote..."Nothing is Easy."

sigh

None of Bob's suggestions are bad ones, but they really ignore the realities of the marketplace experienced by the conscientious retailer. Maybe it isn't clear to the average publisher, but what we perceive as the direct market is actually several different markets crammed on to a single sales sheet. Yes, surely, there are bottom-feeding losers who prey upon the weak or easily swayed – but these retailers do not represent the majority of the volume that moves through the system.

Isn't it just like a publisher (no offense, Bob) to suggest that the reason we can't have "x" is because *some* retailers are screw-ups?

I know this much: there are many (*many!*) retailers who are people of good will. We suggestively sell, we support the medium, we take inordinate risks to bring products to market. We discourage or disallow speculation, we rack the widest selection of material (at cover price) that we humanly can, we're smart and we're savvy, and we run close to the ground.

And yet we still take it in the shorts every month from inconsistent and erratic sell-through on products that should be rock-solid and consistent. And yet we have no real idea how to actually order most new-title launches, or any change in content. And yet we watch as margins get tighter and tighter and tighter until we could probably make more money selling just about any other product than comic books in our store fronts.

The publisher's "solution" is "work harder!" Well, screw you! We're dancing as fast as we can.

There are some 800 comic book available each and every month – even if a retailer only carries a quarter of them, it is *physically impossible* to "support" them all. We can't push, promote and take strong stocking positions on more than a few dozen of them at any one time. It can not be done. At least not on our own.

Speculation was *not* the *cause* of our predicament – speculation was (and is) just a symptom of the problem. And I believe in the deepest part of my heart that had we not had the mid-90s boom and bust we'd've still been having this conversation – it just might have been 2002 rather than 1998.

As I noted at the start, I think the world of Bob, and have great respect for what he says and does, but it's clear that he falls prey to the same trap all publishers do: making the mistake of seeing retailers as an aggregate. Publishers don't have the tools to see the often-drastic proportional change in issue-to-issue sales that individual retailers face day-to-day. They don't see that most of the time we're either selling out way too fast, losing customers long-term because we don't fill their needs; or we're stuck with overages that accumulate quickly and drag down the profitability of even the most accurate orderer. They don't understand that it is a very rare comic that is ordered correctly – filling all reasonable demand, yet having no appreciable overstock. They just don't see that the mistakes that are dragging down the market aren't the *Deathmate*s of the world (though those can sure hurt!), but it is the "Death by a Thousand Papercuts" and the "Suffocation by short-stock Attrition."

I hope this dialogue starts to open the publishers' (and distributor's) minds to these realities, and gives them the will to make the changes that the retail community needs to flourish.

Tilting at Windmills #76
(Originally ran in Comics Retailer #77)

I'm a bit distracted right now; my wife and I have just bought our first house, and are preparing to move in as I type this. Honestly, I should probably just skip this month's column, but I haven't missed one yet, so why start now?

My problem is compounded by not actually having any real good idea for the column this month. I looked at the theme list for this issue, but I just have nothing to say about the Expo other than "it's a good idea to go." But, hey, I need the money, so I'll try to soldier on and see what we come up with. Let's have a beer, first.

(*glug glug*)

Hm, that didn't work.

Man, you cannot even *imagine* how expensive property in San Francisco is! We're paying $350k for a 1300 square-foot house – if I was willing to live almost anywhere else I could get a mansion for that kind of money; but I guess it shows that there *is* money to be made in funny-book selling. Well, O.K., some 80% of my income is going to go to mortgage payments, but in a couple of years it'll work out so I'm way ahead. See, San Francisco has something less than a 1% vacancy rate – the tech-oriented Silicon Valley is but a short drive away, and the rapid explosion of tech has made lots and lots of stock-option millionaires with too much money to spend. They all want to live in The City, so rents have gone through the roof (I saw an estimate that average rent has increased by over *forty* percent in the last year!). Looking at the math, and the political power that landlords wield, I saw that the only rational reaction was to try and build equity. But it's a scary step!

I'm no longer a proletariat anymore, huh? A landowner! Who'd've thunk it? But don't worry, even though I'm now over 30 as you read this (31 on June 15), I'm going to keep my long hair and t-shirts. Some things are better when they don't change.

Would that the rest of the world saw that. Y'all saw *Godzilla*, right? Ow! What a stinker! What the hell was that running-leaping-spinning thing? No Godzilla I know, that's for sure!

Actually, what irks me the most about this was the overships we got from Diamond on those *Godzilla* magazines. Now, look, I think overships can be a valuable tool, but they need to have some basis in rationality. 50% overship, I can understand. 100% is O.K. Maybe even 200%, if your initial quantities are low to non-existent – but we got over *eight-hundred percent* overshipped on the movie magazine at Comix Experience. Good Lord! What are they thinking?!?

(Maybe I should have another beer. *glug glug* Hmph! Still nothing!)

Look, even when we get freight-credited, overships are not "free" – time is money, and time needs to be spent to process and handle these books. We have to count hem in; we have to track them throughout the cycle; we have to store them until they show up as returnable; we have to box them up and ship them back. Hell, we have to *remember* to do so, else we get charged for them – and the information I've received shows that a large number of retailers forget to do so until it is too late.

O.K., maybe this is the retailer's fault, but, damn it, we're busy enough trying to keep our businesses running. We're concentrating on making sure we're getting adequately restocked each month; we're spending hours (if not days) each month writing our orders – tracking returns on products we didn't ask for, and almost certainly don't want is a phenomenal waste of our finite resources.

I ordered three copies of the *Godzilla* movie magazine, and I was being bold by going *that* long. I sure as hell can't sell 25 of them! Who on earth thought it was a good idea to send me that many? I mean, I can't even sell 25 copies of *Batman* any more, and that's one of the best-known comic book properties. Doesn't anyone at Diamond *think*, for even a moment, before taking the money?

To top it off, the real value in overshipping is the follow-through – if you're doing a regular monthly book that you don't believe is being properly supported, and you overship it, there is a reasonable chance that the retail accounts will note the success, and change their orders for the better down the line. Everyone wins in such a circumstance. But on a one-shot? What be learned then? Where can we take that?

Honestly, short-term profits are all well and good (hey, *I'm* going to need them with the new house), but with the market the way it stands (or, actually, kneels), shouldn't we all be putting our efforts to where they will gain long-term benefits?

(Time for another beer. *glug glug* Mm! Tasty!)

Why is it that as an industry we seem unwilling to look past the bridge of our own nose? Fine, so this is somewhat indicative of us as a species, as well – but we deal in heroism, in doing the right thing, in helping others – why can't we even learn from that which we sell?

Look at a company like Top Cow. I mean, it's not bad enough that they'd rather jump into bed with a mail-order company selling exclusive products that the traditional Direct market retailer has no wholesale option to purchase than those same stores which *gave them the ability to make those deals in the first place.* I can deal with betrayal as well as the next man. And it's not bad enough that they take incredibly short-sighted tacks like doing that *Darkness* with eleven different covers (how *was* sell-through on that? Not so hot, I'm led to believe); and it's not even bad enough that they announce "guaranteed" ship dates, miss them, and then do nothing in particular about it – but even *I* can't believe that anyone is so stupid as to do a comic book with variant *interiors*! Good lord!

What? Did Bruce Bristow go get a job in marketing at Top Cow, and not tell us?

Actually, now that I think of it, this *was* done once before – anyone remember *Team Titans* #1? No? I rest my case.

Yes, of course, this will pump the initial sales for *Fathom* #1 (oh, and, naming a book after a character from *Elementals* ain't too bright, either – Comico must be the single most reviled company ever!) much much higher than they would be in any rational world – but is there a single retailer in the world who doesn't foresee dropping orders by 60% or better for #2? (If you don't, you're an idiot.) Moreso, I think the consumer backlash against this stunt will bring even higher percentage drops to this title than traditional.

Why are the big publishers so *stupid*?

(more beer! more beer! more beer! *glug glug*)

Look at our pals over at Marvel. Not only is "Marvel Comics 2" quite possibly the single worst name for a line in the entire history of comics (even those yet to be written!), but c'mon! Look at these books! "A-Next?" "J2?" Can they possibly be *that* bereft of ideas?

In an interview with Tom DeFalco (principal writer on this "line") in the *CBG* a few weeks ago he described the titles as "hoo-hah comics" – he said this phrase at least three times. "Hoo-hah?" This is what they think people want?

Maybe its time that we as an industry no longer allow middle-aged men to try to do comics for "the kids today?" I mean, 90% of the time it is a horrifying and embarrassing mess (ala *Teen Titans* by Dan Jurgens) – can we not stop the insanity?

I'm almost at the end of my word count, so I should wrap this up. Have I ever told you how writing the endings to these columns are the single hardest part of the job? I almost always have a good lead, and the middle writes itself, but wrapping it up on the right tone is a terribly difficult thing. Even harder when there isn't a single topic. I guess if I could summarize this month's bit, it'd be "think first." Distributors, think before you accept product, if the manner with which it will be handled is in the best interests and is salable by your accounts. Publishers, think before you make a marketing decision, to see if you're trading a short-term gain for long-term dissatisfaction.

It's really not that hard.

Tilting at Windmills #77
(Originally ran in Comics Retailer #78)

What's this at the top of my notes pile?

Hm, "Diamond Makes Tuesday Release Available To Qualified Multi-Store Customers."

Wow.

This reminds me of a story, actually. Neil Gaiman once said to me (this was many years ago, back when we were both "breaking in," so to speak), "Brian, you should open a second store. If you don't keep expanding, you begin to be viewed as yesterday's news." That is a paraphrase, of course – the years making things fuzzy – and I certainly wasn't in a position at the time to do so; but I've never thought this line of reasoning was correct.

I made a conscious decision to just have one comic book store. I thought hard about opening a second location, but decided that the logistics involved would mean that I would enjoy it less. I would have to split my attention and would end up with two weaker stores, rather than one thriving venue. Certainly the crash of the market has only reaffirmed that I made the correct decision, at least for me.

And now I am being penalized for that decision.

Let's look at the official press release. Diamond Executive VP and COO Chuck Parker is quoted as saying that Diamond "came to the conclusion that large, multi-store retailers have legitimate business reasons for wanting Tuesday release." Sadly only one of these reasons is delineated. "It takes large chain store operations turning in a single Order Form longer to receive and process their weekly shipments, and without the Tuesday release, they are effectively at a disadvantage to single-store operations, which can more easily have new releases on their shelves when they open on Wednesday."

Now in and of itself, I don't have a huge problem with this. Yes, absolutely, to have to break a shipment into component parts will add some amount of time to the process, and could, potentially, lead to a tactical disadvantage (though in many markets this was completely mitigated by chains having trucks and drivers to get an early-morning pick-up from the central UPS warehouse, while the smaller accounts have to wait around for UPS to show up whenever) – these are facts, and we don't argue with facts around here. However, whether Diamond knows it or not, they've just turned the tables about and given these accounts a definite (not effective) advantage.

To the best of my knowledge, neither Chuck Parker nor any of the other executives at Diamond have any recent (say, in the last decade) comics retail experience. Fair enough – distribution is, I'm sure, a demanding mistress. And so I'm all sure we can forgive them for not knowing how much New Comics Day sucks. Yeah, I can hear every retailer out there nodding their heads vigorously. The rest of you Probably Don't Get It. Let me try to enumerate:

First, there is the Fallibility of Man and the delivery systems he hath wrought. While I no longer use UPS (Lindsey Chu goes out to Bob Borden's warehouse to fetch the drop-ship books for my store and Comics & Da Kind), I shiver in dread the "who has any idea whatsoever when they might arrive?" wait that begun with us camping out at the store at eight am "just in case." Sometimes UPS was merciful and showed up about nine am, but I can vividly recall multiple occasions when they sauntered by at noon, or later (at which point we're frantically trying to get tracking numbers, watching the minutes tick by to find out, "good news! They are reportedly in your city!" You almost never get any more information than that!).

Hell, my buddy Michael Drivas of Big Brain Comics in Minneapolis called me last week with the "Guess who didn't get his comics until five pm?" heartbreak. I remember that. Happened *twice* during our UPS purgatory.

In all defense, UPS was usually *fairly* reliable (at least during January to October) – but I'd lay good odds that there isn't a single Diamond account out there without at least one UPS horror story. Hey, they're human, and that's life, but any plan that doesn't take the Hosing of Retailers by UPS into very close account is not a very good plan at all.

Second, you got a *lot* of things to do and a *very* little amount of time to do them in. When we used to get UPS delivery, we'd average receipt at 9:30 am. The doors open at eleven am. Ninety minutes. In that short span of time, we need to count in and merchandise scores of SKUs; we need to pull subscription copies; we need to deal with overages, shortages, damages, or just plain screw-ups; we need to make sure all special orders are filled; we need to break down and clean-up all the cardboard and paper and general garbage created by shipping; we need to do a billion billion small tasks that are unique to our individual stores (I pull the most interesting comics for display in one of our bays – they have to be bagged and boarded, and the rest of the display has to be rotated). They each only take a few minutes, but when you add them all up you're left with no time to think. We're forced to set new land-speed records every week just so that the whole process doesn't impact upon the customer.

(Of course the absolute worst thing in the whole wide world is having to process that shipment with customers in the store. I recall the period when we were lucky if books arrived at one – and all these people would be standing around, trying to get at the books [even if only with their eyes], asking you questions, etc., while you're frantically trying to *get the job done*! Ugly, ugly situation. I am lucky to no longer be in this club, but I am quite sure that many of the retailer readers of this column still suffer under this yoke. I commiserate with you all.)

Third, (or part of second like above) you then get hit with the customers. Normally this is a good thing, to open the doors and see people standing there, waiting – but on New Comics Day you're a wreck. You've been frantically working for the last umpty-ump, and, realistically, you're probably neither looking your best nor in the most relaxed of moods.

Argh.

I probably haven't adequately conveyed the rollercoaster of agony and ecstasy that is New Comics Day if you haven't lived it yourself. Go tell a blind man what "blue" is and see if you do any better.

The only thing I like about New Comics Day is that I get to be the first person to see the funny-books. Opening a box and seeing a particularly pretty cover is always a special thrill. But it don't make up for the Pain.

I can only imagine, but I would suspect that Tuesday delivery is something like Heaven – you'll have multiple hours to do the job; you'll actually have an opportunity to be aware of the *content* of the comics *before* you have to sell them to someone! Oh! Rapture! And you'll be able to come in fresh and relaxed the next morning before the customers start to arrive. Oh! Joy!

But my brothers, my sisters, they have barred the door to Heaven to you and I. Heaven is a fine concept when no one lives there, but to be shown those fields, then be told you may not enter? The most unspeakable pain!

An emotional subject to be sure, but let us look at it logically. What we once had was an imperfect system where in *some* cases multi-store operations *could* be at a disadvantage in bringing books to market on Wednesday morning. Note the "some" and the "could" – clearly this "problem" only effected a very small number of operations who did business in a very specific way. Moreover, I would think there were already a couple of advantages to processing in this manner (reduced shipping charges, for one) that, overall, would offset being slightly slower than single-stores in bringing books to market (else why have these stores been doing it this way prior to Tuesday delivery being official?).

Now, however, we have an imperfect system where in *virtually all* cases multi-store operations *will* have a significant advantage over their single-store brethren. Multi-store employees now have the opportunity to be educated about what they're selling, before they sell it; they have the ability to be relaxed and rested when facing the Wednesday morning crowd; they will have the time to ensure 100% accuracy in filling subscription orders rather than the 99.5% we get when we rush through the job because the customers are about to arrive. They are virtually *guaranteed* of *always* having new comics up at eleven am (or ten am, or whatever) – even if the driver gets in an accident, you'll still have plenty of time to absorb that delay. They will be able to intelligently merchandise their stores because they will be able to know what the content of their wares are. And, though they are limited to eleven am to call in damages and reorders, they stand a better chance of placing more accurate reorders, again because of greater familiarity with the product.

I don't know enough about it, but I thought I had been told that anti-trust laws prohibited preferential treatment by volume. In any case, this is plainly not fair to those of us who are honest, who are ethical, and who have been asking for this for some time. Single-store owners now have a significant disadvantage until this policy changes.

Pandora, thy name is Diamond.

Tilting at Windmills #78
(Originally ran in Comics Retailer #79)

I hate five-week months.

I hate how irresponsible most publishers are.

I hate the week before any major convention.

There are times I think, "If I didn't just love the product so damn much, I should just ditch this all. It's too much of a headache."

Why is it so few publishers can balance their schedules so they make sense?

Why is it shipments are either feast or famine?

Take the week of 7/29 for example. The dreaded fifth week black hole. Yuck. Tangent II. Maybe another 20-30 comics. That's it. My invoice was something like $1800. Puny. Pathetic.

Then we have this week (by my timeframe) – the week of 8/5. *Everything* shipped. You name it, it shipped. My invoice was nearly $4000. Massively, frighteningly insane.

Do any of you publishers have any idea how *badly* this screws the working retailer?

How can we work under these kinds of conditions?

I mean, I was looking forward to selling the *Red Rocket 7* collection. The *Cages* HC. The *Squee* TPB. The new *Hellboy* collection. Milo Manara's *Click 3*. The *Strangehaven* TPB. The Toth *Zorro* book.

But I can't sell them all in one week.

Can't.

None of my customers have that much money.

This doesn't even count all the actual floppy-books that shipped. *Superman for all Seasons #2*. That shiny cover *Uncanny X-Men*. *The Dome*. *Guns of the Dragon*. *Martian Manhunter #0*. *Bone*. *Starman*. *Preacher*. Screw me, David Lapham makes us wait nearly a year for the next *Stray Bullets*, and, *of course*, it has to ship this week.

It's too much.

We can't handle it.

The customers can't handle it.

Thank God I have long hair, so you can't really notice as it falls out in chunks.

Look at all the titles that came this week that were supposed to ship in July. Look at all the ones that were supposed to ship in June, for God's sake. Hell, there are a dozen *May*-scheduled books!

What the hell is wrong with you people?

We retailers don't have the resources to absorb all this. We don't have the manpower to sell all this. *We can't do it!*

That first week of the month, I always get so sick and frustrated and tired of it all – every publisher that is running late sneaks their books in right under the returnable wire. Squeak!

But who pays the cost?

Not the publisher, surely. They hit their "deadline." They have no penalty. No price to pay.

Not Diamond. Diamond has no responsibility in these cases – they just ship us the books as they come in.

Yeah, it's us, the retailers, out there on the front lines. We have to take the cash flow hit, the pain, the frustration.

You all suck. Every one of you damn publishers.

Look at Kitchen Sink. Don't ship us a thing for weeks, then suddenly we get three cool trades in a single batch. How are we supposed to react to this?

Look at DC. We get a crap week like Tangent II, which we can hardly *give* away, then we get hit with nearly every "good" comic they ship, at once.

Look at Marvel. Thin, thin weeks, then three "Heroes Return" books, added to a virtual onslaught of X-titles.

Figure it out!

We can't function like this.

And you wonder why the market is getting soft. Hah! *You* kill our confidence, *you* shatter our strength, every week; every day, nearly.

I need a vacation.

But the treadmill never stops running, does it?

You know, if I hit the emotional crisis point, I dread to think of those without the burning passion; without the need.

Next week, by my time frame, is San Diego. Maybe there I can rekindle a bit of hope, reattach myself to the dream.

But you make it all so hard.

I dunno, maybe you don't see it, but all we want is you to keep your promises, to show us a little sanity in an insane world.

If you say "my book will ship in June" then you bloody well better ship it in June. There is no more time for excuses, for second chances, for foolish stupidity.

We ran out of time quite long ago.

Do what you say you're going to do. When you say you're going to do it. Act professionally.

How can you expect us to do the same, if we can't get this one little thing from you?

We're on the front lines, bleeding and shattered and trying so desperately hard to make this all work.

And you screw us again and again and again.

I know, really I do, that you're not doing it on purpose – but we can't "win" this fight when you "sabotage" us again and again.

If you expect us to be "professional," then you have to be *ne plus ultra* Professional yourself.

For all of our sakes.

"We are the music makers, and we are the dreamers of the dream."
– Willy Wonka

Tilting at Windmills #79
(Originally ran in Comics Retailer #80)

Another year, another San Diego.

This year, thanks to the new mortgage, I couldn't really afford to go down for very long, so I settled for just the second day of the Expo and the first day of the Con itself.

I don't think it's any secret that I'm not a huge fan of the city of San Diego – it is flat, and it is horribly horribly hot in August. Me? I still wish that WonderCon up in the Bay Area and San Diego would swap calendar positions. Make San Diego the *first* con of the season, and WonderCon the *last*, and then we'd be having some fun – August in the Bay Area is wonderfully pleasant, and I suspect that April in San Diego is much nicer weather.

Anyway, this year Pro/Con came under the auspices of San Diego, and was run parallel with the retailer Expo. A mistake, I feel. The talent and the retailer base should be joined, not separated – it splits attention at a stage where we can ill afford it. In addition, it made the crowd at the Expo look much thinner than usual, to this spectator.

At the very least, there should be more structured cross-over between the two groups. During my day at the Expo there was a unified luncheon with planned "topics of conversation," but they were almost all broken into exclusively talent-oriented, and retailer-oriented topics. About the only crossover that I witnessed was during Punchline Live in the evening (more on that a bit below).

In any event, I would say that a cautious optimism ruled the floor. Most of the attending retailers seemed to be saying that business was at very least stable, and, in most cases, improving. This matches my own experiences quite nicely, though, of course, the retailers attending the Expo are a self-selecting lot. Those that attend are the ones, for the most part, with the spare cash to do so. And so, with greater success.

However, even cautious optimism didn't erase the perception that we still face a lot of problems in our industry – just a sense that many of us are rolling up our sleeves in our individual markets and trying to do what little we are able with limited tools and resources. This is, perhaps, the soundest course – we need to shore up our individual beachheads before we focus on solving the national problems.

I also went to one day of the convention itself. Well, sorta. Maybe it's just because I've been doing this for far far too long, but conventions (even ones as monstrously huge and well put together as San Diego) just don't hold my interest anymore. I mean, its not like I need to buy any comic books, and the possibility of meeting an Adam West or Richard Hatch lost any thrill it might have once had once I got out of my 20s! For me, the only real value of cons is the social aspect, and that really means just one thing – nighttime!

See, during the day, most people are either working or shopping. Fair enough – that's what the con is for. But, as I have long since vowed to never work another con again, and shopping holds no interest for me whatsoever, so then the daytime portions of a convention are of little pleasure.

I found myself, after lunch, at wits end with nothing of substance to do – my business had long been accomplished. My flight was scheduled to leave at like nine pm, which meant I would not *really* have any night time with which to play, so at three pm, I said "screw it" and hopped off to the airport for the next available flight home (about fifteen minutes later).

This is related to what I was saying a few paragraphs before about tending to our own gardens – unless you're buying or selling, a convention itself is a luxury we can ill afford at this moment. I am doing far more for the "industry" by being home in San Francisco than I can ever accomplish at a convention. Expos, trade shows, business gatherings – these are a different beast altogether, and well worth the effort and expense to attend. But conventions are geared towards consumers, and so, have little relevance to the day-to-day functioning of our businesses.

In fact, sometimes such things can actually undermine our businesses.

Punchline Live was a reasonable enough affair – in trying to discuss how retailers and talent can work together, I suspect a few eyes were opened to the practicalities of our industry. But the most thought-provoking comment spoken was from Bill Liebowitz, owner of the Golden Apple chain in the Los Angeles environs.

Bill's position was that the direct selling of wares from talent/publishers to consumers was demonstrably harmful to the retail community. Certainly this is a very common practice with two "justifications." First, given that the publisher or creator *is* in fact selling goods implies, to some degree or another, that retailers are not doing a "good enough" job of selling same. Second, running a table at a convention is a pretty expensive proposition – it is reasonable to allow people a chance to make their investment back in a direct fashion.

For much of the convention trade, this is all well and fine, and I choose to look upon any "loss of sales" that I may receive as a sign that I have to tend my own garden better. But the place where I squarely agree with Bill is on the newest product.

Let me give you a "for example": Graphitti Designs has a bitchin' keen line of toys. The Big Blast line. Madman, Grendel, Mage, and the Jay & Silent Bob figures. They're cool. Very cool. Hell, *I* want a set of them!

As I write this, it is September 9th, and they're supposed to arrive in shops tomorrow – but in the second week of August (and earlier still at Chicago, I am told) Graphitti was selling these figures direct at the convention. Briskly too, so I hear.

About 20 or 30 of my customers made the trip down to San Diego this year. In all odds, the majority of those who did are prime customers for these awesome toys. Knowing human nature, I think it is safe to say that some percentage of them did, in fact, "give in" and purchase them at the con. This could be $30-60 out of my pocket every time one of my customers chose to do so.

Or maybe it came out of *your* pocket.

I don't really blame Graphitti – they were understandably excited about what they had wrought, and they paid through the nose to get them freighted to the convention in time, meaning their gross profit margin was possibly not much higher.

But they took money out of my pocket.

I don't like that.

I *really* don't like that.

And I can't afford it, either.

I agree with Bill that when the retailer makes a commitment on a product, it is irresponsible for the manufacturer to take any action that might minimize the retailer's sales. I don't have a huge problem, for example, with mail order sales – in the majority of those cases, if one of my customers goes that route it is because *I* dropped the ball – in fact, more than once I have encouraged customers to take that route because I knew I would have problems securing a specific item.

But when something is available to my customers *before* I have a chance to offer it to them...well, it really chaps my hide.

I know that toys, being produced outside of the United States, have a different set of timings than comic books, but I have no doubt that, if one looked, it would not be difficult to find twenty or thirty comics in San Diego that one would *not* be able to find in a comic book shop that same weekend. Maybe way more.

If a manufacturer cannot ship a product so that it is available for national sales at the same time as it appears at a convention, why should I allocate my limited resources to supporting that publisher?

What makes me sad some days is the thought that there are so few that do it "right." I started flipping through *Previews* looking for "good" publishers. For the purposes of this discussion, I define this as shipping product on time, keeping product in print and accessible and at a good price. To not undercutting retailers, and to admitting to mistakes, and correcting them. To producing monthly comics, and by living up to their responsibilities so that retailers *know* they can depend on them. Then I called another few retailers to get their opinions too.

And we were only able to come up with four.

Four.

Aardvark-Vanaheim, Abstract, Archie, and DC.

And we wonder why things are in the state they are?

Look, just tend your own backyard. If we all do that much, if we all do what we're supposed to, if we all keep our promises, if we all try support one another, and don't do anything that might harm one another – well, this could be a wondrous and prosperous business.

As it should be.

And for God's sake, people, don't rob Peter to pay Paul – think about what the ramifications of your decisions will be before you act upon them. And we'll all gain.

Tilting at Windmills #80
(Originally ran in Comics Retailer #81)

Well, it sure was...interesting...news that DC bought WildStorm.

I mean, tell me that you saw *that* one coming. I know *I* sure didn't, and I'm pretty good with predicting these kinds of machinations!

So, what are some of the possible ramifications?

Well, the obvious place to start is that DC is now number one. For the better part of a year, I guess, DC has taken the number one spot from Marvel several times, but it is usually by a small enough margin that it is hard to definitively say who is "winning" – further, Marvel tended to "bounce back" in alternating months to "reclaim" the top spot. That is likely over now. Unless there is some sort of odd backlash (which I doubt – if *anything*, DC's stability should help WildStorm's market share grow), DC will have a clear 2-5% lead over Marvel.

I have to admit some mixed feelings over this. Being number two – well, it causes one to try a bit harder, more often than not. Though I think them to be people of good will, I do also think that "always being the bridesmaid" strongly encouraged DC to take a number of chances that they might not have otherwise; and a small part of me feels that taking the clear lead could yield a certain amount of complacency on DC's behalf. I hope I am wrong, of course, and, if I am right, I suspect we won't see its impact for another year or two, but it is a worry to hold nonetheless.

By the same token, I fear philosophical shifts within DC may loosen some of their moral stances on "collectible" comic publishing. By this I mean that DC has largely avoided doing "chase" covers on their titles – I, in fact, can't think of even one right now. On the rare occasions that DC *does* do multiple covers, it is either the newsstand/direct market kind of split (with each being separately orderable items), or straight 50/50 percentages (like with *Green Lantern* #100).

WildStorm, on the other hand, has produced many many comics with, say, 80/20 splits, or percentages to that effect. Making one cover a de facto "collectible" that completists have to hunt for.

Now the open question will be *who* is actually marketing the books under the new world order? If it is DC, I would expect this practice to cease fairly quickly, but if WildStorm continues to control such policies and continues along the same road, I can easily see some rifts starting to form. What happens when, given the same marketing elements (catalog placement, etc.), a "chase-cover" WildStorm book gets significantly stronger orders than its nearest DC "equivalent?" Will there not be forces within DC that will push the company toward adding such tricks to their own line? I fear the answer to that is "yes."

And I dread that.

The market is just beginning to recover – most individual books are still dropping in sales month-to-month, but the *overall size* of the marketplace has, indeed, begun to stabilize, and, in some cases, grow. But until we get a *lot* stronger, and a *lot* more stable, we need to continue to focus on growing our readership – and we do *not* do that by "collectible" trickery.

So, Jim, Paul, if you're listening – let's just make good comic books. One cover is more than enough for any comic book.

Another big question is: what happens to Image?

Image is, financially, an interesting beast. I think I have this clear, but forgive me if I mess up some of the details in my imperfect understanding. If I have this right, "Image Central" does all the dealing with printers, distribution, etc. An individual studio like WildStorm or Top Cow does not deal directly with Diamond or Quebecor, but routes it all through the central offices. That office, however, has no individual control over the component studios. If, say, Erik Larsen wanted to print his comics on individually-wrapped slices of American cheese, the central office can't tell him "no" – but will be responsible for lining up the dairy farms, and the plastic manufacturers, and dealing with distribution. All of the hassles, and few of the perks of being a "publisher."

Image Central *does* work as a "traditional" publisher in some cases – *Mage* might be a good one. If Matt Wagner wanted to print *Mage* on cheese, I believe central could say, "no thanks, not interested in publishing that," and walk away, unlike a dictate from a partner.

The funding of all of this seems to work by some combination of straight per-title fees, and, quite possibly from the partner's studios, a percentage of some sort. Jim Lee was quoted on the Mania web site that, "I think last year,

[WildStorm] put in something like $360,000 to the central Image office as part of our publishing fees."

So, what does the loss of $360,000 mean to the central Image office? That's $30k a month. That's a lot of money. Will central Image be able to keep all their current staff? Will they continue to publish as many titles? To take as many chances? Will the component studios have to kick in a little more to keep operations running?

Another area of concern is that of deal-making. Now, we can assume that both Quebecor and Diamond have a vested interest at this point in keeping Image alive and strong, but WildStorm accounted for somewhere between 20 to 40% of Image's volume. When contract negotiations come up for print costs, or distribution fees, will a smaller Image still be as competitive?

What of discount structures to retailers? One of the great strengths Image has is the studio system – I do extraordinarily well with the Homage books, and so that got me a good discount the entirety of Image's output. But Homage will no longer be part of Image. You may be doing "disproportionately" well with Cliffhanger!, same thing. Image will have to be extremely careful in ensuring that the majority of retailers can at least maintain current discount under the new reality. This is a problem for DC, as well, but it is mitigated to a degree because they are adding volume, rather than subtracting.

It is not inconceivable that all of this could lead directly to a cover price hike for Image titles. Maybe not for a few months yet, but I suspect one will be coming fairly fast as they try to juggle the financial permutations WildStorm's departure brings.

Whichever way it turns out for the publishers, it is clear to me that in all likelihood some percentage of retailers will find their costs of doing business increased. With any luck DC and Image will maintain our current discounts at least through the dead first-quarter – adding expenses in Jan.-Mar. is not something that would be beneficial to the retail marketplace.

One thing I would boldly suggest to Image is that it may be time for them to do away with line-based volume-discounts, and move to title-based. Base of 45%, ten or more copies gets you 50%, 25 or more gets you 55%, something like that, with the numbers tweaked correctly. The idea is that rather than penalize retailers for the "loss" of WildStorm, they should be rewarded for the support that they *do* show.

The one big positive that should come out of this is DC's management of WildStorm's backlist – backlist is one area where DC has no real competition in terms of keeping material in-print and available. Now if only backlist volume had some bearing on discount...

1999 will be an interesting year as we try to adjust to the financial ramifications this move brings (we'll also have a lot of fun as Marvel adjusts to its new ownership, and vice versa) – I just hope that nothing forestalls the slowly recovering market. As we go into the new year, and the last of the nineteen-hundreds (not the end of the 20th Century, though – that's 12/31/2000 [Hi, Maggie!]), keep a close eye on the cash flow and reorder aggressively and we'll all turn the market around.

a   r   t   i   c   l   e

8 1

Tilting at Windmills #81
(Originally ran in Comics Retailer #82)

Some days you just can't get rid of a bomb.

I mean, here we are all still trying to figure out the ramifications of the DC/WildStorm deal (looks like I won't take any discount loss on the DC side), when the next hot potato is dropped into our lap: Steve Geppi's purchase of a controlling interest of American Entertainment (or AnotherUniverse.com, if you prefer — which I don't. I'm going to use "AE" throughout the body of this article).

le sigh

Hrm, I think I better add some disclaimers here. "The contents of this column are solely the opinion of Brian Hibbs, and are not the opinions of *Comics Retailer*, Krause Publications, or anyone officially affiliated with either, in any way, shape, or form. *Tilting at Windmills* is an opinion column, so if you're going to be enough of a baby to actually get upset at any of this, go knock on Hibbs' door and leave John Miller out of it. Hibbs turns in his columns late enough that it's not like J.J. has any time to ask for a rewrite anyway, so just buck up and deal with it."

All right?

OK, let's see now: I think American Entertainment epitomizes just about everything that is wrong with comics retailing. AE has been one of the most flagrantly whorish businesses in comics history and specializes in marketing overpriced, manufactured collectibles with no inherent value to the segment of the market that doesn't even have the basic awareness to understand they are being taken for a ride. AE has raised PT Barnum's "A sucker is born every minute," fleecing the new and unknowledgable, to a (perfect legal, but morally reprehensible) art form. AE insanely inflates the costs of any project with even the barest hint of pop-culture cachet, then aims it squarely at those we can afford to cheat the least — the "civilians." AE's enormous buying power often deflects and undermines the aesthetic underpinnings of our market, reinforcing the (utterly wrongheaded) idea that selling the *same* product to our customers *twice* (or more!) — in the form of "variant covers" — is a "good" idea. AE robs Peter to pay Paul, and their success at the blatant manipulation of the collector's weakness has trickled down so that *most* publishers and manufacturers salivate at the prospect of doing the same.

In short, they make me physically ill.

See, I still want to be selling funnybooks in another decade. It's something I quite enjoy doing. I love the art form, and I love the content (well, the good ones at least), and I know, after a decade in this business already, that the best way to prosper is to give value for the dollar, and to promote reading over all else.

With only having his company's actions to judge by (I've spoken to AE founder Steve Milo for maybe 10 minutes total in my life), I think it is reasonably safe to say that Steve Milo is the anti-Hibbs, or at least that AE is the anti-Comix Experience.

And for those of you who still aren't convinced that aesthetics are more important than raw commerce (though the former invariably leads *to* the latter), might I observe which of us needed a financial bailout, and which didn't?

I mean, here we have a company with the muscle and clout to reach umpty-million readers in *TV Guide*. Now I surely don't expect that when you're reaching umpty-million readers you're going to promote *Sandman*, or *Transmetropolitan*, or *Eightball* — obviously, you need to lead with *X-Files* or *Xena*, or some other pop-culture project that the audience is familiar with. I've no problem with that.

What I *do* have a problem with is appending the words "Hot" or "red hot!" or "extremely limited" or whatever to each and every listing, and adding 1/3 or better to the price of every comic in doing so. What I have a *huge* problem with is presenting the *value* of comic books as being more important than the *content*.

Especially when you're reaching out to umpty-million readers.

Did I tell you they make me sick? To the core of my soul?

Well, ha-ha, it *didn't* work. And it will *never* work on that kind of a scale, because the civilians simply don't care about comics. And why is that? Because we've spent several decades *telling* them the content of comics is a secondary concern at best. A strategy based upon selling a ware on a presumed commercial after-market only functions if there *is* an after-market to sell them on.

Remember when QVC got *really* into comics for like a year? Hawking signed or "limited" or "collectible" comics to the gullible over the boob tube? And you remember that flood of faces that strolled in after that, clutching their "hot" comics in their hand — "I bought this last week on TV for $20, how much is it worth today?!?!" "Um, fifty cents?"

QVC stopped doing big comic pushes after that.

There *is*, indeed, a sucker born every minute — but even the most moronic fool seldom gets burned the same way twice.

If you take a few steps back from our market and look it from the outside, only the most willful of idiots can't see that the strategies we collectively have focused on throughout the years are doomed to eat us up like a cancer. We expand lines and products past the ability for consumers to keep up (this includes multiple covers and the like) and we preach collectibility like it is somehow inherent in 32 comics-format pages and a few staples. And, certainly, the last few years have shown that we're reaping what we did sow.

And AE was the biggest sower we ever did have.

So, if you ask me if I was at all surprised that AE would need a bailout eventually, I will only chuckle softly, and say, "No."

A business based upon selling air will always eventually blow away.

But if you asked me if I anticipated the owner of the sole national full-line distributor being the one to bail out the single-largest account....

Well, I mean, I guess it sorta makes sense, but I sure didn't expect that.

I'm sure Steve Geppi thinks he was doing right by the industry, much like when Diamond bought Capital — this way, I suspect he believes, the business can continue if only to pay off its bills, then everybody will go home happy.

Except...

...this was the lesson that people should have had to pay for.

Maybe it's just me, but I think if you do something fully legal but morally questionable, and your "partner" goes bust, then you deserve to get spanked. Maybe it's just me, but I think if you were running to do deals that are clearly harmful to the long-term health of this business, just to line your pockets with some cash, then maybe you need to take the cash hit when it all goes south. Call it karmic justice?

I think if you jumped to get in bed with AE, and it turns out the tryst is in a seedy tenderloin hotel, maybe you deserve to find your wallet missing the next morning.

Beyond all that, I simply don't trust it when the man who owns the only national full-line distributor also owns the single largest retail entity.

It's not that I expect anything less than a scrupulous attempt to keep the two businesses separate. Steve Geppi has certainly given me no direct evidence that he would use this to a manipulative advantage, but the potentials for wrongdoing are enormous.

Realistically, how could any of us ever know if the Geppi-owned AE is getting sweetheart deals, or special privileges? We're left to rely on some nebulous threat of the Justice Department to make sure, and faith that Geppi won't give in to temptation.

From a morale standpoint, this is a knife in the back of the retailer. Was there a retailer among us who didn't think when they heard the news, "Great, now Diamond owns AE?" I understand and believe that the two businesses will be run separately, but as long as Geppi continues to own AE, our faith in Diamond will continue to erode.

Because we have no assurances but words.

And as much as the optimist in me hates to say it, the cynic in me says "Historically, words are worth the paper they are written on."

If Geppi doesn't want 1999 to be "The Year We Lost Faith," then he needs to vocally and publicly announce his intention to divest himself of AE once it is running profitably again, and give us a clear timetable for such, and frequent updates, or none of us will be able to trust again.

Sorry, Steve, but I'll *never* trust it when the man who controls the flow of product to my store also controls my single largest "competitor." Even if you do *everything* right from here to 2050, I'll never ever ever trust that. And you desperately need the retailer's trust.

The upbeat sidebar:

In keeping with this issue's theme of "Things we give thanks to," let me single out my favorite individual working in the business of comics today (well, apart from my godlike and wondrous staff who keep me sane and honest) — my Diamond Account Rep Scott Johnson.

Scott has the unenviable joy of working with me on a near-daily basis. And yet he has not snapped like a dry twig.

That alone would mark the man a God, but he tops even that accomplishment by solving every problem swiftly and efficiently, knowing the product and Diamond's arcane policies inside and out, and never being less than ebullient when dealing with my concerns.

If there is *one* job in comics that would cause me to go to the top of a tower and start picking people off one-by-one-by-one, it would be customer service at Diamond. And he does it with such charm. Hrm, maybe I need to send him a case of Guinness.

If I wore a hat, I'd doff it for Scott. He's the reason dealing with Diamond *doesn't* send me off to the top of a tower picking people off one-by-one-by-one. And you can't ask for a better reason for praise than that....

Tilting at Windmills #84
(Originally ran in Comics Retailer #85)

It has gotten out of hand.

It has reached ludicrous proportions.

Haven't we learned a thing yet?

No, I guess not – we never learn a thing, do we? This entire industry is like a big, stubborn, old mule – need to whack it upside the head with a two-by-four to get its attention; and even then, you've got to hit it twice.

Well, here is your two-by-four, friends. Head, meet wood; wood, head.

Enough with the @#!$ variants!

Enough!!!

Do you know how bad it has gotten? You hadn't really noticed, I bet. Well, old Uncle Brian did. Brian knows how to count. Brian went through Previews and counted. And you know what?

For every five comic books on the marketplace, there is one variant.

Multiple covers. Nude editions. Leather editions. Autographed versions.

"Exclusive" editions. "Gold foil." "Bikini chrome." "Platinum editions." "Commemorative editions." The list goes on and on (and on and on and on and on…).

Say it again, this time slowly, O mighty Mule – For. Every. Five. Comics. There. Is. One. Variant.

It was cute at one time – charming, even. A novelty, a bit of fun. But we (as always, as always) took it a few steps too far. Entire companies have been set-up to deliver nothing but variants to us. Programs like Marvel's "Two for #2" (or whatever the hell they call it) have been established to institutionalize variants. Some smaller companies produce *more* variants then the original comics themselves (ABC Studios, anyone?).

We've gone over the top.

Again.

It was easy (-ish) to ignore it at one point – at Comix Experience we just didn't order them. Two covers? Pick the nicer looking one. Multiple editions? Well, just pick a pitch, and swing. *We're* not playing those reindeer games.

But you (The collective you)? You're a moron. Sorry, must be said. You embraced it. You welcomed it. You *rewarded* it.

And so they gave us more.

Darkness #11 with 11 covers? Highest-ordered comic of 1997. *Fathom* #1 with variant (@#$!) interiors? Highest-ordered comic of 1998. *Each* and *every* time they do the variants you bite down hard.

And so they gave us more.

And more. And more.

Until for every five comics there is one variant.

"And as ye reap, so shall ye sow."

Like I said, I could tune it out for awhile. Pick a pitch and swing. Just order one version. Ignore it, maybe it will go away. Heck, I get to laugh while you *idiots* foolishly order far more comics than you can sell – "Maybe this time they'll learn," I thought. "Maybe this time, they'll see."

Ha.

This is what I get for being an optimist.

Most of you fools who over-ordered those eleven versions of *Darkness* #11 *still* have copies left. *Fathom* #1? Easy to find. *Slingers* #1? Har!

But you sent them the wrong message. Told them the wrong things. Even though, if you took the smallest step away from it, even *your* tiny, vestigial brain could see you were just repeating the *same* mistake that caused the market to crash in the first place.

But, no – you supported it.

And now it is institutionalized.

And we get what you called for. What you begged for.

Yeah, I sure thought it was dead brilliant when the solicitation copy in the February *Previews* for *Mage* said "*Mage* will return next month with variant covers *and other retailer-friendly* incentives."

Talk about not getting it.

But, what else could they possibly infer? They do a variant, and like a lemming, you rush straight towards the cliff, even though you are about to die.

"Retailer-friendly?"

Two words, friends: Yer. Arse.

Variants create more work. Variants throw off our careful cycle sheets. Variants create "burps" in normal sell-through patterns. Variants often create multiple SKUs for the same product, even though the *majority* of the customers just want a single cover. Variants create more work for the same money – even if it as simple as trying to keep track of them all once they come off the shelf, and go into the bins.

Variants are about as "retailer-friendly" to a comic book store as open flame, or a burst water pipe.

You want "retailer-friendly?" How about a better margin? How about free shipping? How about targeted overships? How about outside media support...?

Or how about just getting your damn comic out on time, eh?

Surely this ain't too much to ask?

Dang, it's not like I am the only retailer in America. You want to do what you perceive to be what we ask for? Power to you. (Though let me remind you that just because someone *wants* something don't mean they should get it — ask a small child if he would rather have spinach or chocolate pudding for dinner, and I think the answer would be clear...but as a parent, do you think pudding is an appropriate dinner for a child?). But don't you *dare* try to convince me you're doing us a *favor*.

Because you're not – you're doing it to pad *your* bottom line. And to claim otherwise isn't just distasteful – it is downright insulting.

As much as that was a punch in the face, the *trigger* for this column came from the January *Previews*.

Page 234.

Dynamic Forces.

Now, mind – I got nothing *against* DF. Actually, in a few ways, their brilliance of subcontracting out variants and signed editions was a good thing for *this* retailer. Didn't clog up the main publisher listings with a bunch of stuff I will never ever ever ever order in a million billion years. Could red-line an entire section of *Previews* without looking back. Excellent.

And this is America – land of the entrepreneur. They saw an opening, and they went out and tried to fill it. Doesn't matter much if *I* think that anyone who would pay five-to-ten times cover-price of a comic book for the signature of some wheezing hack (come now, is Ron Marz's autograph worth $10 to *anyone* he's not writing a check to?) is a rampaging idiot who should be removed from the gene pool – they saw themselves a niche, and they built a business around it.

Power to them.

But they crossed a line with the *"Danger Girl Special Dynamic Forces Exclusive Premiere #1"*.

Actually, let's talk about *Danger Girl* for a second.

I like it.

A good comic.

Lots of fun. "As close to an action movie on paper as can be done." I think J. Scott Campbell is a pretty talented artist, and he's created something which should serve him in stead for many years to come.

But.

It took two months after #1 for #2 to arrive. Fine. Is bi-monthly. Then it took three months for #3. Then four for #4. Let's hope this is a pattern that will be broken, quick, because waiting five months for #5 and six for #6 will kill this book so dead....

And throughout all this, *Wizard* is reporting that Campbell has negotiated for movie deals and video game deals and toy deals and whatever.

Only thing missing is the *reason* anyone wanted this in the first place – the comic book.

Seen it before, will see it again – prime example of "those who ignore history are doomed to repeat it."

But, y'know, rather than trying to keep his commitments on his regular comic, rather than trying to get his damn book out on time, Campbell would rather go and try to do yet another "special."

Even this I can understand – a line expansion probably can't hurt in getting your title in front of as many people as possible.

But then he made the tactical error.

Rather than the special being available from his publisher, WildStorm, at full and regular discounts, Campbell decides to run it through DF.

At a (wait for it) 35% discount.

With a (wait for it) $6.95 cover price.

I believe my response was very very very loud.

And rhymed with "Clucking Runts."

We'll even ignore the fact there is a $15 version, and a $30 version. (For what? I mean, based on solicitation copy, they *could* deliver us twelve pages of comic book, and there isn't a thing any of us could say.)

That's it. We're done. Stick a fork in it. Don't worry, I'll catch the lights and set the chairs up on the tables after y'all are gone, but it's all over now.

Because you're going to buy into it. And large. History shows us that. And, while most publishers will be able to resist; while most creators will avoid the temptation – enough of them won't. Another project like this will appear, then another, and another, and another.

$6.95, 35% off, no data in solicitation copy other than "Exclusive!" "Danger Girl!" "Art Adams!"

10k minimum – maybe a *lot* more. And someone will do the math and go, "Blimey! *I* want a piece of that gravy train." and the floodgates will open.

Let me tell you something – just because something can be done, doesn't mean it should be. Just because money can be made, doesn't mean a path is proper.

I'm sure I said it once: I live for the day when this column is superfluous. When there aren't wrongs that need to be righted; aren't fouls that need to be called; when Justice and Honor are the watchwords of every single one of us — *especially* those of us with the clout to make a substantive difference.

I've also made it a goal to reach one hundred columns. But with behavior like this; with foolish movements like these...I fear I will be writing this column for decades to come. I'll never ever be free.

Clucking runts.

Tilting at Windmills #85
(Originally ran in Comics Retailer #86)

Another year, another DC RRP meeting.

1999 brought us to Baltimore which is, sorry to say, a real running sore of a town – well, maybe that isn't precisely fair. Its not like we really got out of the three-block radius that the hotel was in – but then, I couldn't find any real compelling reason to do so either. All that I was able to see from the hotel window was another grey East Coast city like all other grey East Coast cities.

Maybe I'm just cranky because I'm sick today. Everyone and his brother got the plague this season, but I somehow managed to avoid it – but stick me for four days in recycled air, and I just wasn't able to dodge it. The last leg of the flight home was on one of those little teeny jets with like 20 rows, and when the pressure changed as we came in for a landing in was like my head was strapped into a vise, crushing my skull. I lost half of the hearing in my left ear, and am going to have to go to an ear, nose and throat doctor to become normal again – it just won't un-pop. I'm also sneezing up a storm, and I hate that, and so I hate you.

Right, anyway – RRP. I always forget what the initials stand for. Not like it matters, precisely – but its something along the lines of Retailer Representative Program. Regardless, DC, once a year, brings a cross-section of stores to a common place, and we hang about for three or four days, listening to their editorial presentation for the next year, as well as (this is the important bit) discussing the "Big Issues" of the day, with the intent of figuring out ways to make them better. Sometimes this stuff is eminently visible to non-RRP stores (like last year's *Transmetropolitan* overship), but most times we serve invisibly – getting formats or price points changed *before* the products start shipping; or showing strong support for something and getting it on the schedule in the first place. *Crisis*, I believe, was finally reprinted (putting aside the fact that it sorta became a fiasco), in large part, due to the lobbying of retailers at the RRP meetings.

The thing you have to understand (and is much harder to explain than I like) is that these meetings are truly give and take – and that DC management is utterly candid and frank with us and has no problem whatsoever walking us through their policies and plans. This is *not* like the traveling dog and pony shows you get at "regional workshops" or at a convention – this is a true meeting of the minds between those who make decisions and those who their decisions affect. Small example: One of the discussion topics this year was (I paraphrase) "Who the heck is *Watchmen* selling to?" See, *Watchmen* keeps selling and selling and selling, yet the numbers it has moved suggests that, like, everyone who reads comics already has a copy. So who is buying the book? During this topic, Paul Levitz took fifteen minutes to walk us through the procedures of just how a backlist item is printed and stored, and the velocities they need to see, and which titles are over this line, and which are under, and just exactly how many years' supply they make at one time, and why, economically, it is better for the publisher to hold inventory, and the cash advantages of "just in time" ordering, and, and, and. They have no problem giving us exact numbers of sales and velocity if it will help us better understand our business.

This is pretty refreshing, y'know?

I never feel like I am being talked *at* during these meetings – I (and everyone else in the room) am *part* of the discussion. That candor, that involvement, gives me more hope than almost anything else that happens during a year.

I still recall one of the early meetings – the one that came just after the Death of Superman came out. I stood and said something like, "Well, it's just too damn bad that *Superman* #75 sucked *so* hard – here was a wonderful chance to introduce new people to our medium, and we gave them a substandard editorial package." And Paul responded with something along the lines of, "If we (or anyone else) puts out a crummy comic book, *please do not buy it.*"

You could *hear* my jaw drop. A publisher saying to *not* buy their wares? Yikes! I'd *never* heard anything like that before, and it was, I suspect, the first time I truly realized that they were not the "enemy" – that their goals were (largely) the same as ours; and that they really and truly cared about the long-term viability of the market. Shocking.

Do you really hear what I am saying? Here we have a publisher that *wants* our criticisms, that *wants* to know our problems, and that hears them, and *doesn't take it personally*, and then (and this is the key part) *tries to fix them to our satisfaction*. Compare this to the time I wrote a critical column about, say, Diamond, and

Chuck Parker and Roger Fletcher call me up saying, "You're being too harsh on us, please change your opinions." – in that case they didn't even want to hear what I had to say, they couldn't take the criticisms; in fact, they couldn't even see there *was* a problem. From Diamond, I consistently get the "you are not an average retailer" with the (sometimes) unspoken premise of "therefore your opinions are not relevant" – when Bob or Paul remind me I am not "average," there is *never* a "dismissal" attached to it. Perhaps because they recognize that only listening to "average" retailers only produces "average" results.

This type of compare and contrast is actually pretty relevant, because this year (for the first time ever), Diamond was an integral part of the RRP meeting – we were in their home town, and one of the four days was given over to their presentations and Q&A.

And, boy, did they blow it.

Like I said, there is a pretty excellent cross-section of stores invited to these things – not every single store there is at the utter top of their game, but it is certainly a room filled with the best and brightest of retail minds. These retailers are there because they're smart, passionate, and committed, and because they're trying so very very hard to usher in a grand future.

And from ten am to three pm (with a few quick breaks for us to stretch our legs or whatever) they gave us a static slide show presentation where they talked *at* us, not *to* us. They'd put a slide up, then proceed to *read that slide to us*. Ugh.

It was a death march.

Here we have 100 of the best and brightest retail minds, each with concerns and issues we want to bring up with the upper management team from Diamond...

...and they spent 45 minutes lecturing us about exclusive toy deals they have made.

Not once, but *twice*, I went back up to my hotel room and watched some TV, I was so horrifically bored. And when I came back? They still hadn't progressed to anything resembling communication.

In a room full of graduate-level retailers, they were presenting "Diamond 101." No. Even less than that: "Pre-semester orientation to Diamond."

And when they *finally* got to Q&A (an excruciating *five* hours later) they decided to begin by reading and answering questions that had been submitted in advance – with *no give and take from the audience*

Mustn't...

...black...

...out.

Even that wouldn't have been so horrific if the answers were, say, logical and consistent. I reached my limit when the response to "Question: Why did Diamond purchase Another Universe? Answer: Part of it was that we had to react fast; two other offers were on the table," was followed 10 minutes later by "For the last two months we have aggressively tried to sell off these assets." Now, wait a minute here – you rushed into this deal, in part, because you had strong bidding competition, yet you are "aggressively" trying to divest the company for "two months" and you don't have a single bite? That doesn't parse, folks.

Anyway, *finally* they let us start asking real, live questions, and the first topic up was about Next Planet Over.

Walking into the meeting, I hadn't heard word one about this; and as you read this column, maybe you haven't heard yet either. No one really spelled out the exacts of the deal, but what I was able to gather is this: a pair of (I guess) venture capitalists with too much money on their hands and trying to cash in on the (tulip-like) craze of internet-based public companies, have signed a deal with Diamond where NPO takes web-orders, and Diamond acts as the fulfillment house for these orders. That is: *Diamond* handles picking and packaging these orders *directly to the consumer.*

blinks

Um. Surely I don't have to spell out the myriad of ways this is truly and utterly heinous?

Here's the clever part: apparently, this deal was engineered by Milton Griepp. Yes, that's the same Milton who a year or so ago suggested here in *CR* that it was a good idea to intentionally underprint comics to inflate secondary-market demand for them. Yeah, the bloody font of bloody wisdom. Sheesh!

And not only wasn't Diamond prepared for the vitriol of the room (but, good lord, how could they *not* be?!?! What planet are these guys living on?) – but Chuck Parker (COO) and Steve Geppi (Owner) weren't aware enough of the specific details of the deal to cogently discuss it with us. "I'll have to go check on that," became the common refrain.

The absolute best moment of the entire day came during this discussion. Let me back track a moment to properly set this up. You all know me a bit – I am not shy about expressing my opinion (understatement #1), nor am I particularly constrained by the need to be utterly diplomatic about it (understatement #2) – I'm also a fairly big and loud guy with a certain amount of physical presence. See me in a dark alley, and you might conceivably get nervous. When we were discussing the AU deal, and Parker was defending it on the basis of trying to "preserve the industry" (well, those companies who were about to get burned by going into heavy business with Milo), I leapt to my feet and said something like "If you do a deal with the devil, well, maybe you deserve to BURN IN HELL!!!" The response from the dais was somewhere between slim and none. I bring this up to show they are not easily flustered. Heh.

So, we're having a heated debate about the NPO deal, and someone decides to ask about how shipping works for them. And Chuck Parker says something like "Oh, they have no shipping costs, we're just moving their books from one side of the warehouse to the other – there is no 'shipping' involved"

Now, I don't know how many of you know Paul Levitz, but he is not an...imposing figure. This is not a swipe by any means, but he's a little, weedy, intellectual New York Jewish guy. I don't think if you gave him the armament of Rob Liefeld's Cable that I would ever feel physically threatened by him.

So, Paul stands up and says, "No. You can't do that." Just like that. Simple and plain. No inflection. Not even particularly loud, like my "Burn in hell!!" rant.

This is the reason I am SO sad we're not allowed to videotape these meetings. The looks on Diamond's upper management team's faces were utterly priceless.

Five full seconds of shock and silence. You can *hear* their thoughts: "Did I just hear a voice?" "Whose voice was that?" "It came from that side of the room." "Oh, that was Paul's voice." "He wasn't talking to me, was he?" "Maybe I misheard" "Uh. Oh."

Chuck starts to stammer: "Yes, of course we can."

"No. You can't. You are not allowed to treat any of my customers differently than any other. I don't care if you're only moving them 20 feet across your warehouse to a different area. You have to charge them freight like you charge anyone freight."

Bra-freaking-vo!

See, there is the difference in a nutshell. DC, evil corporate masters at Time Warner or no, clearly recognizes the strengths and benefits of the direct market retailers, and that we are, both collectively and individually, their partners. When they screw up they spend (frankly) stupid amounts of money trying to fix the problems (Paul walked us through the *Crisis* thing – eep!) They value and seek out our opinion, and try to work on a long-term basis rather then strip-mining every profit center for the quick buck. Upper management works very closely and carefully with us not only to be aware of our problems, but to try and stop them from being problems in the first place.

Diamond management, conversely, is wholly out of touch with the needs and desires of the retailers. Rather than focusing on strengthening their existing customers in a hard market, they rush out to make deals which are clearly against any direct market retailer's best interests. When they screw up, they either deny it or try to justify their errors. They seldom seek our opinion, and when they do, they stack the questions to get the answers *they* want to hear ("Is order reduction a good idea? Yes or no?" does *not* translate into "Retailers vote that order reduction is a better idea then returnability on late product"). Diamond strives to preserve the short-term interests of themselves, and some of their suppliers, and doesn't seem to have a long-range game plan that I can discern. Diamond consistently goes for the fastest buck. And when we do have a problem (because they operate in secret most of the time), they effectively dismiss our concerns, then go on to make the same kinds of mistakes again and again.

Anyway, that is why Paul Levitz is my hero. With five calm words, he accomplishes more than 20 minutes of Hibbs invective can. He talks *to* us – it is a dialogue, not the talk *at* us monologues that Diamond management does. And while we sure as heck disagree a fair amount, I have never once thought that Paul wasn't carefully *listening* to everything I said. I've changed his mind, he's changed my mind, and that's something I will always respect.

Why don't we have a dozen more like him?

Tilting at Windmills #86
(Originally ran in Comics Retailer #87)

So, I'm looking through the latest Comics Retailer's market beat, reading the "what topics should be covered" question, and it sure seems to me that if there is a consensus, it is on the topic of back issues.

What the hell, I can be a populist – so back issues it is.

O.K., so the problem is: we buy non-returnably; we order 2+ months in advance; and sometimes the "information gap" from this process (or even simply customers' tastes changing faster then we can adjust), coupled with the short shelf-life most titles have, means we get stuck with a lot of unsalable product.

In addition, every day we get phone calls from customers (or former customers, or folk who "found a box of comics in their attic," or whatever) who want to sell old comics back to us.

The thing of it is, the back issue market is pretty weak, and stuff can flow in a *lot* faster then it flows out.

This, I hope, adequately describes the scenario you see.

About three years ago I realized most of this, and it became apparent that the "standard" model for handling back issues was pretty flawed.

A big chunk of this realization came out of me trying to sell all my old vinyl LPs – I had about 200 or so, so I dutifully carried my big boxes off to one record store after another, and watched in frustration as my collection was cherry-picked through and piecemealed out. I mean talk about annoying! No one store seemed to be interested in more than 10 or 20 records, and after making all the rounds, I still had at least 25% of my collection that no one wanted for *any* price. With all the time and energy I put into it, I nearly *lost* money (based on the value of my time) – I would have been almost better off donating the records to Goodwill or something and taking the tax deduction.

As a consumer (well, seller, but I mean that in the "not a retailer" context) I was utterly frustrated and annoyed.

Out of any 100 random comics a consumer might bring in, the average comic shop might only have "use" for about 10. This is because most of us are focused on selling the individual pieces of the collection.

Why not sell the *collection* instead?

We switched focus at Comix Experience – rather than placing the largest effort on to single issues, individually bagged, boarded, and priced (though we *have* those, of course), we do the bulk of our sales in, well, bulk.

The first part of the equation is the purchasing of the material. I went out and bought a little $50 freight scale – one designed for shipping packages, with room on its body for larger boxes and with a digital readout. These are heavy-duty construction, not like, say, a bathroom scale.

When customers bring in a collection for sale, we plop the entire thing up on it – this is the key, we don't even *look* at the comics inside – and we pay fifty cents a pound for the weight. We deduct 10% of weight for bagged comics, and 33% if they have bags and boards. This works out to approximately a nickel a comic for a standard format book.

Like I said, the central thing that makes this *work* is that we don't "cherry-pick" collections – they bring the books in, we place them on scale, and buy them all, no matter what it is. There are no exceptions to this rule. If someone brings in *Amazing Fantasy* #15, it's still fifty cents a pound (though, of course, we'd encourage such people to take that kind of thing elsewhere, should that ever happen).

In adopting this for your own use, you could lighten this a bit – perhaps make a "single comics buy list" with the "hot" comics you are *actively* seeking, or some other criteria like "pre-1972 Marvels and DC's" or something.

However, the benefit to having it be hard and fast with no singles is that you both eliminate a lot of confusion, and you allow *any* of your staff to buy comics during *all* of your open hours – no more having to restrict it to when you have your "buyer" available.

So, we have a good *buying* system; now to work on the *selling* side of it.

Once we have a collection purchased, the first step is to cull out those few items that have some "value" as single back issues. By "value," I mean that are *worth* putting into the regular back issue bins – things that will turn within a reasonable amount of time. The nice thing is that since you're paying so little, proportionately, for single pieces, you can set very inexpensive prices for common, good-turning books, giving your customers a greater incentive to purchase them.

We've found that, on average, something like 5-10% of a collection is worth single-bagging. About another 5-10% is utter and complete garbage that no one will buy – this stuff you put off to the side, and once a year or so donate off to children's hospitals or homeless shelters, or what have you. The "investment" you are making is very small – small enough that you could even *throw it away* and not impact your bottom line significantly.

So, something like 10-20% of the collection has been removed as either "crap" or "gold" – what happens to the rest?

Simple: sets.

"20 issues of *Batman*," "20 Marvel comics," "20 first issues," "Avengers #272-290," "20 comics featuring women," just about anything you could imagine. We price these sets out at between fifty cents and a buck or so a book, depending on the precise contents. The sets are put in an appropriate clear bag (Golden Age bags work quite well), with a half-sized sheet of paper describing the contents, and, where appropriate, a designation like "cover price/your price" – "20 issues of *Batman*, cover price: $40, your price $20," or whatever. You want to underscore the value of the packs.

Does this undercut the perception of comics being a "valuable commodity?" YES! This is a *good* thing in the long term. I usually give a little speech that goes something like this: "When you buy a video tape or a paperback book, do you have an *expectation* of a value increase, or are you purchasing them for the entertainment within? On the rare occasion that you get something "rare" it is a *bonus*, not the *reason* for your purchase. Why should comics be any different?"

The truth of it, as we all know as comics retailers, is that 95%+ of all comics produced have no after-market value – why not *embrace* this, and start treating the product in this manner?

The actual dollars in profit is reasonably low, indeed, but the margin can't really be beat – we seldom get less than 1000% markup using this method, and sometimes it is significantly higher. Just as importantly, we've re-sparked a lot of interest in simply *reading* comics – exposing people to things they had perhaps a marginal interest in, but couldn't resist the price as a set. Let's face it, the turn-rate on *Avengers* #272-290 as single back issues is vanishingly small, but package those 18 comics in a set for $10, and you can see good velocity. Your investment? Ninety cents, plus labor and supplies.

The only trick is to create sets that people want. By using a clear bag, you have two "facings" with which to show the contents (we never ever let people open the sets – part of the price break is from the semi-"grab bag" nature of it) – place the two best items in a non-contiguous set on the front and the back. If the price is attractive enough, the rest of the contents of a set could be mediocre – they're buying based on the outside packaging. Sorta like those sets you used to be able to buy in airports when we were kids: "Five comics for the price of three!" and there would be some boss-looking *Avengers* on the front, and inside you'd get a cruddy *Conan* or *TeamAmerica* or whatever. You were never upset, because the price was attractive, and the "bad" comics you got were offset by the value on the others.

Once you have an adequate "floating inventory" made from low-cost purchases, the "bite" of (effectively) liquidating your rack overstock is minimized greatly. Seldom are our "Starter Sets" wholly comprised of off-the-rack material – oh, certainly *some* times it is rather unavoidable, and in those cases you're likely taking a break-even position at best on the stock – but the profit margin from the bulk purchases should more than offset the "loss" you're absorbing in that case. The psychological "trick" is to look at all backstock in the aggregate. While that single copy of *Batman* #528 in your "20 *Batman* comics" set that you pulled off the rack is, individually, losing you money – the other nineteen issues of bulk *Batman* more than make up the difference.

In any case, at this stage of the game you should have tight enough ordering procedures that your "off-rack" back issues should be an insignificant percentage of your initial sales – if not, then you need to carefully examine the methods with which you are ordering your frontlist material.

As always, a significant policy change such as this will not yield instant benefits – it will take time to "ramp up" the program and find the pricing structures that *your* customers will respond to the best – but I do believe you will find that a high-margin, low-cost, fast-turn approach to back issues is far more profitable then the traditional methods of turning older stock.

Tilting at Windmills #87
(Originally ran in Comics Retailer #88)

So, I've been sorta quiet lately – I've pretty much stopped hitting the message boards and chat groups, and what have you. There's a couple of reasons for this: #1) it's not like after ten bloody years anyone still needs to know what I think, and #2) it's a waste of precious time. Time away from doing the *job*. In our derisive moments, we call this "pulling a Sim," but, actually, I think Dave has it precisely right: once you've said your piece, its time to shut up and roll up your sleeves, and just work.

It's like this: comics retailing has two parents. One of them is a big fat lazy bastard like, well, the Comic Shop Guy on the *Simpsons* ("Don't make me get off my stool unless you've got cash"), and the other is...is...well, let's be poetic and call it The Community of the Different.

I am, indeed, a Big Fat Lazy Bastard, but the difference is I Believe.

I believe in comics, and I believe in those who create them, and, most importantly, *I believe in those who care about them.* By way of example I've got a customer...well, let's call him Mr. X. Now Mr. X is not a paragon of social skills, I'd be a little shocked if he's ever kissed a girl (let alone had a shot at procreating, which, all things considered may well be for the best), and, you know, I doubt I'd be the first in line to dinner at his apartment. He stammers; his trains of logic are not always grounded in what we so-laughingly-call the real world, but you know what? He's got a good heart, and most of all, he has a passion. You can see the twinkle in his eyes and the fire in his breast when we talk about Jackie Chan movies, or the character interactions of the Legion of Super-Heroes, or the plot of the last issue of Preacher, or the minutia of movie soundtracks. He cares, he really and truly cares, and he knows me and Rob and Larry do too – and because of this, we have, I believe a bond.

See, they're all Mr. X.

Just some of them cover it up better than others, is all.

We're all bonded together in our passion and our love and our enthusiasm – despite race, or creed, or blood, or standing, or jobs, or any of the other social constructs that society tries to foist upon us. We're bonded together because we *believe*.

And that belief is a wondrous thing. A special thing to cherish. Because it is so rare.

Most of the sheep walking the world don't believe in a thing. They just don't care – they have no *passion*, no *enthusiasm* – they're "into" whatever they are not because they *care* about it, but because their peers are, because it can make them accepted.

This might sound vaguely blasphemous, but I think they were a few letters off in the Bible where it says, "And the Meek shall inherit the earth." Me, I think it should read, "And the *Geek* shall inherit the earth."

Because the geeks care. It burns in them.

I don't think that 80% of the kids who come in looking for *Pokémon* cards are looking for it because they like or care about *Pokémon* – I think they're doing it because "it's what everyone else is doing" – because it is "cool."

When I was a kid in elementary school, it was baseball cards. We used to "flip" them for ownership (not totally unlike the "Collectible Card Games" of today) – and I had a fairly huge collection of cards.

And I hated baseball.

I sure as hell couldn't play the game being a (little) Fat Lazy Bastard – and, let's be realistic, *watching* the game is about as exciting as watching paint dry. I mean come on, here we have a sport that is defined as "perfect" when *nothing happens*. Whoopie.

One day (and I don't mean to imply this was a conscious decision) I guess I realized I'd rather like what *I* liked and not what made me "fit in." That's the real definition of a "geek": someone who cares, who believes in what they love without consideration for what anyone else thinks of it.

They run a wide spectrum: from everyone's pal Larry Young who has the single most frighteningly complete knowledge of pop culture of any man I've met – yet can seamlessly interact with any group of people; to our Mr. X who has a hard time fitting in. They're both geeks, and huge ones at that – what separates them is socialization and little else.

So, what does this have to do with comics retailing?

Glad you asked.

Our goal as we go into the 21st Century should be to build that Community of the Different – to foster it, to encourage it, to strengthen it. All while avoiding the Dark Side of the coin.

What is that Dark Side? Among the problems are cliquishness, insularism, jealousy, and contempt. I'm a King Geek, and I can't begin to count the number of stores I've gone in and out of in 60 seconds because it was a private clubhouse – and it was redolent in the air.

Passion is to be embraced, not walled off like your own private fiefdom – not protected fiercely from the "outsiders." And it must be nurtured, not hoarded.

A couple of stories. You'd think with my picture at the top of the page every month for 87 running, I couldn't go into a comic shop freely and observe, but indeed I can. These are things I've witnessed with my own eyes.

Not a month ago I was in an area comic shop poking around as is my wont, when some kid who was truly excited came in looking for *Pokémon* cards. Now, look, I really think *Pokémon* is a cynical and manufactured thing – and I won't touch it with a ten-foot pole personally – but this kid had the Light in his eyes. He cared. He was excited. He was sincere. And the person behind the counter was contemptuous. "Packs are $5," was his only curt response. He was so put out by the (one presumes) constant influx of people looking for the cards that he reduced it all to money and forgot about the passion.

I ended up buying the kid a pack myself. Heh.

It's easy, perhaps *too* easy, to get cynical – to let that initial passion turn to contempt. To watch the "weekend warriors" come in, and let your feelings towards them transform your feelings towards the true fans to the mercenary. Passion can curdle, which is probably the saddest thing of all.

Y'know, we *can* make a good living without raping the fans for every penny – and while, I believe, infecting the borderline with our own passions.

This is like the people who sold *Superman* #75 for $20 on release day. *Sure* there are people who would pay it, and *happily* – but what about all those people out there who simply loved Superman? What did you do to them?

Second story: I was in a shop in New York a few years ago, and someone came in asking about some character or another. Someone who'd changed a lot – maybe Green Lantern, or something. Time has blurred the details. But the customer asked an honest question about the changes, and the response was all sarcasm and derision: "How can you *not* know *that*?!?!"

It's really easy to become insular – to believe you're the only thing that counts in the world.

Me, I tend my garden – I'm largely done with the fighting and the politics and the stupidity that keeps you and me and everyone else in our business from focusing on what we're doing, and why, and who for. All I care about these days is the passion, and supporting and rewarding that.

If I have a point, it is this: if we were all to give 100% effort, to support and engage and nourish passion and enthusiasm to the depths of our abilities – we could break this slump and reclaim the greatness I *know* we're capable of.

Can you do that? Can you be a hero?

Tilting at Windmills #88
(Originally ran in Comics Retailer #89

The first thing I do each month when I start *TaW* (and I'm really bad, I never ever even start until J.J. calls me up and says, "Uh, Bri, you have 48 hours to give me words, or we run a blank page, and Krause fires me, and I fly to San Francisco and beat you to death with my bound collection of Hostess Twinkie ads,") is go back and read *last* month's column.

Ugh, I was like...*nice* last month. No, no, that will never do. Time to reclaim the vitriol.

Actually, I'm truly nervous as to what might happen if I blew a deadline – I mean J.J. not only saw *Batman* far too many times, but *he actually kept the ticket stubs*. Once I found that little tidbit out, I knew I could never do *anything* to get on the man's bad side. Who in God's name *keeps movie ticket stubs*?!?! The mind fairly boggles.

So what pisses me off this month? Oooh, I know – same thing that pisses me off *every* month: *Previews*.

(This is what we call "stealing candy from a baby's mouth" – want to pick on something? Choose an easy target!)

All right, so its easy enough to pick on Diamond itself – the catalog is a nightmare, really: giving equal weight and space to, dunno, *Xena* earrings as to, say, *Cerebus* is pretty inane behavior for a supposedly comic-book-dedicated distributor (note: the name of the company is "Diamond Comics Distributors," not "Diamond Pop Culture Distributors"). I mean, I *worked* distribution back when dinosaurs still roamed the earth – if they can move 20 jewelry pieces per distribution center, then they're doing damn damn well. What well and truly pisses me off is that they take the dog-and-pony show out on the road and talk about how comic sales are flat, and toy sales are up up up, and I can't help but go, "*Really?* Could that have *anything* to do with ratio of color pictures and editorial weight? Nah! Too obvious!"

But, anyway, there's likely not a retailer in America who thinks that Diamond's catalog department is particularly competent or rational (go on, just ask them), but that's sorta akin to saying "Water is wet." I mean, you can *say* it, but people snicker under their breaths at you for stating the obvious. Me, I'm cruel enough to figure that if you're working marketing at Diamond, it prolly just means you're not good enough to get a *real* job. But then I'm, y'know, a horrible bastard.

(You watch carefully as Brian jumps into the time machine, leaps forward 45 days, and picks up the phone to have an incensed Roger Fletcher on the other line. "Why can't you be more supportive?" he asks. "Those types of comments are hardly productive." Yah, well, as long as he's calling me, and not J.J., I sleep just fine at night.)

Anywho, I can't really blame our little friends at Diamond too terribly badly – the majority of upper management doesn't know a thing about funny books (remember the time I spoke to VP of Purchasing Bill Schanes, and he had never even *heard* of 50% of the Eisner nominees?), so the catalog just reflects corporate vision (or lack thereof). I mean, sure, I wish I believed in God, so I could pray to him to set, dunno, a burning bush or something out on Diamond's lawn that said, "And yea, I knoweth you really want to *think* its a consumer publication; but the absolute percentage of comic buyers in America is double-digit multiples of the readership of *Previews*, so maybe you want to ensure it's actually *useful* to the people making purchasing decisions first?" but, hey, they have their own little fantasies and I have mine.

Hrm, so where was I? Oh, right – this column isn't about Diamond's bits of the catalog, but about the parts controlled by the actual publishers. Here we have the grandest thing any publisher could hope to pray for – complete control over the editorial functions of their distribution organ – and, naturally, most of them utterly screw it up ("Yes, Brian," you whisper, "and the sky is blue," too!).

Let's try it in semi-alphabetical order:

Dark Horse: Is, and always has been, the enigma to me. Anyone want to try to tell me the sense of having half-page *ads* (an ad is defined in this context as something that would run in the monthly comics themselves, and with the copy being hook-oriented – e.g. for *Star Wars: Bounty Hunters* it says "No mercy for the hunted..." All right, but what does *that* mean?) *directly opposite* the solicitation copy? Like, the only thing I can think is it lets them move some of their advertising budget forward a few months for tax reasons. The ads themselves are so nicely designed, and the catalog pages so *bland* (that clumsy never-varying six-panel grid with the ugly top-banded "Spotlight" which looks *exactly* the same as the "offered again." Ugh!). I've always thought DH wastes half of the space available to them for no good reason, and that two-page comic deal that runs at the back almost always makes me *less* interested in the comic it is touting (because virtually no one knows how to pace a two-page serial). And what the *hell* is the deal with that *Predator* ad that runs each and every month back in the merchandise section? Another accounting trick? At least the ad copy tends to be reasonably clear.

DC: My three quibbles. 1) the "features" section about half the time just rehashes the solicitation copy. When I see "for more information, please see the features section" then I damn well want to see *more* information there. 2) I hate and always have hated the white-on-light-blue bar at the bottom of the solicitation – I'm getting old too, and it gets harder and harder to read each month. 3) it is now time to figure out a new solution for the backlist section. Look at my order-form book that comes with *Previews*, folks. Usually there are about 3 pages for the DC listings and at least twice that for the backlist. You remember how once long ago I mentioned that when I got *Previews* each month the first thing I did was to rip-out all the double-sided ad pages (which, might I add, was foolish for me to announce, because they're now conscious of that, and seem to make an effort to avoid the old clumping)? Well, now, my new ritual is to cut any page out of the order form that is nothing but backlist. Look, just count any Star System order that is submitted *with* the monthly order as applying towards frontlist discount, if that's your issue. Use the extra pages from that and the "useless" features to widen out the main catalog a bit more. Six solicitations per page seems to be about the right amount with the current layout. Otherwise the copy is good, and it does its job clearly and well.

Marvel: has some of the basic "huh?" problems of the DH ads-on-same-page-as-solicitation approach, but the real problem the Marvel section always has is it suffers from Stan-itis. I know Stan Lee's shadow looms large over Marvel, but, damn it! you're *not* Stan. You don't write half as well as him, and when you try a "bombastic" approach, you sound like idiots. Stan's voice was uniquely his own, so stop trying to copy it! I like the features approach to actually getting some words out of the creator's mouths, but sometimes it sounds too much like hard sell. And one of the differences between Marvel copywriting and that of DC is that at DC when they need an adjective, you get the impression the hand goes out for the thesaurus. At Marvel, it feels like they flip on WWF Wrestling. If I hear the word "slobberknocker" one more time, I will cry. But, even with all its faults, at least it is better than....

Image: Oh. Where to begin? I'd call it the "triumph of art over literacy" but that's almost too easy. But let's try this: given that nearly everything has a full-page ad in the Image section, full-page ads have no value whatsoever there. The only way you can call attention now is to do *double-page spreads*. I mean, jeez. Talk about a waste of space. And if you do *half-pages* then all of us think, "Well, they think this is a dog."

Then there is the problem that 75% (or better) of the solicitations don't include basic information like duration/frequency of publication, things like that. Plus whatever points Marvel loses for empty hype, Image gets a 25% penalty on top of that. In most cases the copy is next to useless in ordering comics, so all we have is that one, full-page picture to judge on.

Plus it all just seems the same – every month, it seems, a third or better of the catalog is half-dressed uber-babes with guns or swords, and it's all about the #1. Will there ever be a #2? Is there any real chance it will come out the month solicited? Is it even a comic, or is it just one prong of a merchandising phenomenon?

Here's the thing that endlessly frustrates me about Image: I believe in creator rights, and I believe in creator control, and yet we've a company set for purely that, and all they do left-and-right and up-and-down is bobble the ball when it comes to the professional aspects of the gig.

As a retailer I really really don't want all that much – most of it comes down to making my life easier. And given that monthly ordering is probably the single most stressful function of the job, I and, I am sure, most of my brethren would really appreciate it if the catalog editors of America would take a very close and careful look at the *utility* of their catalogs. Right now, it is a *chore* to do our order forms. And I think that, as much as anything, is hindering the market's stabilization.

Tilting at Windmills #89
(Originally ran in Comics Retailer #90)

Feast or famine. Those seem to be the only two states shipping weeks have anymore. $1600, $1800, $3500, $1200. That's what my weekly invoices seem to be like each month.

May sucked a lot for Comix Experience. Like a *lot*. We were down about 20% for the month. I can fairly attribute this to the twin engines of destruction: *Star Wars* and *Pokémon*, which sucked the dollars right out of my customers' pockets.

(Why, you ask, didn't we chase after some of those dollars? Fair question, I s'pose. And the only answer I can give is, "We don't do fads." Brief pop-culture blips have an inevitable habit of collapsing like soap bubbles after a short while, and while you have tons of product tied up in the pipeline. I've never been one for gambling, even when the odds look good. Most of all I don't trust our suppliers and our distributors to move the products to me in the tight time frame allowed. I've been stung once or twice, and I've watched several otherwise fine stores drown when the "tulip-mania" runs dry. Heck, it happened with our *core product* – the one we all *understand*. And you want me to invest heavy in fad-driven trading cards or toys? No thanks, compadre. I mean, if we had a *real* mark-up on them ["real" defined as "at least having the chance to double my investment" – not this 35% {or less!} nonsense] then maybe I'd give it a go, but when I can go to Toys "R" Us and pay pennies more at "retail" than my wholesale pricing, that makes little sense.)

June pretty much chewed as well, but this was more a factor of week after week of puny new comics deliveries. Or badly staggered ones.

You'd think that in a down market, and in one where the bulk of the foot traffic is driven by the habitual new-comics buyer, publishers and distributors would not merely understand that even shipping throughout the month is *imperative*, but that they would bust their asses to ensure it occurs.

Yah, yah, I've sung this song before, but why the hell aren't the ones who *control* scheduling and shipping *doing* something about it? Is it willful idiocy? Gross incompetence? Simply not caring? Or perhaps they're happy to shift the burdens of their own bad habits onto the backs of the people who can least-afford to pay it?

Right, *there* is a good recipe for a healthy marketplace.

Every week, when I go to Diamond's web-page to download the week's invoice, I get physically distraught. I'm not frickin' kidding here. My pulse rate begins to climb as I scan the week's shipments for all of the stupid *and easily avoidable* shipping problems.

In God's name, what is *wrong* with you people?

I'm talking to the publishers that publish four or more titles *and ship them in the same week.*

I'm talking to the creators who show no respect or work ethic whatsoever, and ship their book at the last possible second before *they* have to pay any price.

I'm talking to the major publishers who let their schedules get "clumped" (*YES* you, Dark Horse which too frequently drops half or more of your licensed comics out in a single week. *YES* you, Marvel which will ship five titles one week, and fifteen the next. *YES* you, Image where less than 20% of your line comes out the month it is solicited [and a side note to Todd McFarlane: Dude, just come right out and say *Spawn* is a fully-returnable comic. Christ, it will probably help your sales. Has there even been an issue of *Spawn* in the last year that was *not* returnable for being 2+ months late?] and *YES* you, DC, which routinely does such wonders as shipping *both Superman* and *Batman Adventures* the same week; or goes for a month with no America's Best Comics, then ships two at once) – get your act together *now.*

And, most frickin' especially, I am talking to Diamond, the single and sole entity with the clout and authority to either work with the exclusive publishers, or to *force* the non-exclusive ones to *behave professionally.*

What the *hell* is wrong with you people? Can't you see, don't you understand, that *the retailer's* cash-flow is dependent upon even and rational ship-weeks? And that if *our* cash-flow is impeded, the next time we fill out that order form we'll be *more* conservative and punitive in our ordering decisions?

This is basic stuff, people.

I single out Diamond because they have the ability and the power to make the effort to fix this, *if* they care to. Yes, yes, I *know*, "We're sensitive to the concerns of the smaller publishers, and do not wish to convey the impression that we're exerting undue pressure on them." Diamond can't really do any "good" because *everyone* with a beef targets them as the "five hundred pound bear," but for the *stability and health* of the marketplace, it's time to start dropping the hammer.

A couple of examples, perhaps, to underscore the point (and in both cases, I am too lazy and too close to deadline to go look up exact weeks and exact issue numbers. If I'm off by a number or two the point still remains). About two weeks ago (my time) we received both *Poison Elves* #47 & 48 via the L.A. warehouse in the same week. I couldn't tell you if the problem was Sirius', Drew Hayes', UPS', or Diamond's.

And what's more, I couldn't give a rats arse *who* is to blame.

The *only* thing that matters is the result: to whit, I lost 20% of the sales volume on both of those issues. Sirius gets their money. Drew Hayes gets his money. UPS gets their money. And Diamond gets their money. The single person in the chain who is out money is *the retailer.*

If I were Diamond, I'd've told them to put an egg in their hat and beat it. Unless, of course, it was Diamond's fault, in which case I'd've bent over and taken it like a man.

Because that is what you *do* for your customers.

Example #2: we ordered "The Return of the Condor Heroes" through Diamond. I think these are coming from either China or Korea. Prolly on the well named "slow boat from." They were solicited as two-per-month. For the first few months I'd seen pretty decent sales on these items, but it all came to a crashing halt when we received *eight* volumes in a *single week*. Jan. codes, Feb. codes, March codes, April codes. All at once.

I sold *no* copies of these.

Zero.

Zilch.

They're sitting there, rotting on my shelves, representing my power bill for the month in wholesale costs, because no one in the chain took the responsibility to go, "Uh, no. Shipping unsalable product is the wrong thing to do."

Believe me, I understand Diamond's position of not wanting to step on anyone's toes, but it's time for them to start properly serving the economic needs of their *customers*. If the vendors don't immediately get their acts together, there won't *be* any customers left. And, tell you what, you can go ahead and let me be the hatchet man. Go make some copies of this column, and send them off to the publishers, if you haven't the corporate will to make the hard choices that need to be made. Here, this next bit is the relevant part:

"Dear vendor: If you are unable to provide balanced shipping, whether it be shipping your four comics as one-a-week rather than all at once; or having an appropriate interval between "monthly issues" (a *minimum* of three weeks is required unless otherwise solicited *in advance*); or by meeting your advertised ship-weeks; you are hereby welcome to take your comic books and CRAM THEM UP YOUR ASS. If you are unable, regardless of the *reason*, to meet these commitments, then Diamond will meet them for you, assessing you the appropriate penalties for storage and returnability. Very sincerely yours, Every Comic Retailer in America."

That's about it. It's time for all of the creators, all of the publishers, and most especially, our distributors to immediately wake up and realize that they have a *responsibility* to the retailer. If *only* so the retailer is still in a position where they have the cash flow to keep buying these wares.

I know, I *know* you feel like you have good justifications. They might even *be* good.

But the retailers care no longer.

The time for sympathy and compassion has passed, and we're in the Age of Get-it-Done-Or-Get-Out.

I'm getting older, and the last thing I want to do is pop a blood vessel and die slumped in front of my computer one week because my invoice bears the traces of your inability to properly deliver your wares.

I'm sick of it. Deadly, deathly, incredibly hugely (four-letter expletive)ingly *SICK* of it.

And so is every other retailer in America.

a   r   t   i   c   l   e
9 0

Tilting at Windmills #90
(Originally ran in Comics Retailer #91)

Well, apparently my last column (about even shipping schedules) really touched a nerve with many of you – my e-mail volume increased eight-fold! I note this just for the publisher types out there. The overwhelming majority of retailers are sick and frustrated with the lopsided and uneven shipping you foist upon us.

So, energized by this, let me hit another pet peeve of mine: the Diamond Star System list. (This also applies, to a lesser extent, to the backlist catalogs of the other distributors, just so no one feels slighted or singled out.)

This may affect me to a greater extent than most of you: a bit more than one in every three dollars of sales I make is from trade paperbacks and graphic novels. Proportional to the rest of the industry, these numbers are absurdly high. In fact, the last time I had heard statistics on it, only some pathetically low number of Diamond accounts ever even *use* the Star System – less than one in five, if I recall correctly. Nonetheless, this is a *huge* headache for me and those of us who do any kind of volume in backlist.

Parenthetically, if you're not making an effort to stock and promote your backlist, you're doing yourself an immense disservice. There is a *lot* of money to be made from this category.

The problem is that the format in which the information is presented is odd and scattered and so riddled with errors as to make it a mediocre tool to use. You want examples, I bet? Sure, I got examples!

Let's begin with the most basic thing of all: *categorization*. Diamond lists several categories of product: "Comics and Magazines," "TPBs, GNs, and Collected Editions," "Books," and so on. The *problem* is that these categories are not only vaguely understood, but that Diamond seems to have inconsistent standards to apply them. The former is *almost* understandable: I believe that Diamond calls any item that costs more than $4.95 a "Graphic Novel." Now, O.K., that was a fine rule of thumb in, say, 1989, but in 1999 that simply doesn't work anymore. For example: the various DC *Secret Files* projects are, I think, to any reasonable person, clearly comic books: they're sequentially numbered within each series (even if some are meant to be one-shots) and they're (heh) "saddle-stitched." (What we who aren't involved in printing or publishing call "stapled." They call it maize, we call it corn.) Yet, lo and behold, they're in the "TPB and GN" section.

If I may, I will posit a series of "tests" to make these lines a trifle clearer. We can, since I have no modesty of any kind, call this **The Hibbs Test**:

1) Is it held together by staples? If so, *it is a comic book.* The presence of a square binding does not a priori imply it is a "book" (see below), but staples *automatically* make it a comic book or magazine.

2) Is it numbered with a number sign (#)? If so, *it is a comic book.* This test means that *Batman Secret Files* #1 is a comic book. Were it simply *Batman Secret Files* alone, then one might be able to make a case for it being a graphic novel, but that number *automatically* makes it a comic book (or magazine).

3) Is it an incomplete story released periodically? If so, *it is a comic book.* Example: *Batman/Grendel*. Now, these have spines (failing test #1), and they are labeled "Book I" and "Book 2" (so they fail test #2), but they were released periodically, and you *need* to have both issues in order to have anything even vaguely approaching a complete story. Therefore they are "comics."

There is one great exception to rule #3, and that is **3a) If it is reprints, then it is probably not a "comic book."** So when Sirius released *Wandering Star* Books 1, 2, and 3 in three consecutive months (none of which were "complete stories") – books that reprinted the regular monthly run of *Wandering Star* – rule #3 might indicate they are "comics." But, the fact they are reprints *means*, in this case, it is a "Trade Paperback."

The latter part of categorization is one of human error. This is even easier to eliminate. I certainly understand that when entering a stack of data into a computer system, single-bit errors occur you hit the wrong key in one field, and a "book" becomes a "comic." But these kinds of things need to be ruthlessly checked and rechecked. Why? Because they cause problems. Example: Diamond once offered an item in the TPB section called *Book of Nod*. There is a comics title (with a TPB) called *Land of Nod*. I ordered it on at least two different occasions thinking it was the comic book *Land of Nod*. But actually it was some sort of gaming supplement. Now I suppose "my bad" and all for being confused, but if it *had* been listed properly, the mistake *could not have been made.*

A large portion of this is consistency. When #1-6 and #8 of *Acme Novelty Library* are in the comics section, and #7 and #9+ are listed under "GNs," that's bad. When Fantagraphics' *Robert Crumb Library* series is listed under "Cr" for "*Crumb Comics* Vol. (x) (subtitle)" for volumes I- 7 and 9-12, but under "Co" for "*Complete Crumb* Vol. 8," that is absurd.

Or look at *Flaming Carrot*. Vol 2 is *Wild Shall Wild Remain*, Vol. 3 is *Greatest Hits*, and Vol. 4 is *Fortune Favors the Bold*. But in the listings they run like this:

Flaming Carrot Vol. 4 Fortune Favors the Bold TP

Flaming Carrot Wild Shall Wild Remain TP

Flaming Carrots Greatest Hits TP

Does this inconsistency drive anyone else insane? Note the "s" on the last listing, skewing it wider.

(Parenthetically, adding "current printing" or "new printing" to a listing I am sure makes some sort of logical sense for internal Diamond reasons – but Star is [in theory] a *perpetual inventory* list; making it, from the retailer's standpoint, utterly redundant.)

I also get enormously confused (and this is from a marketing standpoint) when "like and like" aren't together. Say how *Joker: Devil's Advocate* is listed under "J" rather than "B" for Batman. Look, this isn't a price guide where we have to match the indicia word-for-word. This is a sales tool for working retailers, many of whom are enormously pressed for time most days. Nearly *anything* you can do to streamline the information and make it easier for them to process is a *good* thing.

The problem at the distribution level is, and always has been, that their systems are designed by people who don't *actually have to use them on a day-to-day basis*. This is why *Previews on Disk*, despite the fact that in the English language we read left to right, has you enter data on the *right*-hand side of the screen. This is why the Star catalog is in straight (and fairly frustrating) alphabetical order. No retailer on Earth would design these systems in such a way!

If a retailer were to design Star, they might behave in ways that would facilitate ease of ordering. Heck, if I could design Star, I'd do something incredibly obvious like take all the manga books and put them in their own section. Gee, it might even help sell *more* copies.

The form of the Star System was largely designed when they had something on the order of 2,500 SKUs. Straight alpha is decent on that magnitude, because you can probably keep a fairly clear idea of each of those things in your head. But Star is now rapidly approaching its 10,000th code. And now, on virtually every page there are two or three items that even *I* go "Huh. I wonder what *this* is?"

Obviously, a total compartmentalization of Star would be a bad idea - there are more than a few titles that are not easily categorized and would suffer in sales for it. But a couple of tweaks, like doing a separate sort for manga and one for media/licensed properties, would help streamline the presentation considerably.

One last note is that the out-of-stock listings need to be much more aggressively dealt with. I swear to God that *Grendel: War Child* (to name but one example) has been listed as "out of stock" for a year or more. If an item goes out of stock for more than 90 days because a publisher isn't filling orders (as opposed to it having greater sales velocity than purchase volume), then it needs to be *removed* from the list.

Now to be fair, apparently contractual deals with DC, Dark Horse, Image, and Marvel limits Diamond's ability to expediently handle listings from those companies. When I've asked, "Why is *Grendel: War Child* still on the Star list?" I am told, "We're not able to change brokered publisher listings on our own. They have to *tell us* to remove it."

I mean, O.K., fair enough. But it seems from my "I am an independent retailer" point of view that we have us a giant blinking contest. Is anyone at Diamond going to anyone at Dark Horse and saying, "Uh, you haven't filled any purchase orders for *The Adventures of Luther Arkwright* TPB in like seven months, may we remove this?"

Is anyone at Diamond going to anyone at Marvel and saying, "It's pretty likely the exceedingly poor sales velocity of *Adventures Boxed Set #36904* is because nobody could tell you what's in it without trying to find the quarterly catalog. Do you think maybe we should describe its contents and try to sell a few?"

Is anyone at Diamond going to anyone at DC and saying, "Gosh, don't you think it's pretty darn silly that even though they're numbered, we're listing the *Sandman* TPBs in alphabetical order by their subtitle?"

Is anyone at Diamond going to anyone at Image and saying, "Hey, we're out of stock on *Kabuki: Masks of the Noh* hardcover, and we're pretty sure you're not going to reprint that. Oh, and by the way? Can we list *Curse of the Spawn* with *Spawn* and drop those silly 'new art edition' subtitles?"

Because no one at the companies is going to Diamond to tell the same to *them*.

And people wonder why my hair is starting to thin? None of this is exactly rocket science, people. So what will it take to get it fixed?

Tilting at Windmills #91
(Originally ran in Comics Retailer #92)

Every year or so I have to cover the old familiar ground of my "favorite" topics. Three guesses?

Yuppers, in one. Returns

I wouldn't keep harping on it (well, not as *much* at least) if Diamond hadn't changed the rules a while back and allowed publishers the right of order adjustment.

Now, look, I'm a sane person (well, *mostly*), so I understand the premise here – in these days of so few warehouses where the enormous majority of accounts are dependent upon UPS to shift product back and forth, it makes a modicum of sense to allow retailers the *ability* to *stop* unsalable product from reaching their doors in the first place. Shipping is, most likely, one of your top five expenses these days.

Oh, how I pine for the old days of the "walk-in warehouse." Certainly coverage wasn't 100% of the country, but I'd guess that at least two-thirds of the retailers in the country at one point had the feasible option of driving out to the warehouse to pick up their comics; as well as (of course) drop off their returns. Hell, back in the day the Bay Area had *both* a Capital City and a Diamond warehouse to choose from. It was purely heaven.

Returns were fabulous in those days. Well, heh, I lie – not fabulous because the policies themselves were much laxer (90 days, back then, except for DC, who's basically always had a 30-day policy), but the *process* was much easier. You just carry them along to the warehouse where you're picking up your funny books *anyway*. No muss, no fuss, no extra charges.

But those days are gone. You have to pay (usuriously, too, I think — paper is *heavy*) to get the product to you, and you have to pay to ship it back, and at the end of the day you end up losing money for no real good reason.

So, like I said, I applaud the *idea* of order adjustment.

The problem, as always, is that implementation...well, it just sucks is all.

Each week you get your nice little "order status report." Here are your reorders, here are your canceled items, here are your returns, and here are your order adjustments. "You may adjust your order on Title *x* because..." then you get a little laundry list of codes. "Mis-solicited," "shipping late," whatever.

Like always, it's a system designed by people who don't actually have to *use* the system. Now, don't get me wrong, I rag on Diamond a lot, but I don't truly believe they are malicious – but time after time they design systems that make good sense from *Diamond's* point of view, and, most likely, the vendors' (especially the exclusive ones), but that fail in implementation by the working retailer.

(Must parenthetically digress here – last week in *Diamond Dialogue* I read a story that stated that the warehouse managers were going to be taking field trips out to a couple of comic shops to help them unpack and receive on New Comics Day. This is one of the brightest ideas that anyone at Diamond has had in a good long time. Here's hoping that it gives these managers good insight and good ideas for making their pull-and-pack procedures a bit more streamlined and functional on the hell that we call New Comics Day. So bravo to whoever suggested that. Do please write a follow-up report on it for *Dialogue* too?)

What's the *problem* with order adjustment, then? Well, there are a couple of them, actually. The most glaring one is that the "laundry list" of "Why?" doesn't give anywhere enough information to make an informed purchasing decision. O.K., so it's gonna be late. *How* late? There's a fairly huge difference between four weeks late and four months. So, it was mis-solicited. How *exactly*? What *precisely* is incorrect? Without this kind of data (and data that I don't think can fit on the Order Status report, at that), we're just playing darts. Blindfolded. While the target moves.

The second problem is that the window in which to make the adjustments is very very narrow indeed. I can't speak for you, of course, but my working day is already fairly packed with things to do. Order adjustments, as useful as they *can* be, tend to be down toward the bottom of my "to-do" list – below the stuff I have to do *right now* like placing orders and reorders, maintaining customer lists, ringing up sales, that kind of thing. And so I often don't get to them. Now, of course, the tight time window is (one presumes) an effort to not make the items even *later* (though of course, the entire process virtually guarantees it will do so regardless), but it's a frustrating process at times.

The third problem is, perhaps, the most insidious. It also, I will grant, is probably not the *intention* of the program, but deed and intention don't always match up perfectly. But, with the way order adjustment *functions* it effectively lays the burden of publisher problems squarely where they don't belong: upon the retailer. Why? Because adjustments are a "take it or leave it" proposition. If you order a book in March, order adjust it in June, and it doesn't ship until September, and you don't sell any copies...oh, well, it is *your* problem now. Indeed, if you do *not* adjust it, it is also *still* your problem.

And that's not just right.

See my bottom line is now and has always been this: it is the publisher's responsibility to deliver me not only precisely what they promise, but also precisely at the time they say.

Now, I'm not an unreasonable man – I understand that errors happen and that often they're even caused by someone else. I understand this, and, indeed, sympathize with it.

However.

It ain't *my* problem.

Or at least it shouldn't be.

Y'know for the longest time, I was operating largely off of...well, let's call it moral certainty rather than absolute proof. I mean, no, I've never published a comic, but I keep promises that I make, even if said keeping causes me stress or strain. That's just the way you're supposed to act, right? But I've never actually *published* a comic.

Well, I still haven't. But I've gotten a *much* closer look at the process thanks to Larry Young.

Larry, for those of you who haven't yet been crushed beneath the juggernaut of his publicity wheels, is the publisher of *Astronauts in Trouble* (from AIT/PlaNetLar) – a modestly successful (and quite entertaining) science fiction series. The comic hasn't set the world on fire in terms of sales (yet. But the TPB is coming soon), and Lar still hasn't been able to fund the gaggle of young, nubile college interns to fulfill his every need, but it's not losing money for anyone either. Larry, like most small publishers, has to do other (better paying) gigs to keep up with things like rent and food, including (this here is the disclosure) working part-time for me.

So, I've been able to observe, even if sideways, the steps involved in producing a monthly comic.

He did his first five-issue miniseries and a special. *Every single one of which came out on time.* Not just the "month" it was scheduled, but the very *week*. And he did this in the middle of buying a house, too.

I mean, here's a guy who understands the responsibility of the creator/publisher to the marketplace.

I see him, under-funded, working in his "free time," out of his (effectively) basement, and yet he manages to do just about everything right.

And I know my moral surety was precisely correct.

The "act of publishing" (not the creative end, but the physical, production-oriented end) is monkey work. If you're publishing, and you're *not* hitting your deadlines, then, by jiminy, you have no damn right to be publishing anymore.

Creativity, I understand the Muse, she comes and she goes (trust me, I know – ask J.J. how close I push my deadlines!) – but the way a publisher avoids this is by *not soliciting until the work is done*. This is not hard. If Larry can do it, then you sure as hell can too.

You would not going to catch me whining (as much) about returns if the following policy changes were to be enacted by Diamond, post-haste:

1) Publishers need to give a *week* in which they expect their comics to ship. Not *merely* a month. Honestly, if you can't do that, you have no damn right to be publishing comics at all.

2) If your comic ships (to *stores*, not merely to Diamond) more than four weeks after your target date, it is 100% fully returnable.

3) Any item that is "order adjustable" is *also* declared returnable. There is no "or" in that statement. If you are late/mis-solicited enough to go adjust, then you are returnable. Period.

There is *never* any good reason for publishers to expect retailers to pay *any* direct price for *any* inability of theirs to get their products to market as solicited.

That's just basic common sense.

I'm all for "open access to the marketplace" – likely even more than the next guy – on the other hand, it is a *privilege*, not a *right*. And it's time, right now, right here, for the only body in this industry with the wherewithal to enforce professional standards of doing business to step up and start enforcing.

Tilting at Windmills #92
(Originally ran in Comics Retailer #93)

As you know, the Distribution Wars (from which our friends at Diamond came out on top) changed our worlds immeasurably. We got a few "benefits" out of it, it seems: perhaps a greater amount of direct accountability from the brokered vendors; a slightly stronger (if still seriously flawed) backlist...well, I could go on, but I'm pushing deadline hard this month (J.J. forgot to remind me!), so I'll leave it at "yeah, it wasn't *all* bad."

But there is one area, for sure, in which we all got massively screwed: freight.

Warehouses got shut down. Free freight deals were cut. And them funny books are *heavy*. Speaking for myself, we went from freight costs of (virtually) nothing to it becoming our number three expense.

The way I figure the math, it's as though retailers lost about 1-1.5% of their discount to cover the shipping charges.

But as heinous as this is (and, yah, it's pretty heinous), I think we all understand that it is "the price of doing business." No one is happy or enthusiastic about it, but no one is storming the castle with torches and pitchforks either, as long as everyone plays fair.

I will admit that most weeks my stuff could be packed a bit tighter – I generally feel like I am getting "one box too many" each week. Sometimes that is because there are two separate 200 count boxes that could, or should, have been put in one of those double-box deals. Sometimes it's because of the Diamond policy that items over $x – like *Archive Editions* – need to be packaged in their own shipment (this policy happened because, they say at least, *retailers* were calling in too many false shortages on these high ticket items – if *you* ever did such a thing, fuck you very much for reaming *each and every one of your fellow retailers* for hundreds upon hundreds of dollars). And sometimes it's because things get picked and packed in separate locations, so I end up with the equivalent of two boxes that are nothing but packing material. I'd say two weeks out of four my perception is that I've got a box too much, but I think most of us can concede they're doing the best they can.

But let me digress a moment and go back to that second point. I think all of us know how easy it is to "fake" a shortage or a damage – it's not like Diamond is standing over our shoulders when we unpack our shipment for the week. The thing of it is that doing this is just *wrong*. Not just merely in some intangible moral way (you are *stealing* at that point), but in a real and practical "you are costing us all money in the long-run." I reference the Diamond expensive-books policy. Because there were a statistically-too-high number of *Archive Editions* "gone missing," Diamond had to put a policy in place that adds an extra box cost to *everyone* who orders *Archives from then on*. If you are a retailer who did this, you are, flatly, a shithead. By all means, call in valid damages and shortages, but balance the true value of this against the increased long-term costs you're making the system bear. I, personally, never even bother calling in those single copy damages. I just figure that the $1 wholesale of that single bent copy of *New Warriors* just isn't worth the costs in either my time, or Diamond's services (*someone* has to pay for that "toll free" call, as well as the manpower to do the paperwork – and if you're asking for a replacement copy….)

A second even-more-digressive digression, this time going back to the days I used to work for Capital City: There was this one account, which I shall not name, who literally would not accept anything less than *perfectly* mint copies of books. I mean *flawlessly, completely, utterly, unCATEGORICALLY* mint. If there was a 1/32nd-of-an-inch dent on the spine, they sent the copies back for replacement. This is why it is good I was never a warehouse manager, or a customer-service cat, 'cuz I'd be telling them to stuff their "damages." This account drained resources in our work week, every single week – time that could (and should, IMO) have been put into solving real problems.

Here's the deal: if your customers "will not buy anything less than perfectly mint comics," it's because *you* told them to act like that. Oh, sure, there's always a few stupidly anal-retentive people in any crowd, but I never bought "none of my customers" unless *you* are encouraging such behavior. It's like the guy in Market Beat last month who said something like "Oh, I can't sell trade-paperbacks to any of my customers; they're just *reprints*." The attitude that the *retailer* has towards a product bleeds off on to your customers. I just wish less of you thought that selling the "collectibility" of comics was the sane or proper move. We should be all about the *content*. Good lord, can you picture a video store returning copies of the new Spielberg tape because "our customers will only buy perfectly mint copies?"

Anyway, end digression, let me get back to the point here.

Shipping charges.

To recap: we very much dislike them, but we recognize there is not much we can do, as long as they are applied fairly and appropriately.

Let me try to give a positive example. DC, as part of Time Warner, does all kinds of cross-promotions. I guess it "raises its corporate value" or something, though I generally find a lot of the promotions of mini-movie posters and such to be fairly poorly targeted to the comics market. But, whatever, I have no problem giving something away for free. When it *is* free. And there's the big batch of points we can give DC: their freight reimbursements are usually generous — often to the point where we might even "make" a few cents for handling the promotional item.

I think that's exactly how a vendor should behave: conscientiously. Especially when the item in question doesn't add any *value* to the retailer or the consumer. I have grown inured to the idea that my customers are going to be advertised to within my realm of my storefront. I don't very much like it, but I, at least, see the practical reasons why it happens. And it is bearable, I suppose, when it is handled like DC does it – advertising partners that aren't inherently counter-productive to my well-being as a retailer; and full reimbursement (or better) for anything that goes outside of the bounds of the traditional ad content of comics.

And then we have Marvel.

November Marvel comics were...interesting.

Now first, let's talk about Marvel's packaging in general. No one really talks about it much, but Marvels generally look poor on the shelf. Not because of trade dress, or cover design, or anything like that (even if it *does* tend to be a smidge garish) – but because of the way they are printed. Its the paper, I guess? I'm not conversant enough with printing terminology to discuss this intelligently, but Marvels generally "puff out" on the racks. Virtually every other publisher's books lay flat. Not Marvel's. Large stacks of them tend to be the first comics to fall off the rack in a pile on the floor.

This natural tendency is made far worse the thicker the Marvels get. And in November they were way thick.

First off, every single book that month had "Fast Lane part 1" included with it – an eight page anti-drug comic. Or, at least, I think that's what it was – lots of visual depiction's of marijuana in the thing, but no character named it, or said the word "drug" directly. In fact, really, the only reference is J.J.J.'s "I won't print this trash" speech. "Don't you think I know what this is REALLY advertising?" Which is kinda ironic given all the pot leaves in the story, yet no one actually *says* "don't smoke pot." Presumably this will come along in part 2, I hope, but so far all the peril in the story came from Mysterio (and doesn't that like completely screw the point of Kevin Smith's *Daredevil* run if he didn't "really" die? Heck, they could have at least waited *two months* to bring him back. *sigh*), not drugs. In fact, it took Scott (My-God-at-Diamond) Johnson pointing out the underlying point of this insert was anti-drug. *shrugs* Maybe I'm just smoking too much dope.

And it's kinda funny, because the December books don't seem to have part 2.

(And one last parenthetical thing, I think this finally ties with the Spidey "Got Milk" ad with "worst placement to destroy a story narrative" – I hit *three* comics this month where I lost the narrative thread trying to figure out why the scene had shifted so intensely. Heh.)

Anyway, so every Marvel for the month had "Fast Lane" in it. Then another chunk of the line (all the best sellers, it looks like) also had a cardboard...bookmark (?) advertising NextPlanetOver and the Fox cartoons.

If there is one thing about Marvel's advertising program that I loathe it's that they let your competitors speak directly to your customers. I think this is a poor tactical choice, if one wants storefront-based retailers to be on your side, but hey, it wouldn't be the first poor choice.

So, we add "Fast Lane" to the bookmark (?), and throw in the double gatefold covers that are (of course) all ads, and you know what you get?

A lot of damn weight.

I took thirteen 32-page Marvels from November (how many I had left over that month that ripping them to shreds wouldn't matter), and threw them on a grocery scale. Those thirteen books weighed 2.11 pounds. I then ripped out the inserts and gatefolds, and they weighed 1.42 pounds. A difference of .69. Or about one-third.

Think about that one second.

One-third of your shipping charges from Marvel that month might have been for paying for someone else's advertising.

This is just wrong.

Marvel has, of course, every right in the world to sell as much advertising as they like. If they want to work a deal with a concrete manufacturer to include a free 10-pound bag of cement with every Marvel comic, hey I won't stop them. But I'll be arsed if they expect me to pay for it.

Retailer margins and business models are tight enough without sticking them with more charges.

If Marvel comics has any sense of responsibility to the direct market, then some time in the next month, you'll see a shipping allowance on your invoice for your November purchases.

That's all we ask from any vendor: responsibility.

Tilting at Windmills #93
(Originally ran in Comics Retailer #94)

My muse, she's a-gone.

For *days* I've been trying to write this damn column, but the words is all stuck.

See, my wife is out of town for two months. She's in New York City on a film shoot (she's in the production end). Two. Months.

We've been married for, whoa, fourteen years now. In all that time, we've never spent more than four days apart. And she's gone for two months.

The thing I never really realized is how much I count on her for the little things. It pains me to admit it, but I barely know how to take care of myself on my own. We met when I was seventeen, and we married ten days after my eighteenth birthday, so it's not like I've ever been a *bachelor*, y'know? I mean, I'd eat, and the dirty dishes would "vanish." Heh. So why do I have this big pile of plates threatening to topple over now?

I'm also ineffably lonely. It's just...wrong to come home every night to a cold, empty, dark house. She's always been the center of my life – someone to whom I could whisper my secret hopes and dreams; someone who always had a soft smile and a warm word; someone who made me laugh and cry and sing.

I begin to understand doves. They mate for life. And when one dies, the other one....just stops living. I know that feeling now. It's like I've lost a limb.

I'll tell you what: I'll never ever ever take her for granted again.

I told her this on the phone˙the other night, and she just laughed. "I don't really do anything," she said.

Mm. Except complete me.

So, if this column sucks, now you know the reason.

The funny thing is, this one should be *cake*. I decided I'd "write to topic" (a rarity, as you all know), and the topic is "what are the strengths of the independent retailer?" I mean, good lord, if that doesn't have "Hibbs" stamped on it in forty-foot high glowing letters, I have no idea what does. Cheerleading (usually) comes easily to me.

cracks knuckles and gets to it

Y'know, here we are on the cusp of the 21st Century, and things are changing rapidly. So rapidly that you might feel you're being left behind.

Well, you're not.

Internet this, and internet that. Lots and lots of words spew out about how this changes everything, about how this is the future of the market. I think it was Chuck Rozanski who said something like how he was putting virtually all of his efforts there from here on out.

While it *is* certainly true that 1) there are *tons* of people who *used* to read comics, but broke the habit; 2) there are *tons* of people who *might* be interested in reading a comic, if only they were exposed to them; and 3) there is an explosion of people coming "online," so much so as to make this a potentially lucrative audience to chase, I surely don't think it is any kind of a "threat" to the "traditional" storefront retailer.

The 'net has a number of fundamental problems, some of which will iron themselves out eventually (things like bandwidth and accessibility), but other aspects are basically insurmountable. The main one is really human contact.

See, man is ultimately a social creature. We don't do well (he said, thinking about his missing wife) in isolation; and while the web has hundreds of thousands, if not millions, of people chattering away on it every night it is, at best, the *illusion* of human contact, not the thing itself.

(Really, I know, that needs some back-up and justification – I could write 5,000 words easily on the subject of contact and virtual contact and the socio-psychological impact of the internet – in fact, I even wrote three or four paragraphs before I realized that was a huge digression, and that I'd blow my word count if I tried to more than shorthand the topic. So, lets leave it at "this is beyond the scope of today's topic" and grant me the given on the subject.)

(And, actually, even this much is painfully broad given my space constraints.)

Ultimately, I guess, it comes down to this: you can't smile on the internet. Oh, sure, you can *smiles*, or even (^_^) (and, yes, the Japanese have superior smiley technology), but you can't actually and truly look someone in the eye, and let them know you are sincere.

Sales come from a lot of things. There are price and availability, of course; selection, convenience, those are important as well – and these are all things that the internet can (though not always *does*) excel at. But never ever downplay the value of personality and passion and socialization.

Try this another way: being in the San Francisco Bay Area I would venture that a greater percentage of my customers are "wired" than most other locales.

Further, we have like five of the ten "best" comic book shops in the country within an hour or less from us. One would think that, if the internet was a "threat" to (ugh) "brick-and-mortar" comic shops, we'd feel it first here. But, in reality, our sales are way up.

Why? Because the (excuse the pun) experience one gets from physically shopping can never be replaced or replicated in a "virtual" space. It just can't be done. Only in a "real" store can someone walk out in 15 minutes with a stack of books when they come in and ask, "Hey, can you help me find drawings of bats?" (happened yesterday, that one.) Only in a "real" store can the bored girlfriend be handed a comic to read while she waits for her boyfriend to finish shopping, and get turned into a regular customer. I could go on and on with examples, but the point is human contact is king.

The web is fabulous if you're a knowledgeable and informed consumer who knows precisely what you want, and are shopping based on price. But I believe that describes very few of our current customers, and even less of the huge potential audience that is waiting out there for us to tap.

So, don't be too worried, really, about business getting sucked away from you, by the web.

As long as you run a good store.

Which, as always, is the key.

If your store is clean, well lit, well-stocked, and staffed with bright, creative, knowledgeable and passionate people you are (more or less) bulletproof.

The same thing applies to any potential threat from chain-businesses. I've spoken on this many times before, but the reality of a chain is that they can't sustain quality manpower throughout the entire organization, past a certain point. They can do clean, well lit, and well-stocked. Maybe, possibly, even better than you can – but staffing is always their weak spot. They can probably even smother you on pricing – but you should always be able to beat them on service.

Service creates loyalty. And loyalty is at the heart of survival as an independent. Not "only shopping with you" kind of loyalty – but the kind who exhort others to check you out.

Service isn't just about programs, which is the fundamental mistake a lot of businesses make. Service is about the attitude and passion and knowledge that supports and creates those programs. As an example, it is a "service" to have a pull and hold system for your weekly customers – but the *true* service would be to know their names, and fetch their books as you see them coming down the block; and learn their tastes, so you realize they missed signing up for something they might like, and pulling it for them anyway, without hard-selling them on it; and having a conversation with them about their interests; and, and and....

Here's the basic problem: I don't really think I or anyone else can really *teach* you this stuff. Making a list of "Ten Winning Service Strategies!" or whatever is really deceptive. Because it's not the nuts and bolts that *truly* matter, it's the passion and vision behind it.

Especially in a creative-based field like comics. We're in the business of selling dreams, after all. And the passion we have for those dreams is our greatest strength.

Dream. Believe. Burn. You shouldn't ever fail.

Tilting at Windmills #94
(Originally ran in Comics Retailer #95)

Some months I struggle mightily for a topic, while others fate provides quite well on her own. This time it was easy — all I had to do was open the latest issue of *Comics Retailer* (December '99, by my time line)

Generally speaking it is said that one should not bite the hand that feeds them. Conventional wisdom says "do not argue with your editor." Thankfully (heh) I'm not precisely conventional. See J.J. made the statement, "I've yet to see a good, sound *business* reason to not carry *Pokémon* cards." Now, I might have let it go, but then he repeats it again in the next paragraph. And I have this recollection (though I can't find the issue) that he said something similar in the *CBG* that came out that week too.

Dunno. Maybe J.J. and I have differing opinions on "*business* reasons," but I see a number of practical and tangible ones, personally.

1) Margins. Speaking as a very general rule, anything less than keystoning (doubling your wholesale costs) is not particularly profitable to carry. It's been a few

years since I've paid attention, but, if I recall the old research correctly, the average comics store was working off something like a 7% pre-tax profit margin. And this was, of course, "in the old days" (pre-exclusives), when the huge majority of stores received at least 50%-off their main suppliers (Marvel, DC, etc.) and had, in many cases, greatly reduced shipping costs.

Basically as you ran the math, every dollar you took in was about seven cents profit, once you accounted for all expenses (rent, utilities, wages, cost-of-goods sold, etc.). Like I said, this is fairly old data, and the numbers may well have changed since I stopped looking at it but given that a) I run a (relative to many shops) tight ship and run at around 9%, and b) that expenses have only climbed in the intervening years; I judge it a reasonable benchmark.

I hate to say it, but we're at the week in the month (as I write this) where all of the ordering information is in my manager, Rob's, hands, so I can't look up *Pokémon* card pricing. But, as a standard rule, cards are discounted at 35-40% off.

What I *can* say for sure is that in my economic reality (at least), items with a 35% discount are (at best) a break-even proposition for me to sell. If I don't get a 100% sell-through, they lose money.

And I really have to assume that your numbers aren't all that different.

In the most rosy of projections, the only way to make any money off of low-margin items is to do high volume. A greater volume than you can likely push-through your single store. There is a reason that local competitors for chains like, say, Wal-Mart aren't generally numerous – the model of low-price, low-margin items utterly depends on pushing enormous volume through. Volume that non-chain entities can seldom match.

I can't do your math for you, of course, but take a close look at your books and tell me if, after you factor out your fixed expenses, you're *actually* turning a *profit* (not merely cash flow) on *Pokémon* cards at SRP. Or, at least, a profit that is worth the expense, relative to other product lines you could be carrying. My guess the answer is "no."

"Ah!" you argue, "I'm not selling them at SRP; and besides, we're selling singles for huge sums." And, I admit, I can't calculate your position on that. What I *can* note is that a) selling singles is very manpower intensive, possibly taking resources away from other more practical places you could be placing it, and b) you, as a rule, are less able to compete at higher-than-SRP if you have any competition at all.

2) Which brings us to competition. Earlier in the product cycle the "big boys" weren't playing. Selling packs for two to three times SRP was seemingly common. But as *Pokémon* "matures," and more and more of them find their ways into the Wal-Marts and Blockbusters of the world (I mean, I saw the things just last week at the *computer* store), your ability to engage in such (realistically) predatory pricing is reduced greatly.

Sure, maybe you have no competition nearby – there's always that chance; but odds are better there is a larger business near you that can and will undercut your price through volume.

If you're selling packs for $5, and the Wal-Mart ten minutes away has them at $2.50, you look bad. Real bad.

The thing of it is, prior to the chains "discovering" *Pokémon* (roughly) this fall, I would have not argued J.J.'s point as hard – but if you try *getting into Pokémon today*, odds are good you will get crushed. Your window of opportunity was nine to twelve months ago. Or to put it another way: last week I heard Kay-Bee Toys radio ads in *heavy* rotation on the local cock-rock station. "Get a free framistat from your *Pokémon* Headquarters!" Trying to compete head-to-head with that is, best case, running on a treadmill.

3) of course, is longevity. *Pokémon* is, odds say, a fad. Fads burn bright and hot, and then they crash and burn leaving a lot of people holding the bag. Sure, I suppose there's a chance *Pokémon* might have another year or two left in it, but given that the imitator products have begun to show up, that's nearly the surest sign it's all over once the new school year starts. Marketing fads aimed at children are infamous for going quickly away.

If you're going to chase a fad (and, sure, plenty of people enjoy that lifestyle) the time to do it is when it is *ramping-up*, not once "everyone is talking about it." Running a successful fad-driven business is all about being "cutting edge." If you're *incredibly careful* with inventory management, you can ride it to its conclusion but oh so few people are careful (I'll discuss inventory in the next point).

It's like that Kenny Rogers song: "You have to know when to hold them, know when to fold them, know when to walk away, and know when to run." And, I hate to say it, most of you don't have that skill.

To me, saying, in fourth quarter 1999 "hey, get into *Pokémon!*" to an independent comic book shop is like saying "Hey, get into black-and-white comics!" the week after *Adolescent Radioactive Black-Belt Hamsters* #1 came out. And, if you don't understand *that* reference, even more reason to avoid *Pokémon* like the plague.

4) Supply and demand. Fads are usually driven by demand outstripping supply. This is why the "early adopters" usually can cash in big – they "control" the market (though lets not forget that for every wild success they get in figuring out the trend before anyone else, they usually have two or three massive flops).

Further, in mass-market driven fads, chains, with their higher buying power, are always going to absorb the bulk of what little supply exists once they "figure it out." I see many reports in Market Beat and on the web that read like "I ordered 50 boxes, and got two, and Wal-Mart has them piled floor-to-ceiling!"

The problem is that most people then begin to overcompensate. "Hm, I'm getting 5% fill rates. Better order 20 times what I need to adjust for that." Which will eventually bite you in the ass. Manufacturers are often not able to keep up with demand on a "hot" product at first...but *eventually* their manufacturing processes will catch up to retailer demand, and you *will* get far far more product than you could hope to sell.

We see this curve time and time and time again. And, in most cases, it's the smallest segment of a marketplace (in this case that would be you, o under-financed comic book retailer) that gets the short end of the supply curve – both at the beginning when demand outstrips supply; and at the end when supply far outweighs demand.

Think for a second of all the other comics/games/hobby retailers that you know that lost all of their wonderful initial profits by not seeing the end of the trend rushing up to meet them like a freight train, and losing it all to dead inventory. And if you don't know any, I can name several hundred.

Another thing about supply: maybe it's because I am fairly risk-averse, but I am far more interested in selling *long-term* than I am in the quick buck. I prefer selling products that have dependable and consistent stock because otherwise *I look bad to my customers*

(This is why, for example, I'm quite happy to deal with, say, DC who have learned inventory control. How many times in the last, say, ten years, has *Dark Knight Returns* been out of stock from DC for more than a week or so? Compare this to perpetual whipping boy Marvel who let their single most-salable backlist item [Ross and Busiek's *Marvels*] drop out of print for at least six months. But I digress.)

Loyalty is better than quick rewards, in my opinion, unless you're planning on retiring in a few weeks. The huge and vast majority that are the current *Pokémon* card buyers will instantly and happily abandon you if they find another store that has better stock/prices.

So, ultimately, I think "No, I am sorry, we don't carry that" is always better than "No, sorry, we're out of stock, and I'm not sure when / if we'll get more." The latter, I believe, makes you look slipshod and a poor business owner – *even when supply issues are not your fault*

Hrm, well, I've very nearly reached the end of my word count, so I guess we can talk about #5 (character and environment) some other day, because I have one other thing I want to quickly address this month. The old "be careful what you ask for" problem. Long-time readers will recall me bitching the last two years or so about not enough "holiday" merchandise arriving *before* the holidays. This year, it seems, largely, as if this problem has been worked out, but with it came a "conventional wisdom" problem. CW says that "the Friday after Thanksgiving is the busiest sales day of the year" and it seems a lot of manufacturers put a whole lot of stock in this nugget – because I have never seen as heavy of a ship week as that Wednesday. Basically every publisher crammed *so* much stuff out that week (and, people, *work with us here* – like, Dark Horse, if you're putting out lunch boxes, *don't send us 6 designs in a single fucking week!!!*) that we were choking on product.

Here's the deal in any specialty shop I've ever noticed: conventional wisdom does not apply to us. That's department stores. Downtown shopping areas. Not specialty shops. Least *never* has been for me, or the half a dozen other small business in the area I polled.

So next year, *please* spread it out a *bit* more?

At least we're getting closer....

Tilting at Windmills #95
(Originally ran in Comics Retailer #96)

Hardest part of writing for me is starting. Usually once I have my opening, I can out-pith just about anyone, but the first few sentences are the hardest part. Actually, it gets even worse at certain times of the year, because there just isn't anything to talk about really.

Take when I'm writing this: in January. I mean, ugh, dead dead dead month this year. January 2000. It's not even like I thought I'd be alive to see it – we're in the *future* now.

'Course J.J. even calls me up, as I sit and watch the cursor go blink-blink-blink on the empty white screen, all happy and stuff. "Brian! Good news! I have extra space for you this month! 1700 words!"

Joy.

Hey, have you noticed that like the last four or five of my columns have started with some variant of "Gee, I don't know what to write about?" When people ask me "Why are you stopping the column at 100?" that is probably my best answer.

I think I'll be really relieved when I get to just write the darn things when I feel like it, and have a *real* topic, instead of this "Hey! Have to fill space!"

On the other hand, I just got a raise to $125 a column, and saying "no" to like $40/hour is *really* hard.

Well, Comics Potpourri for $100, Alex.

"This comics publisher, praised in the past for its policies on promotional items, recently dropped the ball on a 'save the animals' insert."

"Who is DC?"

Correct.

So dig this: DC *always* does freight credit for inserts and stuff. They have traditionally understood that it's just not right to charge retailers for things that they didn't order and don't add to the salability of a protect.

Until now apparently.

Several of DC's...well, hm, "younger audience" titles? (cartoon-based, as well as DCU titles like *Impulse* and *Stars and Stripes*) had a poly-bagged "Superman for the Animals" comic book in it. As far as PSA (public service announcement) comics go, this one was actually well done (unlike the inexcusably ham-fisted "Fast Lane" in the Marvel books)... but it doesn't explain why comics retailers are being asked to foot the bill for shipping it to the stores.

As much as I agree that shooting cats with pellet guns and murdering dogs so you can get a collection of their collars is a *bad* thing, I think I have a right to determine whether I should spend *my* money educating my customers on this issue.

There are a million good issues out there, but given that every three to five cents I spend on shipping for these comics is three to five cents away from where *I* want to spend my charity money, I have to sadly cry "foul."

Just for a point of reference, I'd say that, oh, 99% of *my* customers of the affected titles are actually over 20. The odds of them being animal abusers are, frankly, slim-to-none. I simply do not serve the demographic this is directed at.

On the other hand, when DC did "Death Talks about Life" (John Constantine shows you how to put on a condom!), I was *quite* happy to throw down my shekels for that PSA. We're in San Francisco, after all, and I am reasonably sure that a significant percentage of my customers are engaged in high-risk unprotected sex. Will a comic change their minds? Probably not, but the more facts out in the community, the safer everyone is. And in fact, I ordered many *extra* copies of that PSA, in order to do my little part.

I am told that in this case DC opted to not give freight credit because it had "story content/value." And while this may well be true, it was unsolicited, and to me, no different than any *other* change in solicited content that would make an item returnable or (better solution here) eligible for freight credit.

I'll take Comic Potpourri for $500 please, Alex.

"This publisher should be lauded for their free overship in January."

"Who is DC?"

"I would have also accepted AiT Comics."

Two nice overships this month. DC *just* gets the nudge for the program for *Deadenders*. In case you don't recall, *Deadenders* #1 was shipped to you free in *double* the quantity of your orders for #2. What this means in practical terms is that (if you were thinking) you just didn't order #1 at all, and ordered #2 like a #1. I think this was a tremendously intelligent move, which should (one hopes) also deflect the usual issue #3 order pattern a bit. The nice thing is that it should give *more* than adequate enough copies for you to really nail your order on #4 – too often these days we sell out of debut issues faster than we should, and are working off incomplete information when it comes time to order a book with data for the first time (usually #4). Anyway, I really liked this idea, and I hope it proved successful enough for DC to tweak it a little bit and make it a permanent addition to their arsenal of tricks.

In fact, *every* publisher should look closely at this promotion. A cursory glance at Diamond Dateline makes me believe it did significant things for *Deadenders*. Time will tell if *Deadenders* is a "go book" or not, but for a title with legs, this could be a very significant tool to make a creatively strong book a commercial hit right out of the gate.

Runner up (and like I said, it was close) goes to AiT comics, run by Everyman's Pal, Larry Young. Lar is doing a free 50% overship of *Astronauts in Trouble: Space 1959* #1. *And* he's paying freight. That's a reasonably sizable investment for a small publisher to make, but one that should really pay off long-term, if y'all pay attention properly.

(Full disclosure: Larry works for me at Comix Experience, though I don't see a cent from AiT. Coulda too. He offered me the chance to publish, and I declined being the fiscally conservative scaredy-cat that I am. *sighs*)

Comics Potpourri for $1000, please, Alex.

"This may be the single biggest issue facing comics in the next year."

"Hmm....What is comics pricing?"

Maybe so.

I was trolling J.J. for column ideas, and he mentioned he's been getting a lot of mail about "comics are too expensive" coming from the retailers. From the *retailers*. Man, it's one thing when customers are saying it, but when the very guys who have to be out there on the front lines are saying it too, well maybe this needs to be thought about carefully.

Fuel is added to the fire of a rumor (STRESS: RUMOR, NOT FACT!) that Marvel is planning on raising the bottom price of their line to $2.25. Well, even if they don't do it this year, eventually Marvel and DC *will* do it – inflation dictates that.

But, man, $2.25 for a standard format comic book. Ow.

Thing is, if a product is *quality*, "price is irrelevant." I mean, if *League of Extraordinary Gentlemen* was priced at $4.95 an issue, I think we'd all still be selling stacks of it. Because it's good and people like it.

But you know and I know that the average fan's loyalty for the average comic is hovering somewhere between "weak" and "anemic." And there *is* an amount of money which will cause them to walk away from the habit and not return.

The simple fact, in the end, is that a goodly number of comics are priced at levels above what the quality/entertainment value of the contents are.

I don't pretend to know (or even understand) all of the myriad of decisions that go into pricing funny books. But $3.50 for the Marvel annuals is *too much*. $6.95 each for *JSA: Liberty Files* is *too much*. It's too much for the entertainment value inside; and it's too much for us to risk on non-returnable product.

We've got a horribly viscious circle working right now – prices are raising (in part) because initial orders are dropping...which just causes us to be even more risk-averse, and tighten our orders more, which causes prices to raise...and so on.

On anything more than, say, $2.95, I find that (in general) I under-order, because the price scares me. Even if it sounds really good. It's just too much of a risk if it tanks.

And here's something I'm not *sure* the publishers and talent understand, really (having just read Peter David's column on Captain Marvel not selling as well as he thought it should): a good and conscientious retailer (of which I think there are more these days than the "crappy" kind) does *not like selling out too quickly*.

Honestly, it makes us look bad. We really hate saying "no, we sold out," because it makes the customers dissatisfied and makes us look incompetent.

Anyway, the point I really wanted to make is that I'm fairly concerned that more than $2 for a standard format comic might really be the death-knell of the periodic comic. *Particularly* "franchise" lines. I just can't see all that many people willing to pay $2.25 for *Amazing Spider-Man* **and** *Peter Parker*. Or even something that's decently good like the Superman books. Over $2 will be a huge psychological barrier for people to cross, and I think it will make a lot of people reassess their collecting habits.

The smart retailers are beginning to reposition themselves more as a bookstore (perennial items) than as a newsstand (periodical items), but the challenge is if we're moving that needle fast enough, as a community.

Were I a publisher in the year 2000, I'd be putting the majority of my weight into perennial items, trying to build that segment as fast as I could before the periodical backlash begins.

Because if we cross that $2 line *before* the intelligence, supply and infrastructure for the bookstore model is firmly in place, we're going to have at least another year before the market turnaround comes like we want it.

I wish you all luck as we stride into the future.

a   r   t   i   c   l   e

9 6

Tilting at Windmills #96
(Originally ran in Comics Retailer #97)

I don't know about anyone else, but we had a pretty kick-ass January. Up nearly 15% from the year before. Last month's *Comic Retailer* showed the nationwide preorder trend to be almost exactly the opposite for the month, so I'm not so sure that any of the rest of you are seeing this as well.

Not to keep banging the same old drum over and over again, but the way we were able to post such gains was all from trade paperbacks and graphic novels. Backlist.

Thing is, the charts we get to see aren't, I do not think, giving the entire picture of the market. Boy-editor J.J. does a pretty spiff job digging out good and useful data from what Diamond publicly provides each month, but he can't work with data he's not given.

In fact, I don't think that Diamond provides *any* useful data on backlist, really. And that's a huge shame, because I truly believe that category holds the greatest potential for the growth, and maybe even survival, of the Direct Market.

Information is always your friend. Information shows you *where* the bar is; gives you a standard to judge your (and the market's) efforts by. If we judge by my experience, or of the experience of many other retailers making the adjustment toward a backlist-driven economy, the market is actually *stronger* today than it was a year ago – but the preorder picture doesn't (and can't) show that.

If the information given is incomplete, does this not then, potentially, hold back others from acting upon it? What if there are ten retailers reading this right now who are on the borderline of getting into backlist heavier, not sure if my experience is translatable? What if Diamond's Star orders have grown by (he said, making numbers up) 30% a year? Might that not be a piece of data that could sway those people over to a more bold experimentation in stock breadth? Do you see what I mean? Without fact, all we have is faith.

And faith is not precisely the best model with which to run a business.

I often see comics retailing as a war. This is not a new metaphor for my long-time readers, but it's one that must often be reiterated. Over the last few years certain things have gotten better, as a whole – supply lines are more firmly in place to bring us the weapons we need to advance the war: for example, you really don't need to worry too badly about getting copies of *Dark Knight Returns*, or *Cerebus: High Society* any more. This is a good thing.

But what about our MIA?

Comics have a long and storied past, much of which has been "lost" due to...well, its hard to speculate, really. Pig-headedness? Greed? Foolishness? Take your pick. But the fact remains that there are mountains of work that have been left to vanish out on the battlefield. Strong, powerful, vital work that could help us "win our war." I'm going to devote the rest of this column to our Missing in Action – work that you just shake your head and go "um, why isn't this in print anymore?"

This list is hardly conclusive. Nor is it prioritized in anyway other than me looking over at my bookshelves, and sadly shaking my head. You probably have a list of your own. Do us all a favor and codify it and send it into the *Comics Retailer* letter page. It can't hurt.

Hibbs' MIA list:

1) Alan Moore's *Swamp Thing*. I feel bad for Alan Moore, some days. He came a decade too early. He defined a style and a model of working (don't treat your audience like illiterates and write from your heart), and yet, the greatest successes have really come to those who "followed." Take Neil Gaiman for example: virtually every comic he has *ever* written is in print currently. Sure we're down a few *2000ad* stories he wrote, but, jeez, even scripts he wrote that we never actually produced originally are now in print (cf. *Midnight Days*). Garth Ennis is much the same way. Warren Ellis is getting close. But not poor Alan.

The most egregious absence is, of course, *Swamp Thing*. I just don't understand why there isn't a Complete Moore *Swamp Thing* Library in the same vein as the complete *Sandman* or *Preacher*. Does this make sense to anyone else?

There are like, what, six *Hellblazer* books? But you can't buy John Constantine's first appearances anywhere except as back issues. I don't get it.

What about his earlier work? *DR and Quinch*, anyone? *Halo Jones*? *Skizz*? There is an enormous backlog of material out there that someone should be getting down on their knees and just begging Alan to let them bring back into print.

I mean, *Miracleman* is out of print, even, and *Todd* owns the rights to that. Has for a year or two, and he hasn't done a *thing* with it. Does anyone else think this is maddening?

2) *Akira*. Woof. I get 2-3 requests for this a week. Easy. Is this still trapped in the black hole of Marvel's bankruptcy? They're out of that now, so can someone please reissue the complete series? When you have a Manga series that even people who know nothing about Manga can name, I think someone should bring it back to market.

And as long as we're talking about Manga, four words: *Lone. Wolf. And. Cub.*

3) The Moebius library. Same as above, really. In San Francisco Sony opened an "entertainment complex" called the Metreon. An entire city block of movie theaters, a solid floor of video game arcades. The latter has a Moebius theme. Heck they even have a Moebius store. Tens of thousands of people each year see this place, and a lot of them come past my store looking for Mr. Giraud's body of work. Woo hoo, I have four Dark Horse collections. Marvel had like twenty books in print at one point. Where did they all go, and who do I have to kill to get them back?

People know his name, they know his style, and they want his work. And when I say "people," I mean "people who don't read comics"...which is, like, part of the goal, aye?

4) Bill Sienkiewicz. If you looked through the Star System list, one might conclude that Sienkiewicz never existed. Not *one* thing he has illustrated is actually in print anymore. *Elektra. Stray Toasters. Love and War.* Hell, even his run on *New Mutants.* All lost and gone out of print. Sad. Again, I get tons and tons of requests for his work.

5) *Marvel Masterworks.* To be fair, Marvel *has* just started picking these back up, and there are alternatives (like the *Essential* books) for a few of these — but its not anywhere near enough yet. Clearly DC must be making good bank from their *Archive* editions – we're getting at least four to six new ones a year – so how come Marvel hasn't figured out that the, erm, "upscale market" really desperately wants this material? Why doesn't someone up there go take a look at eBay and quickly understand there is a huge untapped market for quality color reprints of their classic work?

On the other hand, it would really be nice if Marvel could, like, hire a design guy with any aesthetic taste whatsoever. One of these days (we hope) they'll eventually realize it is the talent, the quality of the *work* that made (and still makes) Marvel – not the Marvel brand name. These color-riot, over-designed with convenient pigeon-holed groupings like "Marvel's Finest" or "Marvel Visionaries" just look weird and ugly. Especially spine out.

You'd have thought the post-Image period of Marvel would have told them that *brand* is secondary to *talent.* *sighs*

6) Same idea, why in God's name isn't there a sequential, numbered series of the "Claremont" *X-Men?* Everything from, say, *Giant-Size* #1 to *Uncanny* #200 or so should be in print. The majority of the Byrne *X-Men* are not available in color, not one issue of the Paul Smith period...that's just sad. Especially with the movie coming up (not that, he added quickly, I think it it's going to be a huge success – that *Matrix*-look worked for the *Matrix,* but I don't think it will work for *X-Men*), this material should be in print.

(Let me parenthetically reiterate the "sequential, numbered" part. This goes for any and all reprint series. See, really, people like to know what order to read things in. Retailers, too, usually find it helpful in arranging their shelves, and ordering product. People are kinda funny that way. Who'da thunk it? And subtitles are usually stupid. I'd rather see on my invoice and on my shelf Title: book 1 than Title: long unwieldy subtitle. Its often hard to remember which order books read in when you're trying to sell them to a customer. When I was a kid buying *Hardy Boys* books, I *liked* the fact that they were numbered on the spine. Getting "book 5" didn't *detract* me from a series – quite the opposite, in fact! I went, "cool, if I like this, there is more!")

And Byrne's *FF* as long as we're looking at Marvel.

I'm nearly out of space, so I can't keep making lists – and making them would be easy: Defunct publishers alone could add another 2000 words (Where's *Taboo?* Eric Shanower's *Oz* books? The *Complete Nexus? American Flagg? Tapping the Vein? Stig's Inferno? Mister X?* Etc. etc. etc.) But the point remains there is a massive amount of quality, commercial, and wonderful work that is missing from the marketplace.

To me, not having any of these books available is not unlike, say, *Casablanca* not being available on video.

Retailers, write *Comics Retailer* with your own lists...and publishers: listen!

I mean, we all like making money, right?

Tilting at Windmills #97
(Originally ran in Comics Retailer #98)

It's not that periodical comics are dead, exactly. After all, they provide the cash flow that allows us to keep our doors open; and the steady habit that ensures the bulk of our customers will walk back into our stores week after week. But clearly (it's clear to you, right?) the system just isn't working correctly.

It seems to me that comic shops are doing one of three things in response to the changing climate of periodical sales:

1) Going the "safest route" and reducing the majority of their new comics orders to "subscription only" – with few-to-no "rack copies" of most books available.

While there is a certain kind of short-term economic rationality to this approach (if you're not getting a better than 80% sell-through on a title, you're losing money on it. "Subscription only" *forces* 100% sell-through [unless, of course, you get defaulted upon by the subscriber], thereby yielding a "guaranteed profit"), long-term this approach is a slow, painful death.

Why? Well, first off you're almost certainly creating a situation where, really, numbers can't go anywhere but down. Without the material on the racks, customers can not possibly be exposed to a work, leaving your sole marketing to word of mouth. I think it's fairly obvious that out-of-store entities (the internet, *Wizard, Comic Shop News*, etc.) are the largest source of "exposure" that most comics are getting these days.

Now word of mouth is a wonderful thing, of course, but its a slow build, and more than that, its dependent (as it were) on the "kindness of strangers." If one or more of the "trusted voices" don't recommend a title, it's never going to go anywhere. Even when the "buzz" is really growing, we're looking at three to six months before it has much tangible impact in orders.

For small publishers, where 2000 copies represents break-even, because they're doing it out of their garage in their "free time" and they have another source of income to keep food in their bellies, it's possible to "wait the market out." "If you build it, they will come" is the saying, and, once you hit the right amount of buzz, and once you have enough of a body of work that your backlist is providing you that steady income, you can hit that critical mass of sales enough to support you within a year or two.

Thing is, it's not guaranteed, by any means, and certainly, even small missteps towards the beginning of the curve can cut you off at the knees. For example, Julian Sandsburg does a nice little comic called *Jupiter*. He's got a lot of craft and talent, and, maybe more importantly, you can see he's learning more each issue. This is not a comic that will ever crack, say, 5000 copies in sales, because it is "esoteric," but those 5000, if he can get to them all, should (one imagines) provide a decent enough living to allow him to continue. Julian took the interesting step of providing free sample copies of at least four contiguous issues to comics shops. I'm not clear if those sample copies went to every Diamond account, or just the top (whatever criteria), but he was, it appears, trying to show "look, it has basic craft, and more importantly, it's coming out monthly and on time." Now, I've never spoken to Julian, and I don't have access to his financial picture, but, knowing what I do know, I think it's fairly safe to assume that the costs incurred in sending out these four months worth of free copies will add at least a year to his break-even point on the title overall. The gamble he took (or so I presume) was that the extra sales he'd garner from retailers recognizing his craft and dependability would offset the production cost losses for all those sample copies.

Problem is, of course, that, most comic shops are "subs only" and risk-averse, and will only take that one-copy-for-the-shelf risk when they're heard it from both the "press" (including the internet in that designation) as well as their own customers (largely following up on that press). That kind of broad targeting will almost never work.

Large publishers have a different set of issues. One presumes and hopes that they have a broad enough cash-flow to "nurture" titles that "under-perform" – but conversely, they have expensive offices and production facilities and executives, so their bottom line is much much much higher. "Can't Marvel launch a title that makes it past issue #10?" is something that I hear a lot. And, it sure seems like the answer is "no." At least until they're willing to lose money for (at least) six months to find the book's audience, wait for critical acclaim, and make their money back from the reprints of the work. Problem is for Marvel that "critical acclaim" almost never happens because most titles they launch are marketing exercises rather than content- and creator-driven. Which worked very nicely indeed when rack copies were a common thing. But those days are gone.

Certainly, when a large publisher has the vision and commitment, they can afford to lose short-term money for long-term profit. Let's look at, say, *Transmetropolitan*. Now, again, a lot of this is conjecture, since I don't get to see DC's financial records, and I'm missing several key pieces of data, but my strong guess is that at the level *Transmet* is selling, it's losing a small amount of money every periodical issue. *However* (and it's a big however), now that there are three TPBs out, as well as an action figure, and a statue, and soon those cool glasses – *Transmet, as a property*, is probably very much in the black.

Now, the subscription-model comic shop probably doesn't carry *Transmet*. Or, maybe they've started carrying it recently because enough of a buzz has begun to surround it. But the key point is that they're not going to support it (and, note, "one-copy-for-the-rack" is *not* "support") until enough other people do.

Honestly, I don't blame the subscription-model one tiny bit. Certainly, several years ago I announced in these very pages that I was taking a similar approach to Marvel because of the anti-retailer business practices they were enacting (this was coupled with the low editorial standards they had at the time as well) – this is a stance that I've significantly backed away from once Marvel started distributing through Diamond again – but I clearly saw (and still see) the short-term allure of "since I need 80% sell-through to make a profit, I'll 'force' 100% sell-through by not carrying this."

The difference is I also only did this on one subset of those comics that I carried. What I perceive this type of retailer doing is applying this principle far too broadly, to the point where they've smothered all chance of growth in their comics category.

I've chosen that last word fairly carefully, because it's a key point – comics are simply a category for this class of store.

It's no huge secret that I tend to be a purist in most of my passions. I don't believe that one can be a *good* "comic book shop" if, say, 80%+ of your efforts are focused on, well, "comic books." I don't *personally* believe you can consider yourself a "comic book shop" if you only offer, say, the Diamond Top 100. Rather, you are a "store that carries comics".

Like I said, I am a purist, but let me be clear that there is no shame to be a "store that carries comics." But I feel that we, as an industry, have to be very clear indeed on this distinction because the knowledge informs what we do and how we do it.

February's Market Beat (*CR* #97) maps the "Average per-comics-store share of comics ordered during the month (based on an estimated base of 3600 stores)" (and based, it is implied, on the data that Diamond provides exclusively) as $4010 at retail cover price. For an entire month.

Work with me here: $4000 a month either means comics are a sideline for the majority of stores, or that the majority of stores are "hobbies." Figuring an insanely generous profit margin of 15%...well, not many people can live on $600/month.

What is happening in this type of store is that comics are a marginal item that is not carried in any real depth or breadth, and that the "shortfall" (as it were) is being made up by other product lines. Whether they be games or cards or plush toys or paperback books or whatever. Again, nothing wrong with it, but it very much skews the picture of where the market is, and where it can go.

2) Then we have your "true" comic book shops. Stores where, largely, the periodical is slowly (glacially, maybe) being replaced by the perennial – the trade paperback.

This type of store generally racks a wide and diverse amount of comics, in reasonably deep quantities. This type of store is, on any title they "believe" in (which is a highly subjective and personal barometer) *not* trying for 100% sell-through, really, because they see that without stock, they can't grow a title's base.

Further, they see that the profit-over-time of the TPB is the direction we should be heading, because the format and just-in-time ordering makes "risk" a largely abstract concept.

By this I mean I sell about 5 copies of any given *Sandman* TPB each and every month. At $20 each, we can call this $1200 a year gross. However, my inventory-exposure at any given moment is just five copies, maximum. Or less than $45 (five copies x $8.98 wholesale at 55% off). I *know* approximately how many copies of the book I will sell each month, and I only need to reorder them as the product sells through. I don't need to buy *all* sixty copies that I'll sell in a year up front, and, in fact, if I have a really good ordering system, I could float a mere two to three copies, and just order a fresh replacement copy once a week.

Finally the market has begun to catch up to this method of doing business, and finally we can *see* a point where a "comic book shop" might not even *need* periodical comics to make a handsome profit (note that said point is likely still five to ten years away, and in fact, may never actually arrive. But that we can even *discuss* it being potential is an amazing change from just five years ago).

Note too that being a "true" comic book shop doesn't mean you *can't* carry sidelines, or even that non-comics aren't an equal or slightly greater part of your mix – merely that the product is available on the stands rather than from catalog pre-ordering, my purist tendencies aside. There are certainly stores that run kick-ass comics and gaming departments – but, in most cases it's because they have two different managers, each of whom is keenly focused on thier product line.

3) The third path that has been taken is the worst of them all: going out of business. And nobody wants that.

I'm reaching the bottom of my word count, so I'll do something I haven't done yet in 97 of these things: **To be continued.**

Next month I'll discuss, now that we've drawn a distinction between "comic book shops" and "shops that carry comics" (the main difference can be summed up as "intent"), how each type has wholly and completely different marketing needs and wants from the other; why the sales charts we see have very little basis in the "true health" of the market place; and what we can do to service both types, as well as encourage behavior shifts between one group to the other. See you then.

Tilting at Windmills #98
(Originally ran in Comics Retailer #99)

So, last month I drew a line in the sand. To quickly remind you, I posited the difference between two different kinds of comic shops. There are "shops that carry comics" (usually as a sideline amongst other products) and "true comic shops" (where the primary, if not sole, focus is the comic book).

I really think this distinction is an important one to make because the needs of the two are completely different, and foreign to one another – so much so that we may as well call them different businesses all together.

If one looks at the sales charts *Comics Retailer* provides each month in Market Beat, the market looks like it's taking a huge beating month in and month out. Overall sales are dropping like a stone. But does this accurately reflect the market place, or is the data itself flawed?

It's been suggested to me that the information that *CR* gets each month is both incomplete and too narrow in order to be supremely accurate. Obviously reorders aren't a part of this picture (Diamond isn't providing that data), and a couple of the specific mathematical pieces (such as "what is the relationship of the order index number to real sales") is based on publishers on the lower end of the scale giving detail, and not from the larger publishers, skewing those numbers low.

This, of course, is entirely possible, but given that the methodology hasn't changed in some two years, I assume the numbers are, at least, internally consistent. Plus I trust J.J.'s statistical training to make the proper adjustments.

But, the thing is, when I talk informally to other retailers – those who run full-line full-service comic book shops – our sales figures are completely contrary to the chart. The market as a whole is down some 20% by the charts from Feb '98 to Feb '99, and yet my sales (and the sales of a *whole* lot of other stores) were *up* by 20% in the same period.

So where is the disconnect taking place?

A long time ago, comics were primarily sold on the "newsstand." Well, we called it that at least, but most of those "newsstands" were little mom-and-pop pharmacies and convenience stores or whatever. A little spinner rack full of comics was a standard thing to find in most stores of this type. I bought *my* first comics from a spinner in a bodega in Brooklyn when I was just a kid, and it ignited a life-long passion for the form.

But, as time went on, the "mom-and-pop" was (largely) replaced by large corporate entities. Instead of going down to Pop's Pharmacy, you're probably heading off to Walgreen's (or your regional equivalent); instead of the General Store, you're going to Safeway or CostCo.

These businesses stock by efficiency, looking to maximize revenue per-square-foot. And, hey, it turned out that when looked at in terms of restocking effort, return on investment, and all that other good sound business stuff, it was more *efficient* to have, say, a rack of sunglasses than a rack of comic books.

Enter the comic book specialty store to "save us all."

The "beauty" of the comic book shop in the late 70s to early 80s was that one didn't have to be a rocket scientist to make a profit. Not only was it absurdly easy to open one (a few card tables, and your personal collection, and boom, you were a comic book shop), but there was a reasonably large market of customers who wanted the product that were being "forced out" of their traditional place of buying them. Comics were cheap, professional expectations were low to nonexistent, and, if you didn't sell through your comics in the first month or two after they came out, you could move them as back issues down the line.

But time, as she does, marches on. Paper costs began to skyrocket; publishers began to learn ethical business practices and, y'know, actually start paying the talent commensurate to sales (go figure!), and comic prices started to rise. Each time they did so, we made it a little harder for the "casual" purchase of comics.

We also began to recognize that we could actually target sales to a large degree — given that the comic shop would now order (and receive) every issue they wanted (remember when you bought comics off a spinner at Pop's, and you got *Muscle Boy* #36 and 38, but they never got #37 for some reason?) we as an industry began to truly focus on the "hard-core collector." Surely, before the dedicated comic book store, there were people who made whatever efforts needed to fill in their collections, but now, with this growing network of comics-specific stores, we could *cater* to these people.

Muscle Boy #36-38 were now all part of a story arc; no more self-contained issues.

And it accelerated. Soon publishers and retailers became aware that it was sound business to not only make *Muscle Boy* #36-38 a single story, but that if crossed over into *Fast Lad* #45, everybody won. Hm, then why not also do a book called the *Teen Brigade* staring *both* Muscle Boy and Fast lad? Oooh, that's doing well, lets add in *Teen Brigade West* and *Teen Brigade Adventures* and *Teen Force*, and....

Well, it was fanboy heaven, was what it was. The promise Stan had showed us all those years before ("Look! They all live in the same world!") suddenly became the *only* way to do comics. And while the fan boys loved it, the more casual consumer started getting confused and slowly started to drift away. I mean, yes, they *liked* comic books and all, but they didn't have the time or inclination to follow them all – but that's O.K., because there are plenty of hard-core fans to sustain us all.

Then someone got the bright idea that, "Well, you know, since they're actually *collecting* these things – making sure they don't miss any – what if we did special issues that cost a little more? Everyone will make more money, and the fans will be pleased to get something neat and unique!"

And it *was* a bright idea. The problem was, we did not know where to stop. Until we hit the point in the early 90s where *most* comics were tied into something else, or had a "special" issue, in any given month.

We hadn't really noticed the slow erosion of the casual customer – it was slow, after all. And they *did* come in occasionally. Usually to follow something a little more literate, a little more self-contained. And also, very few people noticed that we'd lost the incoming generation of kids because you had to go to a dedicated comic book shop in order to be exposed to comics in the first place. But what did it matter, really? The hard-core devotees were spending more than enough money to cover that shortfall – heck, we were in our boom years!

And even if things shook up a little, well, we still had the collectibility to fall back upon. If you sold 100 copies of *Muscle Boy*, you ordered an extra ten or twenty for the back room as an investment. And that new *Muscle Boy* #1 relaunch with the foil covers? Well, the hard-core wanted a piece of the pie too – so the fans started ordering ten copies apiece, too.

And everyone was doing great. New publishers were starting up. Distributors were expanding like mad. New stores were opening weekly. Comics were a surefire ticket to success!

Then, all of a sudden, the bottom dropped out. Since everyone had plenty of stock of the "collectible" (and everyone included our customers), it ceased to be collectible at all. There are more copies of *X-Men* #1 in circulation than there are (or even were) people who *read comic books* in this country. By a factor of two. Maybe three.

And the fans started realizing they were being milked.

"Um, wait a second, I don't even like Fast Boy. And while *Teen Brigade* is O.K., why am I buying *Teen Brigade West*? And, yikes, *Teen Force stinks*."

"Hold on, you want *how much* for this shiny cover? Nah, I don't want it *that* bad."

"What do you mean these 20 copies of *Muscle Boy v2* #1 are worthless? *Wizard* says they cost $5 each!"

Enormous numbers of our hard-core suddenly decided they weren't playing any more.

I said "all at once" because, when examined over a 20-year period, the crash was sudden. But, of course, all of the signs and portents were there, if you cared to look for them.

I still suspect that we could have lived through that as a mere aberration were it not for the bad planning and bad timing of Marvel. With the decision to self-distribute at the moment that they did, they plunged the very structure of the marketplace into freefall.

I could be a Pollyanna about this, but I largely believe that if Marvel hadn't made the move to purchase Heroes World, the market would have corrected itself much faster – even that we'd still have two or three competing distributorships.

Instead, what happened was that discounts plummeted and hard costs (shipping, etc.) rose at precisely the wrong time in a failing market. And comics went very rapidly from being a maintainable, if not profitable, business for the less-dedicated stores, to being an unprofitable one.

Well, depending on the retailer's methodology, of course. Those that never stressed the collectible *potential* of comics; those that steered their customers to quality rather than quantity; those that took sane inventory positions – those stores never were really "unprofitable."

But, of course, that was the barest fraction of the total.

For the rest of the stores out there, comics were no longer "efficient" – like the Mom and Pops before them. Instead of sunglasses, these "stores that sell comics" moved more effort into other fan/fringe items: gaming, cards, toys, whatever.

They stock for subscriptions only, leaving just a few titles on the rack. The "biggest" ones usually: *Batman, Spawn,* your X-Books. Pretty much everything else is relegated to catalog shopping.

And *these* are the stores where sales are still dropping, several years after the crash.

Why? Because they don't have the stock. They don't have the passion. They don't have the *vision*

My premise is this: "stores that carry comics" are to the market today what the "newsstand" was in the late 70s – a weak and shrinking marketplace whose time has come, as the paradigm shifts around them. And if we're to move forward, to excel, to take the steps needed to bring comics into the 21st Century, we need to embrace the new paradigm, and identify and work to its strengths.

Like the "true comic shops."

The difference between the Newsstand and "stores that carry comics" is that the former was considered a different mechanism entirely – "stores that carry comics" are listed on the books as "true comic shops," and until we change that method of reporting and identifying the two, we're going to have a cloudy, incorrect and flawed picture of what the future really *is*.

And I'm at 1865 words, so I have to...well, this is suddenly a three-parter. Join me next month for *Tilting at Windmills* #99 where I try to wrap this all neatly up with some tangible and rational ways for us to identify where things *really* are in our new economy. Month after that is *TaW* #100 where I'll try to summarize a little more than eight years of monthly columns, and then we'll relaunch as *TaW* v2 #1 with 8 different hologram foil covers, each with variant insides.

Or not.

Tilting at Windmills #99
(Originally ran in Comics Retailer #100)

Hopefully after the last two installments of TaW I've made a sufficient enough case that within the direct market we've reached a split between the "types" of comic book stores. On the one hand we have "stores that carry comics." These stores, for the most part, order the *minimum* number of comics they can, performing primarily as subscription services and catalog-shopping outlets for their customers. They actually *rack* an insignificant percentage of the titles available, and those they do are in such small quantities as to leave little-to-no room for growth. As a general rule, these stores are seeing decreasing sales on comics because they haven't the stock or capitalization with which to grow. These stores, largely, present comics as one category among a series of categories (games, cards, pop culture, whatever).

On the other hand, we have the "true comics shop" (yes, I know, a horrid turn of phrase) that both carries and *stocks* a wide and diverse range of comics material. While they may, in fact, have subscription services, they make a large point of stocking material casually on the rack, and are, for the most part, attempting to maximize their sales on most creatively-engaging material. As a general rule, these stores are seeing (and have seen all throughout the "bust") growing sales on comics. And these stores, largely, present comics as their primary (if not sole) category – while they may, certainly, stock other things of interest to their customers, comics are what they *do*.

The problem is that both these "kinds" of stores are lumped into the same reporting and tracking systems on the distribution level. There is no distinction made between, say, a Comic Relief, and a Bob's Comics Games and Cards Shack in any disseminated information. And further, it is generally accepted that a disproportionately large percentage of many titles' circulations are concentrated in a generally small number of stores. For example: *Transmetropolitan* sells something like 1/3 of *Batman*, nationwide. But my store sells approximately *four times* the number of *Transmet* as it does *Batman*. Now while I certainly am aware that our *Transmet* numbers are exceptional, it seems to me we can infer that for every store that carries *Transmet*, it is likely there are two to three other stores that simply don't rack it at all.

I believe these distinctions are crucial to make if we wish to both understand and grow our marketplace. The paucity of data provided to both vendors and retailers is simply not sufficient to make any kind of informed judgment about the true merit/sales potential of a work, when the data is "washed out" among "3600 stores", 3000 of which, in all likelihood, aren't "really" comic book stores.

Lazy and inefficient informational systems encourage lazy and inefficient retailing and, it appears, are used to "hold back" resources from projects with true growth potential, on both the retail and wholesale level.

One assumes that it is in the distributor's best interest to strengthen and grow the sales of as much material as they can, so I submit that filters need to be applied to the data coming out so that better purchasing decisions can be made.

The Order Index that Diamond provides, in my opinion, utterly fails in its stated mission as a method of determining comparisons in the relative weight and strength of individual titles. "If you ordered 300 copies of *Batman*, and the index for *Cerebus* is 20.5, you would order 62 copies (300/100x20.5 = 61.5) based on the POI to match the average of all orders placed with Diamond" it says. To which I can but laugh. Any store that tried to apply such a broad stroke to their ordering would go out of business within the first six months.

No. The *true* value will come when the charts are weighed by per-store market share – then the information is presented in a format that is useful and meaningful. Let's pretend that *Batman* sells 50k copies, and *Cerebus* 10k (all numbers here are made up and imaginary, and should not be construed to represent reality in any way – I'm only using these titles because that's what Diamond's order index uses as examples). Further, let us say there are 3500 stores, all 3500 of which order *Batman* and 500 of which order *Cerebus*. Then the chart would look something like this:

Qty	Retail	Order index	Title	Per-store	% store
14	47	100	Batman #579	14.28	100
202	218	20	Cerebus #254	20	14

This tells us the raw data of the primacy of *Batman*, nationwide – it sells roughly five times what *Cerebus* sells – mostly because its going into 100% of the stores. Yet *among the stores that sell* Cerebus, Cerebus *is selling roughly fifty percent better than* Batman! Now, that's only about one in seven stores, of course, but the simple inclusion of two more indexes (average copies per store, and the percentage of stores that are ordering an item) gives everyone two more benchmarks to work from and more goals to shoot for.

That latter point is an important one to me. We as an industry tend to dismiss anything not in the "Top 100," as if nothing else drives the economic engine. This, of course, is patently false for most full-line comics shops. In giving more attainable goals to publishers ("I am shooting for ten copies-per-store," "My goal is 20% market penetration") you dramatically increase the odds that functional and targeted marketing plans can be implemented.

Our own beloved *Comics Retailer* makes a stab at providing this kind of information, of course (flip back a few pages and look at Market Beat), but the problem is the data is both self-selecting and limited to the reported "top 30" lists.

I've posited many times that the minority (10-20%) of the stores provide the majority (80-90%) of the sales, and not once has this claim been challenged (and in fact, it has been supported in private conversation). If this is in fact true, then why do we continue to only view the picture of the marketplace in terms of "all" stores?

To me, this needn't be an either/or situation. Continue to print the charts in the same method, but, on the flip side, sort them by average-sales-per-store, replacing that *inane* "Star Collector of the Month" feature. Quick show of hands? Is there *any* retailer out there that finds that useful, interesting, or compelling information? It's not that I don't see the value of this feature – just that it belongs in *Previews*, not in *Dialogue*.

If one wanted to be *really* gutsy, the information on percentage-of-stores-ordering could be further subdivided by some other criteria. The most obvious (and probably most practical) would be by discount level. For example, it wouldn't at all surprise me to find out that 80% of the 55%-off-or-better stores carry "Cerebus" (at "10 copies per store"), while only 5% of the under-50%-off carry that title (and only in single copies). With such further classifications, this information starts to become directly valuable to the retailer as well. Rather than "order 20% of *Cerebus* as you do of *Batman*" (largely meaningless to the average store), you can compare your efforts like-to-like: "Hm, stores that are 'like' me are drastically outperforming me on title *x*. Maybe this is a title I should take a closer look at?"

At the least, this would allow us to identify books with strong potential that much faster. If a book like, oh, say, *Knights of the Dinner Table* is seeing 500 copies-per-issue increases, this is largely invisible on the charts as structured. Going from an order-index of 11.2 to 11.3 to 11.4 is simply imperceptible on a cursory investigation of the chart and can be easily dismissed as "average market fluctuation." More than that, since the index is calculated based on *Batman*, trying to flag growth in relationship to the POI number only works if *Batman never* changes in orders. Market penetration and average-copies-sold per-venue are more internally consistent numbers that shouldn't be impacted by major "events" in *Batman*.

Data and information are what drive informed choices – "Garbage in, garbage out" as they say – and it frustrates me that we're reliant upon word of mouth to communicate "mover" books, rather than the hard data that the distribution channel should be rationally providing.

I simply don't understand why Diamond is so protective of data that would clearly allow more comics to be sold – isn't it in their best interest to increase volume? If a vendor knows where their product is going – in what quantities, to whom – they're in a much better position to take the steps needed to sell more of it through targeted campaigning.

Oh, sure, you *can* get that data from Diamond but you need to pay them for that privilege, which strikes me as terribly counter-productive from everyone's POV.

Once, a long time ago, the careful sequestering of this data made some sense, I suppose – after all, Diamond used to have to fight it out for market-share with any number of national and regional competitors. However, as we all know, that's not a particularly significant "threat" any longer. Diamond just does not have any significant competition to speak of. And given that Diamond's infrastructure is the strongest (like, for example, they, y'know, actually pay vendors on time), any supplier who'd try to "cut Diamond out" isn't going to be in business too long, anyway.

What needs to be done is for Diamond to draw a line, like I have in this series: "true comics shops" and "stores that sell comics," and to provide that data to the vendors, *at no cost*, so that rational and informed decisions can be made by all levels of the marketplace.

Here's the thing of it: "stores that carry comics" are never going to grow. They're never going to expand. They add nothing to the marketplace. And it's time to stop pretending that they do.

If the proper information is given, then we can make better decisions aimed at moving the needle properly. Let me try to give an example. Back in part one of this series, I mention Jason (not Julian, sheesh. Maybe I should do research before writing?) Sandsberg's *Jupiter*. A fine small press comic that shows both craft and growth potential. Sandsberg sent out (via Diamond) at least four contiguous single issues of his book over a period of months. In addition, I (at least), got copies via direct mail on at least two occasions.

This is a smart plan, this is a good plan – put your comic book directly in the hands of the retailers so they have something to judge other than a little squib of copy buried in 200+ pages of other little squibs of copy in the distributor catalog.

Except....

I was already carrying the book. I was already aware of it. I was carrying more than single copies for the rack to begin with.

So all of the money Sandsberg paid in printing and packaging the "introductory packs" – as well as Diamond's handling fees (not to mention the USPO charges) – was wasted on me. *Because I am already supporting the book*

And if it was wasted on me, I think I can safely assume that it was also wasted on some fairly significant percentage of the other retailers it was sent to, because they, too, are already supporting the title.

I'm not of the mind that having a publisher waste money on presenting a message already known, among the "most likely supporters," is a circumstance that any of us (retailer, vendor, distributor) should be encouraging one tiny whit. The cash, time, and effort put into sending out all of this material to me could (and would) have been better spent in other ways (examples: overshipping, POS sales materials, items for a sales-driven raffle, whatever)

If I were on Diamond's senior management team, I'd be falling over myself to try to help small- and mid-list vendors thread the needle. I'd provide them with lists of stores that fit the "profile" of their type of work, and, further, with that same list broken out by quantity. "Based upon our years of data and experience, here are 300 stores that are not carrying your book, and probably should be. Here are 400 that are carrying it, but at less than five copies. And here are the 100 that are moving more than five copies. Send sample copies to the first 300, overship the second group, and offer a unique piece of original art to the final 100 by way of thanks. And completely forget about the other 2400 retailers for now."

That tactic will increase sales in a rational manner, and produce less waste (for *all* three tiers!) of time and effort than the kind of shotgun marketing Diamond appears to encourage.

The path and directions you take to increase sales in an established venue are *completely different* than the path and directions you take to "get your foot in the door." Any first-year salesman could tell you that.

And lest anyone think what I'm describing only applies to smaller publishers, please think again. The scale is slightly different, but this same methodology applies to Marvel and DC as well. Hell, when Boy Editor J.J. Miller can walk into four comic book shops and only find *X-Men* on the rack (bloody *X-Men*! A month or two before the movie comes out!) of *one* of those four stores, it *must* be clear that we're misclassifying our marketplace and putting resources in all of the wrong places.

It's time to stop pretending it's 1992, folks. It's time to properly identify what books are moving where, and in what manner and quantity. And it's bloody well time to stop pretending there are "3600 comic book shops" and marketing to that assumption.

Does this mean I am trying to imply that "stores that carry comics" are worthless to the overall health of the market? No. Certainly, they are an important component to any overall business plan. However, until we clearly delineate what is going where, we're never going to do more than just spin our wheels.

Garbage in, garbage out.

Time to bring the dump truck around.

a   r   t   i   c   l   e
1 0 0

Tilting at Windmills #100
(Originally ran in Comics Retailer #101)

Wow.

Well, so this is my 100th "Tilting at Windmills" – despite having been published in all 101 issues of *Comics Retailer*. And actually, depending on how you count, one can make a compelling case for this actually being #105 or so (102 of them ran in *CR*, but there are a few that ran in other places than *CR*). But by "official" counts this is #100.

This also marks the end of my guaranteed monthly run in *CR*. Oh, I'll still be writing these things, but I won't be stuck on the monthly deadline grind. I'm expecting something along the lines of six to eight a year – writing as the mood (and topic) hits me.

The first column I ever wrote was titled "Ethics and the Comics Industry" and, largely, it set the tone for the run of "Tilting at Windmills." To wit: You are responsible for your actions. You do not exist in a vacuum. Every decision you make has ramifications. And short-term thinking is nearly always harmful and destructive to our long-term health and strength as an industry.

This applies to every level of the industry and it applies to every player, regardless of his or her size, strength, or position.

That's the real thing: None of you are blameless. Not a one.

It applies to every creator who has hacked out a project for short-term gain.
"I don't need to put thought into this, because people will buy it."
"I don't need to learn craft, because people buy [flavor of the month], and he sucks, too."
"Hey, it's a paycheck."
You're guilty.

It applies to every distributor who has made a decision to save a dollar today at the expense of the future.
"They bought a lot of ad space, so let's reinforce their message that high-end multiple variant covers are a good thing. "
"You can lower your orders, but you lose the possibility of returns."
"Hmm, comics as a category are slipping; let's promote pogs."
You're guilty.

It applies to every publisher who "bows to market forces."
"If one cover is good, 12 are better."
"If a title is selling well, let's spin it off to an entire line."
"People will buy *Mucus Man* no matter who is drawing it; let's not use our best talent."
You're guilty.

It applies to every retailer who looks at his customers as ATMs rather than people to serve.
"People will pay a premium for this comic book, even though I'll never buy it back from them for a fraction of its price."
"If it's not from [publisher], no one will buy it."
"No, our customers won't buy TPBs; they're not collectible."
You're guilty.

It applies to the trade press which happily repackages evil and nonsense as The Way Things Should Be.
"What's hot, what's not!"
"Locking away comics in a bag with a professional grade is a good thing."
You're guilty.

It applies to customers who buy into the hype we shovel down their throats.
"How much will this be worth?"
"I'm going to put my kids through college with this."
"I have to buy all 12 covers, or my collection will not be complete."
You're guilty.

You're all guilty. Every man-jack of you.
"There is right, and there is wrong, and the difference is not so very hard to tell."
But if we accept the possibility that we're responsible for our actions, that what we do matters and has meaning, that there are significance and ramifications to

our actions – if we accept these as truths – then there is an immediate corollary that appears:

We have the power to change things.

You **have the power to change things.**

And that's what this column is all about. That power. That spark of decency and common sense and earned wisdom. That ability to change, to "take arms against a sea of troubles, and, by opposing, end them."

The pessimist in me screams out, "We're surrounded by venal sheep who only wish to fatten their own nests, regardless of the costs of their own soul and livelihood!" (And, yes, that bit of me has a horrible tendency to mix metaphors terribly. Oh, and to use too many adjectives and adverbs.)

But the optimist in me whispers quietly, insistently, "Where there is life, there is hope."

I dunno, maybe I read too many comics as a kid. Maybe I'm foolish to believe that with great power comes great responsibility. Maybe I am ignorant to believe that one person can make a difference.

Maybe.

But I don't think so.

Because I've seen the changes, subtle and small that they are, that have come from this column. I've spoken to the retailers who said, "Man, you really made me think when you pointed out that selling [title] for $5 a throw when I have two cases in my back room and I'd never buy a copy from a customer is wrong."

I've spoken to the publishers who understand that, despite the expediency of putting the burden of mis-solicitation on another party, they have an obligation to take the financial hit themselves.

I've spoken to the distributors who are willing to take the chance and stock a little extra of a quality book, in the hopes that it will make our market grow over the long haul.

I've spoken to the reporters who know that their words hold weight and that it is their duty to use that weight to promote what is good, not what is popular.

I've spoken to the creators who have taken on a project for passion's sake, not for the paycheck.

I've spoken to the fans who finally came to understand that a collection is meaningless, if it gives them no pleasure to collect.

And those rays of light, streaming down on our cloud-ravaged world, are what fill me with hope that one day the skies will clear fully.

We're on the cusp of change. I can feel it. I can see the signs all around us. Whether the change comes because you are proactive and responsible and you help build it; or whether it comes because your venality and foolishness forces and reinforces the crisis upon us: that's the only question.

Because it's really up to you.

You have the power to change things.

Specifically, it's up to us retailers. We've always had the most real power (the purchasing power) of any group and the least will to use it. This disturbs me greatly, since we're also the ones with the most to lose in virtually all things.

Let me try to give the smallest of examples: the policy at Diamond that late books are either order-adjustable or returnable, but never both. This is a bad policy. It doesn't penalize poor publisher behavior (most comics are not getting adjusted downward to any significant degree) and it doesn't particularly address the problems of late shipping titles (not having proper information to judge sales, non-returnable), unless you cut your order to zero.

Order adjustment is a fine idea, but there's *no* need for it to be an either/or remedy .The best situation is where we have the freedom to adjust our orders, but if the issue ships and still stiffs because it is six months late, then it should *also* be returnable.

If *I* say this alone, no one will listen. If ten of you add your voice, they might consider it. If 100 of us asked for this change, it would be policy the next day.

It takes all of two minutes to write a letter to Steve Geppi and Chuck Parker saying, "Please change your policy so that order-adjustable issues are returnable, as well. Thank you."

There are very few policies or procedures that they won't change, if enough of us demand it. But it takes **you** making an effort.

In the same way, we largely dictate what gets published – the *reason* publishers do multiple covers on comics is because you support them; the *reason* they do weak spin-offs of good-selling titles that end up diluting the parent comic book is because you embrace it. Every month you let your desires and wants known when you fill out your order form. Every month you have the power to change the industry by voting with your budget.

We also influence our customers and their tastes. You think a series is great? Talk it up, push it, promote it – the customers will listen. You think it's terrible that not enough kids are reading comics? Offer Archies at half price for a month if your clientele brings a child into the store with them. There are dozens upon dozens upon dozens of things you can do every day to help the industry grow and prosper and thrive.

But they all take an effort; a *commitment*.

The world sees us as a backwards hillbilly medium, run by mouth-breathing fools. We're *all* the *Simpsons* Comic Book Guy ("I will not get off my stool unless you buy something") – and for good reason! Too few of us make the *barest* effort to change things for the better.

And look where it has gotten us.

Just **look**.

If you're happy to be in a shrinking marginal marketplace, then just keep sitting on your ass. Market forces are quite happy to erode your business as you do nothing.

But the basest ethical choice, the one that illuminates and transforms all others, is that you do make a difference; that you *can* foster change.

So that's my message. What you do *matters*. It has *meaning*. It has *merit*. It has *context*. And, because of that, you've an obligation and responsibility to try – to use *your* power for the best future for *all* of us.

I have faith, some days more than others, maybe, but I have faith that we can change things for the better.

It's up to **you**.

Don't let the rest of us down.

Brian Hibbs lives in San Francisco with his lovely wife Tzipora Friedman. Brian opened the award-winning Comix Experience April Fool's Day, 1989. Brian can be reached at 305 Divisadero St., San Francisco, CA, 94117 or by e-mail at brian@comixexperience.com

www.**idw**publishing.com